Positive Child Guidance

Third Edition

Positive Child Guidance

Third Edition

Darla Ferris Miller

Africa • Australia • Canada • Denmark • Japan • Mexico • New Zealand • Philippines
Puerto Rico • Singapore • Spain • United Kingdom • United States

Notice to the Reader

Publisher does not warrant or guarantee any of the products described herein or perform any independent analysis in connection with any of the product information contained herein. Publisher does not assume, and expressly disclaims, any obligation to obtain and include information other than that provided to it by the manufacturer.

The reader is expressly warned to consider and adopt all safety precautions that might be indicated by the activities herein and to avoid all potential hazards. By following the instructions contained herein, the reader willingly assumes all risks in connection with such instructions.

The Publisher makes no representation or warranties of any kind, including but not limited to, the warranties of fitness for particular purpose or merchantability, nor are any such representations implied with respect to the material set forth herein, and the publisher takes no responsibility with respect to such material. The publisher shall not be liable for any special, consequential, or exemplary damages resulting, in whole or part, from the readers' use of, or reliance upon, this material.

Delmar Staff

Business Unit Director: Susan Simpfenderfer
Executive Editor: Marlene McHugh Pratt
Acquisitions Editor: Erin O'Connor Traylor
Editorial Assistant: Alexis Ferraro
Executive Marketing Manager: Donna Lewis
Executive Production Manager: Wendy Troeger
Production Editor: Sandra Woods
Cover Design: Jay Purcell

Printed in the United States of America
1 2 3 4 5 6 7 8 9 10 XXX 03 02 01 00 99

For more information, contact:
Delmar, 3 Columbia Circle, PO Box 15015, Albany, NY 12212-0515;
or find us on the World Wide Web at http://www.delmar.com

Library of Congress Cataloging-in-Publication Data

Miller, Darla Ferris.
　　Positive child guidance / Darla Ferris Miller.—3rd ed.
　　　　p.　cm.
　　Includes bibliographical references and index.
　　ISBN 0-7668-0360-0
　　　　1. Child rearing—United States.　2. Child development—United States.　3. Child psychology—United States.　4. Parenting—United States.　I. Title.
　　HG769.M5325　　1999
　　649'.1—dc21

99-34456
CIP

Contents

Preface

Parents and caregivers worry about discipline: "How do I get kids to clean up after themselves?" "How can I keep my toddlers from biting and pulling hair?" "What should I do when preschoolers call each other hurtful names?" "Am I being too strict?" "Am I being too lenient?" "How can I manage my own feelings of anger and frustration when children throw tantrums?"

Child guidance is the very challenging process of establishing and maintaining responsible, productive, and cooperative behavior in children. Adult caregivers must devote a great deal of time, effort, and persistence over many years to help children become considerate and self-disciplined members of society. Knowledge of the natural stages of child development is the most powerful tool adults have to guide youngsters successfully through this process of maturing. This book provides answers focused on developmentally appropriate guidance.

Self-discipline and self-control do not automatically appear out of thin air. Competent, well-behaved children do not just happen. Dedication and skill on the part of parents, early educators, and caregivers help children to reach their full potential. Effective guidance prevents behavior problems, keeps children safe, minimizes aggression, and builds a solid foundation for children's future participation in society.

This book has been written specifically for those adults who make an invaluable contribution to society by caring for and teaching the youngest and most vulnerable members of society—our children. The book is intended as a road map to guide adults as they strive to meet the developmental needs of children from infancy through early childhood. Every child has unique needs. Consequently, no single guidance strategy will be appropriate for all children at all ages. This book addresses typical characteristics and needs of children as they proceed through chronological and developmental stages. It provides a broad range of practical, effective, and flexible guidance strategies that are based on principles of straightforward communication and assertiveness. The underlying theme is that of respect for the dignity and human rights of the infant and young child.

Much writing in the area of child guidance has focused only on behaviorist learning theory—a view that all behavior can be explained as the result of externally reinforced (or rewarded) learning. This view assumes that because a full understanding of the internal workings of the human mind is impossible, that process is therefore irrelevant. A key problem with exclusive reliance on behavior modification—ignoring negative behaviors and reinforcing positive behaviors—is that it may be carried out in an aloof or manipulative manner.

Additionally, rewarding children for behaving a certain way raises several sticky issues. Since human beings of all ages are infinitely complex, the praise or prize that reinforces one child may embarrass, bore, or alienate another. Doling out privileges and prizes may place an adult in the role of a stingy Santa Claus rather than that of a democratic guide and role model and may stimulate competition rather than cooperation among children. Doling out attention and praise as reinforcement risks implying to children that compliance is a condition for affection, that only "good" children are loved.

Another problem that undermines the effectiveness of behavior modification as a sole strategy for guidance is the contemporary child's frequent exposure to many different adults and settings. Even intermittent reinforcement of a behavior through attention from children or other adults can undo an attempt by a caregiver to eliminate that behavior by ignoring it. The behaviorist caregiver attempts to control the child's behavior by controlling the child's environment—

a very helpful tool for guidance in specific situations but not a feasible overall plan for child guidance.

Strategies for child guidance should not rely only on methods for external control but rather must stimulate the development of internal mechanisms and motivations for self-control. In this way children can be encouraged to become independent and self-directed rather than dependent and other-directed. As they grow toward adolescence and adulthood, they will begin making more and more critical choices about what to do and how to behave.

Because imitation, or modeling, is a key avenue for early child learning, how adults cope with the stress and frustration of handling children's misbehaviors is critical. Children tend to do what we do rather than what we say to do. The purpose of child guidance is to support and direct the growth of effective life skills rather than only to bring about the immediate control of annoying behaviors.

Positive, persistent assertiveness is considerably more painstaking and time-consuming than bullying and intimidating children into compliance by scolding, screaming, or spanking. It definitely requires a great deal more thought and effort than giving up responsibility for children's behavior, indulging their every whim and assuming that maturation will somehow automatically bring discipline and self-control.

In child guidance—as in much of our instant, drive-through, disposable culture of expedience—the slower, more difficult method has special value. In spite of the added skill and effort required to carry out positive, assertive discipline, its impact on the child's personal growth and on the early childhood setting make it a worthwhile method. Positive, assertive discipline bolsters self-esteem, nurtures cooperativeness, and models socially acceptable coping skills. The early childhood program is a training ground in which very young people acquire and practice the skills needed for effective living. The personal characteristics and capabilities needed for survival in an autocracy or anarchy are very different from those needed for participation in a democracy. In a democratic country, early child guidance should begin the development of self-respect, awareness of and consideration for the rights of others, and recognition that persons of all ages, colors, and creeds should be treated with equal dignity, although each may have very different roles and responsibilities.

The ultimate goal of child guidance is the child's development of responsibility, self-confidence, and self-control. Inner discipline, based on an intrinsic desire to be a cooperative community member, is more functional to adult life in a democracy than sole reliance on external discipline based on an artificially contrived desire to gain rewards and avoid punishments. Of course, there is no place in any democracy for laissez-faire anarchy in which people wantonly trample the rights of others in their quest for self-gratification.

This book outlines practical, workable steps for creating a cooperative, respectful community of children and adults. Behavior modification will be addressed, not as the foundation of child guidance, but as a single, carefully placed stone in a solid structure of active guidance. Maturation will be addressed, not as an excuse to relinquish responsibility for child behavior, but as a powerful tool for understanding and responding appropriately to various stages of child behavior. The method presented is one of assertive and respectful enforcement of cooperatively developed rules and persistent protection of individual rights.

Aggression, passivity, and manipulativeness are identified as hindrances to positive child guidance. They trigger negativeness, even rebellion, in children, and they model behaviors that are hindrances to successful participation in democratic community life. The role of the adult, in this book, is that of one who seeks not to gain control over children but rather to guide them effectively while setting for them an immediate and tangible example of appropriate coping and assertive negotiation.

In this model, the adult not only guards the safety and individual rights of children but also stimulates their development of inner control by creating a functioning democratic community of children and adults. Positive child guidance means guiding children as firmly as necessary, as gently as possible, and always with respect.

This book is meant to be a lively, poignant, warm, and very human look at the process of adults guiding, managing, and coping with children's behavior—and children trying to deal with their own emerging needs and feelings as well as with persistent adult expectations. Although the book is readable, and at times even funny, it is based on a solid theoretical foundation drawn from the empirical study of social and emotional development in infants, toddlers, and young children.

Acknowledgments

I am indebted to many colleagues, friends, and family members who gave endless encouragement, assistance, and guidance during the writing of this text. I especially owe thanks to Cynde Miller, Grace Hively, and Rick McDonald for the sensitive and beautiful photographs included in these pages. The children, families, teachers, and administrators of Montessori Country Day School of Houston and Echo Park-Silverlake People's Child Care Center in Los Angeles were most kind in granting permission for photographs to be taken. I also thank my beautiful and wise sisters, Karen Burkhardt and Kathy Searle, for their assistance, feedback, and unflagging support.

I also owe special thanks to my daughters, Michelle Miller, who holds a doctorate in experimental psychology from the University of California—Los Angeles, and Cynde Miller, who holds a masters degree from the University of California—Irvine, and teaches at Chaffe Community College. They both contributed their talents to make this third edition a reality. I also thank my husband, Tommy, for his love and support.

Erin O'Connor Traylor and many other professionals at Delmar Publishing have also been of great assistance. And I offer my sincere appreciation to the early childhood experts who contributed to the readability and usefulness of this book by critiquing it and adding their own ideas and suggestions:

Jeannie Edwards
St. Louis Community College
St. Louis, MO

Teresa Frazier
Thomas Nelson Community College
Hampton, VA

Jann James, Ed.D.
Troy State University
Troy, AL

Elaine Lyons
Luzerne County Community College
Nanticoke, PA

Olivia Saracho, Ph.D.
University of Maryland
College Park, MD

Elaine VanLue, Ed.D.
Nova Southeastern University
Fort Lauderdale, FL

Dedication

This book was inspired by and is dedicated to my parents, Evolee and Roy Ferris. "Papa Roy" did not live to see the book completed, but he had great interest in and enthusiasm for its writing. Because he grew up the youngest child of a troubled single parent during the Great Depression, he spent much of his adult life struggling to learn how to be a good parent and to let his children know that he loved them. When he read the beginning draft of this book, his eyes got a bit misty, and he said, "You've said some important things in here. I'm really proud of you." Of course, no child ever outgrows the need to know she has made her parents proud!

As my husband, Tommy Miller, and I have reared our daughters, we too have struggled to learn how to be good parents and let our children know they are loved. Today we feel awe as we watch the beginning of our next generation emerge. Our beautiful first granddaughter, Fiona Ferris McDonald, slips her chubby baby feet into her mommy's high heels, dons her daddy's big baseball cap, and wobbles off toward the future.

About the Author

Darla Ferris Miller holds a doctorate in Early Childhood Education, Texas and Mississippi teaching credentials, and the American Montessori Society Preprimary Certification. She is presently Vice President for Student and Organizational Development at North Harris College. Dr. Miller has served in a wide range of roles within the field of child care and development. She has been caregiver, teacher, center director, teacher trainer, professor, and consultant, and she has worked with children from infancy to school age. Dr. Miller's publications include:

Room to Grow: How to Create Quality Early Childhood Environments (chapter author) (1990). Linda Ard and Mabel Pitts (Eds.). Austin, TX: Texas Association for the Education of Young Children.

First Steps Toward Cultural Difference: Socialization in Infant/Toddler Day Care (author) (1989). Washington, DC: Child Welfare League of America, Inc.

"Social Reproduction and Resistance in Four Infant/Toddler Daycare Settings" (co-authored with Dr. Mark B. Ginsburg, University of Pittsburgh) (1989). *Journal of Education, 171*(3). Boston: Boston University School of Education.

Every child represents a new beginning full of bright possibility.

Chapter 1

Introduction

Chapter Outline

New Roles and Responsibilities in Child Rearing

Short-Term Objectives for Child Guidance
Respecting the Rights of Others
Avoiding Danger
Caring for the Environment

Long-Term Goals for Child Guidance
The Nurturing Environment and Long-Term Development

Practical Application/Discussion
The Spoiled Child—Myth or Reality?

Questions for Discussion
Points to Remember
Related Readings

Objectives

This chapter will assist you in

- Identifying contemporary practices in child care
- Defining responsibility for healthy child rearing
- Recognizing the purpose of child guidance
- Stating the criteria for creating early childhood rules
- Describing ideal early environments for optimum development

New Roles and Responsibilities in Child Rearing

At dawn every weekday morning all across the country, from bustling cities to tiny rural communities, mothers and fathers struggle to begin another workday. In millions of homes and apartments, parents hurry to feed and dress babies and young children. Without a minute to spare, they grab diaper bags and satchels, buckle little ones into car seats, climb onto buses, or push strollers into elevators. They head for a variety of child care arrangements—ranging from homes of relatives to registered family day homes to proprietary, religious, and government-funded child care centers. Stress begins early for today's parents and children. The world is changing dramatically, but children still need protection, nurturance, love, and guidance. Whether mommy is a full-time homemaker or a business executive with an urgent 8 A.M. appointment makes little difference to a toddler who plops in the middle of the floor and cries because he does not want oatmeal for breakfast. Child guidance is a challenging task for any parent, but if parents work outside the home, managing their children's behavior may be more complicated, and parents may rely a great deal on child care workers to support their children's social and emotional development (Brazelton, 1985; Coontz, 1997; Copeland & McCreedy, 1997; Curran, 1985).

Practical day-to-day responsibility for guiding the next generation is shifting from parents alone to parents and early childhood personnel working together. Today there are fewer traditional two-parent, single-earner families and rapidly increasing numbers of dual-earner couples, single parents, and other arrangements of employed households with young children (Blankenhorn, 1997; Duis, 1997; Elkind, 1997; Francke, 1983; Yarrow, 1991). At the same time that family structures are changing, more and more research has surfaced highlighting the critical importance of early experiences for the long-term development of a child's personality, character, values, and social competence (Adlam, 1977; Amato, 1997; Anyon, 1983; Baillargean, 1997; Bandura, 1977; Begley, 1997a; Braun, 1997; Cook-Gumperz, 1973). Never before has there been such acute awareness of the impact early caregivers have on young lives, and never before has there been such need for people outside the family to assume major involvement in the process of child rearing (Campos, Bertenthal, & Kermoian, 1997; Chugani, 1993; Ehrensaft, 1997; Galston, 1993; Hamburg, 1992; Marshall, 1991; National Commission on Children, 1991).

Years ago, "babysitting" was a custodial time-out from the real business of child rearing (which was most often handled by mothers). Since "babysitting" represented only a brief interruption from day-to-day caregiving, any untrained but reasonably responsible teenager or adult could be relied upon to sit with the baby or child for a short time just to ensure that the child was safe and that basic physical needs were met. Now, however, about half of all babies and young children live in homes where the adults in the family work part- or full-time outside the home. Child care is no longer a brief interruption from routine caregiving but rather a major portion of it. Many children spend most of their waking hours in some form of child care by someone other than parents, from as early as the first weeks of life (Hamburg, 1992; Skolnick, 1991).

These changes place new expectations on parents and on early childhood professionals. Working mothers must face the stress of juggling family and career obligations. Fathers find that modern lifestyles present a new level of paternal involvement in caring for and managing young

Striking Changes in the American Family

- **More Working Mothers.** *Never having enough time is particularly stressful for mothers, who more frequently than fathers work a "second shift" at home, doing housework and caring for the children. Today infants and toddlers are spending less quality time with their parents.*

- **More Single-Parent Families.** *Since 1950, the percentage of children living in one-parent families has nearly tripled. This increase has come about because of rising divorce rates and dramatic increases in the numbers of births outside marriage. One in four American children now lives in a single-parent home. The vast majority of these families—fully 90 percent—are headed by a women. These mother-only families often receive little or no help from the child's father. Nationwide, only 50 percent of divorced fathers contribute financially to their child's support, and most rarely see their children.*

- **More Adolescent Parents.** *The United States has one of the highest adolescent pregnancy rates in the developed world. Of teenagers who give birth, 46 percent will go on welfare within four years. Of unmarried teens giving birth, 73 percent will be on welfare within four years.*

- **More Family Isolation and Violence.** *Most of today's families seem far more isolated from friends, kin, and community life. Even very young children experience extreme violence and everyday aggression as both victims and witnesses.*

- **More Young Children in Poverty.** *By 1990, families with children under three years of age constituted the single largest group living in poverty in the United States: 25 percent of these families fall below the poverty line. The rates are higher still for African American and Hispanic families and single-parent families of young children. The poverty rate among young children has risen even though overall American poverty rates are no higher today than they were twenty years ago. These children are often hungry or inadequately nourished. Many live in overcrowded housing, in unsafe buildings or neighborhoods. Many children are homeless. Studies estimate that, of the approximately 100,000 American children who are homeless each night, nearly half are less than six years of age.*

- **More Children Live in Foster Homes.** *In a mere five years, from 1987 to 1991, the number of children in foster care jumped by more than 50 percent—from 300,000 in 1987 to 460,000 in 1991. Babies under the age of one are the fastest-growing category of children entering foster care.*

- **More Children Are Abused and Neglected.** *One in every three victims of physical abuse is a baby—less than a year old. In 1990, more one-year-olds were maltreated than in any previous year for which we have data.*

Carnegie Corporation of New York. (1994). Starting points: Meeting the needs of our youngest children, the report of the Carnegie Task Force on Meeting the Needs of Young Children. Waldorf, MD: Author.

children. Child care workers find that more and more is expected of them by parents who depend on paid caregivers to be skillful in supporting wholesome growth and development in the children. Even parents who are full-time homemakers find that contemporary lifestyles bring new

Every child, every moment, is in the process of creating the adult she will become.

The teacher of little children is not merely giving lessons. She is helping to make a brain and nervous system, and this work which is going to determine all that comes after, requires a finer perception and a wider training and outlook than is needed by any other kind of teacher.

Margaret McMillan (Bradburn, 1989)

stresses and strains to child rearing. Many feel that their toddlers and preschoolers benefit from participating in professionally run early childhood programs even if a parent is home full-time and child care is not absolutely necessary.

Why Is Parent and Professional Training in Child Guidance Important?

In today's world, many children do not spend the first years of their lives sheltered in cocoon-like home settings. They are up with the alarm clock, their days are structured and scheduled, they come in contact with many caregivers, and they must learn to get along with other young children in groups. Modern parents need help in developing the skill they need to guide young children effectively and prevent behavior problems, since they may have limitations in their flexibility and time to deal with a tantruming toddler who refuses to get dressed or a pouting preschooler who insists that everyone in the whole world hates her. Parents need support with child

Changing attitudes and expectations in society bring dramatic changes in contemporary child-rearing practices.

guidance so that behavior problems do not place additional strain on family life structures that may already be stretched thin simply from the stresses of contemporary living (Amato, 1997; Coontz, 1997; Copeland & McGreedy, 1997; Salk, 1992; Stringer-Siebold, 1996) (See Appendix A for additional resources.)

Early childhood professionals need help in developing effective child guidance strategies so that they can truly meet the social and emotional needs of the children in their care, so that they provide much needed support to family life, and so that they can assume a reasonable portion of the responsibility for teaching the next generation how to be responsible, cooperative, competent citizens. Teachers and caregivers can never replace the important role of caring parents. Parents have an irreplaceable impact on their children's lives simply because of the emotional bonds that are a part of being a family. While caregivers must never compete with or infringe upon this special parent-child relationship, they can be a tremendous support to both children and their families. Parents are the first and most important teachers children will ever have.

Who Should Be Responsible for the Well-Being and Guidance of Children?

We are all responsible for the well-being and guidance of children. In past centuries, children were thought to be their parents' property. In Western Europe only a century and a half ago, babies were not considered to be real persons. It was not even thought necessary to report their deaths (Aries, 1962). In a modern democracy, however, children are not viewed as property of their parents but rather as human beings with inalienable human rights. Governmental agencies hold responsibility for the welfare and guidance of young children because children are the future citizens of the country. Failure to address early needs later costs government millions of

Changing Family Values Over the Last Half of the Twentieth Century

Traditional Families (mid-1940s to mid-1960s)

- *Couples with children were predominant.*
- *Birth rates were high.*
- *Divorce rates were low.*
- *Marriages tended to have a high degree of stability.*
- *Families enjoyed a strong economy with a high standard of living.*
- *Family life was idealized, conformity to social norms was expected, and men and women had clear roles.*

Shifting Emphasis to Individuals Outside the Family Context (mid-1960s to mid-1980s)

- *Population became much more diverse.*
- *Single lifestyle emerged.*
- *Young people postponed marriage.*
- *Birth rate declined.*
- *Divorce rate rose dramatically.*
- *Career was idealized and women began entering the workforce in huge numbers.*
- *Self-expression was increasingly valued and male and female roles became less defined.*

New Families (mid-1980s to late-1990s)

- *Birth rate increased.*
- *Divorce rate leveled off.*
- *Women's entry into the workforce began to level off as availability of high-paying jobs for women declined.*
- *Cultural values included a return to emphasis on family but with much less conformity than ever before.*

Adapted from Barbara Dafoe Whitehead. (1993, May/June). The new family values. *Utne Reader*.

tax dollars in remedial education, indigent support, and crime (Hernandez, 1997; Jackson, 1997; Lindjord, 1997; McAlister, 1997; White, 1995). Business and industry hold responsibility for the welfare of young children, since they will be the workforce of the future, and competitiveness in world markets depends on the availability of competent, cooperative, responsible workers. Civic groups, churches, schools, and each of us are also responsible. Good citizenship obligates us to look toward the future well-being of humanity rather than just our own personal interests. You can help your community build a brighter future by joining with other interested parents and professionals to support advocacy groups that inform and encourage better child care and education. (See Appendix B for organizations that interest you and address issues you care about.)

"Be safe—sand is for digging, not for throwing. Sand hurts if it gets in your eyes."

Throughout the country there is growing recognition that investing efforts and resources to better the lives of children is not only humane but also very cost-effective. Children are open to ideas and experiences, and it is possible to bring about meaningful changes in their lives and to have real influence on their long-term development of values and character traits. Adults, on the other hand, tend to be more rigidly set in their habits and potentials. If we are to continue to enjoy the benefits of living in a democracy, then we must begin by helping children learn personal responsibility and respect for others so that they will know how to function properly as adults.

Short-Term Objectives for Child Guidance

The short-term objective for child guidance is deceptively simple. Children will be helped to follow the same basic rules for decent and responsible behavior that are applicable to all persons living in a democracy. To accomplish this, we can use the following guidelines to determine the appropriateness of children's day-to-day behaviors and help children learn the difference between right and wrong:

- Behavior must not infringe on the rights of others.

- Behavior must not present a clear risk of harm to oneself or others.

- Behavior must not unreasonably damage the environment or animals, objects, or materials in the environment.

To communicate these rules effectively, to translate them to the comprehension level of young children, they must be greatly oversimplified. By oversimplifying them, young children can be

In the sweep of seven decades, the image conveyed is one of children, smaller than anyone else, lighter in physical weight and political clout, easily picked up and blown wherever the winds of economic, political, and social movements were heading.

Rochelle Beck (1973)

guided to make sense of what otherwise may seem to them to be an endless number of unrelated little rules. By lumping rules into three basic categories, young children can be helped to remember and understand the basic guidelines for appropriate behavior—be *kind,* be *safe,* and be *neat.* These ground rules can be stated as reminders before more specific and practical instructions are given, for example:

- Be kind! Wait for your turn.

- Be safe! Go down the slide feet first.

- Be neat! Put your paper towel in the trash can.

Stating the guidelines for appropriate behavior is easy. Evaluating real behaviors in real children is a great deal more difficult—it requires some critical thinking on the part of the adult. A very well-coordinated five-year-old is leaning back on two legs of his chair. Does this behavior infringe on the rights of others? (For example, is the walkway between tables blocked for other children?) Does this behavior risk an injury? (Could the child fall? If he fell, would he hit soft carpeting or a cement floor?) Does it appear that equipment could be damaged by this behavior? (How sturdy is the chair? Are breakable things nearby?) Personal judgment, practical experience, and knowledge of individual children and their capabilities will determine how different adults answer these questions and how they go about setting rules and enforcing discipline. I hope you will answer these questions with enough compassion to see every situation through children's eyes, but enough courage to be true to your sense of fair play and good judgment.

What Are the Rights of Children?

Children Have a Right Not to Be Hurt.   Adults should be very conscientious about protecting every child's right not to be hit, kicked, bitten, or shoved. It is never okay to allow a child to be kicked because she did it first and "deserved to get a taste of her own medicine." It is never okay to bite a toddler back "so that he will learn what biting feels like." An old cliché that happens to be true is:—"Two wrongs do not make a right." The only thing that revenge really does is set the stage for more hurtful behavior. Adults should monitor children carefully and consistently so that aggression can be prevented or interrupted immediately when it does occur.

Children Have a Right to Avoid Unnecessary Discomfort.   They have a right to eat lunch peacefully without an unnerving noise level caused by children around them screaming and yelling. They have a right to listen to a story without being squashed by others who are struggling to see the pictures. And they have a right to build sand castles without getting sand in their eyes because gleeful playmates are shoveling sand into the air just for the fun of it. Although all

Young children appreciate pleasant and comfortable surroundings.

young children begin with a kind of thinking that limits them to a self-centered (or egocentric) view of the world, adults can help children begin to recognize that others have feelings. In time children begin to get a sense of what it feels like to be someone else. A one-year-old may try to give her pacifier to an older child who is crying, or a preschooler may run to tell a teacher that his friend got pushed off the swing. Adults who are consistently sensitive to the comfort needs of children set an emotional tone in which children are much more inclined to be sensitive to each other.

Children Have a Right to Their Possessions. Adults sometimes impose very strange views of sharing on children. In the adult world, government provides very precise laws related to possession and ownership. Law forbids others from tampering with one's possessions without permission. Even social customs follow the same rule. If I take a cart in a grocery store and begin doing my shopping, it would be extremely rude and surprising for another shopper to snatch that cart away and dump my groceries because she wanted "a turn" with the cart. I would greatly appreciate a store manager (authority figure) who intervened politely but assertively and redirected the offending shopper to other available carts. Oddly enough, a child in preschool who complains because another child grabbed the tricycle or snatched the container of crayons he was using is often not helped but instead chided for "tattling" and for "not sharing."

A child's personal possessions are her own, and no one, not even a parent or teacher, should tamper with them without asking the child or at least letting the child know—for example, "I'm going to put your sweater away now." Objects that are available for shared use belong to the person using them at any given time (until, of course, that use infringes on the rights of others). In

This little boy has a right to explore his art materials without unnecessary interference from other children.

a home setting, if one child is watching television, another should not be allowed to march in and change channels without asking. In a group setting, a puzzle belongs to the child who chose to work with it, and no one else should be allowed to touch that puzzle without permission from the child who chose it first. Sharing is only really sharing if it is voluntary. (Involuntary sharing is something we adults affectionately refer to as taxation.)

Children Have a Right to Fairness.   Fairness is a concept that emerges slowly in children during the preschool and early elementary years. Even before that concept is well developed, however, children deserve fair treatment and they need to observe role models of integrity and fairness. If one child is allowed to have a picture book during naptime, then it is unfair to deny that privilege to another child without some logical reason or explanation.

By the time children are around kindergarten age, they can sometimes be heard proclaiming loudly, "Hey, that's not fair." Although their logic is still rather limited, and their actual concept of fairness may be hazy, they are likely to complain if the action of an adult or another child appears to them to be blatantly unequal or out of compliance with a rule. Sometimes, if an adult carries out a disciplinary action that appears arbitrary and capricious to a child, the child will immediately begin enforcing that action on other children, partly as revenge and partly in imitation of the adult. For example, a teacher angrily snaps at a child and yanks his lunch box out of his hand because it is not yet time for lunch. A few minutes later the child mimics the adult's behavior and tone of voice, yanking away a smaller child's toy and snapping, "Gimme that, you baby!"

How Do We Tell the Difference Between Enforcing Reasonable Safety Rules and Being Overprotective?

Just about every interesting activity or environment has some element of risk. Imagine for a moment trying to create an environment that had absolutely no possibility for any kind of accident. Unfortunately, a child can potentially misuse, fall off of, throw, choke on, or bump into just about any kind of equipment or material that can be named. The only perfectly safe environment would probably be a padded cell—and some child would undoubtedly find a way to get hurt there. Of course, a padded cell would not offer many opportunities for exploration and skill development. So, in an interesting, challenging environment, safety is always a matter of compromise. The difficulty for many teachers and parents seems to be in deciding what level of compromise is acceptable and reasonable and what level is not.

Children feel a sense of pride and dignity when they succeed in mastering a difficult challenge that has a bit of risk involved. No baby ever learned to walk without risking a fall, and no child ever learned to jump off a step, climb a tree, roller skate, or ride a bicycle without risking a bump or bruise. Some pediatricians assume that if a child makes it through early childhood without so much as a broken finger, then he or she has been overprotected. The acceptability of risk must be weighed against the severity of possible outcomes. If the worst thing that could reasonably result from a behavior is a two-foot fall onto a thick gymnastic mat, then the risk seems very acceptable. If the child could possibly fall ten feet onto brick pavement, then there is a clear risk of harm; that kind of accident could result in serious or permanent injury to the child.

Adults must be diligent about safety for young children. Environments in which young children play should be checked and double-checked routinely for hazardous equipment, toxic plants or substances, and dangerous but tempting situations. Then, but only then, adults can step back and allow children the latitude to negotiate challenges independently, under a watchful eye rather than hovering control.

Why Should Children Be Involved in Maintaining and Protecting Their Environment?

In order to learn, children need the freedom to make mistakes, to know that it is really not so awful to break a glass or spill paint on a shirt. Most things can be restored or replaced. Stained clothes will soon be forgotten, but a child's first painting may be treasured for many years, and the benefit of the experience of painting may stay with a child for the rest of her life.

Although it is essential to keep a reasonable perspective about neatness, one cannot lose sight of the fact that responsibility, manners, and good citizenship require one to have respect for his or her surroundings. We all share the resources of this planet and have an obligation, therefore, to use them wisely and well. Early child guidance prepares children for good citizenship. When a child remembers to use one paper towel at a time and then throw it away, she is preparing for membership in adult society where everyone benefits if forests cut for paper mills are replanted, water used in factories is cleaned before being dumped, and fish and game are taken according to lawful limits and seasons.

Responsibility and independence develop when children learn to care for themselves and their environment.

In the first years of life, children can gradually learn to take only what they need, use it with care, then restore it (put it away) when they have finished using it. Toys, games, and learning materials should be arranged in an orderly manner on low shelves to be accessible to children. Even a very young child can learn to replace a puzzle if it has its own place on a shelf or in a puzzle rack. A stack of ten heavy puzzles crammed on a shelf makes it difficult or impossible for a child to select and take any but the top puzzle. There should be no more materials available at any one time than children can deal with. And adults must set an example for care of the environment and assist children consistently in learning that things are easier to find if they are always returned to the same spot.

Children should be stopped firmly but kindly when their behavior is damaging to the environment. While playing outdoors, children may innocently break limbs off shrubs, smash birds' eggs, or peel bark off trees. Teaching them about nature and the value of plants and animals assists them in building respect for living things and in accepting responsibility for their own actions. Indoors, children playfully smash riding toys into table legs and stuff tissues down the sink drain just to see what happens. These actions should immediately be interrupted in an understanding but matter-of-fact way. If the child is shown how tables are built, sanded smooth, and painted, or how pipes bring water into and out of our homes, he will be more likely to understand and care for his environment.

Long-Term Goals for Child Guidance

If children are to become responsible adults, they must learn to control their actions and impulses. Unfortunately, self-control is not an easy thing to teach. Children begin life without any self-control whatsoever, so our most critical long-term goal is to assist them in their journey to responsible adulthood by nurturing their mastery of self-control.

Children are not simply lumps of clay to be shaped by caregivers. They are born with individual potentials and personality traits. They are also, however, profoundly influenced by the people, experiences, and events they encounter, especially during the first years of their lives (Baillargeon, 1997; Begley, 1997b; Begley & Springen, 1997; Berk, 1997; Bodrova & Leong, 1996; Eddowes & Ralph, 1998; Jackson, 1997; Stevenson & Lee, 1990). The effect of the environment on children, interestingly, is reciprocal. Children have tremendous impact on the behavior of the adults in their lives. Instead of being passively shaped by adults, children are actively involved in the experiences that influence their own development. Adults behave differently with different children. The actions and appearances of individual children trigger different emotions and reactions in individual adults.

Children are born with individual and distinctive behavioral patterns (Collins & Gunnar, 1990; Santrock, 1997; Sroufe, 1996; Thomas & Chess, 1977; Thomas, Chess, & Birch, 1970; Rutter, 1976). These clusters of personality traits are referred to as temperament. The temperament of an infant or child has an influence on how adults will care for her. Also, the quality and style of the care that adults provide have a strong influence on her continually developing temperament. She affects her caregivers and they affect her—both change and are changed by their interactions. All these influences, both internal and external, ensure that no two people will ever be exactly the same. We must help children celebrate and appreciate their differences.

Furthermore, even if two children's behavior is similar, their gender, size, or appearance may trigger different adult reactions. A thin, frail infant girl may evoke more protective, nurturing behavior in adults than a loud, robust infant boy, who may evoke more roughhousing and active playfulness in caregivers. A child who appears defiant may be treated sternly, while a child who appears contrite may be treated indulgently after an identical incident. A cycle emerges in which the child begins to anticipate a certain kind of interaction with others so she behaves accordingly, actually triggering the expected interaction. What began as incidental action and reaction settles eventually into habit, attitude, and personality. The bottom line is, of course, that early experiences make a difference in children's lives.

We play a critical role in shaping children's future lives. Our long-term goal for guidance is our most important contribution—equipping children with the skills and attitudes they need for happy, responsible, and productive adult life. The early childhood setting, whether in the home or in a child care center, is a miniature community in which children develop and practice the rudimentary skills they will need to cope with the larger community they encounter as they go through school, then finally the big, wide world when they are grown. Child guidance builds a foundation on which everything else in the child's life is built—social interaction with others, academic learning, and personal development. By their very nature, babies come into this world helpless, self-centered, and dependent. Guidance transforms them into full-fledged, functioning members of society.

What Kind of Early Environment Enhances Children's Long-Term Development?

High-quality early childhood settings look so simple that it is easy to underestimate the importance of the interactions there. An appropriate environment for young children is relaxed and playful. Children follow their own curiosity as they freely but respectfully explore objects, toys, and materials in the environment. They move about, chatter peacefully, laugh, and occasionally argue as they explore human social interactions and learn reasonable limits. A home where children are expected to be seen and not heard or a formal school setting with pupils sitting rigidly and silently following teacher instructions or listening to lectures are not examples of optimum early environments.

The rote memorization typical in lessons with workbooks, flash cards, and ditto sheets is definitely something many young children can master—if coerced, pressured, and bribed. The abstract concepts this memorized jargon represents, however, are totally unrelated to young children's level of brain development and therefore rather meaningless for them. Even a very young child can memorize and repeat chants and rhymes with long words, but he is unlikely to have a clue as to their meaning. (That's why one preschooler's favorite hymn included the words "Granny's cross-eyed bear" instead of "gladly the cross I'd bear.") If too much time is spent in such questionable ventures as rote memorization, the loss of time for more wholesome experiences can interfere with the really essential business of early childhood—healthy development of the whole child, socially, emotionally, and physically. The foundation of early learning is exploring, practicing, constructing, pretending, and problem solving (Gestwicki, 1999; Gordon & Browne, 1996a). Experience truly is the best teacher for young children. If a child's early environment does not fully support these experiences, it will be impossible for the child to reach her full potential.

Properly matching early childhood settings to the natural stages of growth and development seen in infants, toddlers, and young children has been termed developmentally appropriate practice. Detailed information about developmentally appropriate practice can be obtained through the National Association for the Education of Young Children (Bredekamp & Copple, 1997). (Further description of methods to "set the stage" for positive behavior by creating a developmentally appropriate early childhood environment is provided in Chapter 2.)

In family settings where parents feel strong bonds of love and attachment to their child, they will quite naturally respond to that child's cries and smiles when she needs attention or care. A healthy, well-developing baby or child gives many signals or cues to indicate what he needs, and a sensitive, caring parent uses trial and error to discover what will work to stop the child's crying and to keep the child happy and comfortable. This same give-and-take can be the heart of group care. If we see child care as a tedious chore that can be made easier by ignoring the child's cries and refusing to become emotionally attached, then nature's way of ensuring healthy development is undone. Caregivers and teachers who do not find joy in working with children may well be advised to seek different careers.

Because early experiences are so important to healthy development, child care outside the family takes on special significance. The first question parents should ask as they examine child

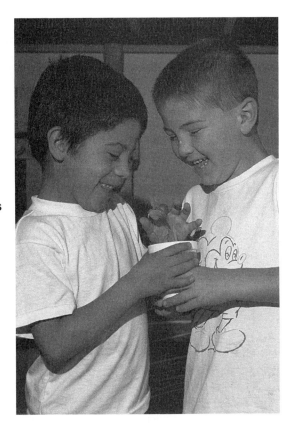

Affection and attention foster the long-term development of children's potential to become competent, confident, cooperative people.

Children—Our Investment in the Future

In some child care situations where working conditions are stressful, pay bottom-of-the-barrel, training inadequate, and staff turnover never ending, teachers/caregivers may not be able to function consistently at a level parents want their children to emulate. Parents, early educators, and public policy makers are becoming acutely aware of the significance of early experience on long-term development. Too often in past years it has been assumed that child care need be little more than a kindly but custodial parking lot for youngsters. Growing evidence from the study of human development indicates that the first years of life may be the most, rather than the least, critical years in a child's emotional, physical, and intellectual growth (Carnegie Corporation of New York, 1994).

Child care centers, preschools, mother's-day-out programs, and other early childhood settings have the potential to help parents create a better future for children and for society in general. To have resources, support, and high expectations from communities, the child care profession must come to be viewed as an integral part of our educational system, as well as a necessary service to support the economic well-being of low-income families (The Brookings Institution, 1992; Families and Work Institute, 1993).

Do adults in the child care center appear to genuinely enjoy and appreciate the individual qualities of each child in their care?

care alternatives is, "Are the adults in this setting warm, nurturing, and emotionally available to the children?" And, since modeling (imitating) and first-hand experience, rather than direct teaching, are the major avenues for learning in young children, the next crucial questions parents might ask are, "Do I want my child to absorb the personality traits, communication styles, and problem-solving behaviors of the adults here?" and "Do these adult role models set an example for behavior that I value and want my child to imitate?"

Positive Adult Role Models . . .

- *Treat everyone with dignity and respect at all times.*
- *Rely on communication, persistence, and patience rather than force.*
- *Respond assertively to misbehavior, with both firmness and gentleness.*
- *Use problem-solving strategies to identify the causes of misbehavior.*
- *Plan and prepare appropriate activities, materials, and routines.*
- *Give unconditional affection and affirmation.*
- *Are polite, honest, and straightforward in communications.*
- *Protect every child's individual rights.*
- *Celebrate differences.*
- *Really listen.*

Practical Application/Discussion

The Spoiled Child—Myth or Reality?

It is a glorious day at the park. Bright sunshine is radiating just enough warmth to balance a flag-snapping breeze. This sudden evidence of spring has drawn families and children outdoors like a magnet. Sitting on the grass alongside a large sandbox is a cluster of grown-ups who are laughing and talking as they watch their youngsters squealing and running or digging eagerly in the sand.

Al and Tamara's four-year-old son Joel makes gleeful whooping sounds as he chases his two-year-old brother Eddy with a wriggling bug he has found in the sand. Eddy screeches and dives onto his dad for protection as his mother beseeches Joel to "stop being so wild."

As he skids to a stop, Joel inadvertently smashes into a double stroller holding the Rodriguez twins. While Al escorts his boys back to their buckets and shovels, Tamara bends down with Elena Rodriguez to make sure the one-year-old twin girls are okay.

Several other parents have stopped talking and are watching attentively as Elena adjusts the little girls in their stroller and smoothes their crisp red dresses with identical embroidered collars.

Other mothers are amazed that the twins have not cried. Tamara takes one little girl by the hand and says, "Shall we get them out and let them play for a while?"

"Oh, no," says Elena, "They would get filthy. They know that they have to stay in the stroller." Al comments that his boys were never that "good." They would have pitched a fit to get out and get right in the middle of the dirt.

Several other parents chime in with awe-struck comments about how good the twins are. Elena responds, "I knew with twins and me working that they had better not get spoiled. In the child care center I use, they are very strict about not spoiling the kids. They only pick up the babies to change and feed them. The babies cried for a few days right at first, but now they're just no trouble at all."

The conversation about Elena's twins trails off as other parents scatter to chase after straying toddlers and to respond to their children's cries of "Watch me," "Push me in the swing again," and "Look at my sand castle." As Tamara rushes to Eddy to remind him not to eat sand, she feels a surge of envy for Elena and her "good" babies who are never any trouble.

Questions for Discussion

1. What do people really mean when they label babies either "spoiled" or "good"?

2. What appear to be Elena's priorities and values in caring for her children? What are her daughters learning about their role in the world?

3. Why do you think the staff in Elena's child care center were opposed to holding, rocking, and playing with babies? Does frequent holding and cuddling create a setting in which adults are "warm nurturing, and emotionally available to the children"? Why is this important?

4. How do you feel about Al and Tamara's relationship with their children?

5. List, in order of importance, the ten characteristics you personally value and admire most in a person (for example, kindness, sense of humor, energy, intelligence, enthusiasm, and so on). Are these the same characteristics you expect caregivers to model in their interactions with babies and young children? Describe a real situation in which you modeled the characteristic you most value.

6. List the ten characteristics you like least in a person. Are these characteristics that you have seen caregivers demonstrate in their interactions with youngsters? Describe a real situation in which you modeled a characteristic you would not want children to imitate.

Points to Remember

- Contemporary family life brings special stresses and strains to children and families.

- Most young children receive at least some of their early care and teaching from adults other than their own parents.

- Ensuring the healthy growth and development of the next generation should be a major concern for everyone.

- The basic rules for responsible human behavior are simple; respect the rights of others, take only reasonable risks, and protect and maintain the environment.

- Children learn by imitating the behaviors and attitudes of others.

- Children learn best in a relaxed environment where play and curiosity are encouraged.

- Early development is fostered by freedom within reasonable limits to explore a safe but interesting environment.

- Properly matching early childhood settings to the natural stages of growth and development is called developmentally appropriate practice.

- Ignoring children's cries and refusing to become emotionally attached damages healthy development and undermines positive guidance.

Related Readings

Contemporary Parenting

Aidman, A. (1997). Television violence: Content, context, and consequences. Champaign, IL: ERIC Clearinghouse on Elementary and Early Childhood Education.

Amato, P. R. (1997). Life-span adjustment of children to their parents' divorce. In E. N. Junn & C. Boyatzis (Eds.), *Annual editions: Child growth and development 97/98* (4th ed.). New York: McGraw-Hill. (Original work published in *The Future of Children,* spring 1994)

> *Paul Amato provides information on children's adjustment to divorce, including their academic, social, and psychological well-being in childhood and as adults. Amato also describes how children's adjustment depends on many factors and explains that differences are generally small between children of divorce and children from intact families.*

Blankenhorn, D. (1997). Life without father. In K. M. Paciorek & J. H. Munro, *Annual editions: Early childhood education 97/98* (18th ed.). New York: McGraw-Hill. (Original work published in *USA Weekend,* February 24–26, 1995)

> *The increase in divorce and in single-mother families has led to a situation that David Blankenhorn calls "disappearing dads." Children without two caring and supportive parents are at risk of future failure in a number of areas.*

Bozett, F. W. (1987). *Gay and lesbian parents.* New York: Praeger.

Christian, L. G. (1997, May). Children and death. *Young Children, 52*(4), 76–80.

Cooksey, E. C., & Fondell, M. M. (1996). Spending time with his kids: Effects of family structure on fathers' and children's lives. *Journal of Marriage and the Family, 58*(3), 693–707.

Coontz, S. (1997). Where are the good old days? In K. M. Paciorek & J. H. Munro, *Annual editions: Early childhood education 97/98* (18th ed.). New York: McGraw-Hill. (Original work published in *Modern Maturity,* May/June 1996)

> *Throughout our nation's history, families have always been in flux. Economic changes have resulted in increasing poverty, homelessness, and distress for young children.*

Copeland, M. L., & McCreedy, B. S. (1997, January–February). Creating family-friendly policies: Are child care center policies in line with current family realities? *Child Care Information Exchange, 113,* 7–10, 12.

Crouson, R. L., & Boyd, W. L. (1993, February). Coordinated services for children: Designing arks for storms and seas unknown. *American Journal of Education, 101,* 141.

Denby, D. (1997). Buried alive. In E. N. Junn & C. Boyatzis (Eds.), *Annual editions: Child growth and development 97/98* (4th ed.). New York: McGraw-Hill. (Original work published in *The New Yorker,* July 15, 1996)

> *In this essay, David Denby argues that "an avalanche of crud" from popular culture television, films, toys, and video and computer games buries today's youth. He offers insight into the impression this culture may leave on children's character and their views of reality.*

deToledo, S., & Brown, D. E. (1995). *Grandparents as parents: A survival guide for raising a second family.* New York: Guilford.

> *More than a million American grandparents today are the primary caregivers for their grandchildren. Most have found their lives altered, their finances spread thin, and their parenting techniques old-fashioned. They find themselves challenged by a new, different, and sometimes traumatized generation. The book is a useful resource for professionals who work with parenting grandparents, and a good reading recommendation for grandparents and family members who need some encouragement and advice.*

Duis, S. S., et al. (1997, Spring). Parent versus child stress in diverse family types: An ecological approach. *Topics in Early Childhood Special Education, 17*(1), 53–73.

Ehrensaft, D. (1997). *Spoiling childhood: How well-meaning parents are giving children too much—but not what they need.* New York: Guilford.

> *In this book, Dr. Ehrensaft discusses the difficulties and stresses that today's parents are creating for themselves and their children. She describes the absurdities, frustrations, and possibilities of contemporary child rearing. She argues that parents today are all too often caught up in a guilt-driven pendulum swing between parenting too little and parenting too much. They are always in a hurry yet anxious for their children to succeed, aware of children's autonomy yet fearful of losing their love. Our culture has created a new kind of child, half miniature adult, half innocent cherub, whose new set of problems creates a divided sense of self and chronic anxiety.*

Elkind, D. (1981). *The hurried child.* Reading, MA: Addison-Wesley.

Elkind, D. (1997). School and family in the postmodern world. In E. N. Junn & C. Boyatzis (Eds.), *Annual editions: Child growth and development 97/98* (4th ed.). New York: McGraw-Hill. (Original work published in *Phi Delta Kappan*, September 1995)

> *David Elkind describes how schools and education have undergone, in the postmodern era, major changes due to broader changes in the family and society. One such change is that schools now assume many parental functions.*

Frieman, B. B. (1993, September). Separation and divorce: Children want their teachers to know—Meeting the emotional needs of preschool and primary school children. *Young Children, 48*(6), 58–63.

Henderson, A. T., & Berla, N. (Eds.). (1994). *A new generation of evidence: The family is critical to student achievement.* Washington, DC: National Committee for Citizens in Education.

Hernandez, D. J. (1995, Winter). Changing demographics: Past and future demands for early childhood programs. *Future of Children, 5*(3), 145–60.

Hildebrand, V., Phenice, L. A., Gray, M. M., & Hines, R. P. (1996). *Knowing and serving diverse families.* Upper Saddle River, NJ: Merrill Education/Prentice-Hall.

> *This book responds to the growing need for programs to work comfortably with all people and to help solve critical societal problems of relating to today's people at home, in the community, the nation, and the world. It examines both ethnic and structural diversity in families in the United States.*

Isenberg, J. P., & Jalongo, M. R. (Eds.) (1997). *Major trends and issues in early childhood education: Challenges, controversies, and insights.* New York: Teachers College Press.

Jackson, B. R. (1997, November). Creating a climate for healing in a violent society. *Young Children, 52*(7), 68–70.

Kagan, S. L. (1997, May). Support systems for children, youths, families, and schools in inner-city situations. *Education and Urban Society, 29*(3), 277–95.

Kagan, S. L., & Neuman, M. J. (1997, September). Highlights of the Quality 2000 Initiative: Not by chance. Public Policy Report. *Young Children, 52*(6), 54–62.

Kagan, S. L. & Neuman, M. J. (1997). *Solving the quality problem: A vision for America's early care and education system. A final report of the Quality 2000 Initiative.* New Haven, CT: Yale University.

Lakey, J. (1997, May). Teachers and parents define diversity in an Oregon preschool cooperative—Democracy at work. *Young Children, 52*(4), 20–28.

Leland, J. (1997). Violence, reel to real. In E. N. Junn & C. Boyatzis (Eds.), *Annual editions: Child growth and development 97/98* (4th ed.). New York: McGraw-Hill. (Original work published in *Newsweek,* December 11, 1995)

John Leland looks at the debate on violence in film and television and challenges the research conclusion that there is a clear causal relationship between televised violence and real-life aggression. Leland critiques many of the famous studies on the topic, as well as discussing the recent controversy over the V-chip.

Lewin, K., Lippitt, R., & White, R. (1939). Patterns of aggressive behavior in experimentally created social climates. *Journal of Social Psychology,* 271–99.

Three leadership styles—authoritarian, democratic, and laissez-faire (permissive)—were studied. Authoritarian leadership resulted in higher discontentment and aggression among the children, but also in more work production. Children in the democratic model showed less hostility, more enjoyment and more independent self-direction in their work. The laissez-faire group accomplished relatively little, and the children evidenced boredom.

Lindjord, D. (1997, November–December). Child care: The continuing crisis for working families and child care teachers. *Journal of Early Education and Family Review, 5*(2), 6–7.

McAlister, B. G. (1997, Spring). Growing up in a violent world: The impact of family and community violence on young children and their families. *Topics in Early Childhood Special Education, 17*(1), 74–102.

McLanahan, S., & Sandefur, G. (1994). *Growing up with a single parent: What hurts, what helps.* Cambridge, MA: Harvard University Press.

McMath, J. S. (1997, March). Young children, national tragedy, and picture books. *Young Children, 52*(3), 82–84.

Mitchell, S. (1997). The next baby boom. In K. M. Paciorek & J. H. Munro, *Annual editions: Early childhood education 97/98* (18th ed.). New York: McGraw-Hill. (Original work published in *American Demographics,* October 1995)

The nearly 76 million baby boomers born between 1946 and 1964 have produced 72 million children of their own, born from 1977 through 1993. This next generation of boomers is very different from the first. These new children and their families often do not have a father living at home. Parent lifestyles and responsibilities have changed tremendously.

Pallas, A. M., Natriello, G., & McDill, E. L. (1989). The changing nature of the disadvantaged population: Current dimensions and future trends. *Educational Researcher, 18*(5), 16–22.

Provenzo, E. F., Jr. (1992, March). The video generation. *American School Board Journal, 179*(3), 29–32.

Roberts, P. (1997). Fathers' time. In E. N. Junn & C. Boyatzis (Eds.), *Annual editions: Child growth and development 97/98* (4th ed.). New York: McGraw-Hill. (Original work published in *Psychology Today,* May/June 1996)

Paul Roberts presents evidence on fathers' roles in the family, their influence on children's emotional and intellectual development, and their distinct interaction styles. Roberts also describes how fathers have only recently received attention from researchers, showing that they are no longer subservient in the parenting realm.

Seefeldt, C., & Glaper, A. (1998). *Continuing issues in early childhood education* (2nd ed.). Upper Saddle River, NJ: Merrill Education/Prentice-Hall.

> *This book contains discussions, debates, disagreements, and disputes, with the expectation that these will lead the reader to explore and question various points of view.*

Shores, E. F. (1991). *Prenatal cocaine exposure: The south looks for answers.* Little Rock, AR: Southern Association on Children Under Six.

Stabiner, K. (1997). Get 'em while they're young. In E. N. Junn & C. Boyatzis (Eds.), *Annual editions: Child growth and development 97/98* (4th ed.). New York: McGraw-Hill. (Original work published in *Los Angeles Times Magazine,* August 15, 1993)

> *Karen Stabiner describes how advertisers set their sights on young children, using sophisticated tactics to shape their consumer habits and tastes to cultivate lifelong loyalty to their products. Also discussed are techniques that parents can use to protect children from the early onslaught of advertising aimed at those too young to understand that commercials are designed to sell a product.*

Stengel, R. (1997). Fly till I die. In K. M. Paciorek & J. H. Munro, *Annual editions: Early childhood education 97/98* (18th ed.). New York: McGraw-Hill. (Original work published in Time, April 22, 1996)

> *The shocking April 18, 1996, death in a plane crash of Jessica Dubroff, her father, and a flight instructor led many people nationwide to question the parenting skills and knowledge of child development of her parents. Should there be a time when decisions made by families are questioned by the government? Just how much are young children today being pushed to achieve goals that may or may not be their goals?*

Stringer-Seibold, T., et al. (1996, Fall). Strengths and needs of divided families. Research Highlights. *Dimensions of Early Childhood, 24*(4), 22–29.

Stroud, J. E., et al. (1997, Summer). Understanding and supporting adoptive families. *Early Childhood Education Journal, 24*(4), 229–34.

Swick, K. J. (1997, Spring). Strengthening homeless families and their young children. *Dimensions of Early Childhood, 25*(2), 29–34.

Children are like little sponges, taking in everything they see, hear, touch, taste, and smell.

Chapter 2

Planning the Prosocial Environment

Chapter Outline

Prosocial Behavior

Setting the Stage for Appropriate Behavior
  The Physical Environment
  Scheduling

The Nurturing Social Environment
  A Relaxed, Playful Atmosphere
  A Cooperative Rather than Competitive Setting
  Developmentally Appropriate Activities, Materials, and Routines
  Consistency and Predictability

The Nurturing Adult
  Modeling Appropriate Behavior
  Showing Attentiveness to Individual Needs
  Providing Affirmation, Affection, and Acceptance
  Providing Recognition and Encouragement
  Being Willing to Enforce Appropriate Rules
  Being Willing to Protect Individual Rights

Practical Application/Discussion
  William and the Nature Walk

Questions for Discussion
Points to Remember
Related Readings

Objectives

This chapter will assist you in

- Defining prosocial behavior
- Identifying components of the nurturing social environment
- Recognizing supportive and effective adult behaviors
- Outlining strategies for initiating positive behavior in children

Prosocial Behavior

Prosocial behavior is the opposite of antisocial behavior. Prosocial behavior benefits others and demonstrates the presence of a social conscience. **Antisocial** behavior harms others and indicates a disregard for the rights and needs of others. The concept of prosocial behavior focuses on three critical elements of a child's beneficial or helping interactions with others:

Since patterns of natural human growth and development teach us that young children always begin life locked into **egocentrism** (or self-centeredness), we know that prosocial behavior is not an inborn trait, but a slowly learned way of acting that wins approval and affection from others.

Three Key Elements of Prosocial Behavior

- *Cooperation—working with others unselfishly toward a common goal*
- *Empathy—putting oneself into others' shoes, to feel what they feel, to have insight into their thoughts and actions*
- *Altruism—behaving generously, acting in a way that benefits others with no motive of personal gain.*

Young children are not likely to postpone immediate gratification in order to work cooperatively with others toward a common goal. They do not start life with a capacity to recognize that others have feelings and needs similar to their own. Also, of course, they do not come into the world equipped with the logical, cause-and-effect thinking skills necessary to understand that generously giving a valued object or favor today may bring affection and loyalty from a friend tomorrow (Peterson, 1983). Children adopt prosocial behaviors only after much experience and practice in an environment that demonstrates and nurtures positive social interaction.

Setting the Stage for Appropriate Behavior

We give subtle messages to children about how we expect them to behave by the surroundings we plan for them. We can prevent many behavior problems before they ever begin simply by careful planning, by understanding children's developmental needs, and by creating a perfect match between their needs and the settings around them.

How Can the Physical Environment Support Prosocial Behavior?

Parents need to adapt home environments to make them safe, child-proof, and interesting for children of various ages. Periodically, as children grow, parents must reexamine their children's bedrooms, playrooms, and play yards to see that the space matches the child's growing skills and interests. Children can gradually deal responsibly with and reliably use and put away more complicated equipment and furnishings.

Children tend to treat other children much the same way they have been treated by the important adults in their lives.

Adults planning living space for groups of children also have a challenging task facing them. The well-planned early childhood environment is orderly but not rigid, clean but not sterile, and interesting but not overstimulating. In other words, it is carefully balanced. The only way to be sure that it is properly balanced is to watch the children who live, play, and work there, to see if the environment seems overwhelming, boring, frustrating, or just right.

What Are Ineffective Child Care Environments Like?

Some early childhood settings have an atmosphere that seems half-way between a festival and a flea market. Almost every square inch of the walls is plastered with pictures, posters, signs, crafts, and notices. Things dangle from the ceiling like a swarm of butterflies, and furniture and toys form a wall-to-wall obstacle course on the floor. Walls and furniture are painted colors such as taxicab yellow or iridescent lime green. Special rugs are purchased with bright, busy, dizzying patterns of letters, numbers, and game boards to "stimulate learning."

This kind of environment invites loud, wild, unbridled activity. Children will probably feel comfortable running, leaping off tables, and bellowing across the room. Adults will probably have great difficulty guiding children into quiet concentration on a puzzle or book, or teaching children to walk rather than run and use soft "inside voices" rather than screaming and yelling. Children may initially have great fun in this environment but will likely become bored, tired, and overwhelmed eventually. Since the adults are likely to have difficulty coping with the children's level of intensity, they may become irritable and restrictive, falling into negative power struggles with the children.

Other early childhood settings have an atmosphere somewhat like a dentist's waiting room. They are stark white, or cool, pale pastel colors, and they smell strongly of disinfectant. The sparse furnishings have an eerie appearance as if they have never been touched by human hands. Insipid elevator music may be piped in softly, and any toys or books seem to be on display rather than intended for actual use (they may actually be arranged out of the children's reach). The adults seem most anxious that the children "don't mess anything up." Painting, water play, and messy clay are out of the question. Everything the children do may be regimented into rigidly controlled activities that the whole class does together.

Nothing about this environment invites children to explore or interact with the materials provided. They become passive recipients of the experiences adults provide, and they are pressured to "sit still, be quiet, and don't touch anything without permission." The children may at first be subdued, restrained, even intimidated by their surroundings, but eventually they will become bored, restless, and rebellious.

How Would I Recognize a Developmentally Appropriate Environment?

Developmentally appropriate early childhood settings are warm and homey. There are focal points of interest at various places in the environment (displays of children's artwork, holiday decorations, or decorative touches), but they are not overwhelming. Ceilings, walls, and floors are muted, neutral tones so that the visual emphasis is on brightly colored toys, learning equipment, and the children's art "masterpieces."

The well-planned environment is warm and homey.

The environment is well-lighted with plenty of sunny windows. Acoustical ceiling tiles soften the sound level. Furniture and equipment are arranged to break the floor space into clearly defined learning centers in order to discourage running, to encourage focused attention on learning materials such as books, puzzles, and blocks, and to allow easy supervision. Messy activities such as food preparation, clay, water play, and painting are regularly available for children past three and structured to be used successfully and independently.

In a developmentally appropriate preschool classroom, painting may be routinely set up with a day's supply of paper available to be clothespinned onto a child-sized easel. Just an ounce or

> *The lessons are individual, and brevity must be one of the chief characteristics.*
>
> Maria Montessori (Montessori & Hunt, 1989)

two of fairly thick paint in a couple of nontip containers with short, fat paintbrushes makes the activity almost "goof-proof" for a young child wanting to paint "all by herself." A clothesline is ready nearby for hanging wet paintings to dry. There are classroom pets such as hamsters and fish, plants for the children to water and enjoy, and many opportunities for children to be involved in real-life activities such as preparing food and cleaning up.

Whether an environment is designed for infants, toddlers, preschoolers, or school-aged children, individual children's levels of development and interests are taken into consideration. Toddlers cannot function properly in environments that are arranged with hazardous and inappropriate furniture and toys, even though that same equipment may be perfectly suited to preschoolers. Infants and toddlers need unstructured toys and materials for sensory exploration and safe motor skill practice.

School-aged children will be bored and offended if they are placed in a room filled with preschool blocks, picture books, and baby dolls. They too need a space suited to their special needs and interests. In after-school care settings, children need a "clubhouse" environment with games, music, and quiet places to study. Outdoors they need a soccer field, a basketball goal, and elementary-sized swings and slides.

What Effect Does the Environment Have on Child Guidance?

In developmentally appropriate environments, behavior problems are minimized simply because children are challenged and their needs are met. They are busy and excited about their accomplishments. At the beginning of the year, adults often have to simplify an environment to ensure that children can manage independently and successfully. Gradually, as the children develop new skills, adults add new materials and increase the complexity of the environment so that it continually challenges the children. Adults are constantly searching for materials that match children's skills perfectly—somewhere right in the middle, between materials that are so simple that they are boring and materials that are so complex they are overwhelming. Adults in the developmentally appropriate environment allow children to carry out play activities individually or in

The well-planned environment is challenging but not overwhelming. (Photograph provided courtesy of CHILDREN AT RISK.)

small groups of their own choosing rather than marching them all lockstep to do the same activities at the same time as a large group. Large group activities for preschoolers are limited to short periods of time for sharing, singing, and hearing stories read. Large group activities are avoided altogether for infants and toddlers.

The adult constantly looks for ways to increase the children's independence and mastery of their environment. She has taught the children how to spread their jackets on the floor, stand with feet near the collar or hood, stick hands in the arm holes, then flip the jackets over their heads—like magic they know how to put their own coats on without help. She has used color-coding to help children know where things go. Everything in a yellow container goes in the art center; everything red goes in the science center. She has even taped pictures of toys and games on shelves to remind children where to put things away. Children are allowed to rearrange the playhouse furniture in the housekeeping center, as long as they remember to be good citizens and put it back when they are finished. They feel the environment is their space. They feel pride and self-confidence. They know the adult is their ally, not their enemy. The stage is set for positive child guidance. (See Appendix B for additional resources.)

How Do Schedules Support Positive Behavior?

Another critical concern in planning for positive child guidance relates to pacing or scheduling. Young children fiercely resist being hurried, and they can barely tolerate being forced to wait.

They have their own pace. Different children have different paces. By scheduling large blocks of time for **child-directed** (independent) activities, children feel freer to work and play at their own pace. One child may take only three seconds to paint a paper plate turkey to her satisfaction, while another child may want to spend twenty minutes painting it just the way he wants. Children appreciate a schedule that is consistent enough to give them the security of predictable patterns, but not so rigid that it cannot adapt to their individual needs.

If children are forced into a rigidly scheduled large group activity, the fast child will be bored and tempted to get into mischief as she waits for others to finish. The slow child will be forced to stop painting before he has fully benefited from the learning value of the activity. He may also feel frustrated and irritable because he did not have the opportunity to finish the project he obviously cared about.

Parents also have to pay close attention to scheduling in order to set the stage for positive child guidance. Bill and Irene both work. They hate getting their three children up in the morning. Because evenings are so hectic, the children often do not get to bed until 9:30 or 10:00 p.m. Of course they are cranky and out-of-sorts when their parents try to wake them at the crack of dawn. Bill and Irene are so rushed in the morning, they wait until the last possible moment to get the kids up. Then there is a mad rush to get them dressed and fed. Almost always there is conflict with one or more of the balky, groggy children.

To plan for more successful behavior, Bill and Irene will have to reschedule their evenings to make sure they and the children have adequate rest. They will also have to get the children up in the morning as early as possible rather than as late as possible, so the children have time to wake up and plenty of time to eat and dress without being hassled. Rushing a sleepy child is an almost guaranteed way to create an unmanageable child.

The Nurturing Social Environment

Adults who hope to stimulate prosocial behavior in young children must first establish a nurturing social environment—a setting in which children feel safe enough and comfortable enough to be cooperative, empathetic, and altruistic. Children who worry about being hurt, feel stressed to perform beyond their capability, or feel pushed into competition with playmates will probably have little interest in prosocial behavior. Children who are afraid that their own needs will not be met may not be able to be generous with others. A child may behave in a prosocial manner in one setting but not in another; her day-to-day behavior depends to a great extent on her surroundings (Hartshorne & May, 1928).

How Does a Relaxed, Playful Environment Encourage Prosocial Behavior?

Early childhood is a special time in one's life. The young of other mammals (puppies, kittens, colts, and so on) frolic and play as they develop the skills they need to survive in adulthood. Adults of various species go about the serious work of providing food, shelter, and protection while the young chase around, pouncing on bugs, climbing trees, rolling in the grass, and having pretend fights. Their gleeful freedom enables them to coordinate muscles and practice skills.

Young human beings need a protected period of childhood in which to play and explore. If children are forced into somber, little-adult behavior, they may turn sour and critical. Instead of taking pleasure in their friends' playful antics, they may feel compelled to report, or "tattle," to adults about even the most trivial misdeed of another child. Children should feel free to complain to adults when personal rights have been violated and to report misbehavior to authorities (adults) when rules have been broken or hazardous behavior is taking place. That kind of "telling" is sincere and should never be labeled tattling. Frivolous or malicious telling, however, is a different matter. The child who obsessively tells, hoping to get peers in trouble, may expect adults to stamp out or punish every silly or childish behavior and to reward him or her for telling, for playing the role of "little Miss Goody Two-Shoes" or "little Mr. Goody Goody." This behavior is inappropriate and should be addressed.

A child who persists in "telling on" others for no good reason will seem antisocial to playmates who have been "told on." The child who tattles, however, will probably have inferred from adult criticisms of childish behavior that it is not okay to be a child, to be "one of the gang." This child may feel aloof and apart from other children—she may actually view herself as a little adult. These feelings hinder the development of friendships that lead to wholesome cooperative play and to optimum social and emotional development, so we need let the child know that it is definitely okay to be a "silly kid" sometimes. Children can be helped to refrain from "tattling on" other children when they are taught to help a friend who made a mistake. "Yes, Shelley, I see that James forgot to take his turn. How can we help him remember?"

The nurturing social environment is relaxed and playful.

A relaxed, playful atmosphere for babies and young children helps them develop tolerance and a sense of humor. Exposure to adults who are tolerant of others and do not take themselves too seriously greatly aids children in developing the ability to feel empathy for others. Adults sometimes forget to step into children's shoes to feel what they feel and see things from their perspective.

Adults consider sitting back, staring into space, and doing nothing an indulgent luxury—children consider this sitting and doing nothing an aversive punishment. Adults have a slower, quieter rhythm or pace than children and may feel annoyed by children's squealing, wriggling, wrestling, and running. Intolerant adults force children to function within the adult's comfort zone for noise and movement. In contrast, when young children sense the generosity of adults who kindly tolerate and gently redirect the bustling chaos of active, noisy children, then the children in turn learn to demonstrate generosity and tolerance for others.

Instead of expressing exasperation, Allen, a young daddy, sits down and has a good laugh when his toddler walks in wearing underwear on his head rather than on his bottom. Mrs. Farrel, a long-time member of Weight Watchers, grins and takes it as a sincere compliment when little Jennifer says, "I think you're beautiful. You're the prettiest fat lady in the whole world." Even Miss Cindy laughs good-naturedly with her school-agers after the gruesome spider that has startled her turns out to be nothing more than a plastic Halloween party favor.

We might be tempted to take normal childish behaviors more seriously than necessary or even become angry and punitive with the children described above. In a relaxed, playful atmosphere, however, children can learn discipline, but they can also learn that it is okay to be generous and forgiving (Mussen & Eisenberg-Berg, 1977). Children learn that it is okay to make mistakes, because parents, teachers, and caregivers are allies, not enemies. It is okay to be playful and silly at times, because others can let down their barriers and share in a good laugh.

Clearly, there is a boundary between silliness and genuine misbehavior, between playfulness and antisocial activity. Playfulness is neither hurtful nor mean-spirited, maliciousness is both. Silly behavior that is not totally appropriate can be dealt with patiently and with a sense of humor even though it may need to be firmly redirected at some point if it begins to interfere with necessary routines or to annoy others.

How Can I Create a Cooperative Rather than Competitive Setting?

When adults say things like "See if you can put your lunch box away before anyone else" or "Whoever is quietest can be first in line," children are encouraged to be competitive rather than cooperative. We are often tempted to use competitive challenges because they work so much more powerfully and effectively than nagging or threatening, and seem less negative. Remember, even if something works well to achieve short-term goals, it may not necessarily achieve the long-term goals we seek. In the long run, getting children's coats on quickly or getting trash picked up without a second reminder is not nearly so important as fostering cooperative and caring relationships among children who will someday be adult citizens.

By urging children to win at the expense of others, we may be establishing patterns of greediness and a lack of regard for the feelings of others. It is far more helpful to redirect children's natural competitive urges into competition with their own best records—"I wonder if you can build these blocks even higher than you did yesterday" or "Deonicia, you are so quiet and still. You must be ready for lunch. Would you like to be our leader today?"

Developmentally Appropriate Activities, Materials, and Routines

Bored children become irritable and mischievous. Children who are pushed beyond their limits into irrelevant memorization or tedious busywork may become antagonistic and rebellious. Unhappy children are more likely to behave in antisocial ways. When adults hold unrealistic expectations for children, stressful, even angry, relations erupt. This friction becomes contagious and soon interactions among the children themselves are tinged with irritability and annoyance. This is quite obviously not a productive situation for children to learn and to practice prosocial behavior.

The secret to a cooperative, caring, and generous atmosphere among young children lies in our meeting children's basic needs—social, emotional, physical, and intellectual. An overwhelming need of early childhood is the need for engrossing, entertaining, and rewarding activity. John Dewey, Maria Montessori, Jean Piaget, and other experts have shown us that children love to learn. These experts have made it clear that children learn easily through spontaneous as well as guided play experiences. Children find fulfillment in activities that are developmentally appropriate. (See Chapter 10 for history and philosophy of early education.)

Children become deeply involved in their play and are amazingly relaxed and compliant when their need for fulfilling activity is met. This kind of productive, fulfilling activity is defined as being developmentally appropriate.

Why Is Consistency So Important?

Teachers, parents, and child care providers quite often are trapped by the idea that if something does not work the first time, then it will never work. Children eventually change a behavior when they finally comprehend and remember that the action will quickly and consistently be stopped or redirected. A caregiver who decides that preschoolers should learn to scrape their plates independently after lunch may feel exasperated when the children mistakenly throw their plates and utensils away on their first try. A kindergarten teacher may throw up his hands in frustration after disastrously introducing finger-painting for the first time to rowdy five-year-olds who leave school looking like splotchy rainbows. And any adult who has ever dealt with toddlers knows that the point simply does not get across the first hundred times one-year-olds are told that sticks and leaves should not go in one's mouth.

Children learn positive ways of interacting with others when we can be consistent and persistent (not angry and impatient). We can avoid a great deal of irritation simply by recognizing that it takes time for children to absorb new skills and habits. Our task is to structure a consistent and

Activities Should Be . . .

- **Relevant**—match the child's capabilities and interests
- **Active**—encourage movement
- **Sensorial**—appeal to the five senses

To Support Positive Behavior . . .

- *Get to know children personally, and respond to their individual capabilities, interests, and preferences.*
- *Plan room arrangements that minimize frustration, congestion, and confusion for children.*
- *Prepare and arrange interesting toys and activities that relate to all areas of children's development—social, emotional, and physical as well as intellectual.*
- *Establish routines that allow uninterrupted blocks of time for spontaneous, self-directed play in a carefully planned environment.*
- *Make arrangements for hands-on exploration of real objects to be a natural and integral part of learning activities.*
- *Allow children to express their own individuality by making their own choices within clearly defined limits, by saying, for example, "Would you rather paint or play with clay?" "Would you rather have orange juice or milk?" "Would you rather wear a skirt or blue jeans?"*
- *Greatly limit situations in which children are forced to sit still, to wait for something to happen, or to stand in line (toddlers are especially unable to cope with these situations).*

predictable environment for children, where they are allowed adequate periods of time to develop new skills introduced in tiny, bite-sized bits.

We adults are prone to set absurd goals. We focus our attention on children's behavior in fits and spurts. We ignore messiness for months or years then suddenly insist on neatness—this minute! Three-year-old Fernando had always traipsed around the house after his bath in a big, soft bath towel. When he was ready to get dressed, he had a habit of dropping the damp towel in a heap on his bedroom floor. Freshly scrubbed little boys wrapped in towels are so endearing that his parents had always quietly tolerated his towel-dropping ritual. One day, however, his poor mom reached the end of her patience and yelled, "Fernando, get this wet towel into the bathroom, and I mean step on it!" After she cooled off a bit, she peeked into the bathroom to check on Fernando—there he stood in the middle of the bathroom, crying pitifully but standing obediently on the towel.

Does Potty Training Always Have to Be a Battle?

We live in an instant society. When we feel a child is old enough to behave in a certain way, we want that behavior instantly. One popular paperback book confidently tells parents that children can be toilet trained in a day. In reality, children can not master toilet training in a day, a week, or even a month. A two-year-old may go from diapers to dry pants literally overnight, but this only happens after the child has mastered hundreds of little prerequisite skills. The toddler must gradually learn how to recognize body sensations, communicate needs, inhibit sudden impulses, consciously manipulate the muscles that control elimination, and even balance on top of a big scary bowl of water—all this just to please grown-ups! Many children will be three or older before they have gained reliable control over bowel and bladder.

Consistent, predictable routines help a child ease comfortably into learning new skills. For months, toilet training may consist only of talking about the potty, looking at it, exploring it, and sitting for a second or two on it, just as a playful part of diaper-changing routine. It may be months before the child's consistent, predictable routines expand to include actually using the potty. The important thing is that the child keeps moving in the right direction. Someday, nobody will remember or care how fast or slow the learning was.

Children are quite naturally inclined to resist when they are confronted with a sudden, unexpected demand that they change a long-standing behavior. Likewise, some of us adults put up quite a fuss when we were first told that we ought to wear seat belts in cars. We argued, "But it feels weird . . . but I'm not accustomed to it . . . but I don't want to change." A toddler who has never had a worry in the world about when or where to relieve himself might well feel those same feelings when we insist that he ought to keep his pants dry by urinating in a toilet.

A great big toilet can be pretty intimidating to a very little person!

Consistency and predictability in our expectations for children helps them accept and gradually adapt to our standards. Children do not instantly develop an ability to take turns or to resist greedily grabbing a toy. Slowly and persistently, however, we can nudge children into behaving in a more responsible and prosocial manner.

The Nurturing Adult

One might jump to the erroneous conclusion that a nurturing parent, teacher, or caregiver is one who is either a saint or a pushover. The word nurture, however, means to train, to educate, or to nourish. The truly nurturing adult is simply an honest, emotionally healthy person who has learned how to be both assertive and caring at the same time.

How Can I Be More Nurturing and Patient?

Teaching children in a way that nourishes them does not mean pointing out every flaw, criticizing every imperfection, and punishing every lapse in judgment. In fact, the first step toward shaping children's behavior positively is simply setting a good example, that is, modeling appropriate behavior. Unbeknownst to us, many of children's most upsetting misbehaviors are little more than instant replays of our own behavior, in a context we do not expect. Take, for example, the classic irony of an adult saying, "If you don't stop hitting people, I'm going to spank you."

Children gradually learn one must *be* a friend to *have* a friend.

If a child is overly loud and boisterous, we may focus on being particularly soft-voiced and calm. If a child is angry and unyielding, we can model patience and forgiveness. If a child is aggressive and hurtful, we can demonstrate gentleness and kindness. Being nurturing must not be used as an excuse to ignore behaviors that must be stopped. Our own prosocial behavior will be a good example for the child as we assertively protect property and personal rights by interrupting and redirecting unacceptable behavior. Additionally, we can make a mental note to find future opportunities, after a conflict situation has been resolved, to continue modeling desired behaviors such as calmness, forgiveness, and gentleness. This focus on assertive but nonaggressive guidance is particularly noteworthy, since many adults rely on angry and aggressive methods of discipline. Between 84 and 97 percent of all parents use physical punishment at some point as a strategy for disciplining their children (Parke & Slaby, 1983).

Ask These Questions About Annoying Behaviors

- *What specific aspects of the behavior are particularly annoying to me?*
- *Is there any way that I may have been inadvertently setting an example for that behavior?*
- *What positive behavior could be modeled and reinforced to replace the undesired behavior?*
- *How can I model appropriate behaviors so the child will be sure to notice and respond?*

How Does a Nurturing Adult Respond to Aggression?

Mrs. Young cares for one-year-olds in a mothers-day-out program. When a toddler bites, she does whatever she has to—as firmly as necessary, but as gently as possible—to stop the biting, to get the bitten child free from the biter. In a deeply concerned (but not angry) voice, she tells the biter assertively, "No biting, biting hurts." She then takes great pains to model touching the bitten child gently. Mrs. Young delicately strokes the bitten child's arm saying in a soothing voice, "Gentle. Be gentle." Often the biter will imitate her and touch the other child, then she responds, "That was so gentle. Thank you." Slowly, the toddlers begin to absorb the gentleness they see in Mrs. Young's actions every day.

When the children are older, Mrs. Young will begin emphasizing another concept, using words rather than aggression to express anger. Since she uses the word *no* very sparingly and only when she really intends for an action to stop, the children learn through observation that it is a powerful and important word. We will not hear Mrs. Young snapping at a child, "Don't you dare say no to me!" She allows children to express their thoughts and feelings verbally.

By being positive and assertive rather than negative and confrontational with children, Mrs. Young does not overuse the word *no* herself. Consequently, she does not hear the word *no* from toddlers very often. When she does, however, she acknowledges the balky child's feelings—

even if the child cannot reasonably be allowed to have his or her own way. She says, "I know you don't want to wash your hands right now, but you must have clean hands in order to be allowed to eat." Furthermore, she actually coaches her toddlers in the skill of saying no. She prompts them, "Can you tell Marcus no? Say, 'No, Marcus. My cracker. Mine.'" In time, children learn by direct teaching as well as by imitation to use words rather than aggression to express their feelings of anger.

Can Children Learn Appropriate Behavior Through Imitation?

Although babies and toddlers are only able to mimic bits and pieces of behaviors they observe, even these first attempts at **modeling** (imitating) are critically important to their development. Preschoolers imitate entire sequences of behavior. Preschoolers are in a particularly sensitive period of their lives for imitation. As they mime adult actions in their play, we get to see them reenact their world as they perceive it (Mussen & Eisenberg-Berg, 1977). These glimpses into their world range from the delightfully funny to the downright alarming. Children's imitative play discloses their innocent misconceptions of the adult world as well as the fears and pains they sometimes feel.

School-aged children imitate, but they are more selective in choosing role models. They are constantly (but unconsciously) absorbing subtle behavior characteristics from those around them. But they are not likely to mimic the behaviors of adults or children they do not like. They will make conscious attempts, however, to talk, dress, and act like those they admire (Bandura, 1977). Adults can enhance positive imitative learning by becoming a respected and admired member of the child's immediate world rather than an aloof and distanced authority figure.

Imitation is an important and logical tool for teaching prosocial behavior. Adults waste a great opportunity to have impact on children if they do not become particularly aware of their own actions and attitudes as well as those communicated by such cultural media as television (Aidman, 1997; Bandura, 1977; Cairns, 1979; Gerbner & Gross, 1980; Lefkowitz & Tesiny, 1980; Leland, 1997; Parke & Slaby, 1983). If children spend long periods of time watching television, they are bound to internalize the language and behavior they see there. The nurturing adult will closely monitor and limit programs to avoid overexposure to violent, irresponsible behaviors.

Rather than focus all our attention on correcting children's behaviors, we must take a cold, hard look at ourselves in the mirror now and again and correct some of our own flaws. Even if we are unsuccessful in weeding out all of our personal quirks and imperfections, we will certainly become more sensitive to the child's dilemma of truly wanting to stop an undesirable behavior but not being able to accomplish it. If our goal is to develop children's self-discipline and self-control, then we had best see how much of those admirable characteristics we are able to muster so we can show children (rather than just tell them) how people should behave.

How Can I Be More Attentive to Children's Individual Needs?

Nurturing adults respond to children's individual needs. Parents generally have no difficulty in seeing their own children as individuals. Family intimacy and shared history throughout a child's

Children are likely to be happy and cooperative
when their needs are met.

Am I a Positive Role Model?

- *Can children easily observe cooperation, empathy, and altruism in my day-to-day actions?*
- *Are my values evidenced clearly in the environment I provide for children?*
- *What kinds of books do I read to them?*
- *What kinds of toys, movies, and television shows do I make available?*

---

life make it likely that there is at least awareness of (if not respect for) individual differences. A key problem for parents may be accepting individual differences among their children and resisting the temptation to compare them to one another. A parent may say, "I'm sure that Ramona will love taking piano lessons just like her older brother did," while knowing full well that little Ramona would much rather do "wheelies" on a bicycle than learn to play the piano.

In a group setting, sadly, young children may be seen as tiny cogs in a very large machine. Babies' diapers may be changed not when they become wet or soiled, but at routinely scheduled times. Eating, playing, and sleeping may take place as scheduled for whole groups rather than in response to children's individual feelings of hunger, playfulness, or fatigue. A child may not be

Adults should become actively involved in the child's world so they will not be seen as cold, aloof authority figures.

hungry for breakfast on a given day or may be really tired before naptime. It is easy for a child to feel very overlooked in a group. While routines are essential to "sanity and survival" for group caregivers, nurturing adults will find ways to be sensitive and to make allowances for children's individual needs.

A nurturing adult will not be callous to children sleeping facedown on uncovered plastic mats in sweaty August heat, or make little ones nap with their shoes on simply because taking shoes off and putting them back on is too much bother. The nurturing adult would not be inclined to toss snack crackers unceremoniously onto a bare table without even the dignity of a napkin or paper plate. A nurturing adult will really care about the comfort and feelings of individual children. Even if every individual need cannot reasonably be met, the nurturing adult will express awareness of and concern for children's individual circumstances. Showing attentiveness to children's individual needs is an excellent way to demonstrate cooperative behavior for them.

How Can I Provide Affirmation, Affection, and Acceptance?

Affirmation, affection, and acceptance assure a child that she is wanted and appreciated. Unconditional positive regard is the process through which affirmation, affection, and acceptance are conveyed. In contrast, conditional affection is attention given to a child only when he pleases the adult. Conditional affection carries the hidden message, "I will only love you if you are good." Unconditional positive regard lets children know they are liked simply for who they are, not for how they perform at any given time. Children absorb the message, "You are a loved, worthwhile individual even if you sometimes make mistakes." According to Clarke (1978), in order for children to develop healthy self-esteem, they must absorb the following clear messages from the words and actions of their caregivers:

Affirmations for Being

- *"You have a right to be here."*
- *"I'm glad you are who you are."*
- *"It's okay for you to have needs."*

Affirmations for Becoming Independent

- *"You don't have to do tricks (be cute, sick, sad, mad, or scared) to get attention."*
- *It's okay to be curious and try new things on your own."*

Affirmations for Learning to Think

- *"You can stand up for the things you believe even if there is some risk involved."*
- *"You can own the consequences of your own actions; others don't have to rescue you."*
- *"It's okay to make mistakes as long as you accept responsibility for making amends."*

Affirmations for Developing an Individual Identity

- *"You can express your own thoughts and feelings without fear of rejection."*
- *"It's okay to disagree."*
- *"You can trust your own judgment."*

Sometimes the preceding messages of affirmation can be verbally expressed to children. They can also be conveyed to children in day-to-day actions throughout children's lives. Affirmation is communicated to a baby by her caregiver's facial expression during such routines as diaper changing. If she looks up and sees disgust or annoyance in the caregiver's face, she will sense that it is not okay to be a baby and to need a dirty diaper changed. If she sees a relaxed smile, she will know that she is welcome and her needs are okay. If a preschooler accidentally tramples a flower bed while trying to pull weeds like his daddy, he will sense affirmation as his dad patiently acknowledges the child's good intentions and teaches him how to weed the garden without trampling.

Nurturing adults care about children's comfort.

Nurturing adults are not afraid to show affection to children (Hoffman, 1979). Smiles, warm hugs, and sincere interest in a child's world let her know that she is the recipient of unconditional positive regard. Appropriate affection should never be intrusive, overwhelming, or one-sided, but rather respectful and reciprocal. A basic human need is for a sense of belonging. We human beings are essentially social creatures. We cannot really be happy or functional without a secure feeling that we have a place in the social order around us. The most desirable social position is one in which we feel admiration, acceptance, and approval from the important people around us.

If that situation cannot be found, people (children as well as grown-ups) may opt for negative substitute relationships to find recognition and acceptance. People assume leadership by becoming gang members, achieve recognition by defying rules, and hold others' attention by shocking, frightening, or angering them. The very last thing children (or anyone else) will settle for is being ignored and left out. Only the most emotionally disabled members of society retreat into and accept a life of total social isolation.

To stimulate prosocial behavior, the nurturing adult will be generous in making sure children know that they are accepted and approved. Instead of focusing only on children's unacceptable behaviors, the nurturing adult makes a point of noticing and commenting on positive behaviors—thanking the child for remembering to wipe his feet, commenting on the lovely colors in his crayon drawing, and listening with interest to his excited but rambling account of a weekend camping trip. The nurturing adult is careful to separate clearly the difference between "bad" actions and "bad" people: "I don't like hitting, but I like you very much. You are a good person. You can learn to use words rather than hitting." In spite of inevitable disciplinary intervention from time to time, the nurtured child always knows she is a good and worthwhile human being.

Nurturing adults who treat everyone with respect become role models of prosocial behavior.

How Can I Provide Positive Recognition and Encouragement?

On special occasions children want and deserve outright praise, just as we do in our own personal and professional lives. An occasional, sincere pat on the back can trigger a surge of motivation in us (Mussen & Eisenberg-Berg, 1977). Too much praise, however, can be burdensome, causing us to feel pressured to live up to unrealistic standards. We either awkwardly stammer thank you or, worse, become addicted to praise, needing more and more every day to maintain our self-esteem. A suddenly famous guitar player was asked recently what he missed most about the formerly quiet life he led before he found fame. He quickly replied, "I miss just sitting down with people to talk about music. Everyone tells me how much they admire my work and how wonderful they think I am, but how can you answer that?"

Recognition and encouragement are more moderate alternatives to an overabundance of gushy or insincere praise. Often we praise a child by stating a value judgment, "Oh, what a good boy you are!" Unfortunately, by implying that cleaning up makes him "good," we hint that if he does not continue the action in the future, he might become "bad." (Young children tend to think in simplistic terms—if you are not good, then you must be bad.)

Recognizing and encouraging are different from praising. To recognize and encourage a child, we might say, "I noticed that you wiped the table with a sponge. The table is clean and beautiful. Thanks!" The recognition is very specific (tells exactly what the child did) and encourages the child by letting him know that we appreciate the action. He is not labeled good or bad, just sincerely acknowledged for a job well done. The nurturing adult says thank you very frequently to children. When children do the right thing, it is not appropriate or helpful to dredge up old problems, saying, for example, "Why didn't you do this yesterday?" or "Well, now that you have done this, you can do everything else I've been telling you to do." Children who are overwhelmed with criticism become very defeatist. They think, "Why should I even try? Everything I do just gets me into more trouble." The child will feel more encouraged if she is allowed to "glow" in every little bit of success before tactfully being guided by a nurturing adult to complete other unfinished tasks. (See Chapter 4 for more about this.)

Praise focuses a child's attention on gaining external rewards. Recognition and encouragement focus the child's attention on internal rewards, feelings of accomplishment, pride, and self-worth. Internal rewards build the child's capacity for self-control and self-direction.

Am I Willing to Enforce Rules Even If It Would Be Easier to Look the Other Way?

The nurturing adult is able to be both assertive and caring at the same time. Mr. Leone really enjoys children. He is tender-hearted and kind but has trouble being assertive. When Jenny runs to him complaining, "Anna pulled my hair and broke my new crayons," Mr. Leone shrugs and says, "I'm sure it was just an accident." When children throw food during lunch, Mr. Leone pretends he does not notice but tries to distract the ringleaders by talking loudly about the weather, "Listen, I think I hear thunder. Do you hear that?" Mr. Leone is kind, but he is definitely not assertive. Lackadaisical permissiveness cultivates antisocial and aggressive behavior in children (Sears et al., 1957).

Children Want and Need Rules. A truly nurturing adult earns children's respect by being firm and fair in a way that reminds children that a sturdy protective wall of reasonable limits surrounds them and keeps them safe. (They also need to know, of course, that this "wall" of rules can and will be broken in specific situations where it becomes a hindrance rather a help to the children.) What they do not need is anger and retaliation. Anger is frightening to people generally because it can cause them to lose control of their actions. Children especially feel vulnerable, since they have not developed the self-control to stop themselves from going too far when they are angry and out of control. Children feel nurtured and safe when they know they can trust a strong adult to stop them before they behave aggressively or destructively. They also want to know with certainty that their safety and rights will be protected if someone else loses control. The nurturing adult is not hesitant to enforce appropriate rules fairly and firmly.

Am I Willing to Protect Individual Rights?

Mary Beth is the mother of two young children, a five-year-old boy, Trey, and a three-year-old girl, Betsy. Betsy adores her big brother and attempts to follow every step he takes. Sometimes, when Trey is alone, he seems proud of Betsy's attention and plays with her for hours, but when he has friends his own age to play with, he chases Betsy away and tells her to leave him alone. One day, while Mary Beth is waxing the kitchen floor, she hears a loud altercation in the backyard. Betsy is crying because Trey and his chums will not let her play with them and are taunting her by chanting, "Betsy is a tag-along! Betsy is a tag-along!"

Since Mary Beth's mind is on the "waxy yellow buildup" problem in her kitchen, she is tempted for a moment to order Trey to entertain his little sister and stop the silly nonsense with his friends. Luckily, however, she stops to assess the individual rights of everyone involved in the situation. As a parent, she has a right to do her housework without interruption—but, of course, she also has an obligation to care for her children (she thinks children are considerably more important than waxy yellow buildup). Trey has an obligation to treat his sister with kindness and to help out by entertaining her from time to time—but he also has a right to lead his own life and to play with his own friends. Betsy has a right not to be called names—but she also has an obligation to respect her brother's privacy and to learn to play alone sometimes.

After Mary Beth patiently listens to complaints from all sides, she says, "Trey, Betsy feels hurt when you call her names. You have a right to play with your friends, but name-calling can't be allowed. Let's make a compromise. Please push Betsy on the swing for a few minutes so that I can finish my work in the kitchen, then I will bring Betsy in the house, and you and your friends can have the backyard to yourselves until your friends go home. Betsy, you may play with Trey for a few minutes, then you and I will go inside, and I will show you how to give your dolls a bath."

Because Mary Beth is a nurturing parent, she is able and willing to make an extra effort to see that everyone's rights are protected and that everyone behaves responsibly. She does not do only what seems expedient or convenient at the moment, but tries hard to create an environment of fairness and mutual respect for the rights of others.

Practical Application/Discussion

William and the Nature Walk

Brenda's three-year-olds were ready to go outside. Several days of heavy autumn rains had kept them indoors in the child care center, so today's clear sky and bright sun were a welcome invitation to break away from usual morning routines and release some pent-up energy.

Brenda and her assistant teacher, Theresa, decided that playing on the playground was out of the question, since there were still big puddles in the sandbox and under the swings. "A nature walk," Theresa suggested, "would be perfect. There are lots of pretty fall leaves, and we could walk to the park to collect acorns and leaves for our science center."

The children excitedly prepared for their walk. Each child chose a "buddy" to hold hands with, and the pairs of young children danced and wriggled with anticipation as Brenda and Theresa helped them get into a straight line on the sidewalk.

"Remember," said Brenda, "we need to hold hands with our partners and walk very carefully on the sidewalk until we get to the park." Before they had gone even a few feet, however, William, who had just turned three, saw a bright yellow leaf and, dropping his partner's hand, bent down to pick it up. Louisa, the older three-year-old directly behind William, immediately tumbled on top of him.

Children want and need reasonable limits.

Brenda helped William and Louisa up, then, kneeling at eye level to William and gently taking his hand, said politely but firmly, "Excuse me, William, you must wait until we get to the park, then you can look for leaves. Remember—be safe! Hold hands with your partner." She then gave William a little pat on the shoulder and a smile as she announced, "Okay, is this train ready to go again? Let's chug, chug, chug down the railroad track! Whooo, whoo—ding, ding, ding!"

Within minutes, William was again distracted and stooped to pick up an irresistibly bright red leaf, and poor little Louisa was sprawled on top of him just like before. This time, however, she quickly scrambled to her feet, took William's hand and said in a confident voice, "Exsqueeze me, Weeyum! When you do dat, I faw down!" (Excuse me, William! When you do that, I fall down!)

Questions for Discussion

1. Why do you think Louisa was able to use words to express her frustration with William rather than biting or hitting him?

2. How should Brenda respond to the interaction between William and Louisa? Should she do anything further to correct William's behavior? Should she attempt to reinforce Louisa for remembering to use words?

3. What should Brenda and Theresa do if William continues to disrupt the nature walk? Can you think of anything preventive that could be done to stop the problem and avoid difficulty on future walks?

4. Are these children learning prosocial behavior? How?

5. Did Brenda and Theresa seem playful, consistent, assertive, and sensitive to the children's basic needs? Did it appear that developmentally appropriate activities and routines were being carried out?

Points to Remember

- Prosocial behavior is that which cooperates with, cares about, and helps others.

- Children gradually discover that their prosocial behavior wins approval and affection from others.

- To develop prosocial behavior, children must interact with peers in a nurturing social environment.

- Children who are afraid that their own needs will not be met will not be able to be generous with others.

- Encouraging children to compete with each other reduces cooperativeness.

- A cooperative, caring, and generous atmosphere evolves when children's basic needs are met.

- Developmentally appropriate activities, materials, and routines are essential to effective child guidance.

- Consistent, predictable routines help children develop self-control.

- The nurturing adult is an honest, emotionally healthy person who is both assertive and caring.

- The first step toward shaping children's behavior positively is simply setting a good example.

- Imitation is an important and logical tool for teaching prosocial behavior.

- Affirmation, affection, and acceptance assure a child that she is wanted and appreciated.

- Unconditional positive regard is the process of conveying affirmation, affection, and acceptance.

- Nurturing adults generously give affection that is not intrusive, overwhelming, or one-sided.

- Recognition and encouragement are an appropriate alternative to an overabundance of gushy or insincere praise.

- Children want and need rules.

- The nurturing adult is able and willing to see that children's rights are protected and that they behave responsibly.

Related Readings

Supporting Prosocial Behavior

Asher, S. R., & Coie, J. D. (Eds.). (1990). *Peer rejection in childhood.* New York: Cambridge University Press.

Bredekamp, Sue, & Copple, Carol (Eds.). (1997). *Developmentally appropriate practice in early childhood programs* (Rev. ed). Washington, DC: National Association for the Education of Young Children.

Burts, D. C., Hart, C. H., Charlesworth, R., & Kirk, L. (1990). A comparison of frequencies of stress behaviors observed in kindergarten children in classrooms with developmentally appropriate versus developmentally inappropriate instructional practices. *Early Childhood Research Quarterly, 5*(3), 407–423.

Burts, D. C., et al. (1993). Developmental appropriateness of kindergarten programs and academic outcomes in first grade. *Journal of Research in Childhood Education, 8*(1), 23–31.

Driscoll, A. (1995). *Cases in early childhood education: Stories of programs and practices.* Needham Heights, MA: Allyn & Bacon.

This book provides case studies showing developmentally appropriate practice and reflective teaching methods. It gives examples of a variety of practices seen in a range of settings. The "snapshots" provide examples of typical situations in early childhood settings and examples of developmentally appropriate practice with the day-to-day problems and issues that happen in "real classrooms."

Gestwicki, C. (1995). *Developmentally appropriate practice.* Albany, NY: Delmar Publishers, an International Thomson Publishing company.

This book is designed to assist teachers in implementing the widely recognized philosophy of developmentally appropriate practice. The text is organized into "environments" for each developmental stage to help focus on specific appropriate responses and to nurture overall development.

Gordon, A., & Browne, K. W. (1996). *Beginnings and beyond* (4th ed.). Albany, NY: Delmar Publishers, an International Thomson Publishing company.

Comprehensive approaches to the curriculum, education, developmentally appropriate practice, and other hot topics in early education.

Hirsh-Pasek, Kathy, Hyson, Marion, & Rescorla, Leslie. (1990). Academic environments in preschool: Do they pressure or challenge young children? *Early Education and Development, 1*(6), 401–423.

Honig, A., & Wittmer, D. (1992). *Prosocial development in children: Caring, sharing, and cooperation: A bibliographic resource guide.* New York: Garland.

Honig, A. S., & Wittmer, D. S. (1997). Helping children become more prosocial: Ideas for classrooms. In K. M. Paciorek & J. H. Munro, *Annual editions: Early childhood education 97/98* (18th ed.). New York: McGraw-Hill. (Original work published in *Young Children*, January 1996)

Teachers can promote positive social development by emphasizing cooperation and conflict resolution as they guide behavior. Families should be involved in programming to encourage social interaction with special needs children.

Hyson, Marion C., Hirsh-Pasek, Kathy, & Rescorla, Leslie. (1990). The classroom practices inventory: An observation instrument based on NAEYC's guidelines for developmentally appropriate practices for 4- and 5-year-old children. *Early Childhood Research Quarterly, 5*(4), 475–94.

Katz, L. G., McClellan, D. E., Fuller, J. O., & Walz, G. R. (1995). Building social competence in children: A practical handbook for counselors, psychologists and teachers. Greensboro, NC: ERIC Clearinghouse on Counseling and Student Services.

Kilpatrick, W. (1997). The moral power of good stories. In E. N. Junn & C. Boyatzis (Eds.), *Annual editions: Child growth and development 97/98* (4th ed.). New York: McGraw-Hill. (Original work published in *American Educator,* Summer 1993)

> *Stories help to make sense of our lives, claims William Kilpatrick, and they offer children vivid examples of morals and good values. This essay urges educators and parents to use stories as a powerful means of communicating about character and virtue to children.*

Mahany, B. (1997). *Mrs. Paley's lessons.* In K. M. Paciorek & J. H. Munro, *Annual editions: Early child-hood education 97/98* (18th ed.). New York: McGraw-Hill. (Original work published in *Chicago Tribune,* June 25, 1995)

> *Vivian Paley was a kindergarten teacher at the University of Chicago Lab School for twenty-four years. She has deep respect for young children and considers the kindergarten classroom an important place for social development. Paley regards teaching as a moral act.*

Ramsey, P. G. (1991). *Making friends in school: Promoting peer relationships in early childhood.* New York: Teacher's College Press.

Effective guidance depends on positive communication.

Chapter 3

Positive Communication

Objectives

This chapter will assist you in

- Identifying effective listening strategies
- Addressing feelings and emotions underlying communication
- Recognizing the rationale for positive statements of instruction
- Listing the characteristics of assertive communication
- Listing the characteristics of nonproductive communication
- Discussing strategies for positive confrontation

Building a Foundation for Positive Communication

Positive communication is like a dance filled with expressive and responsive give and take. Children begin this interactive dance early in life, but effective communication skills are acquired gradually over many years. Children can best learn to communicate effectively by imitating and interacting with adults who model well, setting an example for and participating with children in both conversational roles, speaking and listening—leading and following.

When Does Communication Begin?

The development of communication begins before birth when the fetus hears the muffled tones of his or her mother's voice. The **auditory physiology** (all those little body parts in and around the ears) of infants is relatively well developed at birth. Immediately after birth, the infant may turn toward or startle at sounds and may even be able to distinguish the mother's voice from that of another female (DeCasper & Fifer, 1980). Although newborns have not yet developed any concept of language, they respond attentively to the sounds of speech (Begley, 1997a; Eisenberg, 1976; Kuhl, 1981; White, 1995).

One-day-old infants move their bodies in rhythm to the sounds of a caregiver's speech (Condon & Sander, 1974). One-month-olds are able to discriminate between certain vowel sounds (Trehub, 1973). In time babies learn to mimic bits and pieces of adult communication—inflection, intonation, facial expression, and timing as well as the give and take of dialogue.

How Can Adults Assist the Development of Early Communication Skills in Infants?

From the time children are infants, adults should both lead and follow in communication with them. An adult may lead by talking to an infant in a way that is sensitive to the baby's mood and attention span. An infant will participate in this interaction by watching and responding as the adult speaks and then, when the interaction becomes too intense and tiring, by looking away, grimacing, or yawning to signal fatigue and the need for a time out (Brazelton, Koslowski, & Main, 1974; Field, 1982; Shore, 1997; Stern, 1974; White, 1995).

A sensitive adult will follow the baby's lead by being quiet until after the baby rests for a few seconds then looks back indicating that he or she is ready to interact again. The adult may also follow the infant by waiting for the infant to make some sound and then repeating the baby's gurgling, cooing, or babbling. This form of babytalk (or "parentese"), in which the baby leads, is very useful for helping babies get a sense of conversational give and take long before they are able to say or understand any words (Bruner, 1978a, 1978b).

When adults pace their interactions with infants so that a specific infant behavior elicits a predictable adult response, infants begin to learn that their environment is controllable and predictable, which increases their motivation for involvement in surroundings and stimulates learning. Infants who sense they are powerless over interactions may become distressed, irritable, or passive and withdrawn (Watson, 1973).

The beginnings of communication take place in infancy.

Older babies learn to look back and forth between an object and a caregiver, grunting, pointing, or reaching to indicate desire for the object (Harding & Golinkoff, 1979). This effort to communicate reflects the child's dawning ability to bring about a desired action by communicating with adults. Well-developing toddlers grasp the essential elements of conversation—meaningful words, intonation, inflection, facial expression, gesture, and give-and-take. It may be impossible, however, to make much sense of what the toddler is trying to say. An adult who is tactful will find ways to avoid repeated requests that toddler repeat herself.

A positive and supportive response to children's early attempts at speech will encourage continued effort (Hess & Shipman, 1967). Excessive correcting or prodding discourages further practice. Even after two-year-olds have mastered many of the words and phrases of the language, they will need a bit of gentle prompting to carry on a dialogue. Adults can help by asking simple questions (for example, "Is this your big teddy bear? What is your teddy bear's name?") to maintain the child's active participation in a conversation (Honig & Wittmer, 1997; Kaye, 1982).

What Are Typical Characteristics of Early Speech?

Usually, toddlers seem oblivious to the notion that one should speak only when a listener is present. One- and two-year-olds sometimes carry on animated self-talk while engaging in solitary play (Weiss & Lillywhite, 1976). In fact, toddlers may stare blankly and silently when urged to talk, then jabber freely later when alone or with a very trusted caregiver. Toddlers who are new to a group care setting may attend for weeks or months before trying to communicate verbally with a nursery school teacher, even though parents report they talk a great deal at home with family members.

Three- and four-year-olds gain the vocabulary needed to understand and express many ideas and feelings, and they become more concerned that there is an audience present for conversations. A preschooler who thinks an adult is not listening may move directly into the adult's line of vision or may even try to hold the adult's face to keep the adult from looking away. It is not uncommon, however, for two preschoolers to be looking straight at each other, chatting excitedly at the same time without either of them seeming to notice that neither is listening. Preschoolers also talk to inanimate objects such as stuffed animals and television characters without seeming to be bothered that these objects are not very responsive listeners.

School-aged children become more refined in their communication. They finally recognize that communicators must take turns listening and speaking in order for anyone to be heard. Their growing vocabulary and maturity increase their capacity. Toddlers and younger preschoolers tend to be physical in their expression of feelings—anger may be expressed by biting or hitting and affection by bear hugs and moist kisses. In contrast, school-agers use words more expertly to express affection or to lash out when they feel angry. They tend to use insults, threats, or name calling to express anger and verbal promises of friendship to show affection. Although school-agers are no longer as sensitive to imitation as younger children, who seem to absorb everything they see, school-agers are still likely to emulate, and thus be influenced by, adults and children they admire (Bandura, 1977).

Why Is Positive, Mutual Communication Important for Child Guidance?

As children develop and their communication style changes from stage to stage, adults must recognize and adapt to the various limitations of children in order to guide them toward effective communication. The achievement of effective child guidance really hinges on the achievement of mutual communication. The ultimate goal of positive discipline is not just to control or manipulate children externally but rather to stimulate inner control based on responsibility and respect for the rights of others. This inner control depends on an understanding of the needs and expectations of oneself and others gained through open, honest dialogue.

Preparing children to function as adults in a democratic political system requires that children become competent communicators. In an autocracy, citizens can blindly and ignorantly follow leaders without ever discussing or questioning commands. For a democracy to work, citizens must accept responsibility to grasp, understand, and take a stand on various issues. These goals are achieved by communication—listening, reading, discussing, and so forth.

The most effective tools for children to learn communication skills are modeling and practicing. Children learn effective skills as they watch, listen to, and interact with consistent adults who set a good example. Children are able to make those skills a part of their repertoire by practicing again and again the words and interactions they have observed. Therefore, adults who care for and teach children need well-developed communication skills. These skills help them to:

- Understand and interpret children's needs accurately
- Clearly express expectations to children
- Teach effective communication to children by modeling

Through daily experience and practice, children learn to listen to others and to express their own feelings and ideas.

Adults often complain that children do not listen. The view presented here proposes that children be taught effective communication skills through exposure to capable models and by participation in appropriate interactions.

Effective Listening

Randall pulls his chair up to the table close to his teacher and spreads out a large sheet of drawing paper and an assortment of crayons. He says, "Hi, Miss Katie. I'm gonna color me a big picture." Miss Katie glances at him and smiles briefly, saying, "Umm humm, that's nice." Miss Katie's attention is focused on a group of children playing across the room. She does not seem to notice Randall as he repeats, "Look, Miss Katie, look here!"

Finally, Randall tugs at her sleeve and says, "Look at this. I'm drawing great big mountains. My daddy took me camping and I found lots of rocks. Wanna see my real mountain rocks?"

Randall jumps up from his chair and begins emptying his pockets onto the drawing paper. Miss Katie suddenly sees his small pile of rocks and pebbles. She says in a stern voice, "Randall! What is all this? Get these dirty rocks off here. Go throw them in the trash. You can't color with rocks all over your paper."

Randall stammers "but, but . . ." as tears fill his eyes. Miss Katie insists, "Randall, would you quit making such a fuss and just do what I said."

Randall hangs his head and drags his feet as he slowly shuffles across the room to the trash can. One by one he ceremoniously drops his pebbles, his "real mountain rocks," into the trash. Miss Katie did not listen.

How Can Attentive Listening Nurture the Child's Developing Sense of Self?

The greatest need children have is for attention, recognition, and a sense of belonging. If a child is routinely ignored, he or she may begin to feel invisible. Much that is called misbehavior is simply an attempt by a child to become visible—one way or another. A child who does not feel a sense of belonging may gradually become alienated, rebellious, or withdrawn.

The more sure a child is that he or she is an accepted member of a group, the more confident and cooperative that child will be. Adults can indicate their recognition and acceptance of a child by listening well. Attentive listening includes:

- Maintaining eye contact

- Giving relevant nonverbal gestures such as nodding, smiling, and appropriate touch

- Giving relevant verbal responses to draw out and encourage the child to continue

- Waiting patiently for the child to complete what he or she is saying, without rushing the child or trying to finish the child's sentences

This polite, attentive listening not only gives children the confident feeling that what they have to say is important enough for the adult to listen, but also teaches children by modeling how they should listen to others. Also, careful listening will help the adult to hear, interpret, and respond accurately to children's needs.

What Are the Three Basic Human Needs Underlying Requests for Help?

Gazda et al. 1990 define three needs that are at the heart of communications indicating a desire for some kind of response or help. Adults and children have the same basic human urge to get their social, emotional, intellectual, and physical needs met. Young children (and sometimes older children and adults) function at an unconscious level in which they react to a vague feeling of need without recognizing or understanding that need. There are an infinite number of complicated ways that people of all ages approach others to get help, but at the bottom of all that complexity are three simple human needs. These three needs are expressed as requests for:

- Action or information—Please do . . ., or Please tell me . . .

- Understanding and attention—Please listen and show concern for me . . .

- Inappropriate interaction—Please let me cling, whine, complain, undermine, and so on . . .

Time, effort, and practice are required if one is to become skilled at recognizing the underlying needs hidden in everyday communications. A question such as "Where is my Mommy?" may be a simple request for information, or it may be an emotion-packed request for understanding and attention by a child who knows very well where Mommy is. A major source of miscommunication is the tendency of persons in the helping role to jump to the wrong conclusion and respond in a way that does not meet the real need of the person requesting help. Listening carefully and waiting attentively for the child to find words to express herself encourage the child to practice speaking. Impatience can discourage the child and delay language development.

Are These Listening and Helping Strategies Only Appropriate for Use with Young Children?

The following sections will give strategies for identifying and responding to expressed needs. These strategies are not intended as gimmicks or as a bag-of-tricks to manipulate children's behavior but as a respectful and effective way of communicating with children and adults. As has been previously stressed, children learn by modeling. Children will quickly recognize an adult who is snide and sarcastic with other adults but artificially sweet or patronizing with children. Parents and early childhood professionals set the emotional tone for children's interactions and personal relationships. The communication method presented here can be most effective only if it is applied to adult-adult, adult-child, and child-child interactions. We can't say, "Do as I say and not as I do."

The phrase "children are people too" has become such a cliché that the significance of its meaning has been lost. But, children really are people who deserve the same dignity and human rights as anyone else. Children's perceptions are different, their logic and experience are limited, and their needs, roles, and responsibilities are not the same as those of adults, but they can

"No one will listen to me!"

Learning to communicate effectively is an important part of daily life.

definitely feel the sting of humiliation and the pain of rejection. Most adults can remember in vivid detail some painful experience that occurred early in their childhoods. And yet we often act as if children's feelings do not really merit much consideration. Every baby or child is, in fact, the very same person who will someday be a teacher, senator, artist, or carpenter. The events of that person's early childhood will be an integral part of his or her character and personality, whether these events are consciously remembered or not.

Children learn as if by **osmosis** (absorbed through one's skin). They soak in information simply by living day to day in an environment. Effective listening is not only a learning objective for children but also a necessary component of children's daily lives, to be used directly with children as well as among the various adults who interact with children. For example, an ancient proverb says:

- Tell me and I forget;

- Show me and I remember;

- Let me experience for myself and I understand.

Children learn to listen well by experiencing respectful listening as a regular part of daily life. Simply telling children to listen is not enough.

What Are Appropriate Responses to Requests for Action or Information?

Joey, an eighteen-month-old, sits on a small stool, rocking and crying, "Beah, beah, ma beah." Miss Rosario squats beside him and gently coaxes him to show her what he wants. Joey quickly leads her to the bathroom. He stretches his arm toward a high shelf where diaper bags are kept. Urgently, he opens and closes his hand pleading, "Beah, beah!"

Miss Rosario takes his diaper bag from the shelf. Immediately she sees that Joey's fuzzy white teddy bear is inside. She says, "Oh, you want your bear. Is that right, Joey, bear?"

Joey nods and says, "Ma beah." He hugs his bear and toddles away dragging it by one leg.

Even though Miss Rosario could not understand Joey's words, she recognized that Joey was requesting action from her. People who work with young children spend a great deal of time responding to requests for action or information. Some requests are straightforward and simple to understand—"Is it time for snack yet?" or "Tie my shoe, please." Other requests, like Joey's request for his bear, are difficult to interpret.

Requests may also be hidden or masked. What sounds like a simple statement may really be intended as a request for action. "I can't sleep," may really mean, "Come sit by me and read me a story." A comment may really mask a request for information. "Latecia's mama is too fat" may

Very young children must gradually learn to express their angry feelings in words rather than action.

really mean, "Latecia told me there is a baby in her mama's tummy, and I am very frightened and confused." Since children do not have fully developed communication skills, adults must accept additional responsibility for keeping the channels of communication open and clear.

Five-year-old Malika is standing on the playground beside her teacher, Mrs. Johnson. She sees a caterpillar crawling toward her and starts to shriek. Mrs. Johnson bends down and gently allows the fuzzy caterpillar to crawl onto a leaf she is holding. Malika screams, "It's gonna kill you! Is it gonna kill you?"

Mrs. Johnson says, "No, Malika. This little caterpillar has a very tiny mouth and no teeth and no poison. He likes to eat leaves. When he gets very fat, he will wrap himself in a cocoon that is like a little blanket. While he is inside, he will change into a beautiful butterfly. Then, after a long time, that beautiful butterfly will come out of the cocoon and fly away." Mrs. Johnson helps Malika make a suitable home for the caterpillar in a large jar. Later, at circle time, she reads a book called The Very Hungry Caterpillar.

Mrs. Johnson has redirected Malika's fear of bugs to curiosity about science and nature. Mrs. Johnson recognized that underneath Malika's shrieking and screaming was a need for information. Mrs. Johnson responded to a hidden request for information.

After a birthday party, four-year-old Seth sees that his mother is wrapping leftover cake. He says, "Mommy, I want more cake, please." His mother says, "No, Seth. No more cake." Seth begs, "Please, I'm hungry. I want more cake."

Seth's mother bends down to Seth's eye level and takes his hand gently. In a sympathetic voice, she says, "Seth, I understand that you really want more cake. That cake tasted great, didn't it? But a lot of cake is not good for you. I love you and I want you to have a healthy body and healthy teeth, so I have to say no. No more cake."

Seth pulls his hand away, bouncing up and down, whining and flapping his arms like an angry old hen (the preschooler's dance of frustration and impending tantrum). Seth's mother does not flinch a muscle. In a very calm tone she says, "It's okay to feel angry. Sometimes I feel angry too. Sometimes I get so angry I feel like crying. Sometimes I feel so bad that I just need a hug."

Without looking at her face, Seth climbs into his mother's arms and gets a long hug. Suddenly, he brightens and says, "How 'bout apples. They make you get strong teeth like Superman." His mom smiles and replies, "You know, Seth, that sounds like a great idea." Seth's mother clearly understood her son's request for action, but she also knew that providing what he wanted was not in his best interest.

Seth's mother loved him enough to say no to his request and enough to accept an appropriate compromise. Adults are ultimately responsible for the health, safety, and welfare of children in their care. Complying with potentially harmful or unfair requests hurts children and, eventually, damages adult-child trust and respect. Sometimes adults are tempted to comply with questionable requests to avoid conflict or in a misguided attempt to win the child's affection. Not only has Seth's mother stood firm in making the decision that is in Seth's best interest, but she has also taught a very valuable lesson.

Her gentle strength has shown Seth an example of self-discipline, doing the right thing even though it would be easier to give in and avoid a fuss. Her calm, patient persistence, even when he threatened a tantrum, has shown him an appropriate example of coping with a stressful situation (some adults reinforce children's tantrums by pitching tantrums of their own). And, most importantly, her sensitive understanding of his feelings helps him know that he is loved and respected even while a limit is being enforced.

What are Appropriate Responses to Requests for Understanding and Attention?

Some requests may appear on the surface to be requests for action or information, but they are not. The real need at the core of this type of communication is for someone to listen and show interest.

Mr. Wilke watches as his kindergartners work and play in various learning centers. Angelica, a shy five-year-old, is alone in the art center. As Mr. Wilke walks past, she calls out, "Mr. Wilke, I need some help." He smiles and perches his tall frame onto the little chair beside her. Angelica hands him her paper and plastic scissors and says, "Help me cut, I don't know how to."

Mr. Wilke has always made careful observations and kept records of his students' levels of skill with learning center materials. He feels sure that Angelica does know how to use scissors. He looks at the situation and mentally rules out possibilities such as broken scissors or thick paper that is too difficult. He decides that Angelica may not really be seeking action (cutting for her) or information (teaching her how to cut) but, instead, seeking understanding and attention.

Mr. Wilke knows it will not help Angelica to embarrass her by confronting her in a harsh way. He also knows that he does not want to reinforce her perception that she can get the attention she needs by feigning incompetence. He says, "Sometimes cutting seems really hard, doesn't it?" He gently pats her shoulder and adds, "Would you like for me to sit beside you while you try cutting this yellow paper?" Angelica eagerly cuts her jagged paper while Mr. Wilke watches attentively. After a few minutes, as he gets up to leave, he says, "Angelica, you must really feel proud that you cut that out all by yourself."

Mr. Wilke was correct in his assumption that Angelica was really requesting understanding and attention. Seeking attention is not a perverse behavior that must always be extinguished in children. Human beings are primarily social beings; we all need attention from others in order to thrive. The goal with young children is not to stop attention-getting behaviors but to teach children how to get an appropriate amount of attention in a socially acceptable manner. If Mr. Wilke observed that Angelica continued in a pattern of pretending ineptness to get attention (see requests for dependency and inappropriate interaction), it might become necessary for Mr. Wilke, privately and tactfully, to confront her behavior by saying, "Angelica, you seem to need some attention. It's okay to need attention. Please say, 'Mr. Wilke, I feel lonely. I need some attention.' That will help me know exactly what you need."

Sometimes all that is needed is a little understanding and attention.

In an environment in which needs are respected, children come to know that it is okay to have needs and feelings. Sometimes adults inadvertently give children the impression that their needs or emotions make adults angry. This problem often occurs when the adults are having a difficult time getting their own emotional needs met.

A particularly helpful strategy for dealing with feelings and needs honestly and respectfully is through a technique called **active listening** (sometimes referred to as reflective listening, empathetic listening, or responsive listening). In active listening, the listener refrains from lecturing, advising, or informing. She simply listens and reflects back the feelings she perceives from seeing and hearing the other person. This gives the listener plenty of time to really hear the other person, to let the other person know her feelings and needs are important and respected, and to think of ways to help the person resolve his problem.

Jenny, who directs an infant/toddler child care program, treats the teaching and caring staff with the same respect and dignity she expects them to extend to the babies. She knows that even infants and toddlers are unconsciously absorbing the behaviors around them. She also knows that caring for little ones can sometimes be incredibly stressful.

Fred, a four-month-old whose mother has just returned to work from her maternity leave, is crying. He has attended the child care program for only a few days, and he has cried most of the time. Kate, his primary caregiver, has tried everything she knows to calm him. She has walked him, patted him, rocked him, and is at the end of her patience.

Kate storms into the director's office and demands, "What is that child's problem? Nothing I do works. What am I supposed to do?" Luckily, Jenny realizes that Kate is not really seeking action or information. What Kate needs most is understanding, so Jenny offers her a chair and closes the door for privacy. Instead of focusing on solving baby Fred's problem, Jenny focuses on hearing and understanding Kate's feelings. In a caring voice, Jenny says, "Kate, you seem really frustrated."

"You bet I am," replies Kate, "I don't think I can deal with his crying another minute. I don't even know if I ought to work with children. I am really at my wit's end."

Wisely, Jenny refrains from making judgments, giving information, or taking action. Gazda et al. (1990) notes that rushing to give a helpee a quick solution is "cheap and dirty" advice, since the helper has not had a chance to learn all the facts. If one's problems were so easy to solve that an "off the top of the head" solution were adequate, one would wonder why the person suffering the problem had not already thought of it.

Instead of rushing to tell Kate why she has a problem or how to solve it, Jenny simply mirrors to Kate (through active listening) what she hears Kate saying. She responds with nonjudgmental active (or reflective) listening statements that begin with phrases such as:

- What I'm hearing you say is . . .

- In other words, you are saying that . . .

- It sounds as if you feel . . .

Jenny says, "Kate, it sounds like what you're saying is that you're feeling so frustrated that you're afraid you've lost your patience. You seem to be wondering if you're really cut out to work with children." A calmness settles over Kate as she realizes that she is not being judged or told what to do but that her director is really listening and understanding what she is saying. She thinks for a moment and says, "I guess I'm just having a bad day. I really do love working with babies. It's just that Fred keeps screaming no matter what I do." Jenny leans close and touches Kate's arm. "You know, it sounds like you feel inadequate because you can't stop Fred's crying. I think Fred is lucky to have someone like you to care so much and try so hard to comfort him."

Streams of tears spill down Kate's face. She feels enough trust to let go of her feelings and let everything out that has been bottled inside her. Now that her own needs for understanding and attention have been met, she can return to her nursery classroom and try again to meet Fred's needs for understanding and attention.

Even though Fred did not see or hear the adult interaction (and would have been too young to make sense of it if he had), he most certainly will feel and benefit from the calmer, more accepting attitude Kate will have when she returns to care for him. By sensing the patience and understanding of his caregiver, Fred will begin learning the coping skills he will need to develop confidence and self-esteem as he grows older.

How Should Caregivers Respond to Requests for Dependency or Inappropriate Interaction?

Adults who care for young children often have difficulty knowing where understanding ends and dependency begins. A child begs, "Hold me," "Put my coat on for me," or "Help me finish my puzzle." Many adults struggle to know what is right for the child. Is holding, helping, and nurturing meeting the child's needs or reinforcing a pattern of dependency?

Under usual circumstances, as soon as children are able, they spontaneously break away from various levels of dependence on adults. Toddlers stubbornly resist the hovering care that was necessary to their survival as infants. Adolescents rebel against the close parental attachment that protected them in early childhood. For most children, achieving independence is the motivating force behind the process of growing up. But this force does not always move steadily forward. Even highly competent, well-developing children regress from time to time and need the security of someone big to depend on. A bit of babying, on infrequent occasions, does little harm to well-developing children. This regression only seems to recharge their energy and desire for independence. But for chronically dependent children, coddling undermines self-esteem and destroys initiative.

In certain situations, children learn to be helpless (Altenor, Kay, & Richter, 1977; Finkelstein & Ramey, 1977). Some adults have difficulty accepting change and may fail to recognize a child's emerging capabilities. Other adults may inadvertently interfere with children's efforts at learning to function independently because they may simply not understand the process and importance of the development of autonomy.

Even highly competent, well-developing children regress from time to time.

Children's first efforts to do things by themselves are often messy and fraught with mistakes. Babies learning to feed themselves splatter, smear, and spill food. Toddlers learning to dress themselves put both feet in the same leg-hole of their training pants. Preschoolers learning to tie their own shoes create nightmarish knots in their shoelaces. And, school-agers learning gardening walk on the seedlings they have just planted. Little mishaps such as these are a necessary part of learning by experience. In a demanding, perfectionist, or punitive atmosphere, where a child begins to fear making mistakes, he or she may learn to avoid risk by becoming passive, by not attempting anything that requires initiative or involves the chance of failure.

Children who have learned to be helpless and dependent (learned helplessness) need special guidance and support to break away from patterns of dependency. Children sometimes express requests for dependency through such actions as persistent whining, clinging, or regularly demanding special favors such as being first in line, sitting in the teacher's lap, or being carried. Indulging these inappropriate requests is not helpful for children.

Solicitations for dependence should be redirected in a way that encourages more appropriate behavior. An infant who whines for help after one half-hearted attempt at reaching a toy needs to be encouraged to try again rather than simply be given the toy. A preschooler who whines, feigns exhaustion, and begs for help putting blocks away may respond to a game—"I'll close my eyes. You tell me when to open them, and I'll count how many blocks are on the shelf." Or a kindergartner who follows the teacher, clinging and asking for help, may need to be given some important responsibility such as helping a younger child.

In some cases, redirection is not enough. It may be necessary to clearly communicate unwillingness to participate in interactions that indulge or solicit inappropriate dependency, spread gossip, reinforce inordinate complaining, or involve actions that turn adults or children against one another. Gazda et al. (1990) state that, "If you encourage inappropriate behaviors, even by silence, you may lose your opportunity to help and you could unwittingly become a model for negative or hurtful behavior."

Gazda further adds that this rule is easier to preach than to practice because it is necessary to end the inappropriate interaction without offending the person initiating it. Offending a child or other adult damages trust, closes off communication, and projects an image of haughtiness. The recommended response is a polite but firm refusal to be part of the inappropriateness accompanied by a straightforward, warm, and respectful indication of caring about the person as an individual (Gazda et al. 1990).

Tactfulness, fairness, and warmth ease the sting of a refusal to participate in an inappropriate interaction. For example, Mr. Hernandez arrives one afternoon and prepares to teach his after-school gymnastics class. Sarah and Cynthia, twin third graders, eagerly volunteer to help spread mats. As Sarah and Cynthia help, they confide to Mr. Hernandez how much they dislike James, one of the least popular boys in the gymnastics class.

Sarah says, "Ugh! We can't stand James. He's fatter than an elephant." Cynthia chimes in, "Have you ever listened when he laughs? He sort of snorts and makes some weird sound." They giggle uproariously.

Mr. Hernandez values the positive relationship he has with Sarah and Cynthia and does not wish to embarrass them, but he also knows that to smile and say nothing would be tacit approval of their remarks about James. That would be hurtful to James and fails to guide Sarah and Cynthia toward more appropriate behavior.

Mr. Hernandez carefully chooses his words then bends down, touching each girl lightly on the shoulder. He says gently, "I don't feel good talking about James." Then his tone brightens and he deftly changes the subject, "But, you know what, I surely do like all this great help. How about this balance beam, girls—do you think you both can get at that end and help me move it? Thanks."

Mr. Hernandez has not been judgmental or critical. He has simply and politely declined to participate by focusing on his own feelings. The girls probably felt a moment of embarrassment, but they also knew their teacher accepted and cared about them. As a result of this encounter, the girls may become more thoughtful about ridiculing others, not because of an external fear of punishment or chastisement, but from a growing internal sense of right and wrong bolstered by a strong and admired role model in the person of Mr. Hernandez.

Are These Listening and Helping Strategies Relevant to the Care of Babies and Toddlers?

The complexity of words and sentences must always be adjusted to the level of maturity of one's listener. However, the integrity and content of one's message need not be diluted. Physical actions, facial expression, intonation, and gestures convey a sense of one's message even to an infant.

Mrs. Wang, who cares for infants in her church's mother's-day-out program, hears eleven-month-old Kyle crying. He is banging on a low cabinet door that is locked with a child-guard latch. Mrs. Wang perceives the baby's cry is a request for action. Kyle wants the cabinet door opened. Mrs. Wang tries to distract him with several toys, but he continues to cry and pull at the door.

Mrs. Wang picks Kyle up, kicking and screaming, and carries him to her big rocking chair. She rocks and pats Kyle as she says in a caring voice, "I really understand that you want to explore that cabinet, but the things in there could hurt you. I can't let you play there because I like you and I want to keep you safe." As Kyle begins to calm down, Mrs. Wang carries him around the nursery showing him alternative areas to explore and continuing to talk to him.

> *Kyle does not understand her words but he definitely can sense her warmth and empathy, and he can sense the firmness of the limit she has set. He may test the limit many more times, but Mrs. Wang's warmth will communicate to him that he is still accepted as a person. Her consistency will communicate to him that limits are sometimes a part of life. Sherecognizes that babies explore limits because they have a limited capacity to understand or remember rules and because they learn through trial and error. She will refuse Kyle's demands that she open the locked cabinet, but his actions will not change her feelings about him.*
>
> *Additionally, by talking to Kyle, Mrs. Wang is able to focus her own thoughts and feelings on the situation. She, as well as Kyle, needs to hear the words she has said. By expressing in words the reasons she is doing what she is doing, she feels reassured that she is doing the right thing. Also, by putting her feelings into words, she is able to make sure her facial expression and body language are consistent with the message she wants to convey to Kyle.*

Mrs. Wang, knowing that Kyle could not really understand her words, might have said instead, "Listen, I'm tired of fooling with you. Are you just trying to bug me?" However, it is nearly impossible to say these words in a sincere, warm, and caring way. Mrs. Wang's face and tone would probably have conveyed sarcasm, impatience, and blaming to Kyle. In an unconscious way, he would have absorbed these negative feelings and reflected them in his behavior. Also, words like *brat, fooling,* and *bug* are ambiguous cliché words that do not help Kyle learn language. Luckily for Kyle, Mrs. Wang would not think of behaving rudely to him any more than she would be rude to anyone else she respected and liked as a person.

Addressing Underlying Feelings

Any discussion of communication would be incomplete without a consideration of underlying feelings. Most people who work with children would agree that child care and early childhood education are emotionally draining occupations. Young children ride an emotional roller coaster. They can go from laughter to tears in the blink of an eye. Responsive adults who are closely involved in the lives of young children are pulled along in the wave of emotions—from the elation of a new discovery to the heartbreak of a best friend who says, "I hate you."

Children's emotions are real. Before six months, infants are only capable of three undifferentiated emotions—pleasure, wariness, and rage. By nine months the baby has a dramatically increased range of emotional responses. By age three, children have virtually the entire panorama of human emotions (Sroufe, 1979).

An important part of early childhood learning is the child's gradually developing awareness of feelings and the child's growing ability to express those feelings. Very young children react unconsciously. A toddler may whine and act out in an aggressive way without realizing that he or she is feeling hunger, discomfort, fatigue, and so on. Adults play an important role in identifying, labeling, and explaining children's feelings to them. Adults also give children important feedback about certain behaviors by expressing relevant adult feelings.

Babies and toddlers pay close attention to an adult's face and tone of voice, even if they do not understand the words that are spoken.

When and How Should Adults Express Their Feelings to Children?

Discretion must be used in expressing adult feelings. Young children can be overwhelmed if adults unload too much on them or if the expression is too intense. Simple, clear statements of feeling limited to relevant situations are most helpful. Following is a fill-in-the-blank statement called an "I message" that is very helpful for stating feelings appropriately and in a nonthreatening way (Gordon, 1970):

When_____happens, I feel_____ because_____.

This statement does not contain the word *you.* Statements such as "You make me angry," or "You are hurting my ears with your yelling," may induce an unnecessary feeling of guilt in the child by suggesting blame. Positive discipline should bring about responsibility rather than guilt. It is more helpful to say simply and sincerely, "When there is loud screaming, I feel uncomfortable because the noise hurts my ears. I need for you to use a soft voice." "Biting makes me feel really upset because biting hurts and biting is dangerous. It is okay to bite crackers and apples, but it is never okay to bite people."

Attempting to identify the child's feelings focuses our attention on the underlying causes of misbehavior.

If adults consistently use assertive yet controlled words to express strong feelings, then children will eventually imitate by using words instead of physical attacks to express their own anger and frustration. A child will also feel more compliant when the adult's anger is focused on the action rather than on the child.

Additionally, adults can clarify and express positive feelings using the same sample sentence. For example, "When I see you share a special toy, I feel proud because I know you are growing up." (In positive contexts, the word you does not suggest blame.) "When the sun is shining, I feel elated because we can go outside and enjoy the grass and trees." "When I discovered that you had put every single block away all by yourself, I felt like jumping up and down because I was so happy and proud."

Positive and negative expressions of feelings can have a powerful impact on a child's behavior, but only when the person expressing those feelings is admired and liked by the child. Neither adults nor children are particularly concerned about the feelings of someone who is not liked or respected. In fact, knowing that a disliked adult's ears hurt with loud noise would stimulate screaming from some children, who may purposely intend to inflict pain or to manipulate attention from the adult.

How Can Children Be Helped to Understand Their Feelings?

In the previous section on requests for understanding and attention, nonjudgmental active (or reflective) listening was described. This kind of listening and responding can assist children in identifying, labeling, and understanding their feelings. A major difference here is that often the child's feelings must be inferred from his or her behavior.

Carolyn is a child care professional teaching and caring for a group of four-year-olds. As her children come inside for a snack from the playground, she says, "Ummm, I feel hungry. Do you feel hungry, Clay?" Clay agrees and the children expand on Carolyn's expression of hunger—"I am as hungry as a tiger." "I'm so hungry I could eat this whole building." "I'm so hungry I could eat the whole world!"

The children giggle about eating the whole world as they find their seats at the table. Clay rushes to sit by his best friend Misha, but Ellen has already taken the chair. Clay stamps his foot and complains loudly as he shakes the back of the chair he wants. The child in the chair stubbornly holds on.

Carolyn quickly comes to intervene in the brewing fight. She kneels down at eye level to Clay and says, "You feel angry because someone took the chair you wanted. Can you use words to tell Ellen how you feel?"

Clay shouts, "I want that chair. Gimme it, now!" Ellen grips the chair tighter and ignores him. Carolyn turns to Ellen and says, "Ellen, can you tell Clay how you feel?" Ellen looks at the floor and shakes her head no. Carolyn asks her, "Would you like me to tell Clay how you feel?" Ellen vigorously nods yes.

Carolyn says, "Clay, Ellen is feeling very upset because you are shaking her chair and yelling at her. She got here first and she doesn't want you to take her chair away." Clay begins to shake the chair again, so Carolyn firmly removes his hands from the chair. Then, restraining his hands, but with concern and empathy in her voice, Carolyn says, "Clay, I know you feel really frustrated, but you have two choices. You may choose another chair and have a snack, or you may come out in the hall and talk with me until you feel better. What do you choose?"

From experience, Clay knows Carolyn is gentle and caring, but he also knows that she always means what she says. He does not relish the idea of throwing a tantrum that will only succeed in delaying his snack.

Carolyn sees a look of indecision on his face and quickly says, "Look, Clay. There is an empty chair right at the end of the table by Joey. Would you like to sit there?" Clay decides that Joey would not be so bad to sit by after all and shuffles along to take a seat.

Carolyn smiles and pats his shoulder.

How Can Children Be Helped to Confront Troublesome Feelings?

Adlerian psychologists focus on exploring the motives for negative behavior. Dreikurs and Cassel (1972) list four goals of misbehaviors that are based on children's mistaken logic:

- Children who are deprived of opportunities to gain status through useful contributions often seek attention by acting helpless, silly, bratty, artificially charming, lazy, inept, or obnoxious.

- Children who do not feel they are accepted members of their family or social groups may seek power by acting bossy, rebellious, stubborn, vengeful, or disobedient.

- Children who feel so beaten down that they no longer care about struggling for power retaliate by seeking revenge by hurting others the way they feel they have been hurt. They may injure peers, destroy property, express contempt, distrust others, and defy authority.

- Children who become trapped in passive, destructive forms of attention getting by being overly criticized may eventually become so discouraged they give up all hope and expect only failure and defeat. They seek only to be left alone. They may be passive, withdrawn, and depressed—paralyzed by feelings of inadequacy and hopelessness.

Dreikurs recommends that older children be confronted in a friendly, noncritical way at a relaxed time rather than during a time of conflict. The child can be engaged in conversation exploring the motives for his typical behaviors, then tactfully asked the following questions:

- Could it be that you want attention?

- Could it be that you want your own way and hope to be boss?

- Could it be that you want to hurt others as much as you feel hurt by them?

Could it be that you want to be left alone?

Although these questions are not appropriate to ask infants and very young children, adults may find it helpful mentally to run through the list of questions to gain insight into possible unconscious causes of misbehavior in children under three. For children of any age, identifying the underlying feelings that motivate behavior makes it possible to respond to children's emotional well-being rather than only chasing and eliminating symptomatic misbehaviors.

Once the motive for behavior is diagnosed, adults can better respond to the misbehavior. If attention is the goal of the misbehavior, it can be removed as a response for inappropriate behaviors and given bountifully for appropriate or constructive behaviors. If bullying is the goal, adults can extricate themselves from power struggles and allow children to feel they are respected and responsible group members. If revenge is the goal, adults can assist children in making friends and experiencing successful accomplishments. If solitude is the goal, adults can offer encouragement, persist in including the child, and find ways to make the child feel worthwhile.

By seeking understanding of behavior rather than blame for it, adults have an opportunity to open new doors of communication with children. As children mature and develop self-awareness, open lines of communication will help them assume greater responsibility for their own actions and choices. By the time children reach adolescence, it is especially important that they have developed some conscious awareness of their own motives and goals. It is essential that open, honest communication has become an accepted and routine part of every child's daily life.

Effective caregivers are assertive and caring at the same time.

Positive Instructions Versus Negative Commands

A key factor in positive communication is focusing on identifying and stating desired behaviors rather than focusing on inappropriate behaviors. Children and adults tend to respond more cooperatively to positive requests than negative admonitions. For example, a parent would probably feel more responsive to a request from a child care worker worded, "Please check to see that Kelly has enough diapers for the day," rather than, "You never bring enough diapers for Kelly." The difference in children's responses to negative and positive commands is stark.

Additionally, toddlers are so limited in their comprehension of language that they only tend to hear and respond to key words in sentences. If an adult tells a toddler, "I do not want you to touch this cake," the toddler may actually hear, "Do . . . want . . . touch . . . cake." And of course, since the toddler wants to touch the cake, he or she probably will. The adult could bring about better communication by designating a desired activity to replace touching the cake. The adult could provide paper and crayons at a location away from the cake and say, "Please color on this big piece of paper," which the toddler may accurately interpret as, "Color . . . big . . . paper."

Not only do toddlers and young preschoolers have difficulty hearing and interpreting every word of sentences, they also have difficulty thinking about a behavior then inhibiting that behavior. Thinking and doing are almost inseparable at this stage of development. For example, if an adult says firmly, "No spitting," to a young child who has not even yet thought of spitting, he or she may comprehend both words but, as he or she thinks about not spitting, it is almost inevitable that the child will act out the spitting. The statement "Don't wet your pants" causes the child to have a mental image of wetting pants, which may trigger urination. The statement "It is time to use the potty" evokes a mental image of sitting on the toilet, which is desired.

Following is a list of typical negative commands and alternate positive commands:

Negative Commands	Positive Requests
☹ *Don't run in the hall.*	☺ *Walk slowly, please.*
☹ *Don't spill your milk.*	☺ *Use both hands, please.*
☹ *Quit poking at Jimmy.*	☺ *Hands in your lap now.*
☹ *Shut up.*	☺ *Please listen quietly.*
☹ *Stop interrupting me.*	☺ *It is my turn to talk now.*
☹ *Don't talk with a full mouth.*	☺ *Swallow first, then talk.*
☹ *Quit shoving in line.*	☺ *Walk carefully, please.*
☹ *Stop yelling my name.*	☺ *Say my name softly.*

Negative commands are strongly entrenched as habit patterns for many of us! Time, commitment, motivation, and persistence are needed to break any habit pattern, and communication habits are no exception. Many adults find that as they try to improve their communication style, they first begin to hear themselves using ineffective phrases but cannot seem to stop using them. A toddler standing in a puddle with an innocent and surprised look saying, "Go potty," is taking the first tentative step toward changing a habit pattern. An adult who feels guilty about yelling "shut up" to a child may be taking the first step toward consciously controlling and changing an ineffective communication strategy.

Characteristics of Assertive Communication

Communication is always intended to convey a message, just as a radio transmitter is intended to transmit a radio program. In order for the music of a radio program to be heard, the waves sent from the transmitter have to match the receiver equipment in one's radio. The communication transmitted from an adult must match the mental and emotional equipment of the child or the message will simply not be received.

Children, and adults as well, will close off communication that is incomprehensible, threatening, vague, or rude—like tuning out or turning off a radio with unpleasant static noise. Although one may sometimes feel justified in lecturing or lashing out, there is no value in conveying a message if the message is rejected. Our goal is to have messages accepted and acted on.

What Are the Key Factors in Assertive Communication?

Simplicity Is the First Rule for Assertive Communication. While babies, toddlers, and young children need plenty of opportunities to hear the rhythm and flow of complex adult language, assertive statements need to be short and to the point. Decide what needs to be said and say it in as few words as possible. Verbal clutter gets in the way of stating a desired action.

The younger the child is, the more essential simplicity becomes. Toddlers need simple two- or three-word sentences, such as "Sit, please," or (if a child has already bitten), "No biting. Biting hurts." Preschoolers need only slightly longer sentences, such as "Apples are for eating, not for throwing," "Please hold your glass with two hands," or "A chair is for your seat, not your feet."

Honesty Is Essential for Assertive Communication. Children quickly identify adults who do not really mean what they say. Empty threats are counterproductive. They only teach children that adults cannot be relied on to do what they say, no matter how many times they insist that "this time I really mean it!" It is never acceptable to lie to children or to trick them into compliance. They should be told honestly when a parent is leaving, even if that causes tears. Feeling sad is a natural and healthy response; feeling tricked is not.

Directness Helps Communicators Get Right to the Point. Rambling, hinting, and insinuating are of little value to adult listeners and are totally lost on children. Instead of saying, "The art area is getting pretty sloppy, children," say "Please pick up all of the scrap paper and put it in the trash can. Thank you. Now get a sponge and wipe the table." Instead of saying, "Let's keep it down now," say "Please walk softly and speak quietly." Words used with children should be literal words with clearly definable meanings. A phrase such as "You two cut it out now" should mean that scissors and paper are involved.

Tactfulness Keeps Channels of Communication Open. Gushing sweetness is usually not any more palatable to young children than it is to adults, but tactfulness and sincerity are greatly appreciated. It is tactful to say, "Your glass may tip off the table. Please push it back away from the edge. Thank you." It is not tactful to say, "Stop being so careless with your glass of milk." It is overly patronizing to say, "Here, sweetheart, let's push our little glass back so we don't spill it, okay honey?" Children can be given affection and kindness without being drowned in cloying sweetness.

Concreteness Makes Communication Clear. Abstractions like goodness and badness can be very confusing to children. The statement that lying is bad, for example, may cause a child to think he or she is a bad person. It is more concrete to say, "If you lie, other people may not trust you. They may learn not to believe things you say." With younger children, concreteness is expressed through actions. It is not concrete to tell a toddler, "Be nice to your friends." A toddler has no real concept of the word *nice*. It is a vague, value-laden term for which no two adults would have exactly the same definition. A toddler would not know precisely what one does to be nice. It is concrete to repeat, "Touch softly," while demonstrating stroking the friend's arm gently. The toddler can see and comprehend exactly what action is expected.

Respectfulness Is an Integral Part of Assertive Communication. It is impossible to have open, honest communication with someone for whom one has disgust and disdain. In a democracy, one should have as much respect for the personhood of a garbage collector as for the President, even though each has distinctly different roles and responsibilities. One should have as much respect for the personhood and human rights of a newborn as for any other member of society. Respect for children is expressed by recognizing and protecting their dignity and rights. A police officer may stop a citizen and issue a penalty that makes the citizen feel very unhappy, but the officer has no right to hurt, humiliate, or threaten the citizen. Respectful adults assertively enforce fair rules without name-calling, teasing, embarrassing, hurting, or bullying. A respectful adult confronts children privately and focuses on improving behaviors rather than on punishing children.

Optimism Boosts Cooperativeness by Sharing Hope. A child trying to cope with an assertive adult needs to know that the adult really believes he or she can succeed. Confrontation is softened and made more acceptable by reassurance that problems can indeed be solved. After confronting Jennifer, one might say, "Jennifer, everyone makes mistakes. Our mistakes help us learn. Perhaps tomorrow you can help by reminding the younger children how important it is not to run out of the gate without permission."

Flexibility Is Necessary to Distinguish Assertiveness from Stubbornness. No matter how firmly one intends to carry out a plan of action, the possibility always exists that additional information could indicate the need for a change in plans. Young children need consistency to make sense of what is expected of them, but that need is not contradictory with their need for flexibility. (The trick is finding the right balance.) Effective, assertive, guidance requires that adults provide as much consistency as possible but also as much flexibility as needed to make discipline humane and reasonable.

Adults must constantly seek a balance between firm, predictable limits and the flexibility to listen, adapt, and compromise appropriately. For example, an adult might firmly refuse to talk about or compromise a stated rule while a child is pitching a tantrum and behaving very inappropriately. Later, however, when the child is calm and able to explain logically her problem with the rule, the adult might decide that justice is best served by bending or eliminating the rule. With a very young child, the adult may rely on direct observations rather than verbal discussions to determine if a rule is fair and reasonable.

Confidence Strengthens Assertive Communication by Projecting Assurance That What Is Being Said Is Really Meant. Children are especially sensitive to nonverbal signals or cues from facial expression, intonation, body positioning, and the use of hands and feet. Adults who do not really believe children will do what is asked of them project an air of uncertainty and weakness. A clear-eyed look of confidence greatly increases the probability of compliance from children as well as from listeners of any other age. Fidgeting, speaking in a weak or shrill voice, and avoiding eye contact hint to the child that compliance is not really expected.

When adults say sarcastic things, such as "Well, let's see if you can keep from being a little monster, as usual, running around and tearing everything up while we wait for the doctor," children know immediately that they are expected to behave badly. In contrast, a confident adult

When we truly understand a child's feelings, we can more accurately identify possible reasons for his inappropriate behavior.

might say firmly but caringly, "Here is a book to look at quietly while we wait. We must sit very still. People are not allowed to be rowdy and noisy in a doctor's office." This indicates assurance that the adult believes the child can and will behave appropriately.

Persistence Makes Assertive Communication Work. Punishing, threatening, and intimidating get quick results on the surface but undermine discipline in the long run. Assertive communication does not always bring about an immediate solution, but persistence over time makes it an effective and lasting technique for solving problems. Adults are sometimes tempted to surrender to children's demands when first efforts at communication do not bring about an immediate resolution. However, a generous amount of persistence will reap important benefits by letting children know that we really mean what we say. A child may stubbornly reject a rule on a whim, but if we persist in letting her know we expect the rule to be followed, she will almost surely comply eventually. As with the tortoise and the hare in their fabled contest—slow and steady wins the race.

Empathy May Seem out of Context with Assertiveness, but Instead It Is Absolutely Essential. Sympathy means feeling sorry for others; empathy means walking in their shoes, feeling what they feel. Assertiveness without empathy is hollow and insincere. Assertiveness with empathy is strength and love rolled into one. A little person with grimy hands, a runny nose, and a knack for creating havoc does not always trigger feelings of warmth and empathy in parents and caregivers. Nonetheless, effective communication requires sincere understanding and caring. Empathy is expressed to listeners, from infancy to adulthood, primarily through the eyes and face, but all other verbal and nonverbal cues can also express empathy (or the lack of it).

For example, adults can begin reprimands by making an initial positive statement of some kind to show empathy. An adult might take a child by the hand and say, "I know you just want to play with the kitty, but chasing him and pulling his tail really frightens him. Would you like to feed him to show him you're his friend?"

Characteristics of Nonproductive Communication

Adults use many different communication styles. Of course, some styles are more effective than others. The least effective styles usually deal only superficially with the content of the communication and fail completely to address the feelings or emotions of the persons sharing in the communication. It is most important that adults avoid the communication pitfalls that inhibit dialogue and alienate children (or others of any age).

Gazda et al. (1984) lists nine common stereotypes of ineffective communication styles:

1. Florist—avoids issues through flowery euphemisms
2. Detective—skirts issues by persistently prying with questions
3. Magician—vaporizes problems with the wave of a wand
4. Drill sergeant—avoids conflict by barking orders
5. Foreman—clouds issues by the use of compulsive busyness
6. Hangman—induces guilt to avoid confronting problems
7. Guru—covers over issues by giving a cliché for every occasion
8. Swami—smoke screens issues by predicting dismal outcomes
9. Sign painter—dismisses problems by tacking labels on them

While two-dimensional stereotypes do not reflect the complex facets of real people, they are helpful for identifying characteristics real people display from time to time. One stereotype may be the predominant way an individual responds, but others might recognize a little bit of each stereotype in their behavior occasionally. The purpose of these stereotypes is not to label children or adults but to better recognize and understand ineffective communication styles.

How Do People Behaving Like These Stereotypes Respond to Problem Situations Involving Children and Adults?

Florists simply do not see any problems. If a child communicates that he or she has been hurt by another child, the florist ever so sweetly croons, "Why Suzy, I'm sure he didn't mean to hurt you!" If a tearful child sobs, "I hate my mommy," the florist teacher just smiles knowingly and says, "Of course you don't hate your mommy. Children don't hate their mommies." The florist loses many opportunities for communication by tossing garlands of optimism rather than confronting and exploring problems.

Detectives want answers—"Why did you do that?" "Who did it first?" "Did I tell you not to do that?" "What do you think you're going to do now?" The listener is not only dazed by the battery of questions but also tempted to lie or to give whatever answers the detective seems to want.

Magicians dismiss issues conveniently. If a child says, "Someone pushed me off the swing," the magician says with flourish, "Yes, but playtime is over now so it really doesn't matter does it?" If a father expresses concern that his baby's pacifier is lost, the magician responds, "That's okay. Sarah really doesn't need a pacifier. She'll scream for an hour or two then forget all about it."

Drill sergeants do not have time to communicate; they are too busy barking orders. The drill sergeant nursery school teacher hears a heated argument in the block center. Instead of encouraging communication, she says, "Get these blocks picked up off the floor. Kaleb, tuck in your shirt. Samantha, you wouldn't have these problems if you'd pay attention and mind your own business."

The *foreman* keeps everyone so busy they cannot think about problems. A mother confides to her child's kindergarten teacher that her husband has left her and she has lost her job. She is worried that her son, Joshua, is being affected by her stress and depression. The foreman teacher responds, "You need to get out of the house and stop feeling sorry for yourself. Take an art class. Volunteer at the hospital. Throw a party." The mother leaves feeling even more guilty and overwhelmed.

The *hangman* dishes out blame. The hangman's favorite phrase is, "Well, I'm not surprised. You know, it's your own fault." When Jamey asks his hangman preschool teacher, Miss Judy, for help printing his name, she says, "If you had paid attention last week, you would already know how to do this." When the director asks Miss Judy for help with a new child who is crying for his mother, Miss Judy says, "Of course he's crying. What do you expect? Did you see the way his mother let him manipulate her? She's to blame for this."

The *guru* has a mental storehouse of meaningless clichés to scatter like rose petals over problems. A mother asks her toddler's nursery teacher if she thinks speech therapy is needed for the child. The guru teacher answers brightly, "Well, a stitch in time saves nine!" A nine-year-old boy asks his guru dad why countries have scary things like nuclear bombs and is told, "An ounce of prevention is worth a pound of cure." A four-year-old cries, "Nobody likes me. I don't have any friends." Her guru teacher responds, "Well, you have to be a friend to have a friend." The guru's pat answers end dialogue rather than stimulate insight and understanding of problems.

The *swami* is not exactly a comfort in time of need. He or she is always prepared to predict all the terrible and hopeless things that will probably happen as a result of the listener's actions. When a three-year-old runs into the house crying because she has a splinter in her finger, her swami mother says, "I told you not to play on that seesaw. Now you're going to get an infection and I'm going to be stuck with a big doctor bill. Look at this, your fingernail will probably turn black and fall off." Of course, there is the classic swami response, "Johnny, when you fall out of that tree and break both your legs, don't come running to me."

Sign painters make quick work of problems by assigning labels. A nursery school teacher complains to her coworker that she is having difficulty with one of her toddlers having temper tantrums. The sign painter coworker shrugs his shoulders and says, "I don't know of anything you can do about terrible twos. They're just that way." In a parent conference with child care staff, a single mother asks, "What is happening to my son? He seems to be trying to hurt everyone and everything around him." A sign painter teacher pats her on the shoulder and says, "Hey, all hyperactive kids do that." Meaningful communication is hindered by sign painters. There hardly seems to be any reason to discuss a problem after a label has been stamped on it with such finality.

If These Stereotypical Communication Styles Are Ineffective, What Will Work?

In each of the above stereotypes, the communicator avoids, dismisses, evades, or thwarts feelings. An effective, assertive communicator addresses feelings with kindness and respect, but also with honesty. Often, it seems easiest to do whatever is expedient to stop a child's crying, end a dispute, or make a parent or coworker feel better. Unfortunately, when feelings are pushed under the rug, they can fester into even more unmanageable feelings.

Managing the Positive Confrontation

When confronting a problem issue, one should first use active listening to allow the child or adult to identify, explore, and express feelings related to the situation. "Cheap and dirty" advice should not be tossed out lightly. Instead, persons being helped can be guided to recognize the choices they have and the possible outcomes of those choices. Only then can a person be assisted in solving his or her problem. Adults must assume responsibility for solving their own problems before real help can be given. Imposing unwanted help on another adult is almost always counterproductive. Helping children is another matter. If a child does not show motivation to solve a problem, parents and caregivers must assume that responsibility for the child. The child should be assisted as firmly as necessary but as gently as possible in confronting and solving problems.

When Is Confrontation Appropriate?

Albert is waiting excitedly for his dad to pick him up from his child care center. He and his buddy, Joshua, have been planning to ask if they can spend the night together. As they dig in the sand, they giggle and scheme about the fun they will have watching television and eating grape Popsicles.

Finally, Albert sees his dad. Both boys run to the gate and watch as Albert's dad parks his car. Before his dad is even inside the gate, Albert is talking so fast that his dad cannot understand him. Albert's dad hoists him into the air saying, "How's my big boy?" Albert excitedly says, "Daddy, can Joshua spend the night? Can he? Huh? Can he?"

Albert's dad takes both boys by the hand and as they walk up the sidewalk, he says quietly, "No, son, I have some paperwork I need to do tonight. This is not a good day. I will be happy to call Joshua's parents, though, and arrange for him to stay over one night next week."

Albert pulls his hand away and starts to cry. His dad bends down and says, "You really had your heart set on having Joshua spend the night, didn't you?" Albert nods yes through his tears. His dad continues, "You feel sad and angry because next week seems a long time away." Albert nods again.

> *His dad hugs him and says, "It's okay to cry. Even grown people cry sometimes. I bet Joshua feels pretty bad too." Albert stops rubbing his eyes and looks at Joshua. Albert throws his arms around his dad's neck for one last round of begging—"Pleeeeease, Daddy, I promise we won't bother you." His dad's expression remains calm and empathetic. He says, "Albert, it is okay to ask, and it is okay to cry and feel sad, but the answer won't change. Joshua can't spend the night tonight."*
>
> *Albert's next tactic is pouting, but his dad remains calm and firm as he gathers Albert's belongings and prepares to leave. As his dad buckles him into his seat belt, Albert plants a wet kiss on his cheek and says, "I love you, Daddy." His dad grins and says, "I love you too, son."*

Albert's dad successfully avoided the stereotypes described previously. He did not delay confrontation by saying, "We'll talk about it later." He did not avoid confrontation by giving in to something he knew he would regret. He did not squelch confrontation by saying, "I don't want to hear another word about this. Hush right now or I won't let Joshua stay with you next week either." He did not try to force Albert to like the decision by arguing with him, and he did not try to make Albert agree with him and stop being mad.

Instead, Albert's father confronted Albert simply, directly, and immediately but with a great deal of empathy and respect. He listened, made what he believed was a fair decision, allowed Albert to express his feelings, and then recognized and reflected those feelings. In the end, Albert probably felt very secure in knowing his dad was a strong authority figure to be relied on rather than a weakling to be manipulated or a tyrant to be dreaded.

How Can Confrontations with Children Be Made Positive and Assertive?

Anger undermines assertive confrontation. An adult who becomes enraged with a child should do only what is necessary to protect the child's safety and well-being on an immediate basis. He or she could ask for assistance from another adult who is calm, leave the baby screaming in the crib and do deep breathing and relaxation exercises, or say to an older child, "I feel angry now. I will talk to you when I feel calm."

Confrontation should be delayed until the adult feels in control and is able to muster some level of empathy. Hurtful confrontations attack children in an angry, punitive way. Effective, assertive confrontations guide, protect, and nurture children; they do not intimidate them.

An angry adult may find it helpful to think about and answer the following questions:

- Why do I feel the way I feel?
- What did I feel before I felt anger? Was it frustration? Fear? Embarrassment?
- Am I simply afraid to say no to this child?

- Am I tired, hungry, not feeling well?

- How would I feel right now if I were the child?

- Are my expectations reasonable?

Adults who lack assertiveness are usually afraid to use the following three phrases in their daily speech: "I want . . .," "I need . . .," and, "I feel. . . ." Parents and other caregivers often try so hard to keep children happy that they suppress their own wants, needs, and feelings. Then, instead of being appreciated as long-suffering martyrs, they are taken advantage of, and eventually they explode in anger and resentment. They are rarely appreciated. The more they try to give, the more children and other adults expect of them. As they learn to take an assertive stand, they discover that they are less angry, more appreciated, and a great deal happier.

How Can Attention Be Kept Focused on Confronting the Issues at Hand?

The stereotypical communication styles previously presented were described as adult characteristics; however, these same evasion tactics are often used by children. (Remember, children learn by modeling.) Children who have imitated parents and caregivers with poor or manipulative communication styles are especially prone to using those styles to evade issues.

Children evade confrontations by persistently asking questions, by issuing bossy little commands, and by giving cliché responses, such as "Everyone else's mother lets them stay up as long as they want." Children not only learn roles directly by imitating them, but also create roles as mirror-image opposites of those to which they are exposed. The child of a drill sergeant parent may learn to behave as a magician—"Get that trash picked up off the floor!" "What trash? I don't see any trash. Where? That's not trash. That's my cans I'm saving."

The more adept adults become in direct, assertive communication, the more successful they will be in keeping children's attention focused on confronting and resolving problem issues. Children will not need to evade issues when they trust adults to confront issues in a gentle but firm and fair manner. For many children and adults, the thought of a confrontation triggers terror, since their primary experiences with confrontation have been frightening interactions filled with rage—their own rage as well as the rage of powerful, threatening adults.

Confrontation, without anger, is an essential and healthy part of social interaction.

How Can Children Be Taught Responsibility?

Responsibility cannot be taught through lectures. Responsibility can be shown through example, it can be nurtured and reinforced, and, most importantly, it can be learned first hand by dealing with the consequences of one's own actions. Adults often feel compelled to prevent children from experiencing consequences—"You have to eat this! You might get hungry later." They rescue children—"You were careless and left your doll in the rain. Now I'll have to buy you another." The child feels only the adult's annoyance. He or she is not allowed to feel the natural consequences of behaviors.

We can tell a great deal from body posture and facial expressions. What do you suppose these two boys may be feeling? (Photograph provided courtesy of CHILDREN AT RISK.)

It is better for the child to have support and warmth from adults as he or she feels and owns the sting of unpleasant consequences from poor decisions. Adults must prevent dangerous or damaging consequences. A child cannot learn firsthand the consequences of such things as running out into a busy street, or never brushing teeth. However, exploring and discussing possible consequences should be a part of confrontations.

Rather than lecturing children about consequences, adults should make simple statements ("If you throw food, you will have to leave the table.") and ask simple questions ("What do you think could happen if you stood on the edge of the balcony?"). Children can be encouraged on a regular basis to explore potential consequences. Children who have a habit of considering and weighing consequences are well on their way to becoming responsible and self-directed.

Practical Application/Discussion

"I'll Leave You Here Forever"

Marlene pauses in the shopping mall waiting for her two-year-old to catch up with her. Her four-month-old, who is asleep on her shoulder, is beginning to feel very heavy. "Crystal," she calls to her two-year-old, "Please come on. We need to get home."

Crystal stalls as she climbs on and off benches and stops to look at other shoppers. Her mother loses patience, "Crystal! You come here now or you're going to be sorry." Crystal ignores her.

Marlene walks quickly back to Crystal and, taking her firmly by the wrist, says, "Let's go." Crystal responds with the rubbery-legs strategy toddlers use when they rebel. Her legs go limp as she slumps to the floor, dangling from the wrist her mother is clutching and whining, "Don't want go home."

Marlene realizes that she cannot safely carry her baby and Crystal both out of the shopping mall. In exasperation, she snaps, "That's it, I'm leaving. If you won't come, then I'll just leave you here forever. Good-bye!"

She turns and begins to walk briskly out of the mall. She hears Crystal howling and running to catch up with her.

Questions for Discussion

1. What would you have done in Marlene's place? Why?
2. What has Crystal really learned from the interaction?
3. Could anything have been done to prevent Marlene's predicament?
4. Role play the scene using positive, assertive communication and confrontation, then compare possible outcomes.

Points to Remember

- Communication skills are developed early in life.

- Adults influence children by setting a good example for them and by encouraging them to practice appropriate communication skills.

- Responsive, active listening is essential to child guidance, but dependency and inappropriate interaction must be firmly and respectfully redirected.

- Feelings and emotions must be considered in order to provide appropriate responses to behaviors.

- Adults can help children to understand the motives for their own misbehaviors.

- Positive instructions are more likely to elicit cooperative behavior than imperative commands or negative statements.

- Assertive communication is honest but not brutal.

- Assertiveness always requires respect and empathy in order to be effective.

- Adults often behave in stereotypical ways to avoid, squelch, dismiss, or deny feelings.

- Tactics that avoid addressing feelings are ineffective and harmful to open, honest communication.

- Positive confrontation is a healthy and natural part of social interaction.

- Consequences (that are neither dangerous nor unreasonable) provide children feedback about the appropriateness of their behavior.

- Adults can assist children in developing responsibility by encouraging children I th   to talk about and think about the potential consequences of their behavior.

Related Readings

Effective Communication

Cooney, M., et al. (1996, Fall). From hitting and tattling to communication and negotiation: The young child's stages of socialization. *Early Childhood Education Journal, 24*(1), 23–27.

Diffily, D., & Morrison, K. (1996). *Family-friendly communication for early childhood programs.* Washington, DC: National Association for the Education of Young Children.

Edwards, C., Gandini, L., & Forman, G. (1993). *The hundred languages of children.* Norwood, NJ: Ablex.

French, L. (1996, January). "I told you all about it, so don't tell me you don't know": Two-year-olds and learning through language. *Young Children, 51*(2), 17–20.

Friedman, E. H. (1990). *Friedman's fables*. New York: Guilford.

> *Teaching by parable has an old and honorable tradition. Ed Friedman, rabbi and family therapist, writes stories that are funny, but also profound, even shocking, as they present lessons of family life in a slyly modern, hard-nosed re-evaluation of the wisdom of the ages. Dr. Friedman presents stories to show that neither insight, nor encouragement, nor intimidation can in themselves motivate an unmotivated person to change. These provocative tales playfully demonstrate that new ideas, new questions, and imagination, more than accepted wisdom, provide each of us with the keys to overcoming stubborn emotional barriers and facilitating real change both in ourselves and others.*

Mahoney, G., & Neville-Smith, A. (1996, Summer). The effects of directive communications on children's interactive engagement: Implications for language intervention. Topics in Early Childhood Special Education, 16(2), 236–50.

Marschark, M. (1997). Raising and educating a deaf child. New York, NY: Oxford University Press.

Swick, Kevin J., et al. (1997, Summer). On board early: Building strong family-school relations. Early Childhood Education Journal, 24(4), 269–73.

Turnbull, A. P., & Turnbull, H. R. (1997). Families, professionals and exceptionality: A special partnership (3rd ed.). Upper Saddle River, NJ: Merrill Education/Prentice-Hall.

> *Collaboration means sharing resources and creating a context that empowers families and professionals alike. The book presents comprehensive, data-based, and conceptually consistent approaches for families and professionals to collaborate for empowerment.*

Positive, assertive guidance strengthens children's confidence and self-esteem. (Photograph provided courtesy of CHILDREN AT RISK.)

Chapter 4

Positive Action

Chapter Outline

Objectives

This chapter will assist you in

- Creating a setting that is supportive to positive child guidance
- Focusing on the role of nonverbal communication and body language in assisting positive behavior
- Defining logical and natural consequences and understanding their importance in guidance
- Identifying reasonable and effective circumstances for the use of external reinforcement

Nonverbal Cues, Body Language

Not only does the environment give messages to children about what we expect from them, but also our own physical postures, movements, and gestures communicate a great deal of information to them. We may not even be aware of the body language signals we are sending out and the children are receiving and reacting to.

What Is the Significance of Nonverbal Cues for Young Children?

Before verbal language is well-developed, young children rely heavily on our body **nonverbal communication** (body language such as gestures, facial expressions, and tone of voice) in their interactions with others. Infants pay attention to the touch, facial expressions, and sounds of their caregivers to interpret the adult's moods and expectations. Even a six-month-old baby can recognize clear differences between the meanings of a frowning parent with his hands firmly on his hips and a smiling parent with his arms stretched toward the baby. Rather than interpreting the meaning of a caregiver's words or sentences, very young children focus all their attention on sense perception. They pay attention to things they can actually see, hear, feel, taste, or smell.

As children reach preschool age, they gradually pay more attention to the actual words in adults' speech, but they are still very sensitive to nonverbal cues. (Drumming my fingers on the table may be my cue, or signal, that I am feeling annoyed.)

Why Should Nonverbal Cues be Consistent with Verbal Communication?

Adults must take nonverbal expressions into consideration whenever they attempt to communicate with children. A typical situation in which children receive conflicting messages between verbal and nonverbal cues occurs when children are brought to an early childhood setting for the first time. Typically, a parent will say, "You'll have a lot of fun playing with other children, and I will be back later to pick you up. It's okay now, go ahead with your teacher." The words are full of confidence and optimism. The adult, who focuses only on the words, may not notice that she is tense, strained, and anxious in appearance.

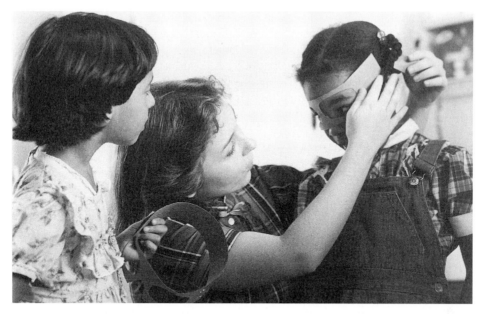

Children pay close attention to the nonverbal signals adults give as part of their communication.

Elena, a preschool teacher in a child care center, took her youngsters outside to play early one summer morning to avoid the midday heat and humidity. As the children played happily, Elena looked up and noticed swarms of hungry mosquitoes circling in clusters near the eaves of the building.

She stood silently, with her arms tightly folded across her chest, staring at the buzzing dive bombers and wondering what she should do. Should she take the children back inside? Should she spray the children with repellent? She felt a tug at her skirt. Willie, a three-year-old who had been riding around Elena on a tricycle and watching her carefully, blurted out in a sad voice, "Miss Elena, how come you're mad at me?" Willie read Elena's body language and sensed tension and frustration. Since he was a normally developing preoperational child, he naturally (and egocentrically) assumed that he was the cause of Elena's unhappiness.

Elena had not realized the effect her nonverbal body language could have on the children around her. Since the vocabulary and language comprehension skills of young children are so limited, their understanding of their environment hinges on their ability to be very alert to nonverbal cues from those around them.

The adult's facial expression is one of uncertainty, her voice sounds uncharacteristically high, and her hands are wringing and twisting nervously. Instead of leaving quickly, she hangs near the child while insisting that the child "act like a big boy and go play." The parent says she is going, but she looks as if she is staying.

Of course, the child pays more attention to the nonverbal cues than to the spoken words. He will sense that his parent is frightened and unsure about leaving him, so he will probably feel frightened and unsure about being left. He will probably resist being left—with a great deal of volume and energy. If, on the other hand, he senses that his parent is confident and optimistic, he may feel a bit uncomfortable at first, but he is likely to adjust more quickly and easily to the separation. He absorbs the confidence of his parent as she smiles and says in a relaxed tone of voice, "I know you will have a great time today," then leaves.

Why Should We Focus Attention at the Child's Eye Level?

If an adult stands across the room from a child and casually looks over a shoulder, saying, "Letecia, don't touch those scissors; you'll cut yourself," Letecia will probably interpret that the adult is not too concerned about the danger of the scissors and will probably not enforce the command. It is likely that Letecia will continue to touch the scissors while watching the adult carefully for stronger or more direct cues about the scissors.

If the adult stops what she is doing and bends down to the child's eye level, holding out a hand for the scissors and saying, "Please give me the scissors. These are too sharp—they could cut you. We'll find you a plastic pair," the adult's assertive nonverbal communication matches her verbal communication. Letecia is likely to perceive that the adult "means business" and is willing to follow through to see that the sharp scissors are removed.

As Letecia decides whether to comply with the command she has been given, she will read the adult's facial expression (Is there a playful twinkle in the eye or a look of concerned resolve?), tone of voice (Is there a weak tone of uncertainty or a tone of absolute confidence?), and hand gestures (Are hand motions assertive or physically threatening?). If the adult's nonverbal cues are too playful or casual, Letecia will assume that she really does not have to comply. If they are too threatening and intrusive, Letecia will be likely to bristle and resist the command. If they are assertive, caring, confident, and no-nonsense, Letecia may decide that it is a good idea to comply quickly and willingly.

Helping Children Resolve Problems Independently

A primary goal for early childhood development is the growth of personal responsibility and independence in children. Learning how to behave appropriately requires self-control, which is closely related to responsibility and independence. In order to become socially competent, children need to learn to **negotiate** (settle disputes through discussion) so they can successfully resolve at least some of their own problems.

Children often come to adults begging to be rescued from various unhappy situations. Sometimes, the child's grievance is legitimate. Children have a right to call on someone bigger, stronger, and with more authority when their rights have been violated—just as I have a right to request legal help if my own rights have been violated.

If I call a police officer for help because my purse has been stolen, I will feel very resentful if the officer responds by saying things like:

Children have a right to ask for adult help when their rights are infringed upon.

- "Don't tattle!"

- "Don't be so stingy, the thief probably needed the money worse than you do anyway."

- "You got what you deserved. You shouldn't have been carrying a purse that would tempt people anyway."

- "Well, did you tell the purse-snatcher you didn't like that?"

We are a tiny bit embarrassed by some of our most frequently used expressions when we step back and compare them with what we expect from others.

Nevertheless, there are occasions when the child should not be rescued by an adult. In order to foster independence, children should be helped to do as much for themselves as they can reasonably be expected to handle successfully. Common sense will tell us that there are times we need to firmly nudge children into assuming responsibility for resolving problems they encounter.

How Can We Help Children Learn to Use Words to Express Themselves to Each Other?

Toddlers scream, hit, shove, and bite primarily because they lack the verbal ability to express themselves otherwise. They are transparent and physical in letting another child or adult know they feel angry. We may regret the onset of name-calling in children past three, but we are very likely to see a decrease in physical aggression as verbal communication skills are mastered. Preschoolers discover they can cause a peer to dissolve in tears just by calling her a "weenie baby" or by tauntingly chanting nonsense words, such as "Nanny, nanny, boo, boo! Nanny, nanny, boo, boo!"

In positive child guidance, children are taught ways to communicate feelings honestly and assertively without having to resort to verbal aggression. Following is a list of adult statements that facilitate child-to-child communication:

- "Jarrod, please say, 'Excuse me, Christie, I need to get past.' Christie doesn't like to be shoved."

- "Alva, use words. Tell Erin you feel very angry when he grabs your crayons without asking. Would you like for me to help you tell him?"

- "Erin, Alva feels really mad when you grab her crayons. Can you ask for a crayon? Can you say, 'Please, may I have a crayon?'"

- "Jerusha, thank you for saying, 'Excuse me, this chair is mine.'"

- "Adam and Beth, you need to sit here on the step and talk until you both feel better."

- "Beth, your friend Adam says you scratched his face. Adam, Beth says you wadded up her drawing and threw it in the wastebasket. Adam, you're upset because your face really hurts."

- "Beth, you're sad because you really wanted to take that picture home to your mother."

- "Can either of you think of some way to make your friend feel better?"

- "That's a great idea, Adam, you could get the drawing out of the trash can and try to smooth it out."

- "Yes, Beth, I think Adam would really like a wet paper towel to hold on his scratched cheek."

By giving children help in knowing exactly what to say to playmates when trouble breaks out, we encourage them to use appropriate words rather than inappropriate physical or verbal aggression. It is okay (even desirable) for children to express strong emotions. We should never push children into being so "nice" that they hold their emotions inside. Our goal is to channel their emotional expression into words that inform rather than words that hurt.

Should We Force Children to Apologize?

It seems very odd that we tell children, "Be honest—always tell the truth," and then proceed to order them to "tell so-and-so you're sorry" (never even wondering if they actually feel sorry). No child should be encouraged to say she feels something that she really does not feel. It is more appropriate to simply point out how the other child feels. She may spontaneously give some indication of remorse or regret—if she really feels it.

If a child appears to be sorry for something she has done, it may be helpful to say, "Would you like to tell Ricky that you're sorry about what happened?" "Would you like me to tell him for you?" It is even more important for us to find some way to help the child make amends to Ricky. She will feel good about herself if she has a chance to make things right. We discourage children terribly when we imply to them, "You have made such a mess of things that there is no way you can undo what you've done."

How Can We Encourage Voluntary Sharing?

Sharing should also be voluntary. If my friend picked up a book I was reading and walked off with it, I would think her very rude. Strangely, when one child is looking at a book and a peer takes the book without asking, we are tempted to say, "You need to share. Look, there are lots of books. Just choose a different book. Don't be so stingy with the books."

I have a right to my own property and possessions. I can offer someone the use of my scissors, but they really should not barge in and take them—especially if I am using them at the moment. I expect guests in my house to be respectful of my personal possessions, yet parents often allow visiting children to barge into their own child's room and play with any toy they want. If their own child puts up a fuss, we hear them say, "You have to share."

We all want children to be generous and polite, but we can encourage generosity most by protecting a child's property rights, so he feels it is safe to invite others to share. The more vulnerable the child feels about losing his possessions, the more tightly and greedily he will guard them.

Graciela quietly moved from cot to cot in the darkened child care room as restless four-year-olds settled in for naptime. Several of the children could always be counted on to fall sound asleep almost before she got the light off. Most took ten or fifteen minutes to wind down and fall asleep. Then, of course, there were the really challenging three who squirmed and fidgeted and tried everything in the book to keep themselves awake! Graciela never knew if she would eventually get them to sleep or not. She especially worried about Brett, because his parents had complained that he was so exhausted when they picked him up from child care that they were not able to spend enough quality time with him in the evenings.

Brett was lying on his stomach with his chin resting on one hand and the other hand twisting a loose thread hanging from his blanket. Graciela moved quietly to his side. She sat down cross-legged on the floor beside him and gently stroked his back. She bent close to him and whispered, "Brett, thanks for being so quiet and still. You were so quiet, I couldn't hear a single sound."

Brett grinned and felt very good about himself.

How Can We Recognize and Encourage Internal Control?

Nurturing adults should always be alert to opportunities for recognizing and reinforcing little indications that a child is making progress in controlling impulses and resisting tempting but inappropriate behaviors.

Logical and Natural Consequences

Children learn skills and information through active involvement in their day-to-day environment. They learn by watching others, by being told things, and, most importantly, by experiencing life. In life, actions are often followed by logical or natural consequences. If I forget to water my potted plant, it will probably die (a natural consequence). If I am regularly late to work, I may lose my job (a logical consequence). No one is trying to hurt or annoy me. These consequences are merely the way the world works. Through them, I learn that I must behave in certain ways if I want to avoid undesired results and achieve desired goals.

Should Children Be Rescued from the Consequences of their Actions?

Sometimes, when we see a child feeling disappointed or sad, we may be tempted to interfere and rescue her from the consequences of her own actions. It is not, however, a useful practice for us to rescue children from the logical and natural results of their actions and choices—so long as the consequences are reasonable and safe! We would never risk a child being run over as a natural consequence of running into the street or allow a child to go hungry as a logical consequence of spilling food.

> *Tina arrived home after a family outing to a downtown movie theater and suddenly yelled, "Oh, no! I left my purse in the theater." Her dad fumed and sputtered, "Tina, why are you so careless? It'll take me a half hour to drive back downtown, and by then the purse will probably be stolen. You'd lose your head if it wasn't tied down." After yelling at Tina for twenty minutes while she sniffled and made excuses for her behavior, he called the theater and drove back downtown alone to search for the purse.*

Even though Tina's dad reprimanded her loudly and angrily, in actuality he **rescued** her from any responsibility for her forgetfulness. (He absorbed the consequences for her.) He was the one who made the phone calls, drove all the way back to the theater, and did the searching. Tina had nothing to do but feel miserable and stupid. Tina's dad would have used natural consequences if he had said:

> Tina, I'm sure you feel awful about losing your purse. Can you think of anything we could do to find it? Would you like for me to help you look up the phone number of the theater? Would you like for me to drive you back to the theater so you can look for it? I don't know if we'll find it or not. Purses left in public places often get stolen.

Tina's dad would have used logical consequences if he had said:

> Tina, it isn't fair for me to have to drive all the way back to town. Next time we go to the theater, you will have to leave your purse at home. When you're a little older, you can try again. Perhaps by then it won't be so hard for you to remember your things.

By helping Tina find ways to solve her problem (rather than solving it for her), Tina's father guides her to focus on her forgetfulness as the problem—not her father's anger. She realizes that her discomfort results from the natural or logical consequences of her forgetfulness, not from someone trying to punish or embarrass her. She will become responsible when she learns to remember her possessions simply because it is frustrating and inconvenient to lose them, not just to please her father. If Tina learns to behave appropriately only to please her father, she may be tempted to behave inappropriately just to annoy him when she is angry with him or feeling rebellious.

What is the Difference Between Punishment and Guidance?

Punishment is negative. It is intended to hurt, humiliate, or pay a child back for something she has done. The purpose of guidance, in contrast, is to teach children (assertively and respectfully) to behave appropriately. Discipline is a part of positive child guidance; punishment is not. Following are examples of punishment versus discipline as used with a preschooler:

Punishment

☹ *"Don't you dare touch that cake. Get away from here and go play. If I catch you fooling around with it, you're really gonna get it!"*

☹ *"I saw you touch that cake. Get in the time-out chair and stay until I say you can get up. Everyone's going to see you sitting in the 'naughty' chair and know that you were being bad."*

☹ *"I'd better not see you get up! If I see you try to get up I'll make you stay twice as long."*

Punishment is used to bully or coerce children into behaving the way we want them to. Following are some of the ways adults punish children:

- Spanking, slapping, arm-yanking, and shaking

- Biting, hair-pulling, or pinching (so he will know how it feels)

- Withdrawing affection, ignoring, avoiding eye contact, not speaking

- Humiliating the child, putting her in a position to be ridiculed

- Endlessly lecturing, nagging, or harping on problems that are past history (they are done, the child cannot undo them)

- Forcing the child to sit or stay somewhere for a set period of time regardless of whether the child is sincerely remorseful and ready to make amends

- Arbitrarily taking away privileges, forbidding activities that the child particularly enjoys (especially privileges that are totally unrelated to the child's offense)

Discipline/Positive Guidance

☺ *"This is Stephen's birthday cake. No one is allowed to touch it. It isn't fair to mess up Stephen's beautiful cake. You may look at it—but only if you keep your hands in your pockets."*

☺ *"You seem to be having a hard time remembering to keep your hands in your pockets while you look at the cake. You need to come sit on the time-out chair until you feel sure you can remember our rule about not touching the cake. Come and tell me when you are sure you can look at the cake without touching."*

☺ *"I like the way you are keeping your hands in your pockets while you look at Stephen's cake. Stephen will be so happy when he sees his beautiful birthday cake. Ummm, it smells good, doesn't it?"*

Positive guidance is used to nurture and shape children's behavior. Following are some of the ways adults discipline children:

- Changing the surroundings to remove the likelihood or temptation for misbehavior

- Focusing the child's attention on logical and natural consequences that will, or may, follow a specific behavior

- Expressing concern for the child's feelings, but refusing to rescue the child from reasonable and safe consequences that are natural or logical results of his behavior

- Carefully supervising the child to prompt or cue appropriate behavior and remind the child of rules

- Firmly but respectfully redirecting the child's behavior away from inappropriate actions and substituting more appropriate activities

- Decisively stopping or interrupting any behavior that is clearly dangerous or unfair—responding as firmly as necessary but as gently as possible

- Physically removing a very young child from a conflict or during a tantrum (even if the child is kicking and screaming) when it is necessary to protect the child and the environment

- Letting an older child know that you refuse to join her in her tantrum, but that you will be glad to talk when she is ready to speak calmly and respectfully

- Assuring the child that he is loved and valued; letting him know that you accept and respect his negative feelings, even if you must stop his negative action (it is okay to feel angry, but not okay to hurt others)

There is a very fine line, sometimes, between punishing and guiding. A controversial concern for many early childhood educators is whether to use something called "time-out" as a consequence for inappropriate behavior. In their efforts to avoid overtly negative punishments, many early childhood professionals have for years responded to misbehavior by having children sit in time-out, by "the thinking wall," or in "the thinking chair." More negative versions have banished children to the "bad chair," the "baby chair," or the "naughty corner." Several early childhood experts have cautioned that children should not be required to sit any longer than three minutes for every year of the child's age, for example, nine minutes for a three-year-old, fifteen minutes for a five-year-old. In reality, it is not uncommon for children in some settings to be forced to sit many times that length of time.

Today, some experts say that time-out is a viable and positive method of guiding behavior while other experts insist that time-out just allows children uninterrupted time to plot their revenge. The real issue, however, is not whether a time-out chair is used or not used (or whether a penalty is imposed, or whether a privilege is denied). The concern lies in how the adult goes about his enforcement and why he does what he does. Following are several ways to tell the difference between punishment and guidance:

Punishment

Lowers self-esteem	*Embarrasses*
Humiliates	*Discourages*
Degrades	*Belittles*
Hurts (physically or emotionally)	*Socially isolates*
Angers	*Emotionally abandons*
Frustrates	*Denies affection*
Thwarts efforts	

Guidance

Builds self-esteem	*Gives confidence*
Strengthens	*Encourages*
Respects	*Enhances self-image*
Heals	*Facilitates trust*
Gives hope	*Gives emotional support*
Models coping skills	*Is loving and caring*
Enables efforts	

Sitting in time-out can feel lonely and embarrassing.

At this point, one might respond by saying, "Those lists are lovely, but when little Elroy draws on my freshly painted walls with his crayon, I'm furious. I don't care about enhancing his self-image, I just want to wring his little neck!" Actually, Elroy's infuriating behavior gives us an excellent opportunity to put our preaching into practice. We can show Elroy, through our own behavior, that feeling angry is natural and normal—but hurting, humiliating, or belittling others is simply not okay. Socially accepted rules for appropriate behavior do not apply only to children; they apply to all of us.

Having Elroy tediously scrub the crayon marks off the wall and taking the crayons away until he can be more carefully supervised are both assertive and effective disciplinary methods. They are a part of positive child guidance—but only if the adult's attitude is optimistic and assertive rather than mean-spirited and punitive. Our attitude toward Elroy should be one of helping him succeed in behaving more appropriately in the future, not making him miserable to punish him for his bad deed.

> *These children, to be well trained and educated, should never hear from their teacher an angry word, or see a cross or threatening expression of countenance.*
>
> Robert Owen (1958)

How Can I Be Firm Without Seeming Angry?

In order to be firm and fair in guiding children, deeds must be seen as separate from the person who did them. In other words, what a child has done may have been dishonest, but that does not mean the child is now a dishonest person. Since children are prone to become what we tell them they are (remember that prophecies are often self-fulfilling), we must be very careful about what we tell children they are. It is helpful to tell a child, "Pouring water on a cat is a thoughtless and unkind thing to do. You are a kind and thoughtful boy—but even kind, thoughtful boys make mistakes. The important thing is to do better next time."

Following are some helpful and some not-so-helpful phrases:

Not Helpful

☹ *"You are a naughty girl!"*

☹ *"Why are you so bad?"*

☹ *"Don't act like a dummy."*

☹ *"You lazy thing! Look at your messy room."*

Helpful

☺ *"Spitting at people is not allowed!"*

☺ *"Why do you feel angry with your brother?"*

☺ *"What will happen if you spill the paint?"*

☺ *"After your room is clean, then you may watch TV."*

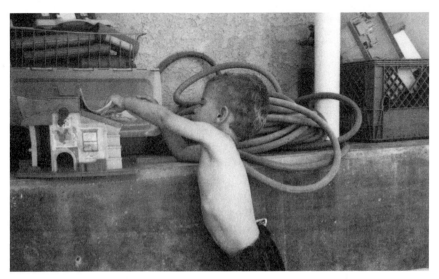

"I am still a good person even if I sometimes break a rule."

Phrases that are not helpful do little more than stereotype children in negative roles (naughty, bad, stupid, lazy). Helpful phrases give children very specific information about what is expected, without labeling the child in a negative way. Children always appreciate being reminded, "I'm very upset with what you did, but I'm not angry with you—I still love you a whole lot, even when you make mistakes."

How Can We Avoid Overindulging and Overprotecting Children?

Caring adults know how to say no. The idea of positive child guidance is sometimes interpreted to mean that adults are slaves to children, that adults must somehow keep things happy, glowing, and idyllic for children at all times. This could not be further from the truth. We have an obligation to be fair, caring, and available, but we are not responsible to make sure that children are completely happy at every moment of their lives.

Caring for and guiding children is physically demanding, emotionally draining, and intellectually taxing work—and growing up is not an easy task for the children either. Adults and children will sometimes be at cross-purposes, so there are bound to be conflicts. Overindulgence and overprotection (sometimes referred to as spoiling) are not a part of positive child guidance. Not being firm enough is just as damaging as being too firm.

One mother says, "But I have to give Lindy ice cream while I'm preparing dinner. If I don't, she screams and holds her breath until she turns blue. I have no choice!" Of course, Lindy's mother does have a choice. She is the only one tall enough to reach the freezer!

Lindy's mother needs reassurance that it is perfectly okay for Lindy to cry. Lindy feels frustrated, and crying is her way of expressing herself. When Lindy was a helpless newborn, her mother needed to respond quickly to her cries of hunger to instill in her a sense of trust. Now Lindy is older. She can **delay gratification** (wait a few minutes) for her needs to be met. In fact, she must learn how to delay gratification if she is ever to develop responsibility and self-control.

Her mother needs to feel more relaxed about Lindy's breath holding. Babies and toddlers often forget to breathe for a few seconds when they are very stunned or hurt. Parents often hear the loud thump of their toddler falling, then a moment of silence, then finally loud, howling cries. The toddler isn't holding her breath to be manipulative, that's just how her body works. If, however, a great deal of attention is paid to that pause in her breathing, the child might eventually learn to hold her breath just for dramatic effect. Unless Lindy is suffering from a disorder such as **apnea** (a breathing abnormality), the worst that will happen is that Lindy will succeed in causing herself to faint, at which time breathing will automatically resume.

The most effective way for Lindy's mother to deal with the child's behavior is to assertively and caringly acknowledge that wanting ice cream is okay, but that no ice cream will be served until after dinner. The mother could tell Lindy, "I know you wish you could have ice cream. It's all right to cry. Sometimes I cry when I'm mad or upset. You may cry as long as you need to. If you need to cry for a long, long time, then you must cry in your room so that you don't hurt other people's ears."

After Lindy has finished crying (remember, no child ever cried forever), her mother can redirect Lindy's hunger (present a compromise) by offering peanut-butter crackers or apple slices. Or, if she senses that even bringing up the subject of hunger would cause another scene, she may wait and offer a nutritious treat the next time she anticipates a problem—before Lindy even has a chance to mention ice cream. She can also choose not to purchase ice cream for a while to reduce Lindy's temptation (as well as her own temptation to give in). Whatever she does, she must not give in to Lindy's tantrum and reinforce her inappropriate behavior by rewarding it with ice cream.

Giving in to Lindy's demand while at the same time yelling, complaining, or making her feel guilty is inappropriately overindulgent and very confusing. Lindy may not learn that the word no really means no, or she may come to view herself as an unlovable and spoiled brat—thinking badly of herself but not really knowing how to behave differently.

How Can We Help Children Learn to Make Choices Within Limits?

Children need freedom within clear limits. Freedom without limits is not really freedom. Instead it is chaotic and dangerous. Jesse's parents have tried to give him complete freedom.

Jesse rules the family with the total abandon of a dictator. Whatever is being served for breakfast is not what he wants. Even if he is asked in advance for his breakfast order, he goes through several changes of mind. His parents meekly pour out bowls of cereal and make waffles or throw away waffles and make oatmeal.

Whatever clothes Jesse's mother has chosen for him to wear are almost never to his liking either. He stamps down the hall like a little emperor and ceremoniously stuffs the clean clothing into the laundry hamper. His mother meekly offers alternate selections of clothes she hopes he will like. Sometimes Jesse goes to school wearing clothes that are totally inappropriate for the weather or the setting.

His parents wonder why he is so demanding. They are so proud of their beautiful little boy, and they want so much for him to love them that they fail to use good judgment. They also hate to confront him and risk an ugly scene. They do not realize it, but what Jesse really wants and needs are strong, loving parents who are willing and able to help him grow up. Secretly, Jesse realizes he is acting like a baby.

Jesse did not become a dictator overnight, and he will not be able to change into a reasonable and polite person overnight. With time and patience, however, Jesse can learn to make choices within clearly defined, reasonable limits. Jesse can be given a choice between eggs and cereal, between the red shirt and the blue shirt, and he can be allowed to deal with the natural and logical consequences of refusing to accept the limits he has been given.

His parents can explain, "Jesse, if you're not hungry enough to eat the corn flakes you asked for, then you're obviously not very hungry for breakfast." "You may take ten minutes to choose what you want to wear from these clothes. If you are not able to choose, then I will choose for you. If you are not dressed and ready for school on time, you will be tardy. I will not write a note to your teacher excusing your lateness." "If you stuff clean clothes in the laundry hamper, you will have to help with the extra laundry by sorting and folding clothes instead of watching television."

In order to enforce freedom of choice within reasonable limits, Jesse's parents will have to make a commitment to confront Jesse with love and persistence. Of course, in the long run, Jesse will be a happier, friendlier, more likable person.

External Reinforcement

Developing children's inner control and motivation for behaving acceptably have been addressed throughout this text. Previous sections have emphasized the concept that children must want to behave well, that they must assume responsibility for their actions. Positive child guidance is not a gimmicky strategy to manipulate children into behaving according to our specifications, but instead a process of guiding children to become competent, confident, and cooperative human beings who behave well not to win favors but because behaving well is the right thing to do.

Now, however, it is time to look at the opposite side of the coin—techniques for refining external control. Some behaviors do not come from internal motivation. They are unconscious habits that are very resistant to even the most sincere desire for change. We know from our own experiences that wanting to quit smoking, lose weight, or exercise regularly is not always enough to make those things happen. I can want desperately to lose weight, but if I am unconsciously conditioned to open the refrigerator every time I pass it, I may be my own worst enemy.

Jeremy tells his mother that he does not want to practice the piano each day (as his piano teacher has asked him to do). Consequently, his mother delves into the Jeremy's inner motivations. She talks with him about his hope to become a famous musician and his feelings of pride when he masters difficult pieces of music. If Jeremy really has an inner desire to play the piano, and the lack of practicing is simply a matter of establishing new habits, then giving him a cute little sticker as a reward each day that he practices may work wonders. If he does not practice because he lacks inner motivation, then stickers will be a waste of time. In fact, they may be worse than a waste of time—Jeremy may make his decision not to practice based on the fact that he is only giving up a little sticker that really is not very valuable anyway. Also, if Jeremy is coerced into practicing to get a reward, he may respond to future reminders of things he is supposed to do by saying, "What will you give me if I do it?"

In contrast, when Jeremy decides to train his pet chicken to "play the piano" for a county fair, he does not waste any time telling the hen how proud she will feel; he just drops a pellet of corn into her dish each time she inadvertently steps on the keyboard of the toy piano he has placed on the floor of her cage. Before long, Jeremy's chicken clucks loudly and pounds on the piano keyboard every time she sees him.

My placing coins in a candy vending machine every day may be every bit as mindless as the chicken's stepping on the toy piano keyboard to get pellets of corn. I may need to change my external surroundings to break my habit cycle. Perhaps I could walk a different route so that I do not pass the vending machines, think of a reward to give myself if I resist candy bars for a whole week, or even bring nutritious, low-calorie snacks with me as a substitute when I am tempted to eat candy. We can assist children in breaking undesirable habits in exactly this same way.

What Are the External Conditions That Support Appropriate Behavior?

> *Stephanie runs up to her mother when her mother arrives to pick her up from her child care center. Stephanie has a handful of drawings, and she is dancing around her mother squealing, "Mommy, look what I made! Look what I made!" Stephanie's mother is busy chatting with other mothers, so she ignores Stephanie. Finally, Stephanie throws the drawings down on the ground and yells, "I hate you, Mommy!" Instantly, her mother bends down and says (with a tone of disgust), "Stephanie, what do you want?"*

Stephanie has learned a lesson that her mother did not intend to teach her—"When you want your mother's attention, be hateful and destructive because you will get attention faster than by just asking for attention."

Children generally do whatever they need to do to get their needs met. Many unconscious habits are formed simply because they work. We need to analyze our daily procedures very carefully to identify how children get the things they want and need in the environment.

Does the child who pushes and shoves the hardest always get to be first in line? Does whining and arguing always succeed in extending bedtime or television viewing time? Does pitching a fit mean the child does not have to buckle her seat belt? Does the child who misbehaves the

"Biting hurts. Be kind. Touch gently."

most during story time get almost all of the adult's eye contact, verbal contact, physical contact, and name recognition? Remember, even negative attention is preferable to being ignored.

We also need to consider the powerful effect of **intermittent** (occasional) **reinforcers**. People in Las Vegas do not need to get a reward every time they put money in a slot machine. They will keep feeding money to "one-armed bandits" for hours just to get a chance at one really big payoff. Children, likewise, can pester for hours on the chance that a disgusted adult will finally give in and reward their inappropriate behavior with the desired privilege or response. Without realizing it, we may be reinforcing and rewarding dysfunctional and annoying behaviors on a daily basis. By consciously looking at what a child gets out of various behaviors and changing our own behaviors, we may take big steps in preventing or resolving many frustrating misbehavior patterns.

What Is Behavior Modification and How Should It Be Used?

Behavior modification is a specific method for changing a child's behavior by following a highly structured process. In this process, the adult:

- Observes a child's present behavior

- Identifies a desired future behavior

- Breaks the distance between the two behaviors into tiny steps

- Systematically reinforces each small step as the child moves closer to the desired behavior

Behaviorists see learning as a process of piecing together a chain, one link at a time. The process is external to the child, since the adult chooses the skill to be learned and then rewards that behavior in the child.

Elinor is a beautiful little girl who is a victim of autism. She cannot speak and she constantly flutters around the room flapping her arms and making small grunting sounds. Pleading with her to stop these behaviors would only confuse her, making her so anxious that the behaviors would probably increase. Using behavior modification, however, would be an effective and caring way to shape her behavior into more socially accepted patterns.

Elinor's teacher, Thomas, simply ignores the flapping and watches carefully for the instant that Elinor stops to look at something. Immediately, Thomas gives Elinor a tiny paper cup of Cheerios, her favorite cereal, and says, "Good girl, Elinor." Over a period of months, very quietly and unobtrusively, Thomas has conditioned Elinor to focus more of her attention on the toys and books in the classroom and to spend a great deal less time flapping and grunting. Very importantly, Thomas ignored Elinor's undesirable behavior—he never ignored or withdrew affection from Elinor herself.

Thomas's next task is to gradually wean Elinor off of the cereal and replace that reinforcement with shiny plastic coins he calls tokens. Eventually, he hopes that Elinor will comprehend that if she collects a certain number of tokens, she can trade them in for a special treat, privilege, or snack.

Children with developmental delays, learning deficits, and language disabilities may lack the ability to discuss or reflect on their inner motivations. Behavior modification may truly be a godsend for guiding these children.

Behavior modification can be used very successfully with well-developing, even gifted, children. It is, however, essential to enlist the bright child's voluntary and active cooperation. Adults and children who are capable of examining their own and the motives of others will feel betrayed or coerced if they realize that their behavior has been manipulated without their knowledge. If I, for example, suddenly realize that someone has rigged the candy vending machine to steal my quarters (so I will stop buying candy), I will feel furious. I may stubbornly eat even more candy just to assert my own autonomy.

Behavior modification works most effectively with bright children when adults are straightforward about their plan. An adult might say, "Ginger, let's make a little booklet to help you remember to go to the bathroom on time. I will set the timer for one hour, and each time it rings, if your pants are still dry, you may paste a special sticker in your book. Do you think that would help you remember? Would you like to try it?"

Obviously, the sticker booklet will only help if Ginger is wetting her pants simply because she has a habit of delaying visits to the bathroom. A young toddler will not suddenly be able to master toilet training just to get stickers. The strategy also will not work if Ginger has inner motivation problems (such as needing to be a baby to compete for attention with a new baby in her family). If, however, Ginger really wants to stop wetting her pants, and she just needs a little boost to break a bad habit, she is likely to cooperate fully and feel very proud of herself when she succeeds.

Why Does Behavior Modification Not Work All the Time?

Behavior modification is a powerful tool when used appropriately. A primary concern, however, is that ignoring inappropriate behavior may become an excuse to give up responsibility for children's unacceptable behavior. Tactfully overlooking certain inappropriate behaviors may be helpful in some situations, and reinforcement has tremendous impact on habit patterns. There is a risk, however, that if used inappropriately, behaviorist tactics can become manipulative and aloof. Ignoring can become punitive and hurtful when the adult is working on the child rather than with the child.

As adults, we have a responsibility not to stand by passively while a child is labeled as bad or wild, but to actively involve ourselves in making it easy for children to behave properly and very, very difficult for them to behave improperly. We may not always succeed—but we can give our most persistent and energetic effort! Then, at least, a child with behavioral problems will know we care very much about her and that we will not give up on her, no matter what she does.

Practical Application/Discussion

The Big Boys and the Very Muddy Day

Mrs. Belk taught first graders in a neighborhood public school for several years. She already had her undergraduate degree in early childhood education but had decided to upgrade her skills by taking a graduate course in psychology at a nearby university. She had only been enrolled in the class for a few weeks, but the professor had already lectured on various methods for reinforcing positive behaviors rather than focusing only on inappropriate behaviors. What a great idea, she thought—ignore the negative and reinforce the positive.

Mrs. Belk was eager to try some new disciplinary techniques on several of her more difficult children, especially Chad, a six-year-old who tended to be her group's ring leader for inappropriate behavior. Chad was tall for his age and wiry. He appeared to be a thin child, but he was surprisingly muscular. His calf muscles were rock-hard and bulged conspicuously on his skinny legs. Mrs. Belk thought that he probably worked off every ounce of fat by being in a constant state of motion.

For two years, he had been taking daily prescription doses of a medication for **hyperactivity** (which his doctor referred to as hyperkinesis or attention deficit disorder). His parents and teachers agreed that the medication helped him to function at home and at school, but he still had a difficult time dealing with the limits that adults set, and adults had a difficult time coping with his frenetic level of activity and wildly impulsive behavior.

The past week had been particularly stressful for Mrs. Belk. Chad had been even more out of control than usual. It had rained for so much of the week that the children had not gotten to play outside a single time. Mrs. Belk was beginning to feel as if the classroom were shrinking and the children multiplying.

She looked out the window. The sun had come out and the only problem with the playground was that there were still some very large mud puddles here and there. Mrs. Belk flipped the light switch on and off several times to signal the children that it was time to put away their work and gather on the rug for storytime. When the room was clean and the children were all sitting around on the floor in a big circle, Mrs. Belk said, "How would you like to go outside to the playground?"

To their gleeful shouts of, "Yes, yes, yes!" Mrs. Belk answered, "We can go outside on one condition. Everyone has to agree only to play on the dry areas. There are mud puddles and you will have to remember to walk around them." The children eagerly agreed to stay on dry land. Chad and his buddies were so excited that they could hardly contain themselves, but they promised Mrs. Belk that they would not forget about the mud puddles.

Mrs. Belk opened the door and was stampeded by squealing, laughing children. As Mrs. Belk walked out into the bright sunlight, she took a deep breath of fresh air and felt a great sense of relief to be outside the stuffy classroom.

After only a few seconds, she saw Chad running backward to catch a ball, and splat, he stepped right into the mud. Mrs. Belk stood with her hands on her hips, glaring at Chad and thinking about whether to have him sit on the bench for ten minutes for breaking a class rule.

She knew that it was a real effort to keep Chad sitting for ten minutes. Mrs. Belk dreaded a confrontation and decided that she just did not have the energy to deal with Chad at the moment.

She started thinking about what her professor had said about it being helpful to ignore inappropriate behavior—and besides, she thought, maybe his stepping in the mud was really an accident—so she looked the other way and decided to ignore Chad. Within seconds, several children were pulling at her shirt sleeves saying, "Mrs. Belk, Mrs. Belk, look, Chad is in the mud!" Mrs. Belk told them, "Go play and don't pay any attention to Chad."

Within minutes, two of Chad's favorite cohorts, Eddie and John, also six, were hollering as Chad stamped his foot in the mud, splattering mud on them. They found it necessary, of course (after they nervously looked back to make sure Mrs. Belk's back was still turned), to stamp their feet in the mud, splattering Chad from head to toe. The chase was on with half the class frantically telling Mrs. Belk, "Look, look at Chad!" and the other half squealing and laughing as the three boys chased and slid in the mud.

Mrs. Belk saw that her strategy was not working. With the look of daggers in her eyes she shouted, "Okay, everybody line up at the door to go inside." All of the children (except Chad, Eddie, and John) hurried to the door and made a straight line. In a loud voice, Mrs. Belk stared straight at the three boys and said, "I'm waiting. Not everyone is ready to go inside." She thought, "There is no way I am going to chase those three around in this mud. They are just doing this to get attention. They'll come as soon as they think we are really going inside."

Mrs. Belk opened the door and said, "Everyone walk quietly in the hall, please." While the group of children were being led inside, they nervously glanced back and forth at Mrs. Belk and the three boys running around outside. They knew the three boys were in a lot of trouble, and they knew Mrs. Belk was angry. The three boys chased and played in the mud, pretending not to notice that the others were going inside and trying to look tough and macho. By this time, their shoes and clothes were caked with mud and they were beginning to feel very uncomfortable.

As soon as Mrs. Belk had ushered her line of children inside, she asked another teacher to watch her class while she stood behind the door where the boys could not see her and watched them through the glass. The other teacher's mouth dropped open as she saw the mud-covered boys. Mrs. Belk said, "They're just doing this for attention, so the best thing is to ignore it. I'm sure they'll get tired of it in a few minutes when they realize they don't have an audience, and then they'll beg to come inside."

Within five minutes, a teacher whose room overlooked the playground ran down the hall and said, "Mrs. Belk, you've got to get those boys inside! They've taken off all their clothes and they are on top of the fort throwing mud balls at the building and at cars."

The playground was a mess. The building and cars were a mess, and the boys were a mess. The situation was no longer salvageable. The boys had to be forcibly brought inside. The principal called their horrified parents to come and get them. There was no easy way for the boys to make amends for their behavior or to save face in front of their peers, parents, and teachers. They had taken part in an open rebellion, a serious and scary step for a child and a damaging precedent for future behavior.

Questions for Discussion

1. What are some possible reasons for Mrs. Belk's ignoring the muddy boys? Evaluate those reasons.

2. List some ways that you think these problems could have been avoided.

3. What could Mrs. Belk have done that might have prevented or stopped the inappropriate behavior?

4. What do you think the muddy boys were thinking and feeling throughout this episode?

5. What do you think the rest of the children were thinking and feeling?

6. How would you have responded if you were the principal? The parents? Another teacher in the building?

7. If you were Mrs. Belk, what would you say or do when the boys came back to school the next day?

Points to Remember

- We give subtle messages to children about how we expect them to behave by the surroundings we plan for them.

- We can prevent many behavior problems before they ever begin simply by careful planning, by understanding children's developmental needs, and by creating a match between their needs and the environment.

- Behavior problems are minimized simply because children are busy and excited about their accomplishments.

- Our physical postures, movements, and gestures communicate a great deal of information to children.

- Infants and young children rely heavily on nonverbal communication in their interactions with others to interpret moods and expectations.

- Adults must take nonverbal expressions into consideration whenever they attempt to communicate with children.

- Nonverbal communication must match verbal communication.

- If nonverbal cues are too threatening and intrusive, children bristle and resist commands.

- If requests are assertive, caring, confident, and respectful, children are more likely to comply quickly and willingly.

- A primary goal for early childhood development is the growth of personal responsibility and independence.

- To become socially competent, children must master negotiation skills and resolve minor problems independently.

- Children should not be rescued from the unpleasant (but reasonable and safe) consequences of their own actions.

- Children should be encouraged to do anything for themselves that they can safely and reasonably manage.

- Toddlers behave aggressively because they lack the verbal ability to express themselves otherwise.

- In positive child guidance, children are taught ways to communicate feelings honestly and assertively without having to resort to verbal aggression.

- We should never push children into being so "nice" that they hold their emotions inside.

- Our goal is to channel their emotional expression into words and actions that inform rather than words and actions that hurt.

- Insisting that children apologize, whether or not they feel regret, is neither an honest nor effective way to guide children.

- The more vulnerable the child feels about losing his possessions, the more tightly and greedily he will guard them.

- Children learn skills and information through active involvement in their day-to-day environment—by watching others, by being told things, and by experiencing life.

- In life, actions are followed by logical or natural consequences.

- Punishment is intended to hurt, humiliate, or pay a child back for something she has done.

- Guidance is intended to teach appropriate behavior.

- Deeds should be seen as separate from the person who did them.

- Not being firm enough is just as damaging as being too firm.

- Children need freedom within clear limits because freedom without limits is chaotic and dangerous.

- Positive child guidance is a process of guiding children to become competent, confident, and cooperative human beings who behave well not to win favors but rather because behaving well is the right thing to do.

- It may be necessary to change external surroundings to break a mindless habit cycle.

- Children generally do whatever they need to do to get their needs met.

- Behavior modification is the most humane and effective strategy for guiding exceptional children who lack the ability to discuss or reflect on their inner motivations.

- Behavior modification can be used successfully with well-developing children if the children's active, voluntary cooperation is obtained.

- Behavior modification is a powerful tool when used to modify habits and not as an excuse to abdicate responsibility.

- Ignoring can be punitive and hurtful, manipulating the child rather than working with the child.

Related Readings

Helping Children Develop Self-Control

Caulfield, R. (1996, Fall). Social and emotional development in the first two years. *Early Childhood Education Journal, 24*(1), 55–58.

Crockenberg, Susan (1997). How children learn to resolve conflicts in families. In E. N. Junn & C. Boyatzis (Eds.), *Annual editions: Child growth and development 97/98* (4th ed.). New York: McGraw-Hill. (Original work published in *Zero to Three*, April 1992)

> *According to Susan Crockenberg, children learn how to settle conflicts from early experiences in the home. When faced with a child's behavior problem or conflict, parents can model and provide their young children with practice in conflict negotiation skills by using strategies that*

include directives, explanations, and compromise. Acquiring these skills early should have many long-term benefits.

Crosser, S. (1997, March–April). Helping children to develop character. *Early Childhood News, 9*(2), 20–24.

Dowrick, N. (1997, October). "You can't shout at them because they just cry": Student teachers with nursery children. *International Journal of Early Years Education, 5*(3), 255–261.

Eaton, M. (1997, September). Positive discipline: Fostering the self-esteem of young children. *Young Children, 52*(6), 43–46.

Gatrell, D. (1997, September). Beyond discipline to guidance. *Young Children, 52*(6), 34–42.

Grossman, S. (1996, September–October). Passing Vickie's test: Building self-esteem and trust by following through with rules. *Early Childhood News, 8*(5), 6–12.

Honig, A. S. (1996). *Behavior guidance for infants and toddlers.* Little Rock, AR: SECA.

Honig, A. S., & Wittmer, D. S. (1996). Helping children become more prosocial: Ideas for classrooms, families, schools, and communities. *Young Children, 51*(2), 62–70.

Vander Wilt, J. (1996, Winter). Beyond stickers and popcorn parties. *Dimensions of Early Childhood, 24*(1), 17–20.

Wallace, E. (1997, May–June). Do you recognize this parent? *Early Childhood News, 9*(3), 32–33.

Healthy, well-developing children are naturally lively and full of silliness. (Photograph provided courtesy of CHILDREN AT RISK.)

Chapter 5

Guidelines for Effective Guidance

Chapter Outline

Ignore Mildly Annoying Behavior That Is Neither Harmful nor Unfair
Focus Attention Elsewhere
Discreetly Redirect Slightly Inappropriate Behavior to More Positive Substitute
    Behavior
Assist the Child in Recognizing the General Effects of Positive Behaviors

Immediately Interrupt Behavior That Is Harmful or Unfair
Intervene as Firmly as Necessary but as Gently as Possible
Maintain Objectivity
Remove the Child from a Problem Situation

Assertively Shape Positive Behavior
Teach Ground Rules
Clarify Expectations
Maintain Consistency
Adapt Objects, Events, and Attitudes to Remove Possible Causes of Problem
    Behavior
Offer Assistance and Encouragement
Give Undivided Attention
Redirect Inappropriate Behavior Firmly and Respectfully
Clearly Express Appropriate Feelings
Explain the Potential Consequences of Unacceptable Behavior
Provide Persistent Follow-up
Emphasize Unconditional Caring and Affection
Maintain and Express Confidence
Protect the Child's Dignity and Privacy
Be Willing to Start Over—To Forgive and Forget

Practical Application/Discussion
Will and the Cream-Cheese Won Ton

Questions for Discussion
Points to Remember
Related Readings

Objectives

This chapter will assist you in

- Developing specific strategies for effective guidance

- Formulating guidelines for responding to inappropriate behaviors

- Identifying methods to shape positive behavior

Specifying techniques for assertive redirection and follow-up

Ignore Mildly Annoying Behavior That Is Neither Harmful nor Unfair

Children are not helped by intrusive and overwhelming attempts to change too much of their behavior at one time. Adults do well to focus disciplinary actions on urgent priorities while overlooking mildly annoying behaviors that are neither harmful nor unfair to others. In dealing with a child who has behaved aggressively but who also bites her fingernails and rocks her chair back and forth, an adult should initially focus attention only on the aggression. A mental note could be made to address the other problems in a more subtle and indirect manner at a later time, well after the aggression has been resolved. We adults sometimes have a tendency to "unload all barrels," overwhelming children with too many demands, especially when we are angry and upset.

Focus Attention Elsewhere

When a child does something that is mildly annoying or embarrassing (but not unacceptable), the adult may resolve the problem simply by focusing the child's attention elsewhere. A baby who is banging a spoon on a metal high-chair tray in a restaurant may be distracted by a parent who plays peek-a-boo or dangles a softer, quieter toy. A thumb-sucking toddler may be distracted from the sucking by being given an interesting toy to explore. A curious preschooler may be distracted from handling items on shelves in the grocery store by being allowed to help push the grocery cart or to help arrange foods in the basket as they are selected.

Discreetly Redirect Slightly Inappropriate Behavior to More Positive Substitute Behavior

Slightly annoying behaviors can also be redirected by involving the child in an activity that **replaces** (cannot be done simultaneously with) the undesirable behavior. For example, a child who is picking at his nose can be directed to use a tissue to blow his nose. Without ever even mentioning the nose picking, the adult can explain how using a tissue, throwing away the tissue, and then washing hands may keep others from catching a cold.

"Here is a tissue. After you blow your nose, I will help you wash your hands."

In order to redirect slightly inappropriate behaviors, we can identify activities that involve the part, or parts, of the child's body currently being used in the undesirable action, then an alternative action involving those body parts can be substituted. For example, a child who is using her hands to feel the blossoms of a neighbor's delicate and expensive garden plants could be shown how to put her hands behind her back or in her pockets while she leans over to smell the wonderful fragrance of the gardenias. She could also be redirected to use her hands to gather interesting leaves and acorns from the ground.

This helps the child know that it is okay to explore and enjoy nature but not okay to damage another person's property. Snapping, "Don't touch those plants!," discourages curiosity—a key factor in the child's long-term ability to develop intellectually. Of course, standing by passively while one's child damages a neighbor's prized gardenias would be rude and disrespectful.

Assist the Child in Recognizing the General Effects of Positive Behaviors

Another method for gently redirecting minor misbehaviors involves focusing the child's attention on the positive outcome of more desirable behaviors. The adult gives information to the child. The adult might say, "If you put your glass of milk on the top corner of your place mat, it will be safely out of your way until you want to drink it." A teacher might say, "If you erase mistakes slowly and lightly, your paper will look very nice." A toddler can be told, "I like to hear 'thank you.' Oh, how nice! Brett remembered to say 'thank you.'"

Immediately Interrupt Behavior That Is Harmful or Unfair

Children rely on adults to enforce rules and protect individual rights. Children will be willing to "play by the rules" only if they come to believe that rules are meaningful. Consistency and fairness in the enforcement of rules help children learn to trust authority figures. Behaviors that are harmful or unfair must be interrupted immediately by a responsible adult.

Adults do not help children become cooperative and respectful by passively watching them fight, saying, "They'll just have to learn to stand up for themselves. When Jimmy has had enough of Gerald hitting him, he'll learn to hit back." We also fail to help children when we say, "Don't come tell me that someone hit you. I don't want to hear about it!" Children can be helped to resolve their own disagreements, but they must know that adults will reliably stop unacceptable, hurtful behavior.

Intervene as Firmly as Necessary but as Gently as Possible

When we find it necessary to stop an unacceptable behavior, we should always proceed as firmly as necessary to stop the unacceptable action, but as gently as possible to remind the child that he is accepted and respected as a person even if his behavior must be ended.

As Miss Melanie firmly pries a toddler's clenched fingers one-by-one out of another screaming toddler's hair, she says with a tone of urgent concern (not anger) in her voice, "Ouch! Pulling hurts. No pulling. Touch gently, please!" After the toddlers are safely separated, she softly strokes each toddler's hair saying, "Gentle, be gentle. Please touch hair gently." Miss Melanie has interrupted a harmful behavior as firmly as necessary but as gently as possible.

Roger grabs a little car from his friend Chris and runs away. Chris yells and starts to cry. Mr. Reese follows Roger (persistently but without chasing him), saying in a deeply concerned tone, "Stop, please. Roger, I need you to stop so we can talk about Chris's car." When Roger finally pauses for a second, Mr. Reese says, "Thank you for waiting. Let's sit down and talk about Chris's car. You like Chris's car, don't you? It's really a neat car, isn't it?"

Mr. Reese does not immediately attempt to snatch the car away from Roger. He patiently asks, "What should you do if you want to see someone else's toy? Should you ask, 'May I play with your car?'" Roger hungs his head and says, "But if I ask him, he might say no." Mr. Reese answers, "You're right. He might say yes or he might say no. Would you like for me to come with you so you can ask? If he says no, I will help you find a different toy to play with. Remember, taking things without asking is not allowed—so when you choose a toy, no one will be allowed to take your toy away without asking you first, right?"

Roger's unfair action has been stopped, firmly but gently, and Roger has had a chance to learn a very important lesson—although rules sometimes stop him from doing what he wants to do, they also assure that his own rights are protected.

Enforcing fair rules protects the rights of all children.

Maintain Objectivity

Marilyn's three-year-old daughter, Stephanie, waited patiently (although she was becoming very bored) while her mother shopped for new towels in a department store. Stephanie caught sight of a little boy about her age shopping with his mother on the other side of a large pillow display. Stephanie peeked around the edge of the pile of pillows to get a better look at the little boy. He grinned at her. Embarrassed, she quickly scrambled back out from behind the pillow display. Unfortunately, in her haste, she dislodged the display, and an avalanche of pillows piled down on top of her.

Two salespersons rushed over (looking very annoyed), and several other shoppers stared at the mess. Marilyn was startled and horrified to see what Stephanie had done. She grabbed Stephanie by the arm and marched her off to the ladies' lounge to have a "few words." Marilyn did not manage to stay objective about her daughter's behavior. She took her own feelings of embarrassment out on Stephanie. She could have been more helpful to Stephanie if she had been able to maintain a more objective and less emotional perspective.

We can greatly assist the development of self-control in children by staying focused on the reality of a situation rather than on adult feelings that are not relevant to the child's problem, preconceived notions, and biased attitudes that do not relate directly to what the child has done. Marilyn's guidance will be more effective if she can push aside her feelings of humiliation (and apprehension that complete strangers will think she is a bad mother). Marilyn should focus on the objective reality of the situation—Stephanie had been trying to wait patiently, she did not intentionally do anything wrong, and she was obviously feeling upset and embarrassed already.

Even a child who has misbehaved deserves reassurance that he is still loved.

Positive child guidance is a teaching process. As in any educational process, powerful emotions such as anger, disgust, or the threat of harm, damage rather than assist the process of learning. People, children included, are better able to concentrate and absorb information when they are reasonably calm and relaxed. A terrified child may remember vividly the look of daggers in a parent's eyes but completely forget the whole point of the reprimand and not be able to recall what behavior caused the problem in the first place.

It is perfectly normal and healthy for us to feel waves of sheer fury now and again. Because of our size and power, however, it is appropriate for us to release most of those feelings of frustration and rage away from young children, by jogging, punching and kneading bread dough, or by pounding out melodies on a piano. It is not fair or helpful to blow children away with powerful and scary expressions of anger. We can be honest without being overpowering.

Remove the Child from a Problem Situation

Removing a child from the scene of a conflict allows a cooling-off period for the adult and child, removes whatever temptation the child is having difficulty with (out of sight, out of mind), and ensures that a gawking or giggling audience is not watching and triggering further misbehavior. Although compromise should never be considered during the heat of a full-blown tantrum, compromise after the child has gained control may serve as an effective role model for the child to imitate as she learns to talk rather than scream to get what she wants.

Occasionally, adults have no choice but to pick up a young child, who may be kicking and screaming, and haul the child (as gently as possible but as firmly as necessary) away from a scene of a conflict. A preschooler who is having a tantrum in a grocery store because she cannot have the candy bar she wants should probably be escorted or, if necessary, picked up and carried out of the store. She can be helped to understand that she has two, and only two, choices—she can sit and cry for a long, long time in the car with her patient but assertive father, or she can return to the grocery store and continue the shopping trip, accepting the fact that there will be no candy bar.

If the father, through consistent verbal and nonverbal communication, convinces his daughter that he will not become angry or argumentative, but that he will also absolutely not back down, the little girl will soon recognize the futility of a long, dramatic, exhausting fit of crying. She will learn that that sort of thing simply does not work.

When she seems ready to throw in the towel, recognizing that she cannot bully or manipulate her father, she should be given an opportunity to "save face." At this point, restraint, tactfulness, empathy, and perhaps an appropriate compromise (letting her choose a nutritious snack to take home) would keep the situation from having a winner and a loser. The little girl's future cooperativeness will hinge on her feeling confident that she can be cooperative without losing her dignity and autonomy, and without having her past mistakes thrown in her face.

Assertively Shape Positive Behavior

When a child must be subjected to an unpleasant occurrence, the situation should be discussed squarely and honestly to give the child a chance to cooperate voluntarily. The situation should not, however, be allowed to stall or become a stalemate if the child refuses to cooperate. When medicine must be applied to a scrape on an unwilling child's knee, the adult must quickly and matter-of-factly explain what must be done, then get the unpleasant task over. The longer discussion, whining, and arguing are tolerated, the more unpleasant and stressful the task of applying medicine will become.

Separation is a good example of a necessary but unpleasant occurrence in the lives of toddlers. Before a separation, parents must be given all the time they want to visit with their child and express affection. A parent should not be rushed but should clearly indicate to the caregiver when she is ready to leave (and willing to actually walk out the door). At this decisive moment of separation, a skilled caregiver will firmly but lovingly state, "Mommy needs to leave now. You may give Mommy a hug and wave bye-bye through the window—or, if you need, I can hold you while Mommy leaves." If the child is clearly not willing to hug mommy and wave good-bye, then the parent and caregiver can move quickly and assertively to get the separation over with, even if the child resists loudly and has to be held.

The caregiver can express empathy, "Yes, you love your mommy. You miss her when she leaves. Sometimes I miss my Mommy too. Did you know I have a Mommy? Let's go see the dolls. Would you like to feed a bottle to our baby doll? Which baby doll do you want?" One can shape positive behavior by making sure that it happens. Adults can often help children avoid situations

Separating from parents may be especially frightening for some children, especially those who have had little experience getting to know caring adults outside their family.

in which they may experience failure by quickly and decisively making the right thing happen and then rapidly moving on to happier activities—all this without giving an appearance of frustration, anger, guilt, or disgust with the child's inability to actively cooperate or comply. Children's negative feelings should be acknowledged and accepted, but they do not necessarily need to be dwelled upon for a lengthy period of time.

Teach Ground Rules

Children need to know exactly what is expected of them. Simple, consistently enforced guidelines help children learn to respect and abide by rules. Children, however, must have adult help to understand and remember ground rules. Following are several ways adults can actively teach children about rules.

Role Play

Give children a chance to "act out" or practice the correct following of rules. For preschoolers, switch roles so that the child can see and experience an appropriate response. Pretend to be the child and allow the child to pretend to be the adult, or pretend to be the child's troublesome friend, for example, "I will pretend to be Bert. Let's pretend I just pulled your hair. Can you point your finger at me, make a frown, and say, 'Don't pull my hair. That hurts!'?"

Repetition

Children need many opportunities to hear a rule repeated before knowledge of that rule has fully reached the child's long-term memory bank. Any adult who has experienced an electrical power failure but mindlessly continued attempting to turn on appliances and lights knows that having knowledge of a thing does not necessarily bring about an immediate change in habit behaviors. We have to remind ourselves over and over, "Oh, yes, I can't listen to the radio. . . . Oh, the electric can opener won't work. . . . Oh, the clock is not right." Children need and deserve patient reminders of rules and expectations so they will be encouraged to change their habit patterns.

Discussion

Rules have a great deal more meaning for children when they really understand reasons for the rules. Adults should remove from their vocabulary that age-old phrase "because I said so," which so often has been used as a blanket explanation for all rules and regulations issued by adults. Positive guidance requires that adults explain things to children simply and honestly, for example, "You must use the blunt knife instead of the sharp knife. I don't want you to get cut." "You may not open the gate without permission, because the street is busy and dangerous." "You must wash your hands with soap and water before you eat. Your hands are dirty and you could get sick from getting germs in your mouth."

Clarify Expectations

If we want children to follow our instructions, we must make sure they really understand what we intend for them to do. Adults often speak in vague, general terms. They say things such as "Be good," "Be nice," "Act like a big boy (or girl)." What children need are simple but specific statements of our expectations. For example, we might say such things as:

- "Sit down please. Make sure your bottom is in the chair and your feet are on the floor."

- "Please hold your milk with both hands."

- "Please wait at the bottom of the slide until the person in front of you has gone down the slide. Then, you may climb up and have your turn."

- "I need for you to use a soft, slow voice to talk to me about your sister. I don't like to hear whining and screaming."

Additionally, adults sometimes assume that children automatically know how objects are intended to be used. Instead, children over the age of three need to be told specifically what various objects are for. Babies and toddlers put bowls on their heads, try to eat decorative plastic fruit, and attempt to pull tee shirts on like underpants! (That's why they're so much fun to be

"Be kind. Please remember to use words instead of hitting. Tell Andy you don't want him to push you off the slide anymore."

around.) One can gently guide them toward the proper use of objects, but they need a great deal of freedom to explore safe objects thoroughly, using all their senses and muscles to discover their world. If a baby or toddler stands up in a chair that could fall, she should tactfully be redirected to a safer place to climb, or else the chair should simply be removed. A child past three, however, can be told, "Please remember, a chair is for your seat, not your feet."

Children past three can be taught the difference between toys, tools, and weapons, for example, "A toy is something you can play with, a tool is something useful to help you, and a weapon is intended to hurt someone. At school we use toys and tools but not weapons." A ball can be used as a toy to play catch, or it can be used as a tool to knock a kite out of a tree—but it must not be used as a weapon to hit someone in the face. A fork should only be used as a tool to pick up food, not as a toy to wave around or as a weapon to poke at another child. School-aged children are especially capable of comprehending and identifying categories of objects and will spontaneously point out to one another, "That pencil is a tool. It's for writing. You mustn't use it like a toy or a weapon!"

Maintain Consistency

In order for children to behave appropriately, there must be consistency, with a reasonable level of flexibility, in the adult's expectations and enforcement of rules. Discipline should not be enforced based on the adult's mood or coincidental circumstances. For example, it would be inconsistent to indicate to a young child (through our actions), "You can walk around the house eating and dropping crumbs, except when I am too tired and crabby to clean up after you—or

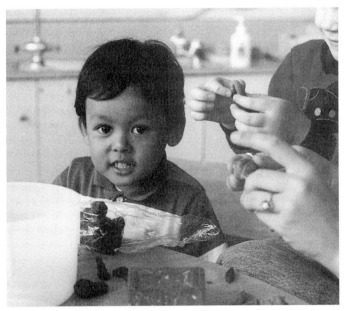

"Be safe. Play Doh is for molding, not for eating."

"Thank you for remembering to put all of the sand toys back in the sandbox."

when we have company." There should either be a consistent rule that eating takes place at the table, or that eating at various places in the house is allowed as long as each family member cleans up after himself or herself.

Older children, who have a clear understanding and acceptance of specific rules, can deal with occasional exceptions to those rules. They can understand that family members are expected to eat in the kitchen, even though breakfast in bed is a perfect Mother's Day surprise, and a pizza around the coffee table might be a perfect treat for a slumber party. Toddlers and young preschoolers, on the other hand, do not have a full grasp of rules. They view the world in very literal, black-and-white terms. An action either is or is not allowed. They become very frustrated and confused and tend to ignore a rule altogether if it seems to them to be inconsistently enforced. For example, little ones should never be allowed, even once, to ride in a car without being properly buckled into an appropriate car seat. If they believe that there is absolutely no chance that the car will move until they are seat-belted, they will accept the car seat as a fact of life rather than something to be negotiated through whining and resisting.

In order to be consistent, adults should make very sure that a child's behavior is not laughed at on one occasion and reprimanded on another. Bathroom terms that brought giggles at home may not be nearly so funny at church or synagogue, or when announced loudly at a family gathering. The toddler with spaghetti in his hair may be adorable the first time, but if he receives a great deal of attention (laughter, photographs, calling the neighbors to come see), he may be inclined to repeat the behavior on a regular basis, which will not be nearly so entertaining to harried parents the second, third, or fourth times. In the early childhood setting, consistency, with reasonable flexibility, is essential.

> *Marty, a toddler teacher, tried to teach her eighteen-month-olds not to climb on the low, redwood picnic table on their playground. Toddlers who climbed on the foot-high plank table were removed and placed on a foot-high, redwood plank deck nearby for a "time-out." Marty knew that decks were to walk on and tables were not. To the toddlers, however, the rule about climbing seemed inconsistent. Both structures looked about the same. They were being removed from one and placed on the other as a negative consequence. Being on the second structure was intended to teach them not to get on the first structure. Of course, the toddlers were never able to make sense of Marty's rule—so, for the most part, they simply ignored it.*

Adapt Objects, Events, and Attitudes to Remove Possible Causes of Problem Behavior

There are many situations in which it is easier to change the circumstances surrounding the child than it is to change the child. Additionally, it is almost always more nurturing and less stressful for everyone involved if adults focus on setting the stage for proper behavior rather than on reprimanding children after they have behaved improperly. For example, if children are running in the classroom, it will be better and easier to change the room arrangement to make running difficult than to endlessly remind children to walk. If toddlers persist in spilling their milk, they can

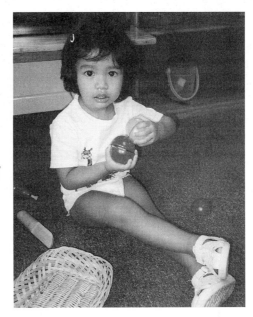

"Those are round and look a lot like our throwing balls don't they? But they are hard. They can hurt, so they're not for throwing. Let's be safe. I'll help you find a ball that is soft and good for throwing."

be given smaller cups with only an ounce of milk at a time. That way, if they do have a spill, very little milk is wasted and very little effort is needed to clean it up.

Rather than yelling to get the attention of rowdy children, an adult can use a dramatic whisper. Children will almost always pay more attention to a wide-eyed, dramatic whisper than to a rude, bellowing voice. If children in a preschool program consistently become tired and irritable on field trips, then perhaps field trips can be rescheduled to a different time of day or to a shorter time period. Or, perhaps trips can be made less often but to more carefully chosen locations. When confronted with troublesome behavior problems, we should ask ourselves, "Instead of trying to change the child, is there any way I can reasonably change the child's environmental surroundings or my own actions or attitudes to ease the problem?"

Offer Assistance and Encouragement

Children thrive on positive attention. They usually become very compliant when adults say, "How can I help you remember this rule?" "What can we do to make it easier for you to get to bed on time?" "Let's practice the words you should say when you feel angry." Positive guidance means that adults work very, very diligently to help children behave appropriately. Their goal is not just to punish children for behaving inappropriately.

Give Undivided Attention

Children immediately recognize whether an adult is serious enough about what he is saying to stop and see that a request is followed. Even toddlers and preschoolers know that instructions do not mean much when they are given by an adult casually glancing back across his shoulder, making an offhanded comment across a room, "Come on now, put those toys away." In contrast, children

Physical touch can be very comforting.

sense that instructions mean a great deal when the adult stops what he is doing, walks to the child, bends down to eye level, gently touches the child's shoulder, and looking directly into the child's eyes, says in a gentle but firm tone, "Sherrie, I need you to stop now and put the blocks away." A half-hour of nagging and threatening from across the room will not have the impact of a gentle touch and one quiet statement made eye-to-eye, using the child's name.

Undivided attention has a powerful effect on children. In positive child guidance, attention focused directly on children will be assertive, positive, and self-esteem building rather than negative, angry, and destructive of pride and confidence. The following four actions can be carried out in a positive way to show children that they have our undivided attention and that we really care about their behavior:

- **Eye Contact**

  Move close and try to establish eye contact. A shy child or a child who has experienced eye contact as part of threatening, angry interactions will feel compelled to look away. Do not force the child to look you in the eye, but rather attempt to win the child's trust by associating eye contact with positive, loving interactions. If the child does look you in the eye, sincerely commend him, "Thank you for listening so well."

- **Body Positioned at Child's Level**

  Bend down to the child's eye level. Staring down one's nose at a child tempts the child to look away. Being stared down on may also seem cold, threatening, or belittling to the child (a little like being formally grilled by an FBI agent).

- **Appropriate Touch**

  Gently placing a hand on a child's shoulder or arm, or lightly holding one or both of the child's hands, helps focus attention. If the child is sitting on the floor, gently touching a foot or knee will obtain the child's attention and communicate caring concern. Appropriate touching is never grabby or forced. Follow the child's signals. Children usually make it very clear whether they find the adult's touch aversive or comforting

- **Use of Child's Name**

  Using a child's given name or accepted nickname is more personal and appropriate than general terms of endearment such as "sweety" or "honey." Adults in early care and education settings must learn every child's name very quickly in order to be effective. Sadly, some young children hear their names yelled so often as a reprimand that they fail to respond as we would expect when their name is used in a positive context. They do not recognize their name as a symbol for who they are, but only as a negative word that means they are in trouble.

Redirect Inappropriate Behavior Firmly and Respectfully

When a child's inappropriate behavior must be stopped, cooperation can be gained and resentment avoided simply by offering the child an acceptable alternate activity. A child who is pouring milk back and forth from cup to bowl during a meal may be told, "You may not play with your food. After lunch (or after nap), I will show you a good place for pouring." The child could then be directed at an appropriate time to pour, squirt, dribble, and splash to her heart's content with dishes and toys at a sink, a bathtub, a commercial water table, an outdoor wading pool, or a plastic basin placed within her reach with an inch or two of water.

When children feel angry, they hit, kick, pinch, and scratch. These typical aggressive behaviors must be stopped. The child's anger should, however, be given an appropriate outlet. When a child is told, "Hitting hurts—no hitting is allowed," the adult should also add, "Use words. Tell Jessica you don't like it when she steps on your fingers. Show Jessica your fingers and tell her how much they hurt."

Common sense and knowledge of the basic principles of behavior modification will guide the effective use of **redirection** (interrupting an inappropriate activity and involving the child in a more appropriate choice). The idea is to replace a misbehavior with a desired behavior so that the focus is on what the child should do rather than on what the child should not do. It is important, however, to ensure that the replacement activity does not become a "reward" for inappropriate behavior.

Miss Kimberly, a toddler caregiver in a child care center, was concerned about the biting that was happening on almost a daily basis in her room. She thought that perhaps the toddlers were biting because their gums were uncomfortable with teething and they needed strong oral stimulation. She decided to offer hard crackers for the toddlers to bite as a

> *substitute for biting each other. Within a few days, she discovered, to her dismay, that the toddlers were attacking and biting each other whenever they felt hungry for crackers. They had become conditioned to expect crackers in response to biting.*

Clearly Express Appropriate Feelings

Although it is very appropriate for adults to be honest in their expression of feelings to children, an adult's expression of anger can be too overwhelming for a young child to handle. Rage has no place in positive child guidance. When confronted by a large, snarling, furious grown-up, a young child has two possibilities—recoil in fear and try to stay out of the grown-up's way, or fight back by being rebellious and insubordinate. Neither of those options help the child become a more confident, competent, and cooperative person.

Rather than focus on feelings of anger, the adult can identify the underlying feelings that caused the anger. We can ask, "Am I feeling angry because I was startled, disappointed, worried, frightened, or frustrated?" Instead of saying, "I am furious with you," we can say, "I felt really frightened when I didn't know where you were. I was afraid you were hurt or lost. I was so upset I felt like crying." Following are several other examples of appropriate verbal expressions of adult feelings that give the child information but do not directly attack anyone:

- **Surprise, Disbelief**

  "I can't believe this beautiful plant has had its leaves torn off. Plants can die if their leaves are harmed."

- **Sadness, Disappointment**

  "I feel very sad when I find books with the pages torn out. Books are beautiful and fun to read, but they aren't of any use when they are ripped apart."

- **Concern, Worry**

  "I feel worried when I see you scratching your mosquito bite. Scratching may cause it to become infected and sore. Let's cover it with a bandage."

- **Apprehension, Fear**

  "I feel very frightened when I see you climbing on the top rail of the fort. You must stay off the rails or else choose a different place to play on the playground."

- **Distress, Frustration**

  "I feel very frustrated when I find the door has been left open. We can't keep our house warm and comfortable inside, when a door is left open. Please check the door each time you go out to make sure it's properly closed."

Explain the Potential Consequences of Unacceptable Behavior

Children past the age of three are usually perfectly capable of mentally connecting the cause-and-effect relationship between their conscious actions and potential consequences. If simple,

"Thank you for turning the pages so gently and carefully."

polite, assertive statements of rules and expectations do not bring about an appropriate response from children, then it is time to discuss potential consequences. Explaining potential consequences is not the same as bribing, intimidating, or giving idle threats. It is intended to inform the child, to give an honest, sincere warning of an impending consequence. It is not intended to manipulate, coerce, or trick the child into behaving a certain way, but rather to give the child honest, reasonable choices—"If you do this, this will happen. If you do that, that will happen." We should only give children reasonable choices that we know we will be comfortable carrying out. It is not acceptable to say, for example, "If you don't come with me this instant, I will leave you here in the store by yourself."

The old cliché "You can lead a horse to water, but you can't make him drink" fits children quite well. We can offer a well-balanced meal to a young child, but we cannot presume to force the child to eat it if she chooses not to. What we can do is say, "You may eat your vegetables and

The nurturing adult resolves conflicts assertively but respectfully.

meat if you feel hungry. If you are not hungry enough to eat your dinner, then you may wait until breakfast to eat. I will put your plate in the refrigerator in case you change your mind." This statement is assertive, confident, and reasonable, but not threatening or punishing. It is merely a recognition that the child has choices about her own body, and the adult has choices and responsibilities about what foods are healthy and appropriate to offer.

Provide Persistent Follow-up, and Enforce Logical Consequences Firmly and Respectfully

A motto to be emblazoned in the memory of all adults who deal with children is, "Say what you mean, and mean what you say." There is no magic wand or bag-of-tricks in positive child guidance—only persistence, persistence, persistence! Adults who persevere in firm, assertive, respectful, and caring discipline will surely see positive results in the children they care for and teach. Children may be very persistent in their patterns of misbehavior. We, as adults, however, must be even more persistent in our supervision, follow-up, and enforcement of reasonable, logical consequences.

The consistency of small but persistent nudges toward appropriate behavior is far more effective than erratic and inconsistent explosions of anger, harsh punishments, or intimidating threats. The gentle, rippling stream etches deep patterns in solid rock. Pounding on rocks with sledge hammers changes the shape of the rocks but risks a lot of damage in the process.

Emphasize Unconditional Caring and Affection

Unconditional caring, the giving of affection without any strings attached, is the foundation on which good discipline is built. Unconditional caring lets children know that they do not have to perform or achieve or submit to be loved and respected. We may disagree with things they do and work hard to change them, but we will still love and care for the child. Adults should create an environment that tells children verbally and nonverbally (Clarke, 1978):

- "You have a right to be here. I'm glad you are who you are."

- "It is okay for you to have needs."

- "You don't have to be cute (sick, sad, mad, or scared) to get attention and approval."

- "It's okay to be smart, curious, and inventive and still get support and protection at the same time."

- "I'm glad you are growing up."

- "I'm not afraid of your anger."

- "You can express your feelings honestly, openly, and respectfully."

- "You can be independent and still have needs."

- "You can think before you make a rule your very own." "You can trust your feelings to help you know." "It's okay to disagree."

- "You don't have to suffer to get your needs met."

- "I love you."

Maintain and Express Confidence That a Problem Will be Resolved

Guiding children can be frustrating and distressing at times. We look at our children and shake our heads, wondering if they will ever gain self-control and self-discipline. We must, however, firmly maintain and express confidence that specific problems will be resolved and our children will learn to behave appropriately—at least most of the time. Our confidence will strengthen children and convince them that control over their own behavior is a reachable goal.

Protect the Child's Dignity and Privacy

When positive, but assertive, disciplinary measures are necessary, children should be afforded the dignity of being talked to in private. They are humiliated by being corrected in front of their friends, or even in front of other adults. Adults should refrain from discussing, in front of a child, all the careless, immature, and improper things the child might have done. Adults should refrain from talking about and laughing about the child's past mistakes. And, most of all, adults should treat children the way they themselves like to be treated—with dignity and respect.

The nurturing adult listens and reflects the child's feelings, then helps her resolve her problems in a fair way. Children's negative feelings should be acknowledged but not dwelled upon.

Be Willing to Start Over—To Forgive and Forget

In positive child guidance, adults should do the best they know how to do and then never look back. Worrying about the past, carrying grudges, or keeping mental lists of past misdeeds all undermine positive child guidance. For young children, every day is a new day. No matter what happened yesterday, today can be a good day and a successful day. When children know that adults are willing to forgive and forget, they will be more compliant and more willing to admit it when they know they are wrong. Forgiveness encourages honesty in children and motivates them to try harder to meet adult expectations.

Practical Application/Discussion

Will and the Cream-Cheese Won Ton

Renee and Tom are loving and assertive parents. They have taught their children, Amy, who is ten, and Will, who is five, to respect the rights of others. They have consistently provided firm guidance tempered with unconditional love.

One evening the entire household was aflutter with excitement—the children's grandparents had arrived for a short visit. Since Renee and Tom both worked, Renee had picked the children up from child care and Tom had picked up Chinese food for dinner from a favorite restaurant. Tom made sure to include an order of cream-cheese won tons; the children were not too wild about Chinese food, but they both especially loved the restaurant's specialty—cream-cheese won tons.

The children helped set the table with festive place mats and napkins and even a candle. Everyone sat around the table chatting and enjoying dinner. Will perched on his knees in the big dining chair so he could see better. He listened attentively to every word of conversation as he slowly nibbled at the food on his plate.

As the family members finished eating, they pushed back their plates and continued to sit at the table, laughing and talking, catching up on family news and funny stories about the children and all their great adventures and escapades. When Tom had finished eating, he leaned back in his chair, stretched out his long legs and draped an arm across the back of Will's chair—Tom really enjoyed these family get-togethers. As he laughed and talked, he happened to glance at Will's almost-empty plate. He noticed one last cream-cheese won ton pushed to the back of the plate. Absent-mindedly, he picked up a fork, stabbed the won ton, and popped it into his mouth.

The instant Tom swallowed the won ton, he saw a stricken look fall across Will's face, and he knew he had made a big mistake. Will leaned close to his dad's ear and whispered intently, "Dad, we have to go to a lonely place and talk." Quietly, Tom got up from the table and followed Will to the bathroom. Tom sat down on the side of the bathtub while Will ceremoniously closed the bathroom door and then, with big tears sliding down his cheeks, said, "Dad, you're not supposed to take other people's things without asking. That was the only cream-cheese won ton left, and I was saving it for last. You did a wrong thing."

Tom lifted Will into his lap and they hugged each other long and hard. Tom said, "You're right, son. I did do a wrong thing and I apologize."

Tom almost had tears in his own eyes, but his heart was filled with pride that his son had been able to stand up for his rights but also had made a special effort to spare his dad's dignity—by asking to talk in a "lonely place."

Questions for Discussion

1. Why do you suppose Tom ate Will's won ton? Have you ever inadvertently hurt a child's feelings? How did the child respond?

2. How do you think Will learned to resolve problems the way he did? Why do you think he asked for a "lonely place" to talk with his father?

3. How would it make you feel if a child responded to you the way Will responded to his father? How do you imagine Will's father felt? What do you suppose he was thinking during his conversation with Will?

Points to Remember

- Children are not helped by intrusive and overwhelming attempts to change too much of their behavior at once.

- Mildly annoying behaviors can be resolved by simply focusing children's attention elsewhere.

- Consistency and fairness in the enforcement of rules help children learn to trust authority figures.

- Behaviors that are harmful or unfair must be interrupted immediately by a responsible adult.

- Adults should always proceed as firmly as necessary but as gently as possible.

- Positive child guidance is an educational process in which anger, disgust, or the threat of harm damage rather than assist the process of learning.

- Removing a child from the scene of a conflict allows a cooling-off period for the adult and child, removes temptation, and ensures that the misbehavior ends.

- Compromise should be considered only after the child has gained control.

- The development of compliance and cooperativeness hinges on children feeling dignity and respect.

- We should get necessary but unpleasant actions over with quickly so we can move on to more pleasant activities.

- Children's negative feelings should be acknowledged and accepted but not dwelled upon.

- Children need to know exactly what is expected of them.

- Simple, consistently enforced guidelines help children learn to respect and abide by rules.

- Children are helped to understand and remember ground rules through role play, repetition, and discussion.

- Children past the age of three should be taught the difference between toys, tools, and weapons.

- Children need consistency tempered by a reasonable level of flexibility.

- The enforcement of discipline should never hinge on the adult's mood or coincidental circumstances.

- Toddlers and young preschoolers do not have a full grasp of rules, so they become especially frustrated and confused if rules are inconsistently enforced.

- It is usually easier to change the circumstances surrounding the child than it is to change the child.

- Adults should not just punish children for poor behavior but rather assertively shape positive behavior.

- Attention focused directly on children should be assertive, positive, and self-esteem building.

- To show children they have our undivided attention, we give eye contact, position our body at the child's level, give appropriate touch, and use the child's name.

- Cooperation can be gained by substituting misbehavior with an acceptable alternate activity.

- Rather than focusing on feelings of anger, adults can identify the underlying feelings that caused their anger—being startled, disappointed, worried, frightened, or frustrated.

- Adults should express surprise, disbelief, sadness, disappointment, concern, worry, apprehension, fear, distress, or frustration without overpowering children with anger or inducing guilt.

- The consistency of small but persistent nudges toward appropriate behavior is far more effective than erratic and inconsistent explosions of anger, harsh punishments, or intimidating threats.

- Unconditional caring is the giving of affection without any strings attached.

- Our confidence will strengthen children's confidence that they can gain control over their own behavior.

- Children are indeed full-fledged human beings and, as such, should be treated with the respect we give to and expect from other people we admire and care deeply about.

- Adults must be willing to let go of past events and look toward the future.

Related Readings

Helping Children Cope with Anger

Brown, J. R., & Dunn, J. (1996). Continuities in emotion understanding from three to six years. Child Development, 67(3), 789–803.

Cummings, E. (1987). Coping with background anger in early childhood. Child Development, 58(4), 976–984.

Fabes, R. A., & Eisenberg, N. (1992). Young children's coping with interpersonal anger. Child Development, 63(1), 116–128.

Hennessy, K. D., Rabideau, G. J., Cicchetti, D., & Cummings, E. M. (1994). Responses of physically abused and nonabused children to different forms on interadult anger. Child Development, 65(3), 815–828.

Jalongo,M. (1986). Using crisis-oriented books with young children. In J. B. McCracken (Ed.), Reducing stress in young children's lives (pp. 41–46). Washington, DC: NAEYC.

Lewis, M., & Michalson, L. (1983). *Children's emotions and moods*. New York: Plenum.

Lewis, M., & Saarni, C. (1985). Culture and emotions. In M. Lewis & C. Saarni (Eds.), *The socialization of emotions* (pp. 1–17). New York: Plenum.

Miller, P., & Sperry, L. (1987). The socialization of anger and aggression. Merrill-Palmer Quarterly, 33(1), 1–31.

Russel, J. A. (1989). Culture, scripts, and children's understanding of emotion. In C. Saarni & P. L . Harris (Eds.), Children's understanding of emotion (pp. 293–318). Cambridge, UK: Cambridge University Press.

Saifer, S. (1996, Winter). Dealing with hitting and aggression in the classroom. NHSA Journal, 15(1), 37–39.

Zeman, J., & Shipman, K. (1996). Children's expression of negative affect: Reasons and methods. Development Psychology, 32(5), 842–850.

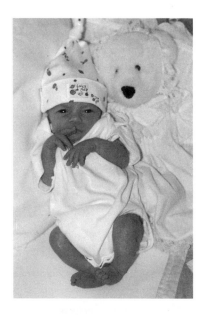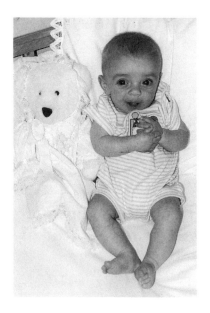

Typical behaviors change quickly as children grow from one developmental stage to the next. Look at the changes in Cory over the first year of his life (clockwise starting on the top left: at three days, four months, seven months, and eleven months).

Chapter 6

Understanding Children's Behavior

Chapter Outline

Early School-Agers (5–8 Years)
    Developing Critical Thinking
    Affirming Self-Worth
    Expressing Anger
    Testing Authority Figures
    Coping with Limits
    Emerging Sense of Fairness
    Establishing Self-Identity
    Becoming Productive
    Maintaining Self-Esteem

Older School-Agers (9–12 Years)
    Striving for Independence
    Changing Roles and Relationships
    Identifying with Peers
    Working Toward Long-Term Goals
    Guarding Self-Esteem

Practical Application/Discussion
"I'm Never Gonna 'Vite You to My Birth'ay!"

Questions for Discussion
Points to Remember
Related Readings

Objectives

This chapter will assist you in

- Recognizing typical ages and stages of early childhood

- Identifying developmental milestones that affect behavior

- Identifying relationships between maturation and guidance strategies

- Outlining changes over time in adult-child relationships

- Tracing the development of positive self-esteem

Typical Ages and Stages

The most important thing to remember when considering the typical ages and stages of childhood is that no child is completely typical—every child is unique. Although typical or average patterns can be identified, real children have individual patterns and rates of development that may be normal but not at all average. The most valid reason for comparing a child's rate of

Identifying individual levels of social, emotional, physical, and intellectual development is intended to assist us in creating developmentally appropriate environments for children. It must never be used to label or stereotype children.

development to standard rates is to be alert to any consistent pattern of differences, or "red flags," that indicate a need for professional screening and possibly the need for therapeutic intervention.

Sometimes, by comparing a child's individual behaviors with typical behaviors, we can better understand the child, recognize that the child is only going through a normal phase, and anticipate phases that the child will soon be entering. Adults are often comforted to know that many children at a certain age behave the same way as the child they are dealing with. Babies shy away from strangers, toddlers become stubbornly assertive, preschoolers worry about who is or is not their best friend at any given moment, and school-agers reject everything that is not considered "cool" by their friends. Adults are also relieved to realize that most children tend to outgrow whatever phase is at issue regardless of how adults try to respond to it.

Typical behaviors tend to be consistently clustered together and in a sequential order so a child's behaviors might be matched to those at a specific age level although her chronological age may actually be younger or older than that listed. A seven-year-old who is developmentally delayed may show a wide range of typical toddler behaviors. However, a gifted four-year-old who can already read may behave a bit like a school-ager in some behaviors but like a preschooler, or even a toddler, in other behaviors. The value of assessing each child individually is to match guidance strategies to the individual child's developmental capabilities and needs—never to label or stereotype the child.

If, for example, a toddler is discovered trying to poke an object into an electrical outlet, the adult may look very concerned and say, "Ouch, that could hurt you. Come play with your toys," but the primary discipline strategy would be to change the environment to protect the toddler more effectively. A specially designed safety guard could be installed to prevent access to the outlet, or the child could be removed to a safer, better supervised area.

A five-year-old, however, who is discovered exploring and trying to insert an object into an outlet should be handled quite differently. The adult must determine whether the child is curious, misinformed, or feeling rebellious. When the adult has a sense of why the behavior has occurred, he might firmly discuss the cause-and-effect dangers of playing with electric outlets. He should then redirect the child's curiosity by helping the child explore the characteristics of electricity using a safe six-volt battery, wires, and a tiny flashlight bulb. The child's curiosity could be channeled into a whole new area of interest and knowledge by reading books about electricity. She can be taken outside to look at power lines, to talk about how workers protect themselves when they repair dangerous electrical wires, and to make pretend wires out of strings to attach to the child's playhouse.

Infants (Birth–12 Months)

Babies are fascinating. Their big eyes and rounded contours are specially designed to turn grown men and women to mush (Alley, 1981). Babies are soft and warm and cuddly, but few parents are prepared for the powerful emotions that well up inside them when they, for the first time, have their own child. Some parents feel a jumble of emotions—outrageous pride, a protectiveness as passionate as a tiger for her cubs, jealousy of any imagined competition for affection, overwhelming fatigue, fear of failure, even grief over the loss of infancy as the child grows and matures so quickly.

Parenting is one of the most significant and challenging adventures adult human beings undertake (often with little or no preparation). If additional caregivers are involved in infant

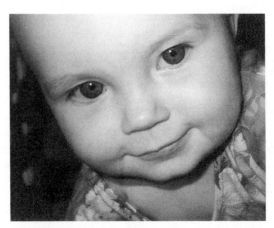

Who can resist the soft, endearing face of a baby?

care, parents may be relieved of some stresses and strains, but other complex feelings or tensions may emerge. Many a mother has left her baby in a carefully chosen child care center for the first time only to sit in the parking lot, collapsed in tears on the steering wheel of her car.

Fathers, grandparents, even siblings also fret over the adequacy of anyone helping to care for the new baby. Jenny, a kindergartner in a day care center, talked her teacher into letting her go to the nursery where her two-month-old brother was newly enrolled. There, she held her baby brother's tiny hand through the bars of his crib for a long time as she carefully watched every move made by the nursery workers. The employees listened smilingly as the little girl pointed out to them, "you mustn't touch his head right up there where it's soft." Although Jenny was only five, she felt protective and concerned about her baby brother.

Do Infants Intentionally Respond by Crying?

Usually, the first kind of upsetting behavior adults must cope with in caring for infants are bouts of crying. A typical scenario pictures the adult trying all the usual problem-solving strategies— warming a bottle, changing a diaper, rocking. Soon, the adult has done everything he knows to do, but the infant cries even more frantically. Some adults hear the infant's wails as a personal indictment of their competence, integrity, or authority—"How dare this baby accuse me of being a bad father (or mother, or caregiver)!" A howling baby can quickly fray the nerves of even the most patient and devoted adult.

A temptation for many of us is the tendency to project intentional motives on the baby for her crying. We say things like, "She's just crying because she knows I'm a pushover," "He always cries when I try to cook, because he thinks he should be the center of attention," or "She's only crying because she's mad at me. She was born with a fiery temper." These rationalizations may make us feel vindicated for angry or resentful feelings that surge through us as we try to deal with the screaming baby, but they are, nevertheless, inaccurate. Infants do not intentionally do much of anything—they just react spontaneously and unconsciously to their environment.

Sadly, some adults with virtually no understanding of the processes of child development see infant crying as such a clear example of intentional, "bad" behavior that they attempt to punish the infant for her crying. Child protective service workers and other social agents often deal with parents who begin shaking, hitting, and spanking babies in the first year of life—a very dangerous and inappropriate practice—in the mistaken belief that they are helping their babies learn to be "good."

Can Babies Misbehave on Purpose?

Regardless of many common misconceptions, in the first months of life infants have no capacity for consciously intentional behavior. They are not able to think about or plan actions to get desired results. Until they have **object permanence** (the mental ability to envision persons, objects, or events that are not in sight), they cannot "think" or "know" that any action will bring about a desired result. They can only react or respond in a very unconscious way to internal feelings such as pain or hunger and to external **stimuli**—sensations the infant sees, feels, hears, tastes, or smells (Piaget, 1968).

Even past six months, some behaviors that may seem intentional are actually **unconscious reactions** based on the child's having absorbed connections or relationships among day-to-day experiences. Unrelated objects, events, and sensations become connected. If a microwave oven is customarily used to warm a baby's bottle, the sound of the microwave timer dinging becomes associated with being given a warm bottle of formula, so the baby gets very excited any time she hears it ring. Similarly, we might expect any nine-month-old to show curious interest in a brightly colored, shiny can. If the child immediately fusses and struggles for the can of soft drink he sees in his mother's hand, though, it is pretty clear his experience has led him to expect a sip whenever he sees a soft drink can.

The Critical Importance of the First Three Years

Recent scientific findings show that babies raised by caring, attentive adults in safe, predictable environments develop more brain capacity and become more competent learners than babies raised with less attention in less secure settings. Today, with the help of powerful new research tools such as brain scans, scientists have learned more about the developing brain than ever before. Here is what we know:

- *The brain development that takes place during the prenatal period and in the first year of life is more rapid and extensive than scientists previously realized.*

- *Brain development is much more vulnerable to environmental influence than researchers ever suspected.*

- *The influence of early environment on brain development is long lasting.*

- *The environment affects not only the number of brain cells and number of connections among them, but also the way these connections are "wired."*

Recent studies have shown the harmful impact of early stress on early brain development. Spending the early months or years of a child's life in an inadequate environment damages overall growth and development, placing the child at much greater risk of developing a wide range of cognitive, behavioral, and physical problems. In some cases, these effects may be irreversible. But the opportunities for early learning are equally exciting. A nurturing start in life can do more to promote long-term capacity for learning and prevent damage than we ever imagined possible.

Carnegie Corporation of New York. (1994). *Starting points, Meeting the needs of our youngest children—The report of the Carnegie Task Force on Meeting the Needs of Young Children.* Waldorf, MD: Carnegie Corporation of New York.

What Are Reflex Responses, and What Is Unconscious Conditioning?

In newborns, almost all actions are simple reflexes over which the child has no control. Infants blink, startle, grasp an object placed in the palm of the hand, and root toward a nipple—but not because they choose to do those things. They do them simply because their brain is designed to make certain behaviors happen automatically. From the moment of birth, however, babies carefully study their

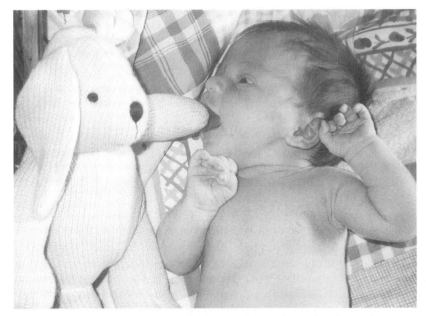

The newborn baby comes into the world equipped to learn by looking, listening, feeling, tasting, and smelling.

environment, at first by staring and eventually by using all their senses. Babies gradually progress beyond reflex behavior. They begin to recognize and associate things they see, feel, hear, taste, and smell with other meaningful sensations or events. A hungry, breast-fed infant will become very agitated when she is held near her mother's breast. The feel, smell, and sight of the breast is closely associated with the memory of the sweet taste of milk.

What is Classical Conditioning?

To a baby, hearing keys rattle means someone is leaving, being placed in a stroller means going for a walk, or hearing the rustle of plastic wrap means getting a cookie. This kind of learning is generally categorized as **classical conditioning**. Looking at a balloon does not normally make babies cry—seeing a balloon is an unconditioned stimuli. Loud noises, however, certainly do make them cry—crying in response to a loud bang is a naturally occurring stimulus-response connection. If a baby has been frightened and has cried on several occasions when balloons have popped, then the baby may begin to cry whenever he even sees a balloon—this is a conditioned stimulus-response connection.

Researchers have for decades attempted to document classical conditioning (pairing an unconditioned stimuli with a naturally occurring stimulus-response connection) in newborns. The best that has yet been documented is a rather rough kind of learning now called pseudoconditioning. Studying early responses is difficult, since so little of the newborn's movement can really be classified as voluntary (Rosenblith & Sims-Knight, 1985; White, 1995). However, by the middle of the infant's first year, classical conditioning is clearly a part of the child's learning.

What is Operant Conditioning?

Operant conditioning is quite different from classical conditioning. It occurs when the child's spontaneous actions (such as crying) are reinforced by pleasurable rewards (such as food). This type of conditioning has been studied and documented in infants from the first days and weeks of life (Sameroff & Cavanagh, 1979). Newborns automatically cry as a response to the discomfort of being hungry. Older babies and toddlers learn to whimper or make a "fake" crying sound to signal that they are hungry. In the classical conditioning example previously described, babies became excited by sensations that unconsciously reminded them of being fed. In operant conditioning, however, hungry babies learn to repeat whatever behaviors have in the past resulted in their being fed. For example, if a breast-fed infant is nursed whenever he roots and pulls at his mother's blouse, then that action (rooting and pulling) may become an unconscious but **learned behavior** that he repeats whenever he is hungry.

A baby first turns toward a nipple in response to an unconditioned rooting reflex. Then, over time, the pleasurable reward of warm milk stimulates more active and goal-oriented rooting. Eventually, the sight of the nipple, recognizing the feel of being placed in a nursing position, or other sensory cues (the smell of milk, the sound a voice) will trigger rooting and sucking. An adult who is unfamiliar with a specific baby may inadvertently cause her to become frustrated and cry simply by holding her, without feeding her, in a position that she associates with nursing.

What Is Metacognition?

Young infants need many repetitions of unfamiliar sensations, actions, and events in order to form associations. By the end of their first year, however, they have learned, through conditioning, to expect many specific responses to accompany certain actions and sensations (Papousek, 1967). This kind of learning is an unconscious process. Although unconscious, conditioned learning continues to take place throughout life, months and years will pass before the child will develop an ability to consciously and intentionally control his own behavior—a process we call **metacognition**.

When a child has developed metacognition, she will be able to think about her own thinking processes and develop strategies to help her manage her own behavior. Children between three- and six-years-old are only beginning to develop metacognition. School-aged children have a much better developed ability to plan strategies, for example, to say, "I'll hide the candy where I can't see it, then I won't be so tempted to eat it before supper." Babies and toddlers possess none of these skills; they just spontaneously react to the positive and negative sensations in their world.

How Do Babies Develop Control of Their Actions?

The first muscles babies can actively control are those around the face and head. (The newborn can move her eyes to follow objects, she can suck effectively, and she can turn her head.) Muscle development proceeds from head to toe and from the trunk to the extremities—**cephalocaudal** (top to bottom) and **proximodistal** (close to far). At first, infants are only able to control a few mouth, eye, and neck muscles. Gradually, the infant expands body control downward into the trunk (she learns to turn over), outward through the arms to the hands (she learns to bat at objects and then to grasp them), and finally down to the legs to the feet (she learns to crawl and then walk). Tiny muscles of the hands and fingers will not be fully developed for years (then she will finally be able to use her fingers to button her sweater, tie her shoe laces, and write her name).

Why Do Babies Cry?

In the child's first year of life, behaviors result almost exclusively from internal developmental characteristics along with gradually increasing conditioned learning. If a baby cries for a prolonged period, that behavior does not stem from manipulativeness, maliciousness, or any other kind of conscious intention, but rather from internal discomfort, stress, or fatigue or from externally conditioned routines. Babies cannot be held responsible or blamed for their behavior. It is more realistic to think in terms of relieving the cause of a crying infant's unhappiness if the problem is internal or of gradually changing adult routines to bring about a different kind of conditioned behavior if the problem has been caused externally.

Adults are the ones who establish routines and habits in infants through day-to-day basic care patterns. Infants become **habituated** (accustomed) to those patterns and object loudly when routines are abruptly broken. If an infant is accustomed to being in constant contact with her mother's body, she will cry pitifully when she is left unexpectedly in a play pen. If an infant is accustomed to quiet isolation, he may be terrified by sudden placement in a noisy, bustling child care center. Psychologists define *stress* as the process of recognizing and responding to threat or danger (Fleming, Baum, & Singer, 1984). While working directly with infants over the years in various child care facilities, I have on several occasions seen babies who seemed especially upset by a separation or by a stark upheaval in their care arrangements. In spite of attentive caregivers,

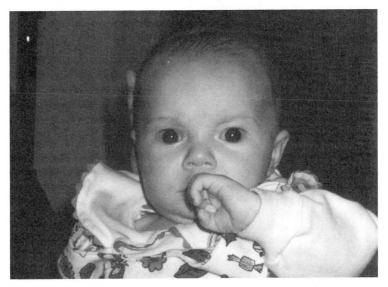

Babies naturally respond to such things as discomfort, hunger, boredom, and fear.

the infants (ranging from three to nine months of age) appeared to slip from a long period of anguished, relentless crying into a period of quiet depression with only languid whimpering.

The infants withdrew from social contact, avoided eye contact, lost appetite, refused to play, slept too much or too little, and, apparently as a result, appeared noticeably less healthy after a time. After various lengths of time (ranging from days to months), each of these babies eventually recovered spontaneously and became responsive, robust, and playful. Today, almost a decade later, the most severely affected of these infants gives every appearance of being a bright, healthy, and well-adjusted young girl. Nevertheless, stress should be considered in dealings with children of any age and avoided or eased whenever possible.

Careful planning of basic care and nurturing routines that can be maintained consistently will help protect the child from abrupt and upsetting changes. When changes in routines must occur, careful planning and gradual orientation should take place—especially before drastic upheavals in child care arrangements occur—in order to avoid subjecting babies to unnecessary stress.

How Does Trauma and Chronic Stress Affect the Infant's Brain Development?

Constant exposure to stressful environments can dramatically change the way an infant or young child's brain develops, making the child more prone to emotional disturbances and less able to learn. Children exposed to severe, prolonged stress often develop learning disabilities and emotional and behavioral problems (for example, attention deficit disorder, anxiety, and

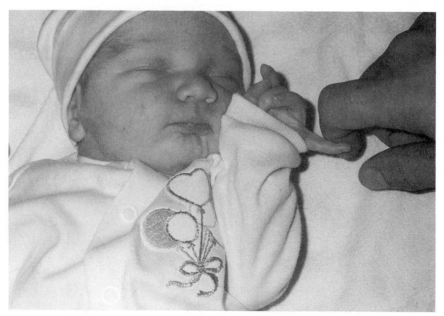

Secure attachment to caregivers is critical to healthy emotional development.

depression). They also become more vulnerable to various medical problems—such as asthma, immune-system dysfunction, and heart disease (Poussaint & Linn, 1997; Pransky, 1991; Prothrow-Stith & Quaday, 1995; Shore, 1997).

How Do Babies Develop Trust?

According to Eric Erikson (1959, 1963, 1982), trust developed in infancy is a primary foundation for the development of healthy emotional attitudes that must be built upon throughout life. Basic care patterns offer our first opportunity to demonstrate our trustworthiness to an infant. Whenever the infant experiences internal distress, she automatically responds by crying. In time, through operant and classical conditioning, she can come to expect a dependable and pleasurable response from the adult caregivers in her life. This trust in the predictability of her environment and in the responsiveness of her primary caregivers helps the baby develop a sense that she is valued and that she can have impact on her surroundings—the first step toward the development of positive self-esteem.

Key Problems That Put Children at Risk

- **Inadequate prenatal care.** *Nearly one quarter of all pregnant women in America, many of whom are adolescents, receive little or no prenatal care.*

- **Isolation.** *More divorces, more single-parent families, and less familial and community support have made parents feel more isolated than ever before in raising their young children.*

- **Substandard child care.** *More than half of all mothers return to the workforce within a year of their baby's birth, but many of their infants and toddlers spend thirty-five or more hours per week in substandard child care.*

- **Poverty.** *A quarter of all families with children under age three live in poverty.*

- **Lack of attention.** *Only half of infants and toddlers are routinely read to by their parents, and many parents give insufficient attention to their children's intellectual development.*

Carnegie Corporation of New York. (1994). *Starting points: Meeting the needs of our youngest children—The report of the Carnegie Task Force on Meeting the Needs of Young Children.* Waldorf, MD: Carnegie Corporation of New York.

What is Learned Helplessness?

Babies who are caught in a flow of events that are unpredictable and clearly outside their control may, in contrast, develop an unfortunate style of response termed learned helplessness (Honig, 1986; Honig & Wittmer, 1997). Heartbreaking but very instructive studies of the Creche, a Romanian orphanage run by French nuns, helped researchers more fully understand the devastating impact of learned helplessness. Babies in this orphanage were adequately fed, clothed, and kept warm and dry, but the babies stayed in cribs with only uninteresting white crib bumpers and white ceilings to look at. There were few playthings and no structured activities. Caregivers were not aware that talking directly to and interacting with babies was necessary.

Because the babies were fed and changed on a schedule, there was no motivation for caregivers to respond to the babies' cries, so the babies soon learned that there was no use in crying. In effect, the children had no impact on their environment. Nothing that happened to them hinged on either spontaneous or learned actions on their part. They had no incentive to function in any way other than as passive objects in the environment, and, in fact, their behavior was soon not much livelier than that of a potted plant. These babies did not learn to sit up until a year or walk until four or five years. By age six their IQs were about 50, which is half the normal IQ and well into the range of serious mental retardation (Dennis, 1960, 1973).

Adults who care for babies should be down on the floor laughing, talking, singing, playing, and interacting with the babies—not sitting in rocking chairs watching television programs while

---

The Concept of Spoiling

Sometimes caregivers are tempted to leave babies in cribs or playpens for the sake of convenience or to put them on a predetermined schedule for feeding, changing, and sleeping regardless of the child's day-to-day rhythms or preferences. A long-standing folk belief in many modern cultures is that responding quickly to babies and holding or playing with them will result in "spoiling" and will make the child excessively demanding and dependent. We know now that lots of holding, touching, talking, and playing with babies is critical for them to grow and learn properly, so do not ever be afraid of giving positive attention.

---

babies are isolated and bored in cribs or playpens. Sometimes adults rationalize this inappropriate behavior by saying, "You shouldn't hold babies and play with them all the time. They'll turn into spoiled brats! It's better for them to learn to entertain themselves."

Obviously, the fundamental needs of an infant for the kind of care that will foster development of social, emotional, intellectual, and physical growth must take priority over questions of convenience for adults. Quality child care, like most other quality endeavors, involves a great deal of effort and hard work. Although overindulgence and overprotection do indeed undermine child guidance, lazy or haphazard care and teaching is never in the best interest of children.

Which is Best—Flexible Spontaneity or Predictable Routines?

Two opposing priorities for infants have been described so far in this chapter. The reader might well ask at this point, "Should I provide consistent, reliable routines or respond flexibly and spontaneously to cues from the baby?" The relationship of these two opposite needs is something like that of the contrasting philosophies described in an earlier chapter. On one hand, the **external environment** (the infant's physical surroundings, daily routines, and patterns of interacting with others) is important because infants tend to shape future expectations through conditioned learning. On the other hand, the infant's **internal sensations** and needs are important as a basis for adult responses because that process stimulates the child to initiate self-directed behaviors and to assume responsibility for making things happen.

This baby explores the physical properties of objects she finds in her environment.

There is a third alternative, however. The "developmental interactionist" perspective describes an interweaving between external forces and internal processes. In terms of guiding young children, this process is called positive child guidance, the assertive but gentle nudge method. A caregiver can be very responsive to and respectful of **cues** (indications of interest or need) from a baby while at the same time gradually nudging the child toward routines that are appropriate and convenient for the adult.

A six-month-old may be allowed to follow her inner drives to explore the sensory qualities of her environment by feeling, squishing, pounding, and smelling her food as she tastes it. However, she can also be gently but persistently nudged over time to handle food in a more traditional manner, gradually to use eating utensils, and eventually, years later, to exhibit polite table manners.

In a domineering (autocratic) setting, the baby would be forced to eat neatly with a spoon or not touch the food at all. In a setting where adults abdicate responsibility (anarchy), they would shrug and passively accept the belief that children are hopelessly slovenly in their eating habits and nothing can be done about it. In a respectful (democratic) setting, adults set very reasonable but slightly challenging expectations for the child based on his needs, interests, and abilities. They assist the interaction between the child and his environment by allowing him freedom to explore, modeling appropriate behaviors for him, and encouraging his first clumsy attempts to master skills.

What Do We Mean by Secure Attachment to Caregivers?

The attachment of babies to their adult caregivers is a critical part of their overall healthy social and emotional development. Early studies looked only at mother-infant relationships, since that was the only interaction that was considered to be of any importance. Freud focused on the attachment of infants to the mother and theorized that the baby considered her a "love object" simply because she provided pleasurable sucking and warm milk. He believed that the process of weaning, whether it was too rigid or too lenient, set the emotional tone for all of the child's future relationships with people and institutions.

Erikson (1963) extended, revised, and updated Freud's theory. He believed that experiences in the first year of life established in infants a general point of view for perceiving the world—either the positive and accepting reaction of trust or the negative and rejecting reaction of mistrust. He theorized that not only interpersonal relations but also competence in learning to use objects was affected by the baby's relationship to the mother. Exploration is essential for skill development, but babies only have the confidence to function competently in exploring the environment when they have an adult who serves as a "secure base" from which to explore.

Konrad Lorenz (1966) discovered a kind of attachment in certain birds (ducks, chickens, and so on) that he called imprinting. The ducks he studied became attached to whatever, or whomever, they saw moving near them when they hatched. Baby ducks that attached to "Papa" Lorenz not only followed him around as they grew up but also tried to mate with his leg when they reached maturity. The ethologists (scientists who study behaviors in naturalistic surroundings)

Babies begin to develop emotional bonds to the "significant others" in their lives.

do not pretend that human beings behave simplistically and instinctively as ducks do, but they do theorize that some early experiences or attachments have long-term impact on human behavior.

Bowlby (1958) and Ainsworth (1973) studied the processes of human attachment as researchers experienced a dawning awareness that biological mothers were not the only people who could develop important emotional relationships with infants. Writers began to use the word *parent* instead of *mother* when discussing attachment, to reflect awareness of the impact of father-child relationships. Gradually, the term *caregiver* came into use to indicate awareness that babies could develop multiple, loving attachments to grandparents, older siblings, and other consistent child care providers outside the family as well as to adoptive and biological parents.

Why Do Babies Cling?

It is essential that the process of early attachment be recognized by adults as a valuable occurrence in babies' early development rather than as an inconvenience to be avoided. Elise, a highly successful career mother, picked up her eleven-month-old son from his child care center one afternoon. The little boy eagerly crawled to his mother and pulled up holding on to her legs. As he clutched at her skirt, clung to her legs, and whined to be picked up, Elise breathed a dismayed sigh, looked helplessly at the infant-room teacher, and said, "Look at him. He just clings to me. What am I doing wrong?"

Elise was not aware that her son was only showing the normal indications of healthy emotional ties to his mother, which Ainsworth called "secure attachment." When babies brighten at the sight of a caregiver, visually follow that caregiver's movements, smile or vocalize to get attention, hold out their arms to be picked up, or cling to the caregiver, they are showing the typical signs of healthy attachment. Babies who turn or crawl away when a caregiver returns after an absence may be expressing the angry, rejected feelings that accompany a disrupted or poorly formed attachment. Babies who alternately cling and reject or show a push-pull relationship with the caregiver may not have built a really secure attachment to the caregiver. Developing secure attachments is an essential step in the growth of normal social and emotional skills.

The positive child guidance concept (assertive but patient nudging) applies well in the area of attachment. Caregivers can best assist infants' healthy social and emotional development by allowing and supporting closeness but also by gradually, as the child seems ready, nudging the child to move out on her own in exploring the environment. A newborn (or a baby in a new child care setting) may need to be held a great deal of the time at first, but gradually she can be enticed to spend increasing amounts of time occupying herself by looking at or playing with interesting mobiles, toys, and other surroundings. By getting down on the floor to play with the baby, a caregiver can be readily available to serve as a the "secure base" to facilitate the baby's moving out into more and more independent explorations of the surrounding environment.

What are Separation and Stranger Anxieties?

Attachment to caregivers serves as a survival mechanism for the species because an infant's safety depends on staying close to a caretaker. Therefore, it follows logically that an infant would quite naturally resist being separated from the parent figure who provides comfort and security.

Sometime between six months and a year, separation and stranger anxieties begin to appear in many children because of their newly developed cognitive adeptness in visually distinguishing between familiar and unfamiliar faces. Coincidentally, many parents first begin to rely on occasional or regular child care at about this same time. We adults are able to think and talk about child care arrangements. We may have studied a substitute caregiver's references or investigated carefully a center's license to provide care, but a baby has no way of comprehending all this.

When a baby looks up and sees that her daddy is not in sight, she feels the same way she would feel if she suddenly realized she was alone in the middle of a big department store. The swarms of strangers hovering around trying to be helpful would, at first, only be more frightening. Amazingly, it is not uncommon for parents or child care workers to be heard chiding a crying baby, "Hush! There is no reason for you to cry." If I were riding in an airplane that made an unexpected landing, or if I were pushed out kicking and screaming and left in a strange land with strangers who did not speak my language, I might cry too as I watched the plane carrying my family fly away. When the parent is out of sight, the child is unable to realize that Daddy is not gone forever.

The more positive experiences a baby has had with meeting new people, the less uncomfortable he will feel when he separates from parents or encounters strangers. In time, the baby develops a concrete understanding that strangers can be relied on to provide care and that after a while parents reappear. Pushing the baby into frightening situations is not helpful, but avoiding encounters with strangers altogether is also counterproductive. Gently nudging the baby into pleasurable and trusting relationships with adults other than parents will assist her in developing confidence and an open, positive attitude toward the world.

Some healthy, well-developing babies cry whenever an unfamiliar adult approaches them.

How Do Babies Perceive Themselves and Their Surroundings?

In the first months of life, babies have not yet gained a mental conception of themselves as separate individuals. Their perception of their own existence is limited to that which they see, feel, taste, smell, and hear. They unconsciously perceive their surroundings as if they were the center of the universe and the people and objects around them were extensions of their own existence. They make no distinction between their own physical being and the surroundings they perceive through their senses.

Caregivers take on a very important role in this context. Caring for a baby means that you literally become a part of that baby's life. Adults facilitate and guide older children, whose interests are focused on each other and on their own activities as much or more than on adults. In the first year of life however, infants focus an enormous quantity of their interest and energy on interacting with adult caregivers. They depend on adults for every aspect of physical care and safety as well as for entertainment and affection. Their interest in peers is purely **egocentric** (centered on one's own needs and desires). A seven-month-old will crawl onto a younger baby and casually grasp a handful of hair to feel and taste, then look quite puzzled by the sudden loud, piercing noises emitted by the little friend.

By rushing to rescue the younger baby and by **modeling** (demonstrating) appropriate behavior—softly stroking the offended baby's head while saying to the offender, "Gentle, gentle. Be gentle"—babies can eventually **internalize** (adopt as their own) more appropriate ways of behaving. Since the baby identifies so closely with the adult caregiver, the baby will automatically mimic behaviors of that adult. Caregivers who respond harshly or aggressively reinforce inappropriate behaviors in babies by modeling loud or rough interactions.

Some healthy, normal babies experience little stranger anxiety, and cope surprisingly well with separation from primary caregivers.

> *In each stage of child development . . . there is a central problem that has to be solved . . . if the child is to proceed with vigor and confidence to the next stage.*
>
> Erik H. Erikson

Toddlers (12 Months–3 Years)

Burton White has termed toddlers "a force to be reckoned with." Any parent or caregiver/teacher who deals with toddlers probably knows exactly what he means. Young toddlers, the one-year-olds, are phenomenal human beings. For the first time in their lives, they have become upright bipeds like the rest of us. Also, for the first time, they do not depend on us to bring rattles or tacky squeak toys to them for entertainment—they can walk through, wriggle under, or climb over any obstacle a grownup can devise in order to get to the really interesting things that attract their curiosity. While the young toddler can be an adorable timid rabbit one moment, sucking a thumb while peeking from behind a well-worn but snuggly piece of blanket, he can in an instant raise the rafters, crumpled on the floor in a full-fledged tantrum.

Can Toddlers Control Their Feelings and Actions?

Young toddlers are totally transparent in their feelings. They are openly affectionate, easily delighted by attention, and full of wonder about their surroundings. They also become confused, frustrated, and overwhelmed by their newfound freedom. One moment they are amazingly grown up and ready to take on the world, the next they regress into helpless clingy babies again. Their needs are simple—they want food, comfort, affection, approval, and to learn about the huge, booming, wide world around them. As babies, they still respond to their sensations of need by crying for caregivers, but as growing children, they also begin responding to their own desires by literally moving out into the environment to get what they want.

They use senses (touch, sight, smell, taste, and hearing) to explore the physical attributes of their environment and both small and large muscles to practice physical skills. They still do not consciously plan or think about their actions much. They just act. If the toddler feels hungry and the box of cereal in the grocery cart with him looks delicious, he may just rip it open and have a snack, then look hurt when his parents seemed shocked by his behavior.

How Does an Awareness of Cause and Effect Develop?

Toddlers have made a huge cognitive leap since infancy in their ability to remember things and in their first crude ability to manipulate ideas mentally. Cause-and-effect relationships become a focal point for their learning. They are fascinated by light switches and will flip the light on and off many times, if they are allowed, alternately watching the switch and the light fixture and mentally connecting the cause-and-effect relationship between the two.

They also tirelessly explore cause-and-effect relationships in social interactions. The toddler will stick her little pointed index finger out to touch the electrical outlet (covered of course with a plastic safety cap) and look up at her caregiver/teacher expectantly as he patiently repeats for

Safety is a major concern in the care of toddlers.

the hundredth time, "No, no. That's not for touching." Finally, the little girl will touch the outlet, shaking her head and repeating soberly, "No, no. No touch." She is preoccupied with connecting the cause-and-effect relationship between her action and the adult's words and has totally missed the point that he would rather she did not touch the outlet. With just a bit more time and patience, she will be satiated in her curiosity about the cause-and-effect connection, will be able to remember the connection each time she sees an electrical outlet, and will probably be quite willing to respect her caregiver/teacher's rule.

Do Toddlers Need to Explore Their Surroundings?

Healthy, well-developing toddlers have a curiosity that is boundless. Their desire to explore at times overshadows all other needs. A toddler who is totally immersed in the miseries of teething will stop crying when his mother carries him to the refrigerator and opens the freezer to get his frozen teething ring. For the moment, his pain is forgotten as he watches the frosty air roll out of the freezer and feels the brisk difference in temperature from this strange part of his environment he has never explored before.

Toddlers learn to walk because their fascination with this form of locomotion outweighs their fear of falling or being hurt. They move out into the environment, away from the security of caregivers, because the exhilaration of discovery causes them to throw caution to the wind.

Babies might stay in the comfort of their mother's arms forever if it were not for the powerfully motivating activator we call curiosity that drives toddlers out into the scary but exciting world. Baby birds are comfortable, secure, safe, and well-fed in the nest. At some point, however, nature intends them to leap precariously into the air and to flap their little wings until they figure out how to fly—a frightening and exhilarating experience for babies, of course, but also a frightening and exhilarating experience for grown-up birds to watch.

Is Safety a Major Issue in Toddler Care?

During toddlerhood, a child's motor development far outstrips her capacity to understand, remember, or abide by rules. Since she has not yet developed metacognition, she cannot look at a situation and then think about and plan for the potential consequences of her own behavior in that situation. Toddlers are still a bit unsteady in their walking, running, and climbing, and they are compelled to taste, feel, smell, and manipulate every interesting object or phenomenon they encounter. All this adds up to toddlers being in the most vulnerable period of their lives for accidents.

Unless toddlers are constantly and diligently supervised, they can inadvertently swallow objects and poisonous substances, fall off or bump into things, and touch things they should not touch despite warnings. If crying is the first major area of potential confrontation between infants and adults, then keeping toddlers from harming themselves or the environment is surely the second big area of stress and difficulty for parents and caregivers.

In past years, parents often bragged that their toddler was so well behaved that the most expensive, fragile, or even dangerous bric-a-brac could be left on the coffee table and the baby

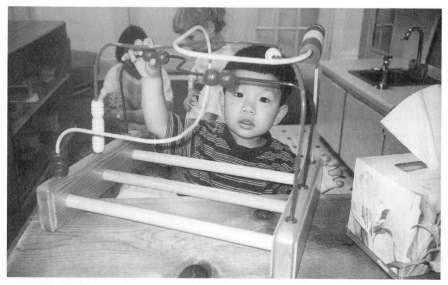

"I need safe, interesting things to explore by touching."

"I need safe, interesting things to explore by doing."

would never so much as touch it. They sometimes accomplished that feat by slapping the baby's hand or saying "no" sharply whenever the child attempted to touch the forbidden items. These adults believed that by teaching the baby to be still and not touch anything, they were helping her become well disciplined and polite.

Information about the processes of cognitive development, generated by research over the past two decades, has changed this old perception. A delightful poster that is very popular among child care workers pictures a young toddler standing forlornly in a play pen. The caption reads, "What do you mean, 'Don't touch'? Touching is how I learn." In order to create a richly stimulating environment conducive to optimum development while at the same time protecting toddlers from unreasonable risk of harm, adults must set about "babyproofing" all accessible areas of children's environments as soon as they develop the motor skills to move about. (See Appendix C for additional resources.)

White (1975, 1995) theorized that the period from ten months to three years is a critical period in the child's life for social, intellectual, and motor skill development. He also theorized that direct sensory exploration of the physical environment serves as a key requirement for optimum development. In his view, keeping toddlers in play pens or restricted in environments that are "hands off," excessively tidy, not baby-proofed, or downright boring risks losing the child's most valuable opportunity for early learning.

What Kind of Surroundings do Toddlers Need?

Toddlers thrive in settings that are made appropriate to their needs and abilities so that they can move about freely and safely exploring and testing every aspect of their surroundings. Of course, they still need careful supervision, even in the most carefully planned environment, but they are provided a much more stimulating range for their play when swallowable objects, toxic plants and substances, sharp corners, and electrical cords are simply put out of the child's reach.

Rather than struggling to force toddlers to behave safely and appropriately, adults should simply change the child's environment to make interaction in it safe and appropriate. As toddlers become older and more compliant, sometime around their third birthday, toys with parts small enough to be swallowed, blunt scissors, water-based marking pens, and other materials requiring special care can be introduced. Gradually, as children are developmentally ready, they can then be gently but firmly guided to understand and follow appropriate safety rules.

Can Toddlers Read Body Language?

From birth children respond to facial expression, tone of voice, and body movement. Long before a child understands language, he will react to cues such as the nonverbal body language, inflection, tone, and volume that is a part of an adult's speech.

Betty Jo, the lively young mother of twelve-month-old Jeremy, comes to pick up her son from the registered family day home where he is cared for during the day. She chats with other parents picking up their children as she zips Jeremy into his snow suit. Jeremy makes a funny sound and his cheeks turn red as it dawns on Betty Jo that she will have to change his diaper.

Everyone downwind of Jeremy is, by this point, quite aware that the diaper is definitely more than just wet. As other parents chuckle, Betty Jo jokingly but energetically scolds Jeremy for being so rude after she has gone to all the trouble of bundling him up to go home. While the little boy clearly does not understand all her words, he unmistakably interprets her fake scowl and sharp tone to mean that she is angry with him. He turns his face away from her and sobs. Betty Jo is quite startled by his reaction. Since he did not know how to talk, she assumed he would not have any idea what she was saying.

The ability of very young children to make some sense of our feelings from our body language and tone of voice gives us an opportunity to communicate with them nonverbally. Before children have mastered **expressive language** (the ability to speak), they have begun to develop **receptive language** (the ability to understand language). Therefore, if we are honest and sincere in the words we speak to babies and toddlers, our body language will quite naturally convey our feelings and attitudes to the child. If we speak to the child for the benefit of other adults, as if the child were not really present or listening, we may miss an important opportunity to build communication with the child.

Adults can begin from the very beginning speaking to babies as if they were (because they definitely are) worthwhile human beings. This has two important benefits for long-term child guidance. First, the child will learn early in life to pay attention to adults, since they seem to say what they mean and mean what they say. Second, adults have plenty of time to practice appropriate communication skills so that they will be prepared when the child really does have a command of language.

Using a kind facial expression and a caring tone of voice, an adult can speak reassuringly to a young toddler who resists going to sleep, "I know you would rather play with your toys, but it's time for nap now. Would you like me to rock you for a minute before you lie down?" Even though the child will not understand all the words, she will sense the adult's caring attitude. She will also have an opportunity to hear language and associate it with objects and events in day-to-day living.

How Does Verbal Communication Begin?

Toddlers seem to explode into language. At a child's first birthday, he may only know words like "mama," "dada," and "baba" for bottle. Within a few months, the child may know many more single word labels plus a number of holophrases (phrases made of words that are joined like Siamese twins and used as if they were inseparable single words). "Gofieys" may mean, "Go to McDonalds and get French fries." "Sousite" may mean, "Let's go outside to play." The child soon learns to mix and match words or holophrases to create two-word sentences. Soon the child's speech begins to sound like abbreviated telegrams, including key words but leaving less critical words out: "Paw Paw doggy big!" "No touch daddy gwas [glasses]." By age three, the child's speech begins to sound surprisingly like our own (with a few quirks here and there): "My daddy goed to work an he gots a big office."

The child's language changes each day as he adds new vocabulary and new levels of expression and understanding. At birth the child had no muscular control of her lips and tongue and no comprehension that language existed or had significance. In only three short years, she has learned how to create many different sounds with her lips, tongue, and vocal cords; amassed hundreds of words in her vocabulary; and grasped the basic syntax (structure) of her native language. Her language comprehension is complex but not at a conscious level. For example, she has simply absorbed an intuitive sense that the "s" sound on the end of a naming word means more than one, and that the "d" sound at the end of an action word means that the action has already happened.

What Kind of Language Experiences are Good for Toddlers?

Infants and children of all ages need to hear the rich, lyrical words of adult conversational speech as well as the musical word patterns in rhymes, songs, and jingles. These kinds of language experiences especially enrich and stimulate language learning in toddlers. For maximum comprehension, however, the child must hear language that is very close to his own level of development. This language should be at or slightly ahead of the child's own level. For example, in developing music appreciation, young children are allowed to hear a wide range of classical, folk, and pop music for enrichment, but for learning actual singing they are introduced to extremely simple songs like "Here We Go 'Round the Mulberry Bush."

If a baby's language development is still limited to the cooing and babbling stage, the adult can effectively communicate through facial expression, tone of voice, and body language. If the child is using single words, the adult can best achieve communication through holophrases ("Allgone") or two-word sentences ("More milk?").

Toddlers may hear and comprehend only a few words in sentences that are above their comprehension. Often they catch a few accentuated or familiar words from the beginning or from the end of the adult's speech. The toddler may innocently respond to the words "You . . . candy . . . mouth" from the adult's complicated sentence, "You need to make very sure you don't put that whole big piece of candy into your mouth." To maximize the toddler's comprehension of important communication, choose key words, speak slowly and clearly, and use facial expression and body gestures to emphasize your meaning.

We might use more elaborate enrichment language to say to a toddler, "I believe you need to have your shoe lace tied. It could make you trip and fall down." But, if a response is needed from the child, bend down, take the child's hand, deliberately establish eye contact, and then pat the floor expectantly as you articulate carefully, "Sit, please." We can then reinforce the child's cooperativeness the instant he looks as if he will comply by smiling warmly and saying, "Thank you!"

Stranger Anxiety

Toddlers show a wide range of reactions to strangers, depending on their own experiences and temperament. Some children go through a distinct phase in which they are terrified of strangers. When confronted by a stranger (or even a less familiar caregiver), many toddlers cling to their parent's or caregiver's clothing, hide their faces, and cry. Other children, especially those who have had broad exposure to many friendly adults since infancy, may show curiosity about new adults, attempt to make friends, and never give any indication of separation or stranger anxiety. To experience stranger anxiety, the child must be able to distinguish familiar from unfamiliar faces, which usually happens around six or seven months of age.

Separation Anxiety

Stranger anxiety is often coupled with separation anxiety—the distress children show when they cry on separation from a parent or primary caregiver. Separation anxiety can be seen at any time from infancy through preschool, but it is usually most pronounced in the second year of life.

How Can I Make Friends with a Shy Toddler?

In order to establish a relationship with a "shy" toddler, it is essential to understand and respect that child's discomfort in interacting with a new adult. Rather than approaching the child directly with a big smile and immediately attempting to touch or hold the child, avoid eye contact with the child at first. Speak quietly and pleasantly with others around the child while moving a bit closer to the child. If the child is standing or sitting on the floor, sit nearby to be at the eye level

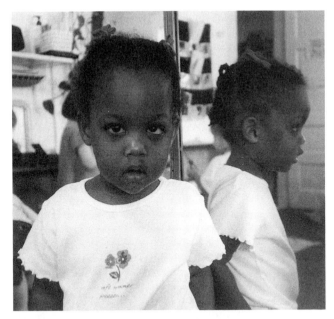

"I need safe, interesting things to explore by looking."

of the child. Glance briefly in the child's direction occasionally to see if he is evidencing curiosity or stress at your presence. Smile, but avoid looking directly into the child's eyes until you are confident he feels comfortable with your presence.

After allowing the toddler plenty of time to stare at you, it may be helpful to touch the child's hand casually for a moment while glancing briefly in his direction with a smile. Eventually, he will probably indicate his willingness to make friends and allow eye contact. At this point, a diversion in the form of a game or toy may be a perfect way to cement the budding adult-child relationship. In a child care center, the teacher may be able, at this point, to interest the toddler in petting the class bunny rabbit, looking at a book, or watching the teacher make a Cookie Monster puppet tell jokes and eat pretend cookies. If no toys are available, sing a song, make up a rhyme, or talk about the child's clothing—"Look at those blue sneakers. You can run really fast in those." An effective diversion at this point will hold the child's interest but not require a great deal of sustained eye contact or active response from him.

Why are Toddlers So Possessive?

Young toddlers callously step on each other to get what they want, take toys from each other, and scramble to grab food. Two-year-olds walk into their child care center in the morning, look suspiciously at their peers, tighten their grip on Dad's hand, and announce defiantly, "My daddy!" Very young children's behavior is not particularly civilized or polite because they do not yet have a well-developed ability to put themselves in the place of others. Some toddlers who have observed and experienced a great deal of **empathy** (kindness) may show concern for others, but their way of expressing concern is totally egocentric. For example, the toddler may try to give her pacifier or teddy bear to an adult who is crying.

There is little to say about toddlers and sharing except that it cannot be expected of them. Instead of attempting to coerce toddlers into behaving in a way that is developmentally incompatible, adults can rearrange the environment, change the routines, or increase their supervision to protect toddlers from inadvertent rough or rude treatment by their peers. In time, children develop the ability to recognize that other people have feelings and rights, and they develop the ability to imagine how others would feel if they were treated a certain way. Then it will be possible to teach them manners. Until then, setting a good example and tactfully but assertively protecting children's (and others') rights are all that adults can do. Having a wide variety of choices available to toddlers will ease this problem. It will also help to have multiples of the most popular objects, such as shovels, balls, and dolls.

Why Do Some Toddlers Become So Attached to Security Blankets, Pacifiers, and So Forth?

Toddlers use many "crutches" to help them cope with being very little and very powerless in a big, fast, scary world. Some adults call toddlers' worn blankets, tattered stuffed animals, pacifiers, or whatever else they hold onto, the child's "cuddlies." Child psychologists call them objects for "cyclical self-stimulation." Caregivers are sometimes tempted to just call them nuisances. Whatever they are called, when they are lost, they can cause the toddler's emotional world to come crashing down around him. As strongly as children are attached to these comfort items, they generally begin to lose interest in them by the time they turn three. Some preschoolers hang onto their

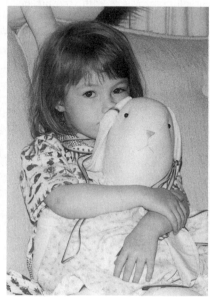

Some toddlers rely on a special cuddly toy to help them cope with the big, confusing, overwhelming world around them.

cuddlies a while longer, but for many of them, their attachment at this point is more habit than emotional need.

In many primitive cultures, children stay in physical contact with their mothers' bodies much of the time during their first three years of life. In modern industrialized societies, children are separated from their mothers at birth to be placed in a hospital nursery, put to sleep in a separate bed (enclosed with bars) in a separate room at home, and buckled into high chairs and car seats. It is not surprising then that many babies improvise "caregiver replacements" to cling to for a while and to help them cope (nipple-shaped objects to suck and soft, warm, fuzzy, or silky objects to hold). The child's need for these objects should be respected, although she can be nudged gently to do without them for gradually increasing periods of time when they have become little more than habit.

Children especially need to be helped to cope without having a pacifier or thumb "plugged in" too much of their day. It is very difficult for toddlers to practice language with their mouths immobilized. It is equally important, on the other hand, to foster language development early in life by allowing infants plenty of sucking to develop the mouth, lip, and tongue muscles necessary for later speech. Since bottle feeding requires less muscular effort and coordination to produce milk than breastfeeding, many babies benefit emotionally and physically from the availability of nonnutritive sucking. Pacifiers are healthier for teeth and thumbs, and usually easier to wean children from than thumbs.

Although some authorities still encourage mothers to wean babies from breast or bottle at about ten months of age, weaning in the first year of life will often cause the child to seek some form of replacement sucking or self-stimulation. We can take good advice from our grandmothers, who have been saying for generations, "If you baby a baby when he's a baby, you won't have to baby him all the rest of his life."

Why Are Toddlers Stubborn One Minute, Then Clingy the Next?

Erikson (1982) focused on the development of autonomy (self-sufficiency) as the second step in his eight stages of **social** and **emotional** (affective) **growth**. After trust has been established in infancy, toddlers become immersed in the conflict between autonomy and shame and doubt. Toddlers are able for the first time to do many things that adults consider naughty or destructive. For the first time adults hold the child responsible for bodily elimination and controlling impulses. The child is torn between assertively resisting adult guidance and feeling fearful and ashamed for getting into trouble so often. She feels she can conquer the world with her new capabilities, but she is constantly getting into scrapes, making messes, and needing adult help and reassurance.

Adults can help toddlers through this period by being very supportive of the child's need to break away from infancy. In order to foster autonomy, we should not do anything for the toddler that she could be helped to do for herself. Toddlers can learn to peel their own banana for snack, pull up their own sock once the adult gets it started, and choose their own clothing from two appropriate choices. They can be allowed to stand on a chair at the sink to wash unbreakable dishes (although Mom or Dad will undoubtedly have to re-wash them later for sanitary reasons). They can even be given a small bucket with a little water, a squirt of liquid soap, and a small piece of sponge or rag to help wash the car or the windows.

Toddlers are interested in having the freedom and independence to be involved in the processes of grown-up activities. They are not at all interested in achieving specific end products to those processes and are confused and discouraged by adult concern over end products or results rather than processes. Adults usually do things the most expedient way to get the result that they want. Toddlers spend long periods of time in the process of dipping, pouring, and splashing dishes in soapy water, but lose interest before the dishes are actually rinsed and dried. Sensitive adults will foster the child's involvement in independent processes but wait until the child is older to expect results. They will redirect unacceptable behavior rather than make the child feel inadequate or naughty for following his curiosity and desire to attempt things he sees adults doing.

Are Toddlers Aware of Themselves?

When babies look in a mirror, they do not necessarily recognize that the image reflected there is their own. At some point in toddlerhood, they finally discover that the face in the mirror is theirs. If they see an unexpected smudge on the nose in the mirror, they touch their own nose to find out what is there. A younger child will only touch the mirror. Toddlers who are not yet aware of their own separate identity seem to think that they cannot be seen by anyone if their own eyes are closed. A toddler being reprimanded for misbehavior may cover her eyes, assuming (because of her egocentricity) that the adults will not be able to see her since she cannot see them.

Toddlers try to imitate the actions and events they see around them.

Why Do Toddlers Get So Excited and Happy When They Imitate Each Other?

Toddlers who have just begun to get a sense of their separateness tend to be very "full of themselves." If a caregiver gathers two-year-olds around him to read a storybook, he will often discover that they are more entertained by each other than by the book. They giggle and poke each other, and inevitably one toddler will begin a gloriously spontaneous action like vigorously shaking her head until her hair stands out all around her head. In an instant this action spreads like a contagion, leaving the poor adult sitting rather foolishly, book in hand, watching a band of toddlers laughing uproariously as they shake their heads (and perhaps wiggle their bodies and stamp their feet for good measure).

As toddlers begin to recognize their existence as a separate person like the people they see around them, they begin to develop a **concept** (or picture) of who they are based on feedback primarily from the adults around them. Sometimes adults make casual comments that are very cutting—"You are as fat as a pig." "Why are you always so mean?" "I think you like to make me mad."—things we would probably hesitate to say to another adult. Sometimes these hurtful comments come from siblings or other children. Toddlers are very naive. They tend to believe what we tell them about themselves through our actions and words. As an older toddler's self-image begins to take shape, we can help her develop a healthy and confident view of herself by being very careful about what we say to her (and what we allow other children to say to her) — "What a big girl you are." "Everybody makes mistakes sometime." "I really like your smile." "I didn't like the hitting, but I will always like you." The toddler's budding self-esteem will serve as a foundation for her growth as a confident, competent, cooperative, and productive human being.

Competent Three-Year-Olds Are . . .

- *Self-confident and trusting*
- *Intellectually inquisitive*
- *Able to use language to communicate*
- *Physically and mentally healthy*
- *Able to relate well to others*
- *Empathic toward others*

Given consistently nurturing and responsive care, healthy babies develop a high level of "competence" by age three. Competent preschoolers are much more likely to be successful and well adjusted in school and throughout life.

Carnegie Corporation of New York. (1994). *Starting points: Meeting the needs of our youngest children—The report of the Carnegie Task Force on Meeting the Needs of Young Children.* Waldorf, MD: Carnegie Corporation of New York.

Preschoolers (3–5 Years)

Can Preschoolers Make Plans and Decisions?

Toddlers are only able to conceive of objects in terms of the way those objects actually feel, look, taste, smell, or sound. Preschoolers have a new mental ability. They can conceive of objects both in terms of what they are perceptually and what they stand for symbolically. For example, a toddler sees a block only as something to bite, hit, throw, or stack. The preschooler can see the block both as a physical object and as a "pretend" bar of soap to bathe a doll or a "pretend" car to zoom around the floor. The block can stand as a symbol for something else.

Preschoolers also become more consciously aware of their own interests and intentions. They look over the toys that are available to them and make intentional choices. While toddlers function primarily by impulse, playing with whatever toy catches their eye for the moment, preschoolers are more inclined to select an activity very carefully and then stay with it longer, sometimes even coming back to play the same game day after day until they finally become bored with it.

Older preschoolers can verbalize what and how they want to play. For example, they may say, "Let's play like this is our house and you are the daddy and he is the baby and that box is the baby bed." They can become very frustrated or angry if things do not turn out the way they expect. Preschoolers often squabble over their conflicting perceptions of how their play should proceed—"I don't want to be the baby. I want to play Masters of the Universe!"

Preschoolers become fascinated with toys that require thinking that is more complicated. They begin to anticipate cause and effect. "I wonder what would happen if I did it this way?"

Adults can help preschoolers during this stage by focusing the children's attention on the probable consequences of their actions. Questions should never be used as verbal battering rams, but adults can gently nudge cause-and-effect thinking by asking, "What might happen if someone ran out into the street without looking?" "Hmmm, I wonder what could happen if you paint without putting a smock on over your clothes?" "How would your friend feel if she never got a turn to be the pretend mommy?" Preschoolers are just beginning to be able to manipulate ideas in their heads and eventually can learn to weigh consequences and make appropriate decisions before acting.

How Does a Preschooler's Language Change?

Because preschoolers have an increasing command of their native language, they can benefit from talking about their own actions and events that have taken place or will take place in their lives. Before an event takes place, they can be helped to understand that event by parents or teachers talking about it in advance in very simple, concrete terms. Parents often try to shield preschoolers from adult concerns by not talking directly to their children about sensitive issues.

A three-year-old, whose parents often affectionately called her "our sweet baby girl," cried hysterically when an aunt said, "I hear there's going to be a new baby at your house." She had overheard her parents saying that they thought it best for her not to know yet that there was going to be a new baby. She knew, of course, that when they got a new car, the old car vanished, and when they got a new refrigerator, the old one was hauled away, and when she got new shoes, the old ones were dropped unceremoniously into the trash can. She could only guess what happened to little girls who she imagined were so naughty that their parents decided to get "a new one."

A four-year-old boy developed nightmares and bed wetting after he heard family members crying and talking in somber but hushed tones about how his expectant mother had lost the baby she was carrying. His problem behaviors increased until a psychologist was consulted and discovered that the little boy had been nervously searching in closets and under beds to find the lost baby. He knew that those were places to look when you lost something. He worried that his parents might lose him too!

How Can I Communicate Successfully with Preschoolers?

By talking to preschoolers in honest but simplified terms, we can help them to understand and deal with events. We cannot take for granted that just because something is obvious to us it will be obvious to young children. There are many things about this world that preschoolers just do not know yet. A caregiver can use very simple but clear sentences to say, "Marcus, your dad just called on the telephone. He will be late picking you up today. His car won't go so he has to get it fixed. It may be dark when he gets here, but it's okay. I will stay with you. We'll get some cheese and crackers and apple juice and play until he comes." Sometimes adults become so preoccupied with their own problems and plans that they forget to tell children what will happen to them. Modeling through dramatic play can help children visualize an expected behavior. Talking through a puppet is a nonthreatening way to get a point across, or model appropriate language.

A parent can prevent potential problems by anticipating and planning for them. Being especially careful not to communicate negative expectations, the parent could say, "Shelley, your friend Jamie will be here soon. Sometimes when she is here it is hard for you to share your favorite toys. That makes Jamie feel sad. Would you like to choose the toys you want to share and put them in this cardboard box? We can take the toys you choose into the backyard, then Jamie will know which toys you want to share and play with." By helping the child positively think through this potential problem before it happens, the child may be able to consciously behave in such a way as to avoid the conflict before it erupts. While a child is angry and upset, it is unlikely that she will be able to listen to logic or behave rationally.

How Can We Teach Preschoolers to Use Words Instead of Hitting When They Feel Angry?

In a democracy, people are allowed to use physical force only as a last resort when other reasonable steps to defend oneself have failed. Children need to know that everyone, children and adults, will use words to express feelings and needs. Force is never used to hurt, punish, or humiliate, but only to defend life and limb.

Preschoolers can be guided firmly to use words to get a point across rather than relying on kicking, scratching, and hair pulling. They can be helped to practice appropriate words and allowed to express strong emotions, even anger, through their words. When a preschooler runs to tell parents or teachers about another child's action, instead of being chided for "tattling," the child can be encouraged to talk to the other child—"Did you tell Kirin that it was your turn for the swing? Would you like for me to go with you to talk to her?"

Adults sometimes try to squelch children's negative feelings. We say things to quiet children like, "Don't cry." "Don't make a fuss." "She didn't really mean to hit you." Maybe the other child really did mean to hit. A child deserves to express her feelings in an honest but respectful way—"I feel angry. I don't like it when you push me off the swing." Preschoolers especially need to be allowed to express their feelings. They can learn that it is okay to feel angry and it is okay to say so, but it is not okay to lash out in a way that verbally attacks or physically hurts others.

Preschoolers can also be helped to verbalize their feelings by having adults **mirror** (reflect back) those feelings. Young children may not realize that they are cranky because they are hot and tired or cold and hungry. Adults can put words to those feelings and assist preschoolers in learning to identify and express what they feel inside—"Brrr, I feel cold! Look at the chill bumps on my arm. Are you cold? Let me feel how cold your hands are."

This mirroring of feelings is called active listening (repeating back what you understood the child to mean). The adult refrains from lecturing, instructing, commanding, or telling. Instead, she listens and sincerely reflects back what she thinks the child is feeling at the moment. In active listening (a useful communication tool for any age), the adult says things such as, "It sounds like you are really feeling angry with Tommy." "In other words, what you are saying is that you feel hurt and sad when you don't get to play." "You seem pretty frightened when the other children pretend to be monsters." The point of active listening is not to solve the child's problem for her, but only to let her know that she has been heard and to give her a chance to talk about, think about, and confront her own feelings.

Why Are Friendships So Important to Preschoolers?

Babies and toddlers are very curious about other children but are most concerned about the adults in their lives. Preschoolers, on the other hand, begin to be interested in their relationships with other children. Throughout the rest of childhood they will rely more and more on their friendships with peers and less and less on their attachment to adults. Between three and five, children need to learn how to be a friend and how to have friends, a very important kind of learning for the child's long-term social and emotional adjustment in life (Corsaro, 1981).

This can be a very trying stage for adults. Children are elated when they feel liked by peers and emotionally crushed when they imagine that no other child in the whole world wants to play with them. Although some children quickly find a best friend or group of friends whom they get along with very well, other children experience a daily emotional roller coaster as they struggle to establish friendships and deal with peers who barter, "I'll be your best friend if you give me your piece of chocolate cake."

Some preschoolers become very cliquish as they decide who is or is not a friend. They say things like, "You can't be our friend because you don't have a football shirt on." "We don't want you to play because you're a boy." "You draw scribble-scrabble so you can't color in our color book." Adults can feel very frustrated trying to decide when or how to intervene in these

Friendship becomes an important part of the day-to-day lives of preschoolers. (Photograph provided courtesy of CHILDREN AT RISK.)

Some preschoolers may still rely on sucking their thumbs from time to time, but it has usually become more of a comfortable habit than a coping mechanism.

troublesome and hurtful interactions. Children have a right to choose their own friends and playmates, but they also have an obligation to avoid being downright cruel in expressing those choices. Adults can gently nudge appropriate behavior by saying, "Please tell Chris, 'I like you but I don't want to play with you right now.'"

How Do Preschoolers Learn to Accept Responsibility?

Erikson (1963) focused on the need of four- and five-year-olds to resolve the emotional conflict of initiative versus guilt. Preschoolers are struggling to become independent of adult caregivers and to find their own limits. Still, however, they want to please adults and feel very guilty when they disappoint or anger parents and teachers. An excessive amount of guilt causes discomfort which the child may relieve by withdrawing from any situation that involves a risk of failure, or by adopting a rebellious "tough guy" facade and appearing to be immune to guilt.

To develop initiative, children must be encouraged to achieve independence from adults. Instead of doing things for preschoolers, adults must tactfully make it possible for the children to do things for themselves. Adults can simplify tasks and then teach simple skills like how to refill the gerbil's water bottle, how to cut safely with a blunt knife, how to clip paper to an easel with clothespins, and how to get a jacket zipper started.

Should Preschoolers Be Allowed to Do Things That Are Difficult?

Preschoolers relish the opportunity to be in charge of their own environment. They make many mistakes and often forget to carry out tasks they have agreed to perform. Adults can respond best by remembering that the process of learning is much more important for preschoolers than the end products resulting from their efforts. Some adults become perfectionist about tasks and say, "It's easier for me to do it myself than to hassle with the kids trying to do it." It may be easier, but it definitely is not better for children who need encouragement and success in accepting and carrying out responsibilities.

With a great deal of practice, encouragement, and patient teaching (one tiny step at a time), preschoolers can learn to carry out fairly complex tasks responsibly and well. They will feel so confident about their accomplishments that they will eagerly show initiative (inner drive) in tackling new tasks or projects without having to be prodded or coerced every step of the way like a child who has fallen prey to feelings of guilt.

How Do We Get Preschoolers to Follow Rules?

Preschoolers are ready for simplistic rules—"Be kind! Wait until it's your turn to go down the slide." "Be safe! Stop at the gate so a grown-up can walk with you across the street." "Be neat! Use a sponge to wipe up the tempera paint that has spilled." Preschoolers are **preoperational** (in

"Uh, oh. I think you forgot our rule. Be kind. Use words instead of shoving." (Photograph provided courtesy of CHILDREN AT RISK.)

Piaget's terms) so they perceive rules in a superficial way. They follow rules more to please adults than because they comprehend the relationship between actions and possible consequences. Preschoolers still must be supervised closely because they are not yet able to follow rules consistently. In their play, they make up rules on a whim and then break the rules they have made with total abandon when a rule no longer suits them.

They begin to make sense intuitively of adult expectations and anticipate what will or will not be allowed in various situations. They tell each other, "Oh! You're gonna get in trouble." They begin to enforce rules on each other, "You didn't flush. I'm gonna tell on you." Adults can redirect this sudden enthusiasm for rules by setting a good example in their own respectful enforcement of rules. If adults are punitive and critical and seem eager to "catch" wrongdoers, children will imitate that. If adults remind children of rules in an assertive but polite tone and then help them comply, children will imitate that too.

Adults can maintain children's interest in rules by making very few rules but making sure that children know and respect the rules that are given. Rules always mean more to children if they played an active role in developing them and in deciding on logical consequences that should be enforced when the rules are broken. Overwhelming preschoolers with picky rules will alienate them and trivialize the whole idea of following rules. Children's perception of the value and importance of rules can be greatly enhanced when they are allowed to be part of the rule-making process. At group or circle time in a group setting, or in a family council meeting at home, children can be invited to think of new rules to solve simple problems like pushing and shoving or taking other people's things without asking. Also, adults can help children by patiently explaining the reasons for rules rather than just saying, "It's a rule because I say so."

Stating rules—"No one is allowed to climb on that fence!" —and then proceeding to ignore children who climb on the fence will convince children that grown-ups do not really mean the things they say and rules are not really to be followed. It is important to remember that following rules is not only to be "kind, safe, and neat" today, but also to develop habits that will result in the child obeying laws as an adolescent and as an adult.

How Do Preschoolers Develop a Positive Sense of Self?

Although the child's self-esteem (or lack of it) has been developing unconsciously since birth, preschool-aged children begin to develop a clear, conscious idea of who and what they are. Self-esteem and self-concept are two closely related concepts. **Self-concept** is one's idea or image of oneself. **Self-esteem** means that one's image of oneself includes a sense of being worthwhile and valuable. Children's ideas about themselves come from others around them, particularly from parents (Coopersmith, 1967; Cotton, 1984). As preschoolers become more adept at language, they also become more susceptible to the opinions of teachers, peers, and others outside the home.

Preschoolers become increasingly aware of their own identity in terms of larger groupings within society. The child may, for the first time, become aware that she is white or black. Self-esteem can grow from pride in one's ethnic, regional, and religious heritage. Sadly, exposure to prejudice devastates self-esteem and creates a cycle of prejudice and low self-esteem, since low self-esteem is one of the causes of prejudice in the first place (Bagley et al., 1979). Every child deserves to know that he or she is special—but, of course, no more special than anyone else!

Preschoolers also become aware, for the first time, that their gender is fixed for life; girls will grow to be women, and boys will grow to be men. Toddlers may distinguish between girls and boys or mommies and daddies, but they think they can turn into the opposite sex simply by wearing different clothing. Preschoolers identify with their own gender and may begin playing only with boys or only with girls.

Parents worry about their physically active daughters who prefer playing with the boys or their quiet, sensitive sons who prefer playing with the girls. Preschoolers worry about playing with toys that their friends consider to be "girl toys" or "boy toys." Preschool teachers often worry about making sure boys feel okay about playing in the housekeeping center with dolls and dressups and girls feel okay about playing in the block center with trucks and cars so that all the children will have well-rounded educational experiences. Everyone worries, but children generally persist in play that reflects the real world as they know it. If they see daddy having a good time feeding the baby and cooking, little boys will probably play house more comfortably than if they have only seen women doing these things. The same is true for little girls who have seen their mothers repair a leaky pipe or wear a police officer's uniform.

Should Children be Encouraged to Compete?

Another factor that affects preschoolers' development of self-concept and self-esteem is competitiveness. Preschoolers have become aware of themselves in comparison to others, so competitiveness reaches a peak during the preschool years (Stott & Ball, 1957). It can be very

Every individual preschooler can be helped to appreciate her own special talents. Hearing adults compare one child's ability to that of a peer is not necessary or beneficial to either of the children.

tempting for adults to exploit that tendency by saying things like, "Whoever can be the quietest at naptime will get a special treat." "The one who puts away toys the fastest will get to be first in line to go outside." "See if you can get dressed faster than your brother."

These challenges may strongly motivate some children to behave as the adult wishes, but the competition also stimulates friction rather than cooperativeness among children. Additionally, whenever there are winners, by definition there will be losers. Winners may feel stressed and compulsive about continuing to win, and losers may feel more and more inadequate.

Early School-Agers (5–8 Years)

Five- through eight-year-old children are very different from younger children, not only because of their gap-toothed smiles and taller bodies, but also because their thinking and language skills are different too.

Why Do Early School-Agers Ask So Many Questions?

As school-agers become more aware of the world around them, they want to know a simple answer to every puzzling phenomenon encountered. Preshcoolers physically explore things that puzzle them—"Do rocks always sink in water?" "What's inside my toy car?" "How high will a swing go?" They ask simple, concrete questions about things around them—"What's this?" "What's that?" "What's your name?" Early school-agers question everything, and often ask questions that are really hard to answer—"Why can't I have pizza for breakfast?" "What if gravity stopped and everything flew off the earth?" "Why do things look small when they're far away?" "Why did Grandma die?" "What makes the car go?"

Early school-aged children are less gullible than preschoolers. They are quick to see discrepancies in adult actions—"You said that nobody could eat or drink unless they sat down at the table. You're somebody and you're drinking coffee." Preschoolers believe just about anything you tell them, but early school-agers become more critical. For example, if you say, "You can't eat candy because it is not good for your teeth," a preschooler might protest and beg, but a school-ager will think about that explanation logically and answer back with her own rationale, "Okay, then I'll brush my teeth after I eat the candy." After the early school-ager has asked a persistent series of logical why or why-not questions, parents and teachers often find themselves snapping with exasperation, "Because I said so!" Of course, this is the phrase we hated to hear as children and promised we would never say when we grew up.

Why Do They Get So Angry If They Do Not Always Win?

Early school-agers make observations and judgments about everything around them. Because of their immaturity, however, their judgment is limited to a simplistic, good-or-bad, win-or-lose view of the world. Naturally, they begin to compare themselves with others. Competition rears its ugly head as children struggle to best each other. They constantly fight over who likes whom best. Adults sometimes throw fuel onto this fire by encouraging competition. For example, teachers say, "Let's see who can be first to get their table clean." "The quietest person will get to go first." "I will put gold starts on the very best papers and put them on the bulletin board for parents night." This tactic is tempting because early school-agers will practically trample each other to be first or best at anything. We should find ways instead, however, to help children get along and cooperate more rather than less. Learning to be a collaborative team member is an important prosocial skill for children to learn during these years. In early childhood, competition should be focused on improving oneself, not on "beating" others.

Why do they call each other names and say such hurtful things? Early school-agers have gained skill in expressing themselves verbally. They use more descriptive words to express their anger, frustration, or jealousy than preschoolers. Preschoolers simply shove or hit someone who upsets them, or bluster, "You're a pooh-pooh head an' I hate you." School-agers are more precise in their words, "Why do you act so bossy? You're not my mother." Their responses become more rational and logical. Angry words hurled at early school-agers can would them deeply, though, so it is important to help them think about the effects their words have on others. Effectively expressing negative feelings in words is an important part of learning to communicate effectively, but cruel or demeaning taunts or epithets must never be allowed.

Why Are Some School-Aged Children Rowdy?

Early school-agers can be intimidating to adults. Younger children who misbehave can be picked up and carried (kicking and screaming) away from a problem situation. School-agers are becoming too large. They can no longer by controlled by physical restraint. We just be able to rely on the child's inner control.

Adults who used spanking to control younger children discover school-aged children may be so emotionally immune to being hit that by this age they only respond with apathy. Or, they may be so angered by being treated like a "baby" that an attempt to spank them could trigger outright defiance. Teachers and caregivers will encounter an occasional school-aged child who has been subjected to a great deal of rough treatment in his life and has become aggressive, toughened, cynical, and very difficult to manage. Our best hope for breaking through this tough outer shell is assertive rule enforcement tempered with unconditional affection and open, respectful communication.

Spanking is always an inappropriate and ineffective method for disciplining children. The powerful negative effect of spanking lies in its ability to frighten and intimidate a child. Although corporal punishment may seem to work quite well at first, when children are tiny and easily intimidated, it models aggressive behavior and accustoms children to being controlled by external physical force. After a child has been spanked on many occasions, he becomes so accustomed to the way it feels that it no longer has the same effect. It may make him furious, but it probably will not scare him. This creates a difficult situation for everyone, as children grow bigger and stronger. Eventually the child will be too large to control physically.

The surest way out of this emotional trap is for the adult to break the cycle by finding some way to prove to each individual child that he or she is liked and respected by the adult. Then, and only then, the adult can begin to gain the children's respect and loyalty. External control methods do not work reliably for bright, capable, thinking children who will feel they are being manipulated into doing things they do not want to do by someone who does not really like them.

The school-aged child begins to worry about her popularity among peers. (Photograph provided courtesy of CHILDREN AT RISK.)

Inner control depends completely on the child wanting to be a cooperative group member. If school-aged children see the adult as someone who is absolutely fair, has a sense of humor, is reasonable, and who really cares about the needs and feelings of the children, they will be more willing to comply with that adult's wishes.

Why Do Early School-Agers Resist Going to Child Care?

Child care workers can especially be intimated by school-aged children who have not yet developed inner control. Often, the youngest and least experienced workers are assigned to care for school-aged children who attend the facility only during the early morning and late afternoon hours, summers, and holidays. After school, these children can be exhausted from long hours of sitting in hard desks, feeling pressured to meet adult expectations. During summers and holidays they may envy friends who are at home or away on vacation. They may come into the child care setting with resentment for having to be in a "day care for babies." They may especially feel frustration over being expected to play quietly with blocks and puzzles they have outgrown in a room filled with all the trappings of a preschool.

In a typical scenario, school-aged children begin to behave a bit wildly. Perhaps they start to throw pine cones at each other on the playground or stir their graham crackers into their milk, giggling and making a disgusting mush. Adults may respond in an abrasive and humorless attempt to stop this silly behavior. The children, feeling their oats, become sassy or perhaps stop the behaviors just long enough for the adult to turn her back for a moment. The angrier the adult becomes, the less compliant and cooperative the children will be. This situation can cause the adult to feel frighteningly out of control or helpless, a phenomenon that has an effect on older children similar to sharks smelling blood. Effective adults are able to model inner control, even in difficult situations.

Early school-aged children will feel more cooperative about rules they have helped to create. Family council or class meetings provide an opportunity for school-aged children to think about potential rules and to give their own opinions. If class meetings are run democratically, with real input from the children, then the children can begin to see rules not as inconveniences capriciously imposed by adults but as necessary protection for the rights and safety of all group members.

Why Do Early School-Agers Get So Upset About Fairness?

Early school-aged children are able to see discrepancies in adult behaviors and so do not gullibly accept everything adults say like younger children do. "But that's not fair" seems to be the battle cry of early school-aged children as they go about daily business. Even though they sometimes gleefully break rules themselves, they may become furious when it seems to them a rule is being enforced inconsistently—"But you didn't make Jerrod go back inside when he threw his book."

At this age, children's concrete operational perspective prohibits them from considering abstract extenuating circumstances that are important to adult decision makers. The school-aged child may not see it as fair when a child who is new to a setting is just given an explanation of rules while a child who is expected to know the rules is given a stiff penalty for the same offense. Adults must constantly examine their own biases to determine if there is any possibility that their treatment of the children is unequal.

Adults should be meticulous not only about their fairness but also about their appearance of fairness. If a situation seems unfair to a child, the adult may assist the child's understanding by giving a concrete explanation for the action taken—"When you were younger, you needed many changes to remember rules. Now that you're seven, you know that throwing books is not allowed. Jerrod is only five now, but when he is seven, he will have to stop playing too if he forgets the rule."

Why Do They Insist on Picking Their Own Clothes?

The early school years are an important period for children to develop their own identity. They develop a sense of personal identity by observing how others perceive them. They are especially sensitive to criticism or teasing about their appearance or clothing. Early school-agers also begin to worry about their status with other children. They assert their autonomy with parents by insisting on dressing like peers or heroes.

Since physical development hinges on the active physical involvement of children in their environment by climbing, jumping, painting, gluing, and so on, parents and teachers can encourage (or require) clothing that is comfortable, washable, and not physically or socially restrictive. It is impossible to be "ladylike" in a frilly, short dress while climbing a jungle gym, and it is dangerous to climb the jungle gym in heavy, slick cowboy boots. Whatever steps adults take, it is essential to remember how desperately children want to belong, to fit in, and to be viewed as special by their friends.

School-aged children want to dress like their friends and their role models. (Photograph provided courtesy of CHILDREN AT RISK.)

How Can We Help Early School-Agers Become Productive?

Erikson (1963) identified the emotional crisis for school-aged children as one of **industry** (being productive) versus **inferiority** (feeling incapable). One of the enjoyable characteristics of school-aged children is their ability to function independently. Younger children need direction and help to do new things. School-aged children have the capacity to think of their own projects, to gather the needed materials, and then to work eagerly. They make miscalculations, messes, and mistakes, but they take great delight in having built their own crooked airplane or art object. Unfortunately, if they receive criticism instead of encouragement for their efforts and accomplishments, they may develop feelings of inferiority ("I'm no good," "Everything I try fails," "My ideas are stupid") and may be discouraged from trying new things.

Adults should not compare children's work to adult standards. One child's cookies may turn out tough and strangely shaped, but who cares? The purpose of the activity is for children to experience and learn from the process. The only importance of the activity outcome is that it makes children feel the pride of accomplishment.

How Can We Support the Early School-Ager's Self-Esteem?

The big, wide world begins to have tremendous impact on the school-aged child. Once she can read, whole new avenues of information are opened. She may see toothpaste ads on television and worry that her teeth have plaque monsters chomping away, or see billboards about fire safety and worry that she will burn up in her bed at night. It is not unusual for school-aged children

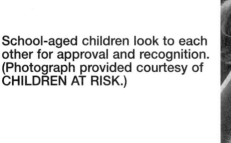

School-aged children look to each other for approval and recognition. (Photograph provided courtesy of CHILDREN AT RISK.)

to experience nightmares or develop irrational fears—"I'm not going to eat that chicken noodle soup because it has mushrooms, and they might be the poison kind that'll make you die."

Older School-Agers (9–12 Years)

Why Do Older School-Aged Children Argue So Much?

As early school-agers become **concrete operational** (at about seven), they spend more time thinking about the things and events in their world. Preschoolers are just barely able to manage thinking through processes or mentally manipulating symbols that represent real objects or events, but by eight or nine, school-agers are usually able to manage manipulating thoughts about entire concrete processes. This enables them to mentally replay an event to evaluate it carefully and logically. Gradually they begin to detect inconsistencies and gaps in logic. For example, an eleven-year-old is likely to say, "Why do I have to wear my bicycle helmet?" A lot more people have accidents riding in cars, and they don't have to wear helmets. Besides, if a car ran over my stomach, I'd be squashed anyway and a helmet wouldn't help." Most children will be adolescents or young adults before they can effectively manipulate abstract ideas and symbols, so they are not yet able to evaluate complex situations. Eleven- and twelve-year-olds may look very mature physically, but emotionally and intellectually, they still need a great deal of adult guidance and attention.

School-agers begin to focus their attention on gender roles and expectations. They may giggle around the opposite sex, pester them, chase them, or avoid them like the plague. (Photograph provided courtesy of CHILDREN AT RISK.)

Older school-aged children love to talk and listen to each other. Younger children are more inclined to play together in a physically active way, using language as a supplement to running, jumping, climbing, and playing make-believe games. School-aged children still enjoy active play but will sit under a tree or get on the telephone and talk excitedly for long periods about themselves, school events, and authority figures. They have discovered there really is no Santa Claus, and are beginning to realize grown-ups are not omnipotent deities but simply human beings who can make mistakes. When talking privately with a trusted friend or group of age-mates, school-agers may give an earful of complaints about parents, teachers, and siblings.

How Can I Get Older School-Agers to Trust and Respect Me?

Older school-aged children can be delightful conversationalists. They will listen attentively and respond appropriately in conversations that hold their attention. They can also build new, more mature bonds of affection and loyalty to adults who are willing to listen to them and treat them fairly and respectfully. Older school-aged children are especially sensitive to being "talked down to" by adults. School places new pressures on them. They are expected to assume a higher level of responsibility for their behavior and schoolwork. They will especially appreciate adults who will really listen to their thoughts and feelings in an open-minded, nonjudgmental manner.

Why Do Older School-Agers Try So Hard to Be "Popular"?

School-aged children have a powerful urge to belong to a peer group. They sometimes make up their own clubs or cliques with some semblance of rules and rituals or even special taboos or requirements in clothing. Younger children may be oblivious to clothing—they wear whatever their parents buy for them, or they may have picky, but individual tastes in clothing. School-aged

As school-aged children become adolescents, school-agers often go through periods of moodiness and insecurity as they cope with their changing bodies and increasing need for peer acceptance. (Photograph courtesy of CHILDREN AT RISK.)

children become very concerned about wearing clothing their friends approve. Even first and second graders today seem to know the popular (and unpopular) brand names for blue jeans and sneakers as well as for dolls and bicycles.

The fact that mom, dad, or teacher prefer a certain style of clothing, shoes, or haircut may mean that the children automatically prefer something else. This tendency to dress for peers gradually increases but does not reach a climactic peak until adolescence. Perhaps some entrepreneur will ease the discomfort parents feel by selling buttons for children to wear that say, "My parents are not responsible for the way I look, I dressed myself."

Adults should first help children feel secure, valued, and accepted, because self-confidence and self-esteem assist children in resisting inappropriate peer pressure. Adults can also help children keep material possessions in a proper perspective by respecting the children's anxiety about peer approval, but also by de-emphasizing the value of objects. They can strengthen children's character by focusing attention on valuing people for their character rather than for their expensive clothing or toys.

Why Do Older School-Aged Children Love Pranks and Jokes?

Older school-aged children are becoming more adept at controlling their impulses. Although they may lapse from time to time into less mature behavior, throwing a tantrum or pouting, they are finally able to wait for a while even though they are bored, hungry, or need to go to the bathroom. As they spend more time conforming to the social and behavioral expectations of authority figures and peers, they eagerly take advantage of opportunities where they feel safe being silly and whimsical. For example, when the teacher walks out of the room for a moment, a child might say, "Hey, wouldn't it be funny to pour this paint into the fish tank and then all the fish would turn purple?" Then, they laugh uproariously and (we hope) resist the urge to really do it. Preschool-aged children are not quite as able to weigh consequences and resist temptations. For toddlers, thinking is doing. Preschoolers can barely resist following their impulses. As children move toward adolescence, they should be developing the ability to persist toward longer-term goals. At this stage, they should not be so easily tempted by instant gratification that keeps them from accomplishing a specific task or project.

How Can We Support Older School-Agers' Self-Esteem?

As children leave early childhood and move toward adolescence, life becomes complicated and stressful. Their bodies seem to take on a life of their own, growing adult genitalia often far too quickly or far too slowly to suit the confused and disoriented owner of the body. We begin to see little children walking around in very adult-looking bodies, and suddenly we expect them to act like a grown-up. Just as in toddlerhood, two-year-olds were torn between the security of infancy and the allure of childhood, preadolescents are likely to waver in their feelings about whether

Behaving in a productive and responsible manner fosters feelings of self-worth.

As school-aged children become adolescents, it is critical for them to have opportunities to practice their prosocial skills in settings where they are really needed and appreciated. They can establish the lifelong habit of giving back to their community by organizing food drives, planning school projects, tutoring other children, and other such activities. (Photograph provided courtesy of CHILDREN AT RISK.)

to be a little kid or a teenager. One minute the child is sitting on a curb crying over a skinned knee and the next she is choosing her favorite color of lipstick.

Adults must provide a great deal of support, affection, and patience during these years so that school-agers' self-esteem and confidence stay intact. Babies, toddlers, and preschoolers get many hugs because they are little and cute. Adolescents and adults get romantic hugs from the opposite sex. Older school-agers are at an awkward stage and, especially young boys, may be left out of shows of affection altogether. Everybody needs an **appropriate** (nonexploitive) hug now and then to feel valued and special, and there are many excellent ways other than hugs to express affection. A big smile, sincere recognition, and listening all let the child know we care (American Academy of Pediatrics, 1995; Charlesworth, 1996; Gartrell, 1998; Gronlund, 1997; Meece, 1997; Steinberg, 1995).

Practical Application/Discussion

"I'm Never Gonna 'Vite You to My Birth'ay!"

Sarah and Lupita, both five-year-olds, have claimed a shady spot under a thick magnolia tree on the playground. It is their favorite place to play. They have staunchly defended their little territory against small bands of marauding playmates by insisting, "You can't play. We got here first. This is our house."

Although their teacher does not allow toys from home in the classroom, they have been allowed to bring their dolls outside with them for their outdoor play period. Sarah has a well-worn Raggedy Ann doll and Lupita has a new, soft plastic baby doll in a pink blanket that looks just like a newborn baby.

They have rocked their dolls to sleep and carefully placed them beside the trunk of the tree while they scurried around gathering leaves and sticks to outline a boundary for their playhouse. Sarah finds a large stick and announces that it is the door, "Nobody can come in unless they open this door. Tick tock. Now it's all locked up."

Robby, also five, has been watching and listening to the girls as he climbed and jumped off a climbing structure "fort" nearby. He cannot resist Sarah's challenge. "I can too get in," he taunts as he dances around the line of leaves and sticks that is the pretend wall of the girls' playhouse. He pokes his foot over the line and darts just out of their reach as he sticks his tongue out, laughing and chanting, "Nanny, nanny, boo, boo!"

Sarah chases and yells at Robby while Lupita furiously mends the pretend wall. Robby retreats to the top of the climbing structure, insisting, "Uh, huh! I could get in there. It's not really your house."

Lupita plants her feet firmly in the grass and stares viciously at Robby, guarding hearth and home, while Sarah runs to tell on Robby.

Robby, of course, loses all interest in Lupita's mean look. He is perched behind a post at the top of the fort watching carefully to see what his teacher, Miss Gresham, will do next.

Miss Gresham bends down on one knee and listens intently as Sarah rants and raves about Robby's alleged offenses. Quietly, Miss Gresham says, "Did you tell Robby how you felt when he messed up your house? Would you like for me to come with you to talk to Robby?" Sarah takes Miss Gresham's hand and quickly leads the way back to the scene of the crime. Robby, meanwhile, is huddled on the fort hoping no one can see him. He forgets that Miss Gresham is tall enough to talk eye-to-eye with him at the highest part of the fort.

With a gentle and reassuring voice, Miss Gresham says, "Robby, let's talk with Lupita and Sarah. I think they're feeling very angry." Robby pauses for just a second, but Miss Gresham holds her hands out and says, "It's okay, Robby. Sometimes I make mistakes and people get mad at me too." Robby leans off the fort and Miss Gresham hoists him to the ground. She looks right in his eyes and pats him as she says, "Thanks, Robby." Then she assumes the role of objective referee as the girls tell Robby, in no uncertain terms, "Don't you break our house no more!"

Robby's lip quivers and a big tear begins to slide down his grimy face as he pulls back his shoulders and announces, "You ain't my best friend and I ain't never gonna 'vite you to my birth'ay party!"

Questions for Discussion

1. Identify characteristics and behaviors of Lupita, Sarah, and Robby that are typical of five-year-olds.

2. List all the reasons you can think of for Robby's interference with the girls' play. Why were the girls so angry?

3. Do you agree with Miss Gresham's handling of the problem? Explain. What would you have done differently?

4. What might have happened if Miss Gresham had responded to Robby with an angry voice and negative punishment?

Points to Remember

- Children have individual patterns and rates of development.

- Comparisons should never be used to label or stereotype a child.

- Newborn behaviors result almost exclusively from uncontrolled reflexes.

- Older babies and toddlers respond to physiological urges and impulses to practice motor skills and explore surroundings.

- Trust developed in infancy is a primary foundation for the development of healthy emotional attitudes.

- Learned helplessness develops in children who have no control over their environment.

- Infants need a balance between predictable routines and flexible responses.

- Babies will explore the environment best if they have a trusted adult for a "secure base."

- Cause-and-effect relationships become a focal point for toddler learning.

- Toddlers cannot understand or follow rules.

- Verbal and nonverbal communication should be honest, sincere, concrete, and extremely simple.

- Stranger and separation anxiety usually peak in young toddlers but the occurrence varies widely among children.

- Toddlers strive to achieve autonomy.

- Preschoolers develop the capacity to manipulate symbols, letting one object stand as a representation for another.

- Preschoolers gradually become more aware of their own interests and intentions.

- Physical force should be viewed only as a last resort when other reasonable steps to defend oneself have failed.

- Preschoolers can be helped to express strong emotions or feelings of anger.

- Some preschoolers become very cliquish as they decide who is or is not a friend.

- Preschoolers need encouragement to do things for themselves.

- Excessive feelings of guilt can cause withdrawal or rebellion.

- Make very few rules but make sure that children know and respect rules that are given.

- Preschoolers' views of themselves are affected by others around them.

- Early school-aged children develop an ability to replay events mentally to evaluate experiences carefully and logically.

- Inner control hinges on the early school-aged child wanting to be a cooperative and accepted group member.

- Early school-aged children are passionate about their perception of fairness.

- Older school-agers have a powerful urge to belong to a peer group and be well liked by friends.

- They are becoming more skilled in controlling impulses.

- Support, affection, acceptance, and patience help older school-aged children keep their self-esteem and confidence intact.

Related Readings

Growth and Development

Baillargeon, R. (1997). How do infants learn about the physical world? In E. N. Junn & C. Boyatzis (Eds.), *Annual editions: Child growth and development 97/98* (4th ed.). New York: McGraw-Hill. (Original work published in *Current Directions in Psychological Science,* October 1994)

> *Based on the pioneering work of Jean Piaget, researchers once assumed that infants lacked a sense of object permanence. René Baillargeon describes her well-known and ingenious research indicating that young infants do, in fact, possess more fundamental and elaborate knowledge about physical objects than once thought.*

Begley, S. (1997). The IQ puzzle. In E. N. Junn & C. Boyatzis (Eds.), *Annual editions: Child growth and development 97/98* (4th ed.). New York: McGraw-Hill. (Original work published in *Newsweek,* May 6, 1996)

> *Scores on intelligence tests have risen dramatically in many countries. Does this mean that children today are smarter than ever? Sharon Begley discusses the possible reasons for these gains—including the popularity of video games and cereal boxes with mazes and puzzles for children—and addresses the debate on whether IQ tests truly measure intelligence.*

Begley, S. (1997). Your child's brain. In K. M. Paciorek & J. H. Munro, *Annual editions: Early childhood education 97/98* (18th ed.). New York: McGraw-Hill. (Original work published in *Newsweek,* February 19, 1996)

> *This article discusses recent research that suggests the human brain is sensitive to experiences very early in life, which influence brain development for skill in language, music, math, and other learning. Sharon Begley describes "learning windows" when children may be most influenced by environmental stimulation.*

Behrman (Ed.), *The future of children: Long-term outcomes of early childhood programs* (Vol. 5, No. 3). Los Altos, CA: Center for the Future of Children.

Berk, L. E. (1997). Vygotsky's theory: The importance of make-believe play. In E. N. Junn & C. Boyatzis (Eds.), *Annual editions: Child growth and development 97/98* (4th ed.). New York: McGraw-Hill. (Original work published in *Young Children,* November 1994)

> *This article describes the view of Lev Vygotsky, a Russian psychologist who emphasizes the importance of pretend play as a forum for learning. In particular, children learn through guidance from parents and teachers that creates a scaffold for experiences, allowing youngsters to take over more responsibility as their skills increase.*

Bornstein, M. H., & Lamb, M. (1992). *Development in infancy: An introduction* (3d ed.). New York: McGraw-Hill.

> *This overview of infant development is intended for experienced infant and child development professionals who want more information about research issues related to infant development.*

Campos, J. J., Bertenthal, B. I., & Kermoian, R. (1997). Early experience and emotional development: The emergence of wariness of heights. In E. N. Junn & C. Boyatzis (Eds.), *Annual editions: Child growth and development 97/98* (4th ed.). New York: McGraw-Hill. (Original work published in *Psychological Science,* January 1992)

> *How do we become afraid of heights? Are we born with the fear, or do we learn it through life experiences? This article by prominent researchers describes careful experiments designed to determine whether babies are born with a fear of heights or if they acquire it only after learning to crawl and the experience of moving around in the world.*

Eddowes, E. A., & Ralph, K. S. (1998). *Interactions for development and learning: Birth through eight years.* Upper Saddle River, NJ: Merrill Education/Prentice-Hall.

> *This book emphasizes the importance of different types of interaction for supporting early development and learning. Research is described showing the importance of appropriate interactions between an adult and child, between a child and older and younger peers, or between a child and an object.*

Elkind, D. (1996, May). Early childhood education: What should we expect? *Principal, 7*(55), 11–13.

French, L. (1996). "I told you all about it, so don't tell me you don't know . . ." *Young Children, 5*(2) 17–20.

> *A developmental psychologist and mother of young children discusses the development of the ability of two-year-olds to comprehend information from language alone. She also explains the negative effects of developmentally inappropriate teaching when inappropriate language expectations are made of children.*

Gibbs, N. (1997). The EQ factor. In E. N. Junn & C. Boyatzis (Eds.), *Annual editions: Child growth and development 97/98* (4th ed.). New York: McGraw-Hill. (Original work published in *Time,* October 2, 1995)

> *Recent brain research suggests that emotions, not the traditional IQ rating, may be the true measure of human intelligence. This article examines this latest trend in the assessment of human ability to cope successfully with challenges.*

Howard, V., Williams, B. F., Port, P. D., & Lepper, C. (1997). Very young children with special needs: A formative approach for the 21st century. In E. N. Junn & C. Boyatzis (Eds.), *Annual editions: Child growth and development 98/98* (4th ed.). New York: McGraw-Hill.

Using a formative, holistic, family-centered approach, it provides comprehensive coverage of normal childhood development—from birth to age six—and a description of over fifty of the most common medical conditions that early childhood educators should understand before working with families and professionals in other fields.

Kantrowitz, B., & Wingert, P. (1997). How kids learn. In E. N. Junn & C. Boyatzis (Eds.), _Annual editions: Child growth and development 97/98_ (4th ed.). New York: McGraw-Hill. (Original work published in _Newsweek_, April 17, 1989)

Between the years of five and eight, children absorb an enormous amount of information. New research indicates that learning is best facilitated when active hands-on exploration, cooperation, and problem solving are emphasized over more traditional forms of passive rote learning of information. Implications for teachers and parents are discussed.

Leong, D., & Bodrova, E. (1996). _Tools of the mind: A Vygotskian approach to early childhood education._ Upper Saddle River, NJ: Merrill Education/Prentice-Hall.

The authors' objective is to enable future teachers to arm young children with the mental tools necessary for learning. The authors view mental tools as a cycle in which ideas are (1) learned from others, (2) modified and changed, and (3) passed back and on to others.

Nash, J. M. (1997, February 3). Fertile minds: From birth, a baby's brain cells proliferate wildly, making connections that may shape a lifetime of experience. _TIME Magazine, 149_(5).

Newberger, J. J. (1997, May). New brain development research—A wonderful window of opportunity to build public support for early childhood education! _Young Children, 52_(4), 4–9.

Peterson, R. W. (1994, April). School readiness considered from a neuro-cognitive perspective. _Early Education and Development, 5_(2), 120–140.

Raikes, H. (1996). A secure base for babies: Applying attachment concepts to the infant care setting. _Young Children, 51_(5), 59–67.

This article explains the basic principles of attachment theory and shows how these principles can be used in infant programs.

Sameroff, A., & McDonough, S. C. (1997). Educational implications of developmental transitions: Revisiting the 5- to 7-year shift. In K. M. Paciorek & J. H. Munro, *Annual editions: Early childhood education 97/98* (18th ed.). New York: McGraw-Hill. (Original work published in *Phi Delta Kappan*, November 1994)

The years between five and seven mark an important milestone in the lives of young children. Educators who have a clear understanding of child development are able to assist children as they make a smooth transition into the primary grades. The onset of this developmental shift depends on the environment, culture, previous school experiences, and the child's unique characteristics.

Schiller, P. (1997, September–October). Brain development research: Support and challenges. *Child Care Information Exchange, 117,* 6–10.

Thorne, B. (1997). Girls and boys together but mostly apart. In E. N. Junn & C. Boyatzis (Eds.), *Annual editions: Child growth and development 97/98* (4th ed.). New York: McGraw-Hill. (Original work published in *GenderPlay: Girls and Boys in School,* Rutgers University Press, 1993)

Gender segregation—boys playing with boys, girls with girls—is very common during the elementary school years. How might this affect boys' and girls' social and interpersonal development? Barrie Thorne describes how not only peers but teachers as well contribute to gender segregation.

U.S. Department of Education. (1997, Spring). What new research on the brain tells us about our youngest children: Summary on the White House Conference on Early Childhood. *Dimensions of Early Childhood, 25*(2).

Maturity and practice are needed for children to learn what adults expect of them.

Chapter 7

Understanding the Reasons for Problem Behavior

Objectives

This chapter will assist you in

- Defining characteristics of inappropriate behavior

- Articulating subjective perceptions of behavior

- Recognizing children's behavioral limitations based on normal stages of moral development

- Listing underlying causes of problem behavior

- Examining causes of misbehavior

Defining Problem Behavior

The process by which children learn acceptable behavior is called socialization. Infants have no comprehension of proper or improper behavior. They would have no ability to inhibit their impulses even if they knew what was expected. Gradually over the first few years of life, however, children develop self-control and learn how to get along with others and how to follow the accepted rules of their family and community. Before self-control develops, children are totally impulsive in following their feelings and desires. They act like children (of course), making mistakes, acting on impulse, and stubbornly resisting external control—actions we consider to be problem behaviors. Chapter 1 identified three specific categories of problem behavior and recommended interrupting or redirecting any child behavior that:

- Infringed unfairly on the rights of others

- Presented a clear risk of harm to the child or anyone else

- Resulted in the mishandling of objects or living things

Those three guidelines were used for defining basic ground rules for children—Be kind! Be safe! Be neat! Next, we need to ask ourselves why children might behave in an unkind, unsafe, or careless manner. *Misbehavior, problem behavior,* and *inappropriate behavior* are used interchangeably, and all three terms tend to be misinterpreted as meaning naughtiness and mischief. Many inappropriate behaviors, however, are not at all mischievous in intent. A child may not even realize that a specific behavior will be viewed as "naughty" by adults. Positive child guidance requires that adults gauge their reaction to misbehaviors by looking at the child's level of understanding, the severity and frequency of the behavior, and possible underlying causes.

A baby who has innocently climbed on top of a coffee table must be dealt with differently than a five-year-old who knowingly uses the couch as if it were a trampoline—although both must be redirected, since the behaviors present a clear risk of harm to the children and involve the mishandling of objects in the environment. To get positive results, we must have reasonable expectations for children at various ages and recognize whether or not they can really be expected to control their actions in particularly difficult or tempting situations.

We sometimes fail to see the world from the child's point of view. (Photograph provided courtesy of CHILDREN AT RISK.)

In many cases, it is far more effective to change the situation than to try to stop a child's behavior. By removing the baby from the coffee table and taking him to a safe piece of play equipment designed for climbing, we can change an inappropriate behavior to an appropriate behavior (even though the child may not yet recognize any difference in the two situations). We assume that the five-year-old knows the difference between a living-room sofa and a trampoline, so our emphasis is on giving the child a clear understanding of pertinent facts, choices, and consequences. For example, we might say, "The couch is not for jumping. If you want to jump, you may jump outside on the soft grass." If the action continued, we should give the child our close, undivided attention at eye level and add in an assertive but sincere tone, "I know jumping on the couch is fun, but it could break the couch, or you could fall on something hard or sharp in here. If you jump on the couch again, then you will not be allowed to play in the living room for the rest of the afternoon." Most importantly, we have to follow through and see that what we say will happen, actually happens.

Assessing the appropriateness of any individual child's behavior requires us to step into her shoes and see the world from her perspective—it requires accurate insight and wise judgment. We are prone, sometimes quickly and flippantly, to label actions that are inconvenient, annoying, or embarrassing to us at the moment as misbehavior, regardless of reasons the child might have for behaving in such a manner.

Children are confused when they do not expect a negative reaction from us and when they cannot make sense of our logic in requiring different behaviors in different situations. They are bewildered when a behavior is praised in one setting but reprimanded in a situation they do not recognize as being very different. Mrs. Perez was exasperated with three of her toddlers who persisted in climbing up on the picnic table in the toddler playground. She had not realized that the wood of the picnic table looked exactly like the wood of the climbing structure nearby. Although the adults were quite clear about the differences between a climbing structure "fort" and a picnic table, a closer look would reveal that both objects are just boards nailed together. Young children's inexperience and naiveté are just a couple of the many reasons they behave in ways that adults perceive as naughty.

Three-year-old Allison Jones's mother opened her dishwasher one morning to discover a pile of dirty towels stuffed where dishes ought to be. Mrs. Jones yelled, "Who put these towels in the dishwasher?" The look of guilt on Allison's face instantly gave her away as the culprit. Although Mrs. Jones asked repeatedly, "Why did you do this? What would possess you to do such a silly thing?," Allison just hung her head and mumbled, "I dunno."

Mrs. Jones never realized Allison intended to surprise her mother by cleaning the bathroom—her intentions were good, but she was just a little bit confused about which "washing machine" one used to wash dirty towels. Allison's behavior was inappropriate (towels should not be put in the dishwasher) but she certainly was not misbehaving. Her behavior did not deserve a reprimand but rather some gentle redirection. An excellent adult response would be for her mother to say, "Thank you so much for wanting to help. Come with me and I'll show you the right place to put dirty clothes."

What Do We Mean by Functional and Dysfunctional Behaviors?

When children evidence a compulsive and chronic pattern of very inappropriate or self-destructive behavior, the behavior can be termed **dysfunctional.** On the other hand, **functional**

The nurtured child is helped to become a responsible adult.

behaviors are various appropriate actions that serve some productive or positive function in a child's life. Functional behaviors help the child get her needs met. Dysfunctional behaviors produce a negative reaction that may be opposite to the outcome desired by the child. The child's strategies for coping and for interacting with others simply do not work, causing the child increasing stress and unhappiness and creating a vicious cycle. A lonely child lacking in social skills may relentlessly tease other children to get their attention, but the teasing is dysfunctional because it does not attract friends; instead it causes the child to be disliked. Consequently the child becomes more isolated and lonely and even more trapped in the existing cycle of dysfunctional behavior.

What Is the Adult-Centered Definition of Misbehavior?

Adult-centered definitions of misbehavior focus on the effect a child's behavior has on the adult. Individual actions are evaluated according to the seriousness of their impact on things the adult cares about as well as the adult's emotional state or mood. If a child spills his juice in the grass during a picnic, the adult may hardly notice, since nothing has to be cleaned up. If the same child spills juice on the kitchen floor, the adult may be annoyed and may reprimand the child. If, however, the spill is grape juice on brand new, light-colored dining room carpeting, the adult may be very angry and punish or spank the child.

The child learns that her behaviors are not always met with a consistent or predictable adult reaction. Children may learn that they can "get away with" inappropriate behaviors when their caregiver is in a relaxed and playful mood. They may also perceive that nothing they do makes any difference when the adult is in a bad mood. They may believe that they will get in trouble regardless of what they do or do not do. (Remember the definition of learned helplessness? We never want children to think they have no control over their circumstances—that things just happen to them randomly.)

Since adult-centered definitions of misbehavior focus only on the adult's needs and desires, desirable behaviors are perceived to be actions that are convenient and desirable to the adult. Being quiet, staying out of the way, and performing the role of a cute (but undemanding) little kid on cue may be seen as the hallmarks of a "good" child. Crying, squealing with joy, being frightened, or being a chatterbox may be perceived as naughty misbehaviors if they are annoying, embarrassing, or inconvenient for the adult.

What Is the Child-Centered Definition of Misbehavior?

In contrast, a child-centered definition of misbehavior focuses on the ability level, motives, and long-term well-being of the child in evaluating the appropriateness or inappropriateness of actions. If an action is wrong or inappropriate, it is judged to be wrong because it infringes on the rights of others, is unsafe, or is unnecessarily damaging to the environment—not because the action is a bother or because the adult happens to be in an intolerant mood. Defining behaviors this way brings about consistency and a sense of fairness. Children learn to be responsible for the consequences of their own actions. They learn that there is a direct relationship between their actions and the reaction they receive from authority figures. (Remember, no learned helplessness, please.)

Children explore their world because they want to learn, not because they want to be naughty.

By taking into consideration the ages and developmental stages of children, adults can recognize that exploring or "getting into things" is normal and beneficial learning behavior for a baby or toddler—not misbehavior. It is the adult's responsibility to baby-proof the environment so that everything accessible to the baby is safe and appropriate. If the baby gets into something inappropriate, the baby is simply moved to an area that is safe for exploration.

Children who are allowed to become actively involved in daily processes will undoubtedly make mistakes more often than children who are encouraged to stand by passively while things are done for them. Allowing young children to help with food preparation, for example, may be messy and time-consuming. It is quicker and easier for the adult to complete such tasks alone, but the confidence and skill development children gain from such experiences are well worth the extra effort. Dropping an egg or inadvertently spilling flour are not seen as mischief from the child-centered perspective but rather as important opportunities for children to learn responsibility and independence. Instead of being scolded for making a mess, the child is taught how to accomplish daily tasks successfully and how to clean up after herself.

Stages of Moral Development in Young Children

A critical priority for parents, schools, communities, even entire countries, is the moral development of their children and future citizens. Morality is the ability to distinguish right from wrong and to act accordingly. Moral development is the process by which human beings learn to monitor their own actions and to decide whether a tempting behavior is a "good" or "bad" thing to do and then to inhibit inappropriate impulses. In other words, morally developed people are able to stop themselves from doing things they know are wrong.

Although the guidance children receive early in life is essential to their moral development, moral behavior is not exclusively a concern of early childhood. Adults who are quick to respond harshly to a young child's misbehavior may forget their own difficulty in inhibiting the inappropriate impulses they have in their own daily life. Even adults with well-developed morals experience difficulty resisting the temptation to gossip, smoke cigarettes, indulge in foods that are bad for them, or tell "little white lies" to get out of tight spots. Remember that one of the key avenues for early childhood learning is imitation. It is essential for adult caregivers consciously to set the best possible example in their day-to-day actions of integrity and strong moral character (Grusec, Kuczynski, Rushton, & Simutis, 1979; Toner, Parke, & Yussen, 1978; Toner & Potts, 1981).

As children observe adult behaviors and experience the cause-and-effect sequences that are a part of interacting with others, they internalize (adopt as their own) the character attributes and ethical standards of the important role models in their lives. Attachment, love, and respect for an adult trigger the child's internalization of that adult's values. When a child has internalized the standards of her adult role models, she begins to experience the emotional component of morality—**moral affect** (the feelings associated with a guilty or clear conscience). Having moral affect means that when she behaves in a way that she knows to be wrong, she has feelings of guilt and shame. When she behaves properly, she feels pride. Moral affect serves as an internal regulator that guides one toward appropriate behavior and away from misbehavior.

Feelings of guilt play a role in regulating moral behavior, but it is not helpful to push guilt on a child by saying such things as, "Aren't you ashamed of yourself, you naughty girl?" Forcing guilt on a young child may actually harden her emotionally and delay her development of moral affect. Guilt that comes from inside us is always more meaningful than guilt imposed on us by someone else. Two specific child-rearing practices are known to help children internalize values and prosocial moral judgment. They are:

- Nurturing and affectionate caregiver behavior

- Consistency in explaining reasons for rules and commands

Adults help children develop moral behavior by being loving and gentle and by putting into words the rationales for imperatives. Instead of just saying, for example, "Don't touch that!," they say, "Please use a different crayon because that one belongs to someone else" (Eisenberg-Berg, 1979).

Another important component of moral development is **moral reasoning** (the thinking processes that guide people in deciding what is or is not moral behavior). The way children think about right and wrong changes dramatically as their intellectual capacity matures (Piaget, 1952). Children younger than seven-years-old tend to focus on the concrete consequences of actions rather than on the abstract motivations or intentions behind them. As they get older and their moral capacity increases, they are better able to take into consideration complicated rationales for various actions (Ferguson & Rule, 1982).

> *We must see childhood as a stage of life, not just the anteroom to life.*
>
> David Elkind (1981)

How Do Young Children Learn Right from Wrong?

Sarah, a four-year-old, was told that Jimmy broke four plates and three glasses while trying to help, and Annie broke one cookie jar lid while trying to steal cookies. She insisted that Jimmy was naughtier and deserves more punishment than Annie. Sarah has focused on the idea that breaking a lot of dishes is worse than breaking one dish. The child is not yet able to think about all aspects of the dilemmas presented or to consider such things as motive. Piaget (1952) studied children's sense of right and wrong through a series of interviews in which he confronted children of various ages with moral problems like the one described above. He found that young children's responses contrasted sharply with the responses of older children. The moral reasoning of young children tends to be simplistic and limited to enforcing the letter of the law (or rule) rather than interpreting the spirit or intent of the law.

Kohlberg (1969; 1976) described the stages through which human beings develop moral reasoning. His three levels and six stages are listed below:

Level One—Preconventional Morality

- **Stage One**

   One obeys rules only to avoid punishment and to gain rewards.

For example, a toddler examining an electric outlet may reach for it, then look up at the adult while saying, "No, no. No touch." The toddler will probably resist the urge to touch the outlet only if the adult appears attentive and ready to enforce the rule.

- **Stage Two**

   One bargains to get one's needs met. Prosocial behaviors are intended to bring about favors from others.

For example, "If you let me ride the tricycle, I'll be your best friend."

Level Two—Conventional Morality

- **Stage Three**

   There is an emphasis on gaining approval from others by being nice, because the focus is on being a "good girl" or a "good boy" to get praise and approval.

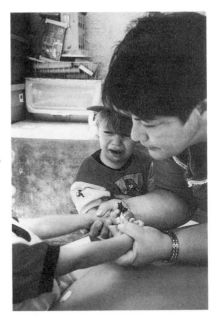

Young children lack the self-control necessary to consistently control their impulses.

For example, when an adult tells one child to taste just a bite of green beans, another child nearby may hurriedly stuff her mouth full of beans, saying, "See me? I'm eating my vegetables!"

- **Stage Four**

  The focus is on "law and order." At this stage, one is concerned that everyone do his duty and follow the letter of the law. It is only okay to break a rule if everyone else is doing it.

For example, school-aged children become very indignant when rules are broken. They may resent the fact that a child suffering from diabetes is given a candy bar by the teacher. Never mind that the child is ill; it just is not right.

Level Three—Postconventional Morality

- **Stage Five**

  At this stage, correct behavior is defined in terms of individual rights according to widely held moral beliefs of society.

For example, a teacher at this level would recognize that the urgent health need of a diabetic child is more important than usual rules about candy at school that are normally fair and reasonable. Protecting the health of a child is more valued in this situation than following a rule.

> - **Stage Six**
>
>   *One decides whether a behavior is moral or not based on a personal decision of conscience in accordance with personal ethical principles that are logical, consistent, and universal.*

For example, a child care center director might risk the solvency of her business by testifying in accordance with her conscience in a child abuse case against a powerful and popular community member.

One distinct characteristic of more advanced levels of moral reasoning is one's ability to consider motivation and intention when evaluating the outcome of a behavior. Young children rarely achieve this, but adult caregivers must achieve this if they wish to be effective in positive child guidance. Adults are also functioning at a low level of moral development when they blindly enforce rules just because rules are rules—regardless of circumstances, motives, or effects on individual children. Adults are also functioning at a very low level of moral behavior if they enforce rules only when it is convenient or in their own best interest to do so. Morally mature adults focus on the intents and motives of children, not on the outcomes of their behaviors. If, for example, Alicia tries to knock someone off of the jungle gym but nobody gets hurt, and Albert is being silly and accidentally knocks someone off who is hurt badly, the morally mature adult will recognize that Alicia's behavior was more inappropriate than Albert's.

"Are my expectations reasonable?" "Does the child really understand what I expect?"

Underlying Causes of Problem Behavior

Lying on a couch and watching cartoons for hours on end is not a desirable use of a child's time. In order to redirect the behavior, an adult may need to think through any potential reasons the child is not involved in healthier, more active play. Is the child reinforced for being quiet and passive? Does the adult respond negatively to active play that is sometimes messy or noisy? Are interesting toys and challenging play equipment accessible to the child? Does the child need someone to play with? Adults must always take into account possible reasons for undesirable behavior in order to have a chance at changing the situation and preventing the behavior from happening. In child guidance, as in health care, the best cure is always prevention! (See Appendix D for additional resources.)

Inappropriate Expectations

Sometimes children's misbehavior is the direct result of inappropriate expectations on the part of adults. We expect children to be able to do things that they simply are not capable of doing.

Helena and Ray are sitting in the pediatrician's waiting room with their eighteen-month-old son, Billy. The little boy is dressed in his very best clothes with shiny black shoes and a tiny bow tie. He is sitting on his dad's knee looking like a fashion model for baby clothes. Billy sits silently for a while, then looks around at the room and at his mom and dad who are preoccupied in their discussion of the questions they want to ask Billy's doctor.

After a few more minutes of sitting, Billy points to a large aquarium with huge tropical fish swimming around and says, "Yook!" (his word for look). After a few seconds, he gestures insistently and looks at his mother, repeating, "Yook, wha' dis?" (What's this?). Helena straightens Billy's tie and says, "Yes, they're fish. Shhh, be still now. You'll get your clothes all messed up."

Billy stares at the aquarium a few seconds longer, then scrambles to get down off his dad's lap. His dad pulls him back in his lap and says firmly, "Those aren't for you to touch. You need to stay here and sit still. If you get down, you'll break something for sure." Billy begins to whine and rub his eyes with his fist, periodically struggling to get down from his dad's lap. His mother pulls a bottle out of her diaper bag and offers it to Billy, but he throws the bottle on the floor and begins kicking and crying loudly.

As the nurse comes in to announce that the doctor is ready to see Billy, Helena and Ray seem to be at their wit's end. With great frustration in her voice, Helena says, "Why does he act like this? What are you supposed to do when they get like this? He's just impossible to deal with sometimes."

Little can be done to resolve the situation at this point in time except to remove Billy from the setting and wait for him to wind down. A great deal, however, could have been done to prevent the situation. If Helena and Ray had known, in advance, more about what to expect from a toddler, they might have anticipated that he really could not sit still for thirty minutes to an hour. Perhaps they could have brought one of his favorite toys or books with them, or they could have distracted him by playing peek-a-boo or by allowing him to scribble on a notepad from his mother's purse.

Or perhaps his dad could have followed up on his interest in the aquarium by supervising him closely and talking with him about the fishes as he looked at and touched the aquarium.

Misunderstanding Expectations

Sometimes children misunderstand what is expected of them:

> *Miss Jean, a preschool teacher, was dismayed to discover that her preschoolers had left the bathroom in a mess. Water was all over the floor and paper towels were everywhere except in the trash can. She turned to three-year-old Misha and said, "I'm going to go get a mop. Can you please put all of the paper towels into the trash can, where they belong?"*
>
> *When Miss Jean returned with her mop, she found poor little Misha struggling to pull clean paper towels out of the dispenser and stuffing them by the handfuls into the trash can. In a pitiful voice, Misha said, "It too much, Teacher. It too much paper towels." Luckily, Miss Jean recognized that although the outcome of Misha's behavior was not the desired one, her intentions were good. Misha simply took her teacher's instructions literally when she said, "put all the paper towels into the trash can." Miss Jean had not specified "wet paper towels on the floor."*
>
> *Miss Jean thanked Misha warmly for trying to help and then proceeded to say matter-of-factly, "Let's put the wet, dirty paper towels in the trash can. The dry ones are good for us to use next time we wash."*

If Miss Jean had scolded Misha or snapped, "Now look what you've done, you silly thing," Misha might not have been so eager to cooperate the next time someone asked her to help.

Immature Self-Control

Sometimes it seems that children really want to abide by an adult's request, but somehow they just cannot seem to manage the self-control needed to accomplish what the adult expects.

> *Eloise provides child care for six children in her home. She is proud to be a registered family day home provider and is committed to being an early childhood educator, not just a babysitter. To help her children learn about science and nature, she has bought a furry baby guinea pig.*
>
> *The guinea pig caused a flurry of excitement on Monday morning as the children arrived for the day. Eloise sat by the cage with two of the toddlers on her lap and talked with the preschool-aged children about the new pet. While the guinea pig ran around in circles making high squealing sounds, the older boys decided that he should be named "Squeaky."*
>
> *Eloise explained that Squeaky would be frightened if people made too much noise or shook his cage. She also explained that although Squeaky was very gentle, he might be confused if he saw a finger sticking into his cage and think it was a carrot or something good to eat and try to nibble on it. The preschool-aged children talked excitedly about Squeaky and managed to keep their hands behind their backs or in their pockets so they did not forget about shaking the cage or sticking their fingers through the bars.*

> *Eloise left the room to help one of the toddlers use the toilet. Suddenly she heard a commotion with shrieks and squeals from the room with the guinea pig. In her absence, the children had gotten a bit too excited, and pushing and shoving in their eagerness to see Squeaky, the children had accidentally tipped the cage off the table, knocking the cage open. Squeaky was running around squealing, the children were running around shrieking, the toddlers were crying, and water and guinea pig food were spilled everywhere.*
>
> *Eloise quickly captured the terrified guinea pig and then, gently stroking the shaking Squeaky, said in a calm voice, "Listen boys and girls, can you hear the little sound Squeaky is making. He's very scared. Let's sing a quiet lullaby to Squeaky so he won't be frightened." Softly, the older children joined Eloise in singing "Rock-a-Bye-Baby" to little Squeaky. The toddlers watched wide-eyed. When everyone was calm and quiet, Eloise put Squeaky back into his cage and said, "We'll put Squeaky's cage in the storage room for a while so he can rest. After naptime, we'll get him out and watch him again."*

Eloise realized that the children had not maliciously intended to harm or frighten Squeaky; they simply were so excited that they could not manage the necessary self-control to deal with the situation successfully. Eloise felt confident that with enough time, patience, and practice, the children could eventually develop the self-control they needed to watch the guinea pig properly. She also knew that until that time, she needed to remove Squeaky, except during the times that she was able to supervise the children very closely as they watched him. Eloise recognized that reprimanding or punishing the children for their lack of self-control was not appropriate or helpful, since the children, at that point, were simply not yet capable of behaving in a more mature

Children's innate desire to explore every possibility around them stretches their learning, but also stretches adult patience!

or controlled way. Instead, she helped them identify with Squeaky's feelings and needs so they could understand why they needed to watch without touching. She also knew that it was better to change the environment temporarily rather than trying to change the children's behavior.

Gleeful Abandon, Group Contagion

Close your eyes for a minute and try to remember the exhilarated sensations you felt as a young child at a terrific birthday party, in a basement full of laughing cousins at a big family celebration, or maybe at a school Halloween carnival. Can you remember you and your friends or siblings going a little berserk? You knew you would get a stern lecture from your parents later, but it just felt so good you could not stop yourself. Whenever we have come to the end of our ropes with gleeful, goofy children, it may help for us to pause for a second and remember those magical moments in our own childhoods. I know I would love to feel that way again—totally uninhibited and free.

Tuesday mornings are always a little strange at the Elm Street Public Library. The sleepy little library comes to life as neighborhood children troop in for the children's story hour and other events scheduled especially for youngsters, such as movies and puppet shows.

Mrs. Asaad, the children's librarian, spends hours each week choosing just the right books and practicing reading them over and over to make sure her program is interesting and fun for the children. One Tuesday morning, Mrs. Asaad was helping an unusually young group of children get seated on the floor and ready for storytime. She positioned a row of the youngest children, a half-dozen particularly enthusiastic two-year-olds, right in front of her as she began singing a song about three little ducks.

One of the toddlers folded his hands under his armpits (to make duck wings) and helped her with the "quack, quack, quack" part of the song. The other toddlers caught on and began wagging their arms and quacking too, whereupon the first quacking toddler began giggling and falling over on the floor. Of course, all the other toddlers imitated by giggling and falling down and kicking their feet in the air.

Mrs. Asaad finished her song and good-naturedly helped Chris, the toddler who appeared to be the leader of the gang, to sit up. "Are you ready to hear a story about a little duck named Ping?" she asked. Chris vigorously shook his head yes. Of course all of the other toddlers began vigorously shaking their heads too.

Mrs. Asaad, with great suspense in her voice, began the story. "Once upon a time in a faraway land, there was a little duck named Ping." All of the children, even the toddlers, leaned forward to hear every word. When Mrs. Asaad, however, got to the very exciting part of the story where Ping gets a spank on the bottom for being late, the toddlers were overcome with their enthusiasm. Several began stamping their feet on the floor and Chris let out a squeal. As the other toddlers joined into the squealing, Chris began shaking his head so vigorously that his hair stood out all around his head.

Mrs. Asaad stood watching helplessly as the toddlers, and even some young threes, seemed possessed by this gleeful group contagion of head shaking and foot stamping. Suddenly, it dawned on Mrs. Asaad that the toddlers were more excited about the social presence of the other children than they were about her planned story. She realized that the story was simply not working at that particular time, so she laid down the book and stood up, saying, "Who can stretch high toward the sky? Great! Now, who can stamp your feet? Terrific! Let's sing 'Head and Shoulders, Knees and Toes.'"

After a few rousing choruses of active movement songs, Mrs. Asaad dismissed the group early, with an invitation to anyone who wanted to hear the end of the story about Ping to come sit with her. Some of the older children clustered around her (after the wild toddlers had left) and listened quietly to the end of the story.

Mrs. Asaad was very insightful to recognize that the toddlers' rowdy behavior was not a personal affront to her. Chris and the other twos were not naughty but just immensely happy. They were thrilled to be in a group of children at an exciting event, and did not have a clue about the life of a duck from a faraway land. Singing and moving as a group met their needs at this particular time, not hearing good literature.

Boredom

Boredom is one of the most predictable causes of misbehavior.

Neighborhood Nursery School was closed for the day, but staff members' children hung around, waiting for their parents' staff meeting to end. The nursery school staff took pride in their professionalism and high standards, and in order to reach their goals for quality, the staff met every Thursday afternoon after nursery school closed to discuss concerns.

Since most of the staff members were also parents, their own children had no alternative but to wait around while the parents met. Staff members took turns bringing a snack for the "staff kids" and attending to their problems and disagreements during meeting times, but it was clear that the staff kids dreaded the long Thursday afternoons. In early December, a meeting went on for hours as the staff planned special Christmas events. The staff kids had eaten their snack, colored pictures, and gone through stacks of puzzles and books. Shelley, five, and Jasmine, four and a half, were terribly bored and beginning to get a little silly. They were going through familiar books, making up ridiculous things for the characters to say and then laughing uproariously at themselves.

Next, they decided that they were "Harriet the Spy," so they sneaked around under tables and behind furniture, trying to get a peek at the adults without being seen, then retreating to the restroom to roll on the floor in laughter. The spies decided that the next time they forayed into the enemy territory (the staff meeting room), they would attack the grown-ups' coffee table. Ever so slowly Shelley crept under the refreshment table, while Jasmine crouched excitedly in the hall, watching with both hands clasped over her mouth to stifle her giggles. While the adults talked on, a little hand slowly made its way up to the box of sugar cubes by the coffee pot, and a strange sound, a muffled giggly sort of chortle, burst from Jasmine in the hall. The adults droned on, not noticing a thing.

The little hand (now grasping a whole handful of sugar cubes) slowly made its way back down the table. Unfortunately, it snagged the cord to the coffee pot on its way, and abruptly, the whole great adventurous fantasy came crashing down around little Shelley.

> *While Jasmine watched from the hall in horror, Shelley huddled under the table, her hands full of sugar cubes, surrounded by a dented coffee pot and huge puddles and rivulets of coffee. Her face flushed with embarrassment as the room full of astonished adults stared at her in disbelief—her mother looked the most shocked of all. Shelley was the kind of child no one ever expected to misbehave.*

Boredom, especially when coupled with lax supervision, is an open invitation to errant behavior (as well as to some extraordinary bursts of "creativity").

Fatigue, Discomfort

If we do not feel well, we may have difficulty behaving appropriately.

> *The Jacobsons had spent a wonderful day at the zoo. They had left home before sunrise and had driven several hours to a large city nearby to expose their four children to the wonders of a first-class zoo. The youngsters, three boys and a girl, ranged in age from fifteen months to eight years. They had enjoyed a near perfect day—the weather was great, the orangutan had hung upside down and delighted the children with wonderful ape tricks, and Allison, the toddler, had learned to say "monkey" and "bird" and make lots of new animal sounds. By the end of the day, the car trip home seemed particularly long and tedious. Al drove, and his wife, Regina, and the kids fell asleep shortly before the family reached home.*
>
> *As they pulled into the driveway and everyone woke up, it was clear that the children were hungry, crabby, and generally exhausted. Al said, "I think I'll make pancakes for supper. That won't take long at all." Regina got the children bathed and dressed for bed, and everyone sat down to big fluffy pancakes, applesauce, and bacon—usually one of the kids' favorite meals.*
>
> *Regina collapsed into a chair as Al lifted Allison (in her cute little "footy" pajamas and thick overnight diaper) into her high chair. He began to cut her pancake. Suddenly, Allison began to whine, shake her head, and push the high-chair tray. Al said, "What's wrong? Didn't you want me to cut up your pancake?" Allison stiffened and struggled, getting louder and louder. Al said, "Here, I'll trade pancakes. Mine isn't cut up." Allison took a swipe at the pancake and it landed on her brother William, causing him to start crying.*
>
> *Al tried to calm William as Regina lifted Allison out of the high chair and said, "Honey, I know you're tired. We're all tired, but you may not throw food." Allison stiffened, struggled, and screamed even louder. Over her screams, Al and Regina wracked their brains to figure out what to do. Nothing they tried seemed to help, and every effort just seemed to make matters worse. They finally decided that the only thing to do was just to put Allison in her crib for the night. She sobbed herself to sleep, finally making the little rhythmic gasping sounds children make after they have cried hard.*
>
> *After the boys were fed and asleep, Al and Regina puzzled over Allison's tantrum but could not decide whether this was a new stage or just the result of her being overstimulated and exhausted from the busy day.*

Boredom and fatigue have a definite effect on children's behavior.

> *The next morning Regina leaned over Allison's crib to say good morning. Allison was all smiles while her mother unsnapped her damp pajama bottoms and pulled off the plastic pants—then Regina stopped. She discovered to her dismay that a diaper pin was open. Allison had several bright red scratches and pin pricks on her left side. Regina removed the offending pin then just stood there with tears filling her eyes. "Why," she asked herself, "didn't I think to check her diaper pins last night?"*

Fatigue or anything that causes discomfort can cause children (and adults) to lose control and act aggressively, defy rules, or behave inappropriately. Being hungry, cold, hot, sick, or hurt are all reasons for children to be cranky and uncooperative. Very young children usually do not even realize that the source of their misery is a waistband that is painfully tight, a sock thread twisted around a toe, or scratchy sand in a wet diaper. Even older children sometimes become negative without recognizing that they just do not feel good. We need to remember that what appears on the surface is not always the whole story.

Desire for Recognition

Being ignored hurts at any age.

> *At three, Kelley was the middle child. His big sister, Kathryn, brought home papers from her elementary school teacher saying how smart and good she was. She also had lots of girl*

friends who came and knocked on the door asking to play with her almost every day. Whenever Kelley tried to play with Kathryn and her friends, they would tell him to go away, and Kathryn would yell, "Mother, make Kelley go away and leave us alone!"

Kelley's baby brother, Nick, on the other hand, always seemed to be in Mommy's arms— getting fed, or burped, or bathed, or rocked. When Kelley asked his mother to read him a book or push him on the swing, she said, "Kelley, please go play with your toys. The baby's crying and I can't play with you right now." Kelley thought his mother did not love him any more—only that stupid baby (and Kathryn with all her important homework and prissy friends).

Kelley wet his pants. His mother said, "Kelley! You're such a big boy. You know how to go to the potty." Kelley sneaked a bottle and climbed into baby Nick's crib. He pretended to be a baby and drank the bottle even though it tasted pretty nasty. His mother said, "Kelley! What are you doing in there? This crib isn't built for a big boy like you. It's for the baby. Look, your shoes have gotten the sheets all dirty."

Kelley pushed an old lawn chair against a tree and climbed up into the tree. Even though it was very scary, he climbed higher and higher, until he could not climb any further. Then he started to cry. Kelley's mother ran outside when she heard Kelley crying. "Oh, my soul!" she yelled, "Kelley, how in the world did you get up there?" She called Kelley's dad and it took two hours and the help of several neighbors to get Kelley safely out of the tree. When his dad got him to the lowest branch, he handed Kelley down to his mother. She hugged him so hard he could hardly breathe, but he did not mind. He was just glad to be out of that tree.

Kelley's dad sat down on the grass. He was still panting and sweating from all the climbing and worrying. He motioned for Kelley to come sit on his lap. "Son," he said, "your mother and I love you. You're the only Kelley we have. We can't ever get another boy just like you. Kathryn is special and Baby Nick is special, but Kathryn can't ride on my shoulders and Baby Nick can't sing all the words to 'I've Been Working on the Railroad.' You are the only one who can do those things."

He gave Kelley a playful squeeze and said, "Did you think we could put a penny in a gumball machine and out would roll another Kelley just exactly like you? That I could just go down to the grocery store and put a shiny new penny in there and, POP, out would come a new Kelley? No siree! We couldn't get a new Kelley that way. You're the only one exactly like you in the whole world."

Kelley sat in his dad's lap, encircled by his dad's strong arms, his face snuggled so close to his dad's chest that he could hear the sound of his dad's big heart thumping, the deep voice, and rumbly laughter. Kelley imagined brightly colored gumballs with his face on them rolling out of a grocery store gumball machine. He took a deep breath and grinned.

Feeling ignored is far more painful and frightening for young children than being in trouble and having everyone angry or upset. All human beings need to feel a sense of belonging, to feel that they are wanted and needed. If a child feels unwanted or left out, he may not be able to cooperate and follow rules.

Discouragement

Becoming overwhelmed by discouragement can cause anyone to feel depressed and angry.

Fiona's family moved to a new neighborhood. In her old school, she had already started second grade and had really liked the teacher there. She had made good marks on her schoolwork, and the teacher often let her help other children when her own work was finished.

The teacher had especially praised Fiona for her careful block printing and often put Fiona's papers on the bulletin board for all to see. In her new school, however, Fiona did not think the new teacher, Miss Crane, was very happy to have her in class. On the first day she attended the new school, Miss Crane acted annoyed, and Fiona heard her complain bitterly to another teacher about having to take a student from a different school district in the middle of the year. When Fiona began carefully printing her name in the new workbook Miss Crane gave her, Miss Crane snapped, "Young lady, in this school, second graders do not print! We write in cursive."

Fiona hung her head and stared at her feet, wondering what cursive was. She knew she had heard her mother say many times that she did not like cursing at all. She wondered if her mother would approve of Miss Crane (with her long, blood-red fingernails, bright purple eye-shadow, and high heels). Miss Crane gave Fiona a little workbook filled with grown-up writing and pale blue straight and dotted lines. She said, "I don't have time to teach you everything I've already gone over with the rest of the class. Just go through this workbook and write the words on each page like the ones in the examples. I don't ever want to see you doing printing in this class again. Do you understand?"

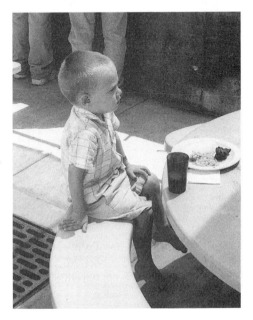

Feelings of discouragement cause
children to be less, rather than more,
cooperative.

Fiona sat at the back of the room by herself, feeling terribly dejected but struggling to copy the weirdly shaped letters in the workbook. Finally, it began to make sense to her that some of the words were made of familiar letters—the letters were just hooked together in a long string like beads on a necklace. She carefully printed the letters she knew and then tediously connected them to make them look like the examples.

Miss Crane did not like Fiona's work at all. She yelled and told Fiona, "This is not how you write in cursive! You will not be allowed to do another thing until you apply yourself and do this work right. Can't you see how the other children are writing?" Fiona was too embarrassed to look around. She hoped none of the other children were staring at her.

Fiona became very quiet at home. She did not bubble with stories about her day. She stopped looking forward to school and began to have stomachaches almost every morning. She begged her mother to let her stay home. She also seemed unusually irritable and often had angry fights with her sisters and brothers. Her mother wondered if Fiona was ill. At school, Fiona went to the pencil sharpener every time she thought Miss Crane was looking or walking in her direction. With so much sharpening, the pencil lead was always too pointed so it snapped every time she nervously pressed down on the paper. She erased until she finally wore holes in the sheets of paper in her workbook, which began to look like Swiss cheese and made her work look even more awful. Miss Crane became exasperated with Fiona and began to wonder if Fiona was a slow learner or just a difficult, uncooperative little girl.

Actually, Fiona was not sick, slow, or difficult—just very, very discouraged. Her self-esteem had slipped, leaving her vulnerable and disorganized and not at all able to do competent school work, make friends, or live up to teacher expectations. Being harshly criticized and "put down" makes it harder, not easier, for a child to accomplish difficult tasks.

Frustration

No matter how old or how young, we all risk losing control when we hit a certain level of frustration.

Benny was two years old. Hardly a day went by without his mother, Virginia, pointing out to someone that he was a "typical terrible two." He vacillated between acting like a baby and trying to act like a grown-up. He whined, "Me do it," whenever his mother tried to tie his shoes. When Virginia became exasperated with him over the shoelaces, she said, "Okay, you tie them." Of course Benny did not know how to tie them, but he stubbornly worked for fifteen minutes, twisting the laces into a scrambled mass of knots.

Virginia said, "Now look what you've done. I told you that you didn't know how to tie them. Be still so I can get these knots out and tie them right." Benny kicked and fought hard to keep his mother from touching his shoes. She finally spanked him to make him let go of his shoes so she could tie them.

Even though Virginia was a single mother with a demanding job and classes two nights a week, she kept her apartment perfectly clean and went to garage sales and resale shops on weekends to see to it that Benny had all the toys and clothes a toddler could need. Every day he was dropped at his child care center looking freshly scrubbed and starched, with every hair in place.

When Virginia got Benny home on the weekday evenings that she did not have to go to class, she always had a lot of work facing her. She usually put Benny on the floor and told him to play with his basket of toys while she cooked, cleaned, and studied. Most often, Benny abandoned the toys and followed his mother around getting into her school books or the kitchen cabinets and making messes. When her patience with him wore thin, she would smack his hand and say "no" or give him a firm swat on the bottom.

Tension built in their little household between the busy, frazzled mother and the clingy, insistent toddler. At his child care center, Benny began biting other children when they refused to give him a toy or let him have a turn on the tricycle. Even being made to sit on the "thinking chair" for a "time-out" by his teachers seemed to have absolutely no effect on stopping his biting—in fact it actually seemed to make him more stubborn and agitated.

One day Benny had been in trouble several times so he was sitting by himself playing with a jack-in-the-box. He cranked the tiny handle and listened to the tune as it played "around and around the cobbler's bench the monkey chased the weasel . . ." until out popped the little clown.

Benny watched attentively then tried to push the little clown back into the box to close the lid so that he could do it again. He pushed the little clown's head down into the box and mashed hard on the lid, but the toy clown's two little flat, plastic hands were sticking out and the lid would not close. Benny pushed on the lid as hard as he could, but his hand slipped and the little clown popped back out.

Benny glared at the uncooperative toy clown then bent down and bit the little clown's hand. Benny bit so long and hard that his whole body shook with the effort and he left a clear imprint of his teeth on the plastic hand.

Much of Benny's aggression probably stemmed from the stress and pressure he was encountering in his daily life. His mother, Virginia, had a lot of frustration building up in her as she tried to survive financially and emotionally as a single parent, a working mother of a toddler, and as a student. She felt frustrated in her efforts to be a perfect mother while also trying to deal with her own personal and social needs. Benny "caught" some of her stress like a contagious illness. He did not know why he felt so tense and stubborn all the time, and he did not know how to make the feelings go away.

Stress is a very real crisis for many children and families today. Children can absorb stress unknowingly from their parents and caregivers, or develop stress symptoms directly from their own lifestyles. Today, there are children who, from earliest childhood, spend their days going from classroom to tutoring to individual lessons to social events, virtually every day from dawn to dusk. Whatever the cause of stress, its symptoms often include inappropriate behavior (along with health, appetite, and concentration problems).

Rebellion

Under repressive enough circumstances, even the most docile of us might be inclined to rebel.

Coach Sam, a tall, muscular nineteen-year-old, had just been hired as the gymnastics instructor in a large, inner-city community center that provided after-school care for six-through twelve-year-olds. His childhood dreams of reaching the Olympics had been dashed by a troublesome back injury, so he found himself teaching gymnastics to small children—something he had never particularly wanted to do.

He decided that in order to create discipline in his class, he would start from the very beginning with his class by being very tough and demanding. He assembled his group of first, second, and third graders on the floor and, towering in front of them with his hands on his hips, announced in a booming voice, "If you talk without my permission, you're out of here. If you don't pay attention and follow my instructions, you're out of here. And, if you even think about being lazy or careless, you're history. Is that understood?" The children chorused back in unison, "Yes, Coach."

At first the children seemed very intimidated by Coach Sam and did everything he said. They were serious and attentive and jumped when he said jump. Gradually, their obedience became more and more strained. Coach Sam never praised the children's accomplishments other than to make a curt comment such as, "Well, finally you're paying attention." He was, however, very quick to mete out caustic criticism such as, "If that's the best you can do, just go sit by the wall. You're not worth me wasting my time." These comments hurt, and the children grew to dislike Coach Sam intensely.

They began to do little things when Coach Sam's back was turned. It became a game for them to see if they could break rules without getting caught. They smuggled candy and gum into the gym. They giggled and whispered whenever Coach Sam tried to give individual attention to a child. Coach Sam yelled and threatened and punished, but the children continued to become even more open in their unruliness.

The children wondered why Coach Sam so frequently threatened to kick them out of class but never followed through on the threat. They did not know that he lacked the authority to expel students from class—they did, however, begin to recognize that most of his threats were empty gestures. In his annoyance and frustration, Coach Sam became colder and more demanding with the children. They became more callous and uncooperative with him. Coach Sam regularly punished children by making them sit by a wall for long periods. Some of the children seemed to be sent to sit by the wall so often that they almost never were allowed to participate. They found ways to use their "sitting" time to create more mischief and disruption for Coach Sam. They expressed their dislike of him and his tactics by causing him endless frustration and interruption. Several children even talked their parents into letting them walk home after school and stay alone rather than go to the community center program at all.

One day, the children in the gymnastics class staged an outright mutiny. They were totally out of control in spite of Coach Sam's yelling and threatening. He ordered a little girl who seemed to be a ring leader to "go sit by the wall for the rest of class." She yelled back, "You can't make me! You're not my mother!" Several other children joined in the confrontation, shouting, "That's right, you can't make me either!"

> *Coach Sam was filled with feelings of rage and helplessness. He knew he would be fired instantly if he struck any of the children, but he was overwhelmed with the urge to show them he had control over them. If he could not use physical force to control them, then he simply did not know how to maintain discipline and order. Coach Sam did not know that positive discipline can best be achieved by establishing an atmosphere of fairness, trust, honesty, and mutual respect—not by trying to create fear and submission.*

The stage is set for rebellion when:

- Children feel anger and contempt rather than affection and respect for the authority figures in their lives who set and enforce rules.

- A situation exists in which it is overly difficult for children to abide by specific rules or live up to expectations.

- Children realize that rules are just hollow threats that will not be consistently or fairly enforced.

- Children reach such a point of discouragement that they feel they are in so much trouble that nothing else they do can make things any worse for them.

These conditions not only trigger rebellion in young children but, in a more general way, are the same kinds of conditions that trigger rebellion and defiance of law and order in segments of adult populations in society at large. Alienation, discouragement, and outrage at inequity are not feelings limited to adults but, on a much smaller scale, also tempt children to defy authority in spite

Frustration triggers misbehavior. Feeling cornered and threatened can trigger rebelliousness.

of the risk of punishment (Crockenberg, 1997; Edwards, 1997; Fields & Boesser, 1998; Gallo, 1997; Gartrell, 1997; Katz & McElellan, 1997; Leach, 1996; McCloskey, 1997).

Practical Application/Discussion

Is a "Really Good Spanking" Really Good?

Edna and Wilbert stopped at a neighborhood fast-food restaurant for a quick hamburger on Saturday afternoon. The place was buzzing with activity, and children of all ages were everywhere. Edna and Wilbert had no children of their own, but they watched in amazement as many different types of adults talked to, played with, and reprimanded children.

Wilbert was especially curious about one harried woman who seemed to be in charge of a half-dozen youngsters. One of the children, a six-year-old, shook salt into her hand, licked it, then laughed as she brushed her salty hands over the children near her. They shrieked with laughter as they dodged the salt, throwing napkins to defend themselves. The woman looked sternly at them and threatened to make them sit in the car if they did not settle down.

Wilbert leaned over and whispered to Edna, "What those children need is a really good spanking!"

Questions for Discussion

1. What could be some possible reasons the children Wilbert was watching were behaving the way they were?
2. Why do you suppose Wilbert believed spanking would be helpful?
3. What do you think would be the most effective and appropriate thing for the woman to do in the situation described above?

Points to Remember

- Over the first few years of life, children gradually develop self-control and learn how to get along with others and how to follow the accepted rules of their family and community.

- Positive child guidance focuses on the child's ability level, the severity and intent of the behavior, as well as possible reasons for the behavior.

- The word inappropriate does not suggest fault or blame, but instead suggests that a behavior is simply not desirable in a specific situation.

- When children evidence a compulsive and chronic pattern of very inappropriate or self-destructive behavior, the behavior can be termed dysfunctional.

- Adult-centered definitions of misbehavior focus on the effect a child's behavior has on the adult.

- Child-centered definitions of misbehavior focus on the ability level, motives, and long-term well-being of the child in evaluating the appropriateness or inappropriateness of actions.

- A critical priority for parents, schools, communities, even entire countries, is the moral development of their children and future citizens.

- Morality is the ability to distinguish right from wrong and to act accordingly.

- Moral development is the process by which human beings learn to monitor their own actions and to decide whether a tempting behavior is a "good" or "bad" thing to do and then to inhibit inappropriate impulses.

- Children internalize or adopt the character attributes and ethical standards of the important role models in their lives. Attachment, love, and respect for an adult trigger the child's internalization of that adult's values.

- When a child has internalized, or accepted as his own, the standards of his adult role models, he has moral affect.

- Nurturing and affectionate caregivers and consistency in explaining reasons for rules help children internalize values and prosocial moral judgment.

- Moral reasoning is the thinking that guides children in deciding what is right or wrong.

- Moral reasoning helps us take into account the causes of children's undesirable behaviors.

- The symptoms of stress can include unhappiness, poor health, and inappropriate behavior.

- The stage is set for rebellion when a situation exists in which a child cannot live up to expectations.

- Children need to know that adults will never give up on caring about them and seeing that they do the right things.

Related Readings

Nurturing At-Risk Children

Barko, N. (1997). Labeled for life? In K. M. Paciorek & J. H. Munro, *Annual editions: Early childhood education 97/98* (18th ed.). New York: McGraw-Hill. (Original work published in *Parents,* September 1996)

Special needs children are often labeled at an early age to initiate services for remediation. Problems can occur when the label is not accurate or the child's development progresses to the point where the special services are no longer required.

Begley, S., and Springen, K. (1997). Life in a parallel world. In E. N. Junn & C. Boyatzis (Eds.), *Annual editions: Child growth and development 97/98* (4th ed.). New York: McGraw-Hill. (Original work published in Newsweek, May 13, 1996)

An increasing number of children are diagnosed as autistic. Autism is a disease; the cause is unknown, but it leaves children socially withdrawn with poor communication skills, compulsive behavior, and, occasionally, savantism. This article describes recent changes in the definition of autism and some theories of its cause.

Benard, B. (1991). *Fostering resiliency in kids: Protective factors in the family, school, and community.* San Francisco: Far West Laboratory for Educational Research and Development.

Brophy, J. (1996). *Teaching problem students.* New York: Guilford.

Brown, J. L., & Pollitt, E. (1997). Malnutrition, poverty, and intellectual development. In E. N. Junn & C. Boyatzis (Eds.), *Annual editions: Child growth and development 97/98* (4th ed.). New York: McGraw-Hill. (Original work published in *Scientific American*, February 1996)

The authors describe research from around the world demonstrating that a poor diet influences children's intellectual development in many ways. The article also addresses other effects of poverty on children's mental growth.

Budd, Linda. (1993). *Living with the active alert child.* Seattle, WA: Parenting Press, Inc.

Bullock, J. R (1997). Children without friends. In E. N. Junn & C. Boyatzis (Eds.), *Annual editions: Child growth and development 97/98* (4th ed.). New York: McGraw-Hill. (Original work published in *Childhood Education*, Winter 1992).

According to research, having friends is crucial for normal development. This article describes the sociometric status of different kinds of children—the popular, rejected, and neglected—and the implications of not having friends. Suggestions are given for teachers to identify and help children without friends.

Coiro, M. J. (1997). *Maternal depressive symptoms as a risk factor for the development of children in poverty.* Phoenix, AZ: Oryx Press.

Davis, M. D., Kilgo J. L., and Gamel-McCormick, M. (1998). *Young children with special needs: A developmentally appropriate approach.* Needham Heights, MA: Allyn & Bacon.

This book proposes that children with disabilities are more like their peers without disabilities than they are different and that we need to provide programming from that perspective. Both beginning students and experienced teachers are facing the reality that early childhood classes reflect increasingly more diverse children as time goes on. Child diversity in terms of race, culture, religion, experience, family, and national origin is related to social and economic realities. Increasing emphasis on inclusion promises to add even more complexity to teachers' decision-making processes.

Eichstaedt, C. B., & Kalakian, L. H. (1993). *Developmental/adapted physical education.* Needham Heights, MA: Allyn & Bacon.

This book focuses on the individual learner rather than the disability, and encourages teachers to emphasize what learners can do, rather than what they cannot do. It is based on the belief that a sound developmental approach to physical education is fundamental to all good learning experiences, both for pupils with disabilities and for those who are able-bodied. Adaptations should be made only to the extent necessary to accommodate a learner's unique developmental needs. It includes children from birth to age three, and discusses developmental milestones in one-year increments, offering guidelines for motor assessment, program development, and physical activities both for infants and toddlers with disabilities and for those who are at-risk.

Frede, Ellen, & Barnett, W. Steve. (1992). Developmentally appropriate public school preschool: A study of implementation of the High/Scope curriculum and its effects on disadvantaged children's skills at first grade. *Early Childhood Research Quarterly, 7*(4), 483–499.

Gamezy, N. (1991). Resiliency and vulnerability to adverse developmental outcomes associated with poverty. *American Behavioral Scientist 34,* 416–430.

Goldstein, Sam, & Goldstein, Michael. (1992). *Hyperactivity: Why won't my child pay attention?* New York, NY: John Wiley.

Karweit, N. (1993). Effective preschool and kindergarten programs for students at-risk. In B. Spodek (Ed.), *Handbook of research on the education of young children* (pp. 385–411). New York: Macmillan.

Landau, S., & McAninch, C. (1997). Young children with attention deficits. In E. N. Junn & C. Boyatzis (Eds.), *Annual editions: Child growth and development 97/98* (4th ed.). New York: McGraw-Hill. (Original work published in *Young Children,* May 1993)

> *Attention-deficit hyperactivity disorder (ADHD) is a frequently misunderstood, complex disorder. This review article describes ADHD, its possible causes, treatments, and the effects of the disorder for children in the classroom setting.*

Noonan, M. J., & McCormick, L. (1993). *Early intervention in natural environments: Methods and procedures.* Needham Heights, MA: Brooks/Cole.

> *Offering readers a variety of empirically validated "best practices," Noonan and McCormick's book focuses on early intervention methods for infants, toddlers, preschoolers, and kindergartners who are developmentally delayed or at-risk.*

Ramler, M., Rice, S. (1997, Summer). Looking beyond chronic illness: Helping children be children. *Texas Child Care, 21*(1), 12–15.

Rief, Sandra F. (1993). *How to reach and teach ADD/ADHD children.* West Nyack, NY: The Center for Applied Research in Education.

Rubin, K. H., LeMare, L. J., & Lollis, S. (1990). Social withdrawal in childhood: Developmental pathways to peer rejection. In S. R. Asher & J. D. Coie (Eds.), *Peer rejection in childhood* (pp. 217–249). New York: Cambridge University Press.

Sroufe, L. A. (1996). *Child development: Its nature and course.* New York: McGraw-Hill.

> *This book has information on gender socialization and gender development; emotional development, prenatal effects of crack, AIDS, and AZT; genetic research; postnatal development, including information on how brain growth is influenced by experience; infant intelligence, assessment, bilingualism, early roots of morality, cross-cultural education; and mixed gender social relationships.*

Stephens, K., et al. (1996, September–October). When children are difficult. Beginnings Workshop. *Child Care Information Exchange, 111,* 43–50, 55–62.

Turecki, Stanley. (1989). *The difficult child.* New York: Bantam Books.

Werner, E., & R. Smith. (1989). *Vulnerable but invincible: A longitudinal study of resilient children and youth.* New York: Adams, Bannister, & Cox.

Werner, E., & R. Srnith. (1992). *Overcoming the odds: High-risk children from birth to adulthood.* New York: Cornell University Press.

Wodrich, David L. (1994). *What every parent wants to know: Attention deficit hyperactivity disorder.* Baltimore: Paul H. Brookes.

Feelings of self-worth make it possible for a child to learn acceptable behavior.

Chapter 8

Managing Persistent Misbehavior

Chapter Outline

Locating Community Resources
Meeting Adult Needs

Practical Application/Discussion
"Thank Heavens for Sarah"

Questions for Discussion
Points to Remember
Related Readings

Objectives

This chapter will assist you in

- Identifying persistent patterns of dysfunctional behaviors
- Categorizing problem behaviors in terms of their misguided purpose
- Defining the typical characteristics of problem behaviors
- Recognizing various hidden reasons for children's misbehavior
- Listing steps to resolve conflicts between adults and children
- Defining strategies for meeting special needs
- Identifying appropriate resources for problem solving

Reacting to Needs—Maslow's Hierarchy

Human beings—children and adults—behave in many complicated ways in order to get their emotional needs met. At the heart of almost any behavior lies the desire to acquire something, whether an object, an experience, or just a feeling. Although some behaviors may be directed toward frivolous whims, many behaviors focus on basic human needs. Maslow (1943) developed a theory of human motivation. He proposed that basic needs are arranged in a hierarchy, a pyramid in which each overriding level of need has to be met before successive levels of need can be addressed. Following is Maslow's list of emotional needs that motivate behavior arranged in the order in which they must be met. People need:

- Freedom from discomfort—to have food, water, shelter, and so on
- Physical safety—to feel secure from danger
- A sense of belonging—to feel loved
- Self-esteem—to feel valued and self-sufficient
- To stretch intellectually—to know and understand

After physical comfort and safety needs are met, children's most pressing need is for a sense of belonging. (Photograph provided courtesy of CHILDREN AT RISK.)

In other words, a child who is starving will not be concerned about anything other than sheer survival. A child who is frightened and insecure will show little interest in making friends or building castles with blocks. A child who feels unloved will not be able to function independently and confidently. In fact, very young children will tend to do whatever seems to work to get their needs met, no matter how annoying or uncivilized their behavior seems to the adults around them, since they have not yet developed the ability to inhibit their impulses. Only after their basic emotional needs have been met can we expect them to be calm, cooperative, and curious learners (Brewer, 1998; Bullock, 1997; Feeney, Christensen, & Moravcik, 1996; Gibbs, 1997; Kagan, 1997; McAlister, 1997).

What Is The Role Of Self-Esteem In Repeated Misbehavior?

Unmet needs are a hidden cause of repeated patterns of dysfunctional behavior in children. In order to behave well, children must have a strong sense of self-esteem. Many behavior-disordered children seem to be walking around with a big, black hole inside them where their self-esteem ought to be. Self-esteem has become more and more emphasized over the past few decades as a characteristic that seems closely tied to school success and social adjustment (Kokenes, 1974; Wittner & Honig, 1997). Early childhood educators have especially focused on activities intended to foster self-esteem. Children, unfortunately, do not suddenly develop a sense of self-worth simply because we sing a cute song about being special and color in between the lines on a ditto sheet that says, "I am special."

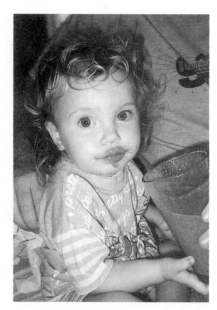

If adults consistently see a child as lovable, capable, and worthwhile, she will probably feel high self-esteem.

How Can I Support The Child's Development Of Self-Esteem?

The perception of "value" children place on themselves reflects the "value" important others place on them (Coopersmith, 1967; Randy, Hoover & Kindsvatter, 1997; Roberts, 1997). If parents and caregivers see a child as lovable, capable, and worthwhile, then the child will probably have a high level of self-esteem. Children begin to develop self-esteem from birth—but only if their needs are met by attentive caregivers, they feel safe and loved, and they are consistently treated with respect (even while they are being disciplined). Although it may be possible to rebuild damaged self-esteem, it is much easier to support the development of a positive self-concept from the very beginning.

If a child's early experiences have been damaging to her sense of self, it is essential to begin fostering self-esteem and to teach her functional ways to get her needs met. With a great deal of support and patience, children can unlearn old, dysfunctional behaviors that may have been the only way they knew to get their needs met in a confusing or unsupportive environment. Repeated cycles of dysfunctional behavior are difficult to handle, and adults easily fall into behaviors that are as dysfunctional as that of the children they are trying to help.

A key to success in dealing with children who have developed habit patterns of inappropriate behavior is for the adult to persistently pull the child up to a more acceptable level of behavior rather than allowing the child to pull the adult down to the child's level of immature and inappropriate interaction—advice that is easy to give but never easy to put into practice.

> *There is nothing so strong as gentleness, nothing so gentle as real strength.*
> St. Francis de Sales (de Sales & Ryan, 1972)

The No-Lose Method of Conflict Resolution

Often, children and adults become locked in a struggle over who will be in control. These power struggles become win-lose situations in which the only way the adults get their needs met is for children to submit to control, and the only way for children to get their needs met is for adults to submit to control. This tug-of-war pits adults and children against each other. Typically, this results in misbehavior patterns becoming well-established. Antagonism between adults and children can also begin to interfere with the pleasurable, nurturing interactions that strengthen self-esteem and are a critical part of daily life for children. Adults find themselves chronically annoyed with children, and children become more and more resistant and noncompliant.

The no-lose method of conflict resolution is a strategy for avoiding power struggles and for adults and children working together to solve problems positively and cooperatively. Following are six steps to use in resolving conflicts (Dinkmeyer & McKay, 1982; Gordon, 1970).

Step 1—*Use reflective listening to clarify feelings.*

Adult: *"Joel, it sounds like you're angry because Amy keeps pulling at your book."*

Step 2—*Generate possible solutions by brainstorming.*

Adult: *"What are some ways you could let Amy know she is bothering you besides screeching?" "You could use words to tell Amy you are upset, or maybe you could move back away from her."*

Step 3—*Evaluate the probable consequence of possible solutions.*

Child: *"If I move back, Amy will still grab my book."*

Step 4—*Choose the best possible solution.*

Adult: *"I see. Perhaps it would be best for you to tell Amy how angry you feel when she takes your book. If she doesn't listen, then you can ask me for help."*

Step 5—*Decide how to carry out the solution.*

Adult: *"Would you like for me to come with you so that you can talk to Amy right now?"*

Step 6—*Evaluate how well the solution worked.*

Adult: *"Joel, do you feel better now? Do you think you will be able to remember about talking instead of screeching?"*

After this interaction, Joel should feel that the adult is really on his side, that the adult is really trying to assist him rather than just take control of him. This guidance interaction is positive because it fosters self-esteem and helps the child feel more confident, competent, and self-reliant. Joel had an opportunity to participate actively in the decision making and to think through the process of problem solving.

Dreikurs's Mistaken Goals

Taking steps to involve a child in conflict resolution is important, but in order to break a persistent cycle of dysfunctional behavior, steps must also be taken simultaneously to see that the child's emotional needs have been met. Adler (1931), a colleague of Freud, theorized that dysfunctional behavior stemmed from inadequate early guidance. He believed that some children were kept from developing a sense of competence and self-worth by doting or dominating parents who saddled them with an inferiority complex, causing them to adopt inappropriate ways to exert control and feel competent.

Dreikurs (Dreikurs & Cassel, 1974) further developed this idea for teachers and parents by proposing four mistaken goals that he hypothesized to be the root of long-standing, habitual patterns of dysfunctional behavior. He theorized that children behave inappropriately because of their overwhelming urge to:

- Get attention from others

- Gain a sense of control

- Get revenge for their own perceived hurts

- Remove themselves from frightening or painful situations

Each of the mistaken goals is directed toward getting an emotional need met—the need for recognition, the need for a sense of control over one's life, the need for fairness, and the need to avoid stressful and frightening situations. Unfortunately, each behavior listed above may seem

Sometimes children need to learn new ways to get their emotional needs met.

to make the child feel a little better temporarily, but it actually compounds and worsens her problem in the long run. There is a snowball effect in which the child's inappropriate responses increase the negativity and hostility in her environment, which in turn increases her emotional neediness and the likelihood of her behaving more and more inappropriately in the future.

Typically, we respond in a way that is precisely opposite to the response actually needed by the child. For example, we are tempted to ignore the child who is acting out to get attention, but that will cause him to have even more need to act out. We are tempted to get into a stern power struggle with the controlling child, "to show her who's boss," but this makes her feel even more powerless and out of control. We are sorely tempted to inflict pain on the aggressive child who bites or hurts another child, but angry aggression on our part can make the child even more resolved to get revenge. Additionally, we are tempted to shrug our shoulders and give up altogether on the withdrawn child who hides under a table, twisting his hair or bumping his head on the wall, but our abandonment only allows him to sink deeper and deeper into his isolation.

In order to bring about real change, we must cure (or at least relieve) the problems that cause persistent patterns of dysfunctional behavior, and retrain children in appropriate methods to get their emotional needs met. It is not effective to tackle inappropriate behaviors as if they existed in a vacuum. When behavior is often dysfunctional, the child's misbehaviors can be thought of as symptoms, and the child's emotional neediness as an underlying disease. Suppressing behavioral symptoms without paying attention to the emotional well-being of the child may only result in the eruption of new or different symptoms, just as treating the fever of an infection without giving an antibiotic to kill the bacteria that caused it will probably mean a return of the fever.

Feelings of positive self-esteem blossom in young children as they live and play in a nurturing environment.

Healing can take place only when the child feels she is an accepted and worthwhile group member, she has some sense of control over her life, she is treated fairly and respectfully, and she feels optimism that she can succeed in whatever is expected of her. If these feelings blossom in the child, then we can say that she has self-esteem, and the four key reasons for persistent misbehavior no longer exist. The child will no longer need to rely on misbehavior for emotional survival and can begin to break habit patterns and learn more effective ways to get along with others.

Attention-Seeking Behavior

Clinging, Feigning Ineptness

Human babies are born helpless and vulnerable. It makes sense that they become emotionally attached to caregivers, that they are most comfortable and secure when they can feel, see, or hear the caregiver's closeness. In a more primitive society, an infant's very survival could depend on staying close to a caring adult. As soon as infants are able to identify and distinguish among family members, caregivers, and strangers, they generally show signs of stranger anxiety and separation anxiety. A baby who has always cooed, gurgled, and smiled for anyone will suddenly cry when a stranger leans close to admire her and tickle her chin. A one-year-old who usually toddles around the house getting into everything may become subdued and clingy while a visitor is in the house.

This **bonding** (becoming emotionally attached to a caregiver) is a healthy and normal phase of development. Attachment to a dependable caregiver is an essential factor in the development of trust. We do no favor to babies and toddlers when we push them too early to break away from the adults who care for them. Babies who are allowed to develop secure, loving bonds with

Children who feel good about themselves feel comfortable behaving in a natural and spontaneous way, but they also are able to accept reasonable limits.

responsive caregivers become friendlier, more independent, and more successful preschoolers later (Bretherton & Waters, 1985; Lamb, et. al. 1985). Close attachment in infancy does not, as parents often worry, cause children to become spoiled, clingy, attention-seekers.

Clingy children who pretend they cannot do anything without help suffer from poor self-esteem. They have not been "loved" too much, although they may well have been overindulged and overprotected in ways that stunted their long-term development of healthy confidence and independence. Overindulgence and overprotection are poor excuses for real love, which is respectful and matched to a child's needs, rather than being intrusive or overwhelming. In many cases, clingy children may have been given too little attention and attachment. Their need to bond may have never been fully satisfied so they cling to baby behaviors. Clingy children only feel comfortable and loved when they are being fussed over and cared for. They long for the adult to cuddle them and to rescue them from their responsibilities.

Artificial Charm, Competitiveness

Children who are insecure in their sense of belonging often adopt an artificial charm. Younger children learn how to play the role of the adorable and irresistible child, while older children gush with insincere compliments. This niceness may vanish instantly, however, whenever the child feels threatened by attention directed toward someone else. The child may swing from absolute charmer to cold competitor in seconds. We need to focus on developing the child's sense of security and self-esteem by giving sincere affection and encouragement at appropriate times. We also need to set firm limits and help the child know that she is loved for herself, not for her fake charm.

Adults can help children become aware of the feelings of others.

Clowning, Acting Out, Silliness

Children use clowning, acting out, and silliness to get attention, not only from adults, but also from other children. Some children only seem to feel sure that they are loved and appreciated when they are at the center of attention with everyone looking at them and either laughing or chiding. Children may be especially likely to get silly when they feel embarrassed or pushed into a corner. For some children, being a clown is a way of saving face and protecting damaged self-esteem.

We need to take care to allow clowning children to save their dignity. They should be corrected privately and respectfully when their acting out is unacceptable. It is also essential that they be given opportunities for responsibility and leadership in positive settings as well as chances to entertain others in appropriate ways. For example, a child might be encouraged to plan a skit for classmates, chosen to pass out napkins or refreshments during a celebration, or allowed to sing, dance, or act out a story at group time.

Laziness, Compulsiveness, Obnoxiousness

Lazy, compulsive, or obnoxious behaviors may be a child's unconscious way of forcing adults to pay attention. They also signal a lack of self-esteem in the child. The child labeled as lazy may receive negative attention when adults nag, take over the child's responsibilities, or insist that other children help or do the child's work for him. Children who overeat, bite their nails, tease, or purposely disgust other children and adults are also giving strong indications that they do not feel good about themselves.

Persistent, assertive, and loving guidance will build the child's respect for herself by helping her know that the adult cares deeply enough to become actively involved in redirecting her inappropriate behaviors. For example, a child who persists in running around the playground terrifying other children with bugs and worms could be firmly redirected from poking the creatures in others' faces to constructing a terrarium for the science center out of an old aquarium, some rocks and dirt, and a few little plants. There the insects and earthworms could be displayed in a socially acceptable manner that does not frighten or disgust others.

Controlling Behavior

Manipulativeness, Vengefulness

Manipulative means trying to trick someone into doing something that he or she really does not want to do. Adults often set an example for this behavior in their attempts to gain control over the child's behavior. We tell children things such as, "Eat your bread crusts because they will make your hair curly" or "Bend over, this shot won't hurt a bit!" We should not be surprised to hear a kindergartner say, "Give me your candy bar and I'll be your best friend forever."

Sometimes manipulativeness can become excessive and vengeful as children struggle to gain control of the children and adults around them. Adults need to define clear limits and help children become aware of the feelings and reactions of those around them. Adults can recognize and

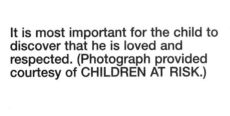

It is most important for the child to discover that he is loved and respected. (Photograph provided courtesy of CHILDREN AT RISK.)

verbalize feelings. For example, "Sallie, I know you really want Alvie's doll, but the doll belongs to Alvie. Alvie doesn't like to play with you when you try to take her doll. You may choose a different toy, or you may play by yourself."

Pouting, Stubbornness

Children who want control but fail to get their way with others may react by pouting, stubbornly refusing to participate, or "causing a scene." The toddler who wants (but does not get) ice cream for dinner, for example, may push her plate off the high-chair tray, kick her feet, scream, shake her head, and generally refuse to have anything to do with carrots and roast beef.

Adults do no favor either by giving in to the toddler (and thus encouraging her controlling behavior) or by forcing nutritious food on her against her will. They can, however, avoid a power struggle by simply removing the toddler from the high chair and allowing her to express her anger. The adults can express sincere empathy, but allow the child to be stubborn without showing a great deal of attention or concern.

For example, the adult may say, "It's okay to cry. When you feel better, you can have dinner." When she has finished screaming, she may or may not want dinner. Either way, she will not starve before the next meal. The child's need for a sense of control can be met by allowing her to choose when she is ready to eat, not by letting her succeed in demanding things that are not in her best interest. Between the lines, the adult is saying, "You may make your own choices—within reasonable limits—but you must also deal with the consequences of your choices."

Bullying, Rebelling

Some children, when failing to gain control by other means, resort to bullying or rebelling. They gain control over smaller children by overwhelming them physically with their size and strength. Grown-ups are not usually so easy to bully, since size and strength advantages fall to the adult. A child, consequently, might be tempted to control adults by being so rebellious, so out of control, that adults feel totally helpless. It is important, however, that adults not allow themselves to lapse into feelings of inadequacy. The child needs strong, reliable adult support in order to give up dysfunctional behaviors and form new habits.

It is also essential for adults to avoid power struggles with the bullying or rebelling child. Head-to-head confrontation will trigger an increase in angry rebellion and will not solve the problem. Aggressive, bullying behavior on the part of adults further establishes the role model for this undesirable behavior. Instead, adults must find ways to build a positive relationship with the child and to help the child feel a sense of belonging. Clear limits are essential, as well as logical consequences, but the most important step is for the child to discover that he is loved, respected, and appreciated. Then he will be able to relax and relinquish his tight-fisted attempt to control those around him.

Disruptive Behavior

Destructiveness, Aggressiveness

Children whose self-esteem is lacking may deteriorate into disruptive habit patterns of destructiveness and aggression. These behaviors tell us that the child feels a sense of hopelessness. She

Healthy emotional development hinges on the development of basic trust.

may believe that she has already been rejected by others so that it really does not matter what she does—nobody will like her no matter how she behaves. These feelings discourage her from developing self-control over her impulses.

The destructive or aggressive child must know that she will be stopped, that others' rights will be protected. Adults must not be afraid to do whatever has to be done to keep a child from harming others. A caregiver in a child care facility who feels helpless and intimidated by a child does great harm to that child by allowing her to bite, kick, shove, pinch, and scratch other children and destroy shared toys. The caregiver must believe that he has two responsibilities:

- To befriend the child during noncrisis times and rebuild her feelings of self-esteem

- To take steps to interrupt outbursts of aggression and protect other children and the physical environment

The caregiver may need to ask for help from another staff member or administrator or from the parents. However tempting it may be for adults to make excuses (no one will help me, I'm a single parent, my director is too busy, there is nowhere else for the child to be, psychologists are too expensive), the adult must not stop until he or she finds the support that is needed. Although it will probably not be necessary to call in the National Guard for help with a fifty-pound child who is throwing rocks, the caregiver must have confidence that if one strategy for stopping the child from hurting others does not work, then other strategies will be tried until something does work! The adult must be willing, in a crisis situation, to physically restrain the child as firmly as necessary but as gently as possible.

In dealing with a very difficult child, behavior modification may be an essential and effective tool for regaining a manageable relationship with the child. A reinforcer (token reward) must be selected that is meaningful and desirable to the child, the specific desired behavior goal must be identified in concrete terms, and a schedule of when, how, and under what circumstances the reinforcement will be given should be planned with the child. Reinforcement must always be immediate. As the child makes little steps of progress toward the desired behavior, she is instantly reinforced with a reward (such as a sticker, a plastic disk, or checks on a chart) that can be exchanged at a predetermined number for special privileges or treats.

Behavior modification will be most successful (especially with an older child) if she has enthusiastically agreed to participate in the plan. If the child likes and respects the adult and really wants to change some behaviors and habits she knows are unacceptable, she may be surprisingly willing to participate in a voluntary behavior modification plan—at least during the brief periods in which she is calm and logical. During the entire process of behavior modification, the child must be helped toward the eventual weaning from external control to internal control. She can be told from the very beginning, "Changing bad habits is very, very hard for anyone! These little prizes will help you remember to use words instead of hitting. After a while though, you won't need little prizes anymore. You'll remember to use words so people will like you and want to play with you."

Children's Books Addressing Aggressive Behavior

Carlson, Nancy. (1985). *Loudmouth George and the Sixth-Grade Bully.* New York: Puffin Books. 32p.

Walker, Alice. (1991). *Finding the Green Stone.* San Diego: Harcourt Brace Jovanovich. 40p.

Bosch, Carl W. (1988). *Bully on the Bus.* Seattle, WA: Parenting Press. 58p.

Naylor, Phyllis Reynolds. (1992). *Reluctantly Alice.* New York: Dell. 182p.

Cohen-Posey, Kate. (1995). *How to Handle Bullies, Teasers, and Other Meanies: A Book That Takes the Nuisance Out of Name Calling and Other Nonsense.* Highland City, FL: Rainbow Books. 91p.

Stoltz, Mary. (1985). *The Bully of Barkham Street.* New York: Harper & Row. 194p.

Contempt, Mistrust

Contempt and mistrust in children sadden and dismay us. The child filled with contempt has so much mistrust of others that he seems to despise everyone. We may find it necessary to backtrack and work on the basic development of trust. Just as a first grader who lacked visual discrimination and vocabulary would need remedial work before he could learn to read, the child who feels contempt must relearn the essential lesson of infancy—to trust others, to believe that adults are reliable, predictable, and accepting—before he can learn to behave appropriately.

A child who feels that he has received a great deal of hurt and unfair treatment in his life will not easily place his trust in adults. Adults will have to earn that trust through consistent fairness

Children learn socially acceptable ways to express negative feelings.

and sincere interest in the child's well-being. Adults can facilitate the development of trust in the child by modeling trust. They can find opportunities to place trust in the mistrustful child in situations in which the child is very likely to succeed and in which a failure to live up to the adult's trust can safely be overlooked.

Fits of Anger, Tantrums, Defiance

Children who regularly indulge in fits of anger, tantrums, and defiance need to know that the adults who care for them are not cowed by these behaviors, but they also need to know that adults will not explode into their own fits of anger. Angry, defiant behaviors may unconsciously be intended to strike back at adults who are perceived to be enemies. Adults, consequently, must take steps to build a cooperative relationship with the defiant child, to become the child's ally and friend while refusing to participate in inappropriate interactions with the child.

We can help children let go of explosive behaviors by responding matter-of-factly but steadfastly to the child's eruptions. An adult may be forced to remove or restrain the child in extreme circumstances, but the adult can be very sure the child recognizes that there is no anger or punitiveness in those actions, just firmness and resolve. Also, the adult can avoid overreacting to expressions of defiance such as vulgar language or spitting.

No adult wants to be spit at or to see other children spit on, but our own angry or violent outburst will make the child's problem worse, not better. Instead, a patient but very firm adult might say, "If you need to spit, you may spit in the sink. Spitting in the sink is fine. Spitting on people is not allowed, though. It makes them angry and it could get germs on them. If you spit, you can't play. You'll need to sit here by me until you are sure you are through spitting."

The child needs to learn that defiant tantrums are really a waste of time, since they have no effect on the adult. The tantrums will not bring about special favors, and they will not succeed in "driving the adult up the wall." Since persistently disruptive behavior is unconsciously intended to hurt others as the child feels she has been hurt, the child may delight in seeing adults frustrated, angry, and helpless.

Withdrawn, Passive Behavior

Cyclical Self-Stimulation

When a child is overwhelmed by fear, stress, and anxiety, she may withdraw into her own little world. Although most children do things to make themselves feel better from time to time, the withdrawn child may sink into constant self-stimulation. This pattern is referred to as cyclical, since the child repeats the behavior cycle over and over. The cycle may consist of excessive thumb sucking, nail biting, hair twisting, overeating, head banging, masturbating, or any number of other self-stimulating actions.

Adults frequently find these behaviors very embarrassing and may focus on forcing the child to end the behavior without addressing the cause of the behavior at all. These behaviors tell us the child is feeling too stressed and overwhelmed to participate in usual activities. By focusing on reducing stress in the child's life and drawing the child out into pleasurable, nonthreatening activities, the child may be eased into more active involvement with things and people around him.

Rejection of Social Interchange

The severely withdrawn child may avoid eye contact, refuse to talk or play, and stay apart from others most of the time. Adults may mistakenly focus all of their guidance efforts on children whose inappropriate behaviors are active and annoying. Teachers, parents, and caregivers may view the child who is a loner as a good child who never bothers anyone. In reality, the child who is a loner may be more at risk emotionally than the difficult, loud, aggressive child. Self-esteem, trust, and a sense of belonging are all essential to building contact with the child who seems to have no interest in others.

Internalization of Stress

Inhibited children sometimes turn all their bad feelings inward. Fear, anger, and frustration are not expressed; they are just held inside—and they may chip away at the child's sense of competence and self-worth. These children need opportunities to learn that they do not have to be perfect, it is okay to disagree, and they have a right to be who they are. As they develop stronger self-esteem, they will feel more comfortable expressing their feelings and actively standing up for themselves.

Children need opportunities to learn socially acceptable ways to express negative feelings. They need assertive role models and the freedom to say what they feel honestly (but respectfully). Adults should avoid telling children that their feelings are not real or valid by saying such things as "That scratch doesn't hurt," "There's nothing to cry about," or "You have no reason to be mad!" Children must be allowed to feel what they feel, even though they must also learn to express negative feelings without hurting, harassing, or humiliating others. When children know an acceptable way to express themselves, they are likely to feel much freer about exposing their inner feelings.

Display of Ineptness and Hopelessness

Feelings of depression are not the exclusive territory of adolescents and adults. Even very young children can show signs of depression. Overwhelming disruption in the child's daily life may contribute to her listlessness and display of ineptness and hopelessness. These children do not involve themselves in spontaneous play or creative expression. They seem to have no energy. They may sleep too much or too little. They are clearly at risk and need special guidance to rebuild self-esteem and give them the spark of hope that fuels healthy curiosity, spontaneous play, and active involvement with others.

Screening for Developmental "Red Flags"

All children behave very inappropriately from time to time—no matter how well they seem to be developing and how cooperative, competent, and confident they are generally. Some children, however, behave inappropriately often enough to cause us serious concern. It is essential that we

Partial hearing loss can be surprisingly difficult to notice.

consider the possibility of physical causes for severe, persistent misbehavior. Various cues or signals could be taken as "red flags," or warning indicators, that something may be awry. Parents, teachers, and caregivers should never attempt to diagnose physical ailments or developmental delays. They should, however, watch carefully for indications that a child needs further evaluation by a physician or other expert to rule out or confirm physiological or psychological problems. (See Appendix G for additional resources.)

Can Hearing Problems Affect Behavior?

The ability to hear properly has an important influence on a child's ability to comply with adult instructions. A child who suffers from frequent nasal congestion, ear infections, and sinus drainage is a prime candidate for hearing difficulty. A young child may have occasional bouts of partial hearing loss or long, persistent periods of hearing difficulty due to these upper respiratory problems. Partial hearing loss can be surprisingly difficult for parents, teachers, and caregivers to notice. Since children pay close attention to body language and nonverbal gestures, they may appear to hear and understand more than they really do.

There are, of course, many other possible causes for partial or full loss of hearing as well. Medical evaluation and treatment may, in some cases, restore the child's hearing completely or at least make adults aware that a communication problem exists. Red flags signaling the possibility of a hearing problem include such things as:

- Pulling, tugging, poking at, or rubbing the ears
- Slowness in learning to speak compared to age-mates

- Muffled or garbled pronunciation of words

- Consistent failure to follow even simple instructions

- Appearance of being socially isolated in group settings

- Unresponsiveness to group activities such as story reading

What Other Physical Conditions Affect Behavior?

Since irritability and discomfort are both likely causes for misbehavior, there are any number of physical illnesses or conditions that could result in behavior changes. Muscular disabilities could hamper a child's ability to carry out tasks that might be expected, or developmental delays could make it impossible for a child to live up to typical adult expectations. Parents, teachers, and caregivers can assist medical personnel in evaluating a child who seems to be displaying signs of difficulty by observing and keeping records of behaviors on a daily basis that seem unusual for a child at a given age.

Can The Presence of Behavioral Problems Signal the Possibility of Child Abuse or Neglect?

A very serious potential cause of developmental and behavioral problems can be the presence of abuse or neglect in a child's life. Although virtually any normally developing child can experience a rare incident of abusive or neglectful treatment, children who lead lives filled with abuse and neglect are profoundly affected by that experience even if they are not maimed or killed. Every aspect of their development is affected—intellectual, physical, social, and emotional

Is the number of child fatalities increasing?

More than three children died each day last year because of parental maltreatment. A national survey conducted by the National Committee to Prevent Child Abuse early in 1995 indicated that the number of confirmed child abuse fatalities increased 39% over the last ten years. This trend is not surprising given the increase in poverty, substance abuse, and violence experienced by so many of our communities. Based on reporting data collected from 37 states and the District of Columbia, a little over three million children were reported for child abuse in 1995, approximately 2% more than had been reported in 1994. Overall, child abuse reporting rates have risen by an average of 4% each year between 1990 and 1995. The total number of reports has increased nationwide by 49% since 1984. Young children are at the highest risk for abuse. Research indicates that between 1993 and 1995, 85% of fatalities occurred to children under the age of five, with 45% to children under the age of one. Child abuse ranks as the second leading cause of death, after accidents, for children between one and five years old (National Committee to Prevent Child Abuse, 1998).

How and why do these fatalities occur?

Between 1993 and 1995, 37% of all fatalities attributed to child maltreatment were the result of neglect, 48% from abuse, and 15% as a result of both forms of maltreatment.

Surrounding circumstances related to these fatalities seem to present themselves year after year. According to a 1995 report by the National Center for the Prevention of Child Abuse (NCPCA), states reported that substance abuse, by the abuser, was involved in anywhere from 4% to 65% of all substantiated cases. Additionally, 46% of children who died between 1993 and 1995 had prior or recent contact with Child Protective Service (CPS) agencies. Children who have been reported to CPS agencies on more than one occasion should be watched very carefully for indications of recurring abuse (National Committee to Prevent Child Abuse, 1998).

How can more child abuse fatalities be prevented?

Communities can help prevent abuse deaths by fully supporting their child protective service agencies and assuring the availability of treatment services for potential abusers. Additionally, alcohol and drug treatment services need to be expanded and made more accessible to pregnant and parenting women. Public agencies, however, cannot prevent all fatalities single-handedly. Other formal institutions such as schools, child care centers, hospitals, and all other members of the community must also play an active role in identifying and getting help for families at risk of abusive or neglectful behavior.

Child abuse is against the law. Every state has a designated agency that is mandated by federal law to receive and to investigate reports of suspected child abuse and neglect. Remember, reporting is a means of getting help for a child or family, not just a way to punish abusers. You do not have to prove that child abuse has occurred, that is up to the investigator to determine. To report a suspected case of child abuse, you should notify the designated agency in the state where the child lives. The agency is listed in the telephone directory, usually in the Government Blue Pages under Rehabilitative Services or Children and Family Services. In some areas, it may also be listed in the Yellow Pages. If you have difficulty finding the agency in your community, call your local police department or call the Childhelp USA/IOF Foresters National Child Abuse Hotline, (800) 422-4453 (4-A-CHILD). Childhelp USA/IOF Foresters keeps listings of child protective service agencies across the country.

(Dean, Malik, Richards, & Stringer, 1986; Finkelhor & Dziuba-Leatherman, 1997; Heineman, 1998; Hoffman-Plotkin & Twentyman, 1984; Ingrassia & McCormick, 1997; Kempe & Kempe, 1978; Lamb, Gaensbauer, Malkin, & Schultz, 1985; National Committee to Prevent Child Abuse, 1998; Wallach, 1997; Wang & Daro, 1998). (See Appendix E for additional resources.)

Abused and neglected children's behaviors tend toward extremes—there seems to be no happy middle ground for these children. They may be diagnosed as learning disabled or they may be compulsive overachievers. They may be hyperactive or lethargic. They may be physically inept weaklings or street-smart, death-defying daredevils. They may either cling relentlessly to others or shun all social interaction. They may appear either dirty and unkempt or rigidly and spotlessly scrubbed, starched, and pressed. They may either defy authority altogether or compulsively try to please everyone at all times, in all ways. They may always play the role of victim or brutally victimize others. The one characteristic that is shared by all abused and neglected children is their lacking or stunted sense of self—they do not have that essential component of all fully functional human beings, the positive feeling of self-worth that comes with self-esteem.

Locating Community Resources

Adults caring for children who have persistent misbehavior problems need help. Once possible causes for behavior problems have been identified, a search for appropriate community resources should take place. Families, schools, and child care facilities all have the potential to serve as resources for each other, to share ideas and methods, and to give each other emotional support and encouragement. Parents can learn a great deal from teachers and caregivers, and teachers and caregivers can learn a great deal from parents. Additionally, almost any community setting offers a wealth of potential resources such as the following:

- The medical community—physicians, psychologists, and other therapists

- Governmental agencies—child protective service workers, child care licensing specialists, health departments, social workers, Head Start, and other publicly funded programs

- Religious entities—churches, synagogues, priests, ministers, counselors, congregational support groups

- Nonprofit organizations—self-help groups, associations focused on specific problems such as diabetes or hyperactivity, and parenting classes or seminars

- Treatment centers—special schools, testing clinics, or therapy facilities such as schools for the blind or physical therapy facilities for such things as cerebral palsy

- Public school systems—educational programs for exceptional children, early intervention programs for children at risk, school psychologists, and counselors

- World Wide Web connections—see Appendix I for Internet starting points for early childhood development care and education

Parents often need help in overcoming feelings of pain and denial when they discover that their child has developmental, physical, or behavioral problems. They may hold an idealized image of their child and resist the notion that their child is, in fact, human and imperfect, having both strengths and weaknesses. They may need to be reminded that there is no shame in having a disability or an imperfection—there is only shame in not dealing with reality and not taking steps to help the child function as well as possible. Many potentially disabling conditions can be prevented or alleviated if they are identified and treated during infancy or earliest childhood, so early screening for developmental problems has special importance. Resource lists in the appendices offer many sources of free or inexpensive help for parents, teachers, and caregivers.

Meeting Adult Needs

Children definitely have needs, but adults have needs too. Caring for children is demanding, exhilarating, frustrating, and rewarding—but it is also exhausting. We can best care for children if our own social, emotional, physical, and intellectual needs have been met. We must set aside time for our own rest and recreation, and we must be able to admit to ourselves at times that we are not able to deal with children in a positive and productive manner. If children are dealt with in a caring and respectful manner most of the time, they will be likely to cope well and respect our own need when we say, "I'm too frustrated and angry to talk about this right now. I just want to be alone for a few minutes."

> *Ever tried?*
> *Ever failed?*
> *No matter.*
> *Try again.*
> *Fail again.*
> *Fail better.*
>
> Samuel Beckett (Knowlson, 1996)

Adult caregivers have emotional needs too. A strong, caring support structure among coworkers helps each individual cope with stress and fatigue that can lead to emotional burnout.

We can be patient and reasonable with ourselves, recognizing that we too are imperfect. It is easy to sit down and think carefully about an ideal response to a misbehaving child, but it is not so easy to respond perfectly when the response is instantaneous and in the heat of conflict with that child. It is important for adults to be supportive, calm, respectful, and consistent, but it is most important for them to do something! Children must know that adults care enough to do something even if it is not the best possible thing to do. (See Appendix F for parent training and information resources for parents and professionals caring for children with behavioral disorders due to psychological or physical disabilities.)

When we attempt to change our ways of dealing with children, we go through the same stages of learning that children go through when they learn new behaviors. For example, a toddler who has no concept of toileting will simply show no awareness when she makes a puddle on the floor. When she has developed a recognition of the desired behavior but lacks practice carrying it out, she will make a puddle, look down, smile sweetly, and say, "Go potty!" Oh course, it will be too late to go to the potty. Finally, when she has fully developed both the awareness and the skill to carry out the new behavior, she will notice the sensation of a full bladder and do what needs to be done to successfully use the toilet.

We go through that same process. At first, we may be totally unaware of the negative, destructive, and hurtful things we say or do with youngsters in the name of disciplining them. As we discover more productive and effective ways to guide them, we begin for the first time to hear ourselves saying or doing negative things. We feel frustration because we only seem to become aware of these actions after we have done them. We become aware of our inappropriate actions, but only after it is too late. Gradually, however, with persistence and practice, we are able to anticipate and respond more skillfully and appropriately. Eventually, our new behaviors become so natural to us that we can behave as we wish with almost no thought or effort.

Positive child guidance is a tool that can be used to help mature, caring adults teach young children the skills they need to lead productive, happy lives.

> *Treat people as if they are what they ought to be, and you help them to become what they are capable of being.*
>
> Johann Wolfgang von Goethe, German poet, 1749–1832 (von Goethe, 1995)

Practical Application/Discussion

"Thank Heavens for Sarah"

Sarah taught and cared for a small group of children in her own home. She felt strong commitment to her work and believed that she made a difference in children's lives. She took great pride in operating her home-based child care program in a professional and responsible manner. She bristled at the term *babysitter,* so she referred to herself as a teacher, because that is what she believed she did with the babies, toddlers, and preschoolers in her care.

Robert was three. Sarah had been caring for him for several months and had become very concerned about his behavior. He always seemed to be in conflict with the other children, and he never seemed to listen or follow even the simplest of Sarah's directions. Sarah began to wonder if Robert had some problem that was causing him to misbehave. She watched him carefully and wrote down her observations about when, where, and why he seemed to get into trouble.

Sarah began to suspect that Robert could not hear as well as he should. She noticed that while all the other children ran to the window each morning when they heard the garbage truck, Robert either did not respond at all or was the last to look up and run to the window. One day, Sarah stood quietly behind Robert and said very softly, "Robert, it's time for lunch." Although other children quickly responded, Robert never even looked up from his puzzle.

Sarah approached Robert's parents about the problem on several occasions. She said, "I'm not an expert in hearing problems, but I'm wondering if Robert could have a hearing problem. Has his pediatrician ever tested his hearing?" Robert's father said, "That's ridiculous. He hears whatever he wants to hear. He just chooses to ignore grown-ups most of the time." Robert's mother said, "His doctor hasn't ever mentioned a problem and I don't see any reason to think anything is wrong."

Sarah continued caring for and working with Robert, but she still had a nagging feeling that his behavior was just not up to par for a child who seemed very bright in other ways. She noticed that his relationship with his parents had deteriorated and that he was almost constantly in trouble with adults or other children. Finally, she set an appointment to sit down privately to talk with Robert's parents.

Sarah, with kindness and respect in her voice, said "I know that you have to do whatever you think is right for Robert, but I have to do what is right for me and for the other children in my care. I have become very attached to Robert. He is so full of creative energy. However, much of the time his behavior is out of control, and I don't know if I am doing the right thing for him. I worry that he may not be able to hear, and I wonder if that is part of the problem. I just don't feel comfortable caring for him without some kind of screening to at least rule out the possibility of a hearing problem."

Robert's father blurted out, "Fine! We'll just find someone else to care for him. We are not about to set out on some wild goose chase, looking for problems that don't exist." Sarah responded, "I understand. You have every right to do only what you believe is the best thing for your child. I'm sure that I would do the same myself. I need you to understand, though, that I am having real difficulty with Robert's behavior, and I just don't feel comfortable caring for him if I'm not sure I'm doing the right thing for him and for the other children. I am willing to accept your decision, and I'll do anything I can to help with the transition to a different child care situation. The important thing is for each of us to feel comfortable with what we do."

Robert's mother was not eager to find new child care for Robert. She really liked the way Sarah cared for the children. Robert's mother had several long discussions with her child's doctor and with her husband and finally convinced her husband that Robert should have his hearing tested in a medical clinic that specialized in that kind of thing.

Within every child is an adult in the making—and within every adult is a child who has just gotten older.

A few weeks later, Robert's father stopped by to talk to Sarah. He said, "You know, I was so sure that nothing was wrong with Robert's hearing that I really resented you insisting on a hearing test. I can't believe it, but the doctor says he has a seventy-five percent hearing loss in one ear and a slight loss in the other. I just didn't know."

Sarah responded, "I could have been right or I could have been wrong. I'm no expert on hearing, but I do appreciate knowing more about why he may have been having such a hard time behaving. Thank you for being so tolerant of my questions and concerns. I think we can all work together now much more effectively to help Robert get his act together."

As Robert's father turned to leave, he patted Robert's head and said softly, "Thank heavens for Sarah."

Questions for Discussion

1. Do you think Sarah's actions were within her role as a caregiver?
2. Do you think Sarah went too far in insisting that Robert's hearing be checked?
3. How do you think this story would have ended if nothing had been wrong with Robert's hearing?
4. Specifically, what things did Sarah say or do that made her assertiveness more tolerable to Robert's parents?
5. What would you have done?

Points to Remember

- At the heart of almost any behavior lies the desire to acquire something to meet some need.

- Maslow proposed that basic needs are arranged in a hierarchy of successive levels of needs.

- Unmet needs are a hidden cause of persistent patterns of dysfunctional behavior.

- In order to behave well, children must have a strong sense of self-esteem.

- Seeing children as lovable, capable, and worthwhile supports the growth of self-esteem.

- Children begin to develop self-esteem from birth if their needs are met by attentive caregivers and they are taught functional ways to get their needs met.

- The no-lose method of conflict resolution is a strategy for avoiding power struggles between adults and children.

- Dreikurs proposed that mistaken goals cause children to misbehave to get attention, gain control, get revenge, or remove themselves.

- Suppressing symptoms without paying attention to the emotional well-being of the child may result in the eruption of new or different symptoms.

- Healing can take place only when the child feels she is accepted, has some control, is treated fairly, and can succeed.

- Attachment to a dependable caregiver is an essential factor in the development of trust.

- Clingy children have not been "loved" too much, although they may well have been overindulged and overprotected.

- Children who are insecure in their sense of belonging should be given positive opportunities for responsibility and leadership and chances to entertain others in appropriate ways.

- Adults need to define clear limits and help children become aware of the feelings and reactions of those around them.

- Children need strong, reliable adult support in order to give up dysfunctional behaviors and form new habits.

- The destructive or aggressive child must know that she will be stopped—that others' rights will be protected.

- In dealing with a very difficult child, behavior modification may be an essential and effective tool for regaining a manageable relationship with the child.

- Adults must earn trust through consistent fairness and sincere interest in the child's well-being.

- Children who regularly indulge in fits of anger, tantrums, and defiance need to know that the adults who care for them will not explode into their own fits of anger.

- Although most children do things to make themselves feel better from time to time, the withdrawn child may rely on self-stimulation.

- The severely withdrawn child may avoid eye contact, refuse to talk or play, and stay apart from others most of the time.

- Overwhelming disruption in the children's daily lives may contribute to their feeling listless, inept, and hopeless.

- Adults must watch persistently misbehaving children for indications that underlying problems may be contributing to their misbehavior.

- Abuse and neglect have a profoundly negative effect on children's overall development and ability to comply with adult expectations.

- Adults must recognize their own needs and imperfections in order to be effective in child guidance.

Related Readings

Children Are Not for Hitting!

American Academy of Pediatrics. (1995). *Caring for your school-age child: Ages 5–12*. New York: Bantam Books.

Flynn, Clifton. (1996). Regional differences in spanking experiences and attitudes: A comparison of northeastern and southern college students. *Journal of Family Violence, 11*(1), 59–80.

Gallo, N. (1997). Why spanking takes the spunk out of kids. In E. N. Junn & C. Boyatzis (Eds.), *Annual editions: Child growth and development 97/98* (4th ed.). New York: McGraw-Hill. (Original work published in *Child,* March/April 1989)

> *Spanking is a very common form of discipline, but is it effective? Perhaps more importantly, does it do short-term or lasting psychological harm? Nick Gallo addresses these issues and offers alternative techniques to help people realize that discipline does not mean spanking, but it does mean instilling self-control in the child.*

Ladd, R. E. (Ed.). (1996). *Children's rights re-visioned: Philosophical readings*. Belmont, CA: Wadsworth.

> *This anthology helps students gain philosophical understanding as they pursue some provocative issues surrounding children's rights in our society.*

Leach, Penelope (1996, July 9). *Spanking: A shortcut to nowhere* [WWW document]. http://cnet.unb.ca/orgs/prevention_cruelty/spank.htm

No Spanking Page. http://www.cei.net/~rcox/nospan.html

Ruben, David. (1996, September). Should you spank? *Parenting,* 136–141.

Samalin, Nancy, & Whitney, Catherine. (1995, May). What's wrong with spanking? *Parents, 70*(5), 35–36.

Straus, Murray. (1995). *Beating the devil out of them: Corporal punishment in American families.* New York: Lexington Books.

Child Abuse

American Association for Protecting Children (AAPC). (1988). *Highlights of Official Child Neglect and Abuse Reporting, 1986.* Denver, CO: American Humane Association.

Conte, Jon R. (1986). *A look at child sexual abuse.* Chicago: National Committee to Prevent Child Abuse (NCPCA).

Douglas, H. (1991). Assessing violent couples. *Families in Society 72*(9), 525–535.

Finkelhor, D. (1986). *A sourcebook on child sexual abuse.* Beverly Hills, CA: Sage.

Finkelhor, D. (1994). Answers to important questions about the scope and nature of child sexual abuse. *Future of Children, 4*(2). Los Altos, CA: David and Lucille Packard Foundation.

Finkelhor, D., & Dziuba-Leatherman, J. (1997). Victimization of children. In E. N. Junn & C. Boyatzis (Eds.), *Annual editions: Child growth and development 97/98* (4th ed.). New York: McGraw-Hill. (Original work published in *American Psychologist,* March 1994)

> *This article gives statistics showing that children are more often victimized than are adults. Victimology of childhood falls into three broad categories: pandemic victimization (e.g., assault by siblings, parents, peers), acute victimization (e.g., physical abuse), and extraordinary victimization (e.g., homicide). The authors call for more research and theory on childhood victimology, using a developmental perspective.*

Finkelhor, D., & Williams, L. (1988). *Nursery crimes: Sexual abuse in day care.* Newbury Park, CA: Sage.

Goodman, G., & Rosenberg, M. (1987). The child witness to family violence: Clinical and legal considerations. In D. Sonkin (Ed.), *Domestic violence on trial: Psychological and legal dimensions of family violence.* New York: Springer.

Heineman, R. V. (1998). *The abused child psychodynamic: Understanding and treatment.* New York: Guilford.

> *The book traces the interplay of neurobiological and psychological facets of behavior to show how abuse derails normal development and how psychodynamic psychotherapy can reestablish emotional connections. Chapters highlight issues involved when working with children who have been physically, sexually, and emotionally abused, exploring memory and disclosure, dissociation and externalization, and the relationship between action and spoken language.*

Hilton, N. Z. (1992). Battered women's concerns about their children witnessing wife assault. *Journal of Interpersonal Violence, 7,* 77–86.

Ingrassia, M., & McCormick, J. (1997). Why leave children with bad parents? In E. N. Junn & C. Boyatzis (Eds.), *Annual editions: Child growth and development 97/98* (4th ed.). New York: McGraw-Hill. (Original work published in *Newsweek,* April 25, 1994)

> *In 1993 alone, there were one million confirmed cases of child neglect and abuse in the United States. Yet, in many states, the child welfare system often strives to keep families intact rather than put children in the care of foster parents (who came into greater demand in the late 1980s when crack use increased dramatically). The authors raise difficult issues about America's care for children at risk.*

Jaffe, P., Wolfe, D., & Wilson, S. (1990). *Children of battered women*. Newbury Park, CA: Sage.

Lung, C. T., & Daro, D. (1996). *Current trends in child abuse reporting and fatalities: The results of the 1995 annual fifty state survey.* Chicago: National Committee to Prevent Child Abuse.

McCurdy, K., & Daro, D. (1995). *Current trends in child abuse reporting and fatalities: The results of the 1994 annual fifty state survey.* Chicago: National Committee to Prevent Child Abuse.

National Committee to Prevent Child Abuse. (1993). *Think you know something about child abuse?* Chicago: Author.

National Committee to Prevent Child Abuse. (1998). *Child abuse and neglect statistics*. Chicago: Author.

Salovitz, B., & Keys, D. (1988). Is Child Protective Service still a service? *Protecting Children, 5*(2), 17–23.

Sedlak, A. (1996). *Early findings from the Third National Incidence Study of Child Abuse and Neglect: 1988.* Rockville, MD: Westat, Inc. (301) 251–4211.

Straus, M. A., & Gelles, R. (1990). *Physical violence in American families.* New Brunswick, NJ: Transaction.

Thoringer, D., Krivackska, J., Laye-McDonough, M., Jarrison, L., Vincent, O., & Hedlund, A. (1988). Prevention of child sexual abuse: An analysis of issues, educational programs and research findings. *School Psychology Review, 17*(4), 614–636.

U.S. Department of Health and Human Services, Children's Bureau. (1997). *National study of protective, preventive and reunification services delivered to children and their families.* Washington, DC: U.S. Government Printing Office.

Wang, C.T., & Daro, D. (1998). *Current trends in child abuse reporting and fatalities: The results of the 1997 annual fifty state survey.* Chicago: National Committee to Prevent Child Abuse.

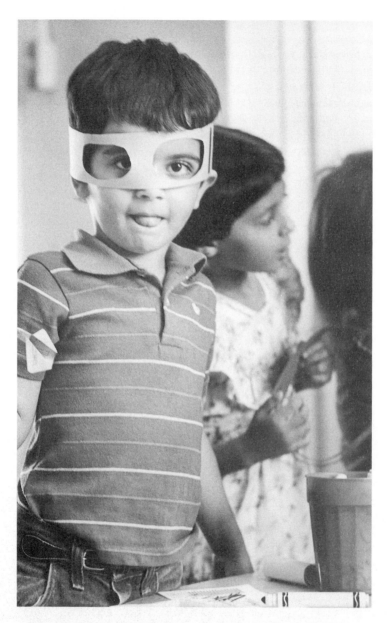

To guide children effectively, we must become skillful observers.

Chapter 9

Taking a New Look at Children

Chapter Outline

Objectives

This chapter will assist you in

- Identifying personal biases that affect guidance
- Recognizing the difference between objective and subjective observations
- Listing effective observation strategies
- Using observations for prescriptive guidance
- Identifying components of the observation sequence

Identifying Personal Biases

Gilda is a bright, gregarious ball of energy. When she was in kindergarten, she popped out of bed every morning before the sun was up because she loved going to school each day. Her teacher, Mr. Costa, seemed to really like her. He often invited her to help with classroom chores like feeding the goldfish or passing out napkins for snack. Since she learned concepts very quickly, he encouraged her to help other children, a responsibility she took very seriously. Gilda liked pretending that she was a teacher, and the younger children thrived on her persistent tutoring. Whenever anyone asked her what she wanted to be when she grew up, she always answered quickly, "A schoolteacher just like Mr. Costa!"

During Gilda's first day of first grade, she eagerly tried to get the attention of her new teacher, Mrs. Redwing, and jumped up to help pass out papers. Mrs. Redwing reprimanded Gilda for getting up out of her desk without asking and said, "Please stop asking me questions and just sit quietly and listen." Mrs. Redwing thought, "Oh, no, another hyperactive kid. That's all I need."

Over a period of time, Gilda has become impatient and unhappy. She cries in the morning and tells her father that she does not want to go to school anymore. Mrs. Redwing is upset too. She is becoming more and more frustrated with Gilda's behavior, which eventually has become disruptive and, at times, even defiant. Mrs. Redwing has become especially exasperated with Gilda's attempts to help other children do their work whenever they have trouble, an action Mrs. Redwing considers a kind of "cheating."

One day Mr. Costa and Mrs. Redwing are sitting in the teacher's lounge drinking coffee. Mr. Costa says, "How is Gilda doing this year? I really miss her . . . what a terrific little girl she is." Mrs. Redwing chokes on her coffee and sputters, "Gilda? You've got to be kidding! She drives me absolutely up the wall."

How is it possible for two people to see the same child's behavior so differently? We see children differently because we are different. Everything that we perceive with our senses (eyes, ears, and so on) is filtered through layers upon layers of our own personal views. Our **biases** are these sets of beliefs, values, and assumptions that develop from our upbringing, our past experiences, and our personal philosophy of life.

Mr. Costa responds favorably to Gilda's energy and spontaneity because she reminds him of himself when he was younger. He values creativity so he is delighted by Gilda's bright mind. In contrast, because of her very strict upbringing, Mrs. Redwing learned early in life to suppress any fidgety impulses she had, so she finds it particularly annoying to deal with Gilda's chattering and bounciness, behaviors her parents would never have tolerated. These behaviors strike Mrs. Redwing as rude and reckless, even though she can remember resenting her parents' rigidness toward her when she was a child.

How Can I Respond More Objectively to Individual Children?

It is inevitable that some children will be more appealing than others to any given adult. Our own personality and style cannot be perfectly matched to the needs of every child; however, we can at least be fair in our treatment of different children. Within families, parents sometimes admit that one of their own children seems easier to understand and manage while another child's behavior seems totally incomprehensible. In group settings, an adult may have difficulty admitting that he or she feels more comfortable with children who are small or large, male or female, black or white, rich or poor.

In order to respond more to children's behaviors, we must focus on our own areas of bias. What preconceived notions do I have about children? Do I expect certain behaviors or motivations from children based on ethnic, gender, or appearance differences? How can I focus on who an individual child really is rather than on the stereotypes I associate with generalized groups or categories of people?

One way to increase objectivity is to consciously separate facts from opinions. What do I actually **perceive** (through looking, listening, touching, tasting, and smelling), and what do I interpret intuitively based on my knowledge, experience, and/or bias? By sorting through our own thinking processes to separate facts from opinions, we can more accurately focus on actual child behaviors and scrutinize our interpretations of the meaning of those actions.

If Mrs. Redwing had separated the facts from the opinions in her own observations, she might have seen Gilda differently. For example:

Objective Observations (Mr. Costa and Mrs. Redwing both agree that these are accurate facts): Gilda talks frequently; begins tasks quickly; completes work before others in class; is active and quick in physical movements; expresses interest in the progress of classmates.

Mr. Costa's Interpretations: Gilda is very capable in verbal communications; she is a competent, bright student; she is enthusiastic about her schoolwork; she has leadership potential; she cares intensely about others.

Mrs. Redwing's Interpretations: Gilda ignores the teacher and class rules about talking; she rushes through her work because she does not take it seriously enough; she is overactive; she worries about the affairs of other children when that is none of her business.

When one's opinions are stated separately from observable facts, and those opinions are clearly labeled as "subjective interpretation," then it is much easier to recognize and deal with personal bias. If we trick ourselves into believing that our opinions are objective facts, then we lose an opportunity to see children as they really are. We can consciously learn to be more objective in our thinking.

For example, the following observation is filled with opinions: "Erik angrily stomped into the kitchen trying to pick a fight with someone. He taunted his sister and hurt her feelings just to see her cry. He hoped she would hit him so he would have an excuse to get her in trouble." These statements are pure fantasy. We cannot see into Erik's head to look at his intentions or hear his thoughts.

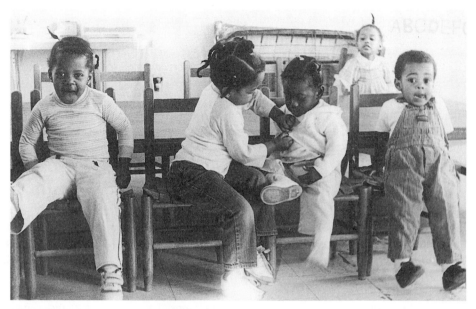

To be objective, we must focus on the things we actually see and hear.

What we can actually see and hear is that Erik "stomped into the kitchen. He looked around with a frown on his face. He pointed to his sister's sandwich and said, 'Yuk, are you going to eat that gooey mess?' His sister began to cry and threatened to hit Erik. Erik said, 'If you hit me, I'll tell Mom.'" What we may interpret is that Erik seemed irritable—unhappy and in a mood to agitate his sister.

The first opinionated description tempts us to punish Erik for his obnoxious behavior because we assume we know why he behaved the way he did. The second, more objective way of reporting Erik's behavior reminds us that we do not know everything that is going on in Erik's mind and heart. Objective observation encourages us to look further for reasons for actions, and to better understand troublesome behavior.

The Observation Sequence

To be effective in working with children, we must become skilled observers so that we can constantly improve the quality of the care and education we provide. Our ongoing observations should result in concrete plans and changes in the curriculum and environment. Child guidance is much more an art than a science.

There is no clear-cut recipe for handling children that works for all children in all circumstances, but with careful observation the adult can gather the information needed to make intelligent decisions and to select appropriate methods to prevent or respond to various problems. Later, the adult can observe to evaluate how effective the chosen guidance technique has been in solving the problem.

How Does Observation Support Positive Guidance?

In order for any effort at resolving a behavior problem to be effective, it must be well matched to the child's ability and frame of mind as well as to the circumstances surrounding the behavior. Does the child appear to be feeling angry and destructive or just bored and silly? Is the behavior habitual or a rare event? Is the child capable of benefiting from verbal reminders or is direct physical redirection required? What actually is the problem—when, where, and why does it occur? These are all questions that should be answered through careful observation.

What Do I Need to Get Started?

There are many excellent checklists, kits, and observational instruments (tests) available commercially to assist early childhood professionals in observing children. For most parents, caregivers, and preschool teachers, however, the most useful record-keeping tool (and definitely the least expensive) is simply a pocket-sized spiral notepad and a pencil. If paper and pencil are available whenever something interesting occurs, it will be a great deal easier to get something written down. No record-keeping instrument of any kind is of value if it stays in a desk drawer or a file cabinet.

With a little pocket notepad, an anecdote can be described before the details are forgotten, tidbits can be added regularly to a running account, or some type of sampling checklist can be maintained. It is easy for us to think, "I don't need to write this down. I'm sure I'll remember it." But then, of course, we forget whatever it was that we were so sure we would remember.

What observations can you make from this picture? (Hint: His big sister painted the box and he is not happy.)

How Will I Use My Observations?

Interpreting observations is the process of **inferring meaning** from what has actually been sensed (seen, heard, touched, tasted, or smelled). In order to interpret what has been observed, one has to rely on a knowledge of child development in general as well as of the unique development of an individual child. One can additionally rely on firsthand experience with other children as well as with the individual child in question. All of this means we should take what we sense at the present time and mull over it using all of our past knowledge and experience to create new ideas about why the child may need to behave as she does.

Looking back over observation notes can be surprisingly enlightening. Children grow and change so quickly that we may be startled to look back at our notes about little Bronwyn and see that only three months ago she cried and clung to us when other children were around. Now she confidently approaches others to initiate play. By seeing a child's progress over time, we can make better sense of the child's immediate behavior, and know what help and guidance the child needs in order to behave more appropriately.

Personal bias must be kept in check while interpreting one's observations. Observation records, particularly objective checklists, may provide convincing evidence that our intuitive assumptions about a particular child have simply been wrong. Interpreting observations also gives us an opportunity to see things from the child's point of view. We may be annoyed with a child for interrupting our conversations but, after observing her carefully, realize that she really deserves to be included more in adult interactions and just needs to be taught how to join a conversation politely.

How Does My Observation Become a Plan?

In a doctor's office, a patient is seen and observation records are written into a chart. The observations of the physician are then carefully interpreted (diagnosed)—what is the meaning of the rash? . . . of the fever? . . . of the pain in the left foot? Then, most importantly, a plan is formulated (a prescription) to remedy the problem. The doctor prescribes bedrest or an antibiotic. We prescribe five minutes away from an activity, an understanding, heart-to-heart talk about hurting people's feelings, or a change in our own behavior toward the child by giving more positive attention or more developmentally appropriate activities.

What If My Plan Does Not Work?

After a plan is formulated, the next step is action. Some adults take a fatalistic attitude toward children's misbehavior. They think children will not change and consequently do not bother doing anything other than complain about their inappropriate or immature behaviors. Young children are avid learners. They learn new habits much more easily than older children or adults. They just need time, effort, encouragement, and a great deal of practice to master the social skills and control of impulses they need to be responsible, cooperative group members.

Sometimes, even if the action we attempt does not really work very well, the simple fact that we are focused on the child's problem (and care enough to try to resolve it) may stimulate the child's own awareness of the problem and commitment to correct it. It will be very therapeutic for the child to see evidence from our actions that "I care about you. I am willing to make a real effort to help you learn to use words rather than fists to express your feelings. I won't give up on you."

As long as the action is positive and respectful of the child, it is far more important for us to formulate a plan and do something than to worry about being right every time. Perfectionists are often so paralyzed by their fear of making mistakes that they never get around to doing anything. Children can learn valuable lessons from our handling of our own mistakes. They can learn that everyone makes mistakes from time to time and that admitting mistakes is nothing to be ashamed of. We could set a good example by saying, "Joshua, I asked you to hold my hand on our walk to help you remember to stay on the sidewalk where it's safe. I made a mistake. I didn't think about how that might make you feel like a baby. Let's think of a different way to help you be safe."

How Can I Be Sure My Plan Is Working?

Is what we are doing effective? In the evaluation phase, we make a complete circle and come back to observing. The only way we can be sure if we were on target in our first observation, interpretation, plan, and resulting action is to observe again and look for indications that our plan is or is not working. If it is working, we can relax and go on to the next problem. If it is not, we return to square one, collect more information through observation, and develop a new and improved plan of action. This cycle repeats until we successfully hit a plan that works (or the child outgrows the behavior, becomes the responsibility of the next teacher, or gets married and moves to another town).

Observation Strategies

Researchers use carefully orchestrated strategies to collect objective data. Adults who care for young children rarely need such formal methodology; we just need a workable plan for finding out the "what, when, where, and why" of children's problem behaviors so that we can respond effectively and appropriately. The following sections describe some useful methods for keeping track and making sense of puzzling or upsetting behaviors (Barko, 1997; Bentzen, 1997; Billman & Sherman, 1997; Bredekamp & Copple, 1997; Green & Stafford, 1997; Harms & Clifford, 1998; McLean, Bailey, & Wolery, 1997; Mindes, Ireton, & Mardell-Czudnowski, 1996).

What Is an Anecdotal Record?

An anecdotal record is an attempt to record in detail a specific episode that is of particular interest or concern. A specific event takes place that catches the attention of the adult. As soon as possible, the adult writes a narrative account; she tells the story of the event. She describes all of the pertinent details that she can recall—what she actually saw, heard, or otherwise perceived with her senses. She will include verbatim quotes whenever possible to further clarify the interaction. Any personal opinions or interpretations will be set apart and clearly identified as observer's comments by such phrases as "It appeared to me that . . ." or "Therefore, it was my impression that. . . ."

Following is an example of an anecdotal record of a toddler biting incident:

Observations: *Ricky wandered slowly around the room, whining and shaking his head. After about five minutes, he abruptly dropped to the floor and began to cry. Periodically he stopped crying to sit up, suck his thumb, and twist a tuft of his hair while he looked around, then he would close his eyes, drop back on the floor, and begin sobbing again.*

I picked up a handful of picture books and sat down on the floor beside him. I said, "Ricky, would you like to read a book? Look, it's a book about kitty cats." At first he ignored me, but finally he crawled into my lap and laid his head on my chest as he continued to suck his thumb and make the jerky little sniffing sounds that follow a bout of hard crying. I began to read the story about kittens.

After only a few minutes, Katherine toddled over and plopped into my lap practically on top of Ricky. Before I had even a second to respond, Ricky had grabbed Katherine's face and hair and had sunk his teeth into her cheek.

Comments/Interpretations: *Ricky was probably frightened and anxious because he has not been away from his mother very often. He seems to be showing evidence of a great deal of separation anxiety. He may have felt threatened by Katherine's presence, since he has no sisters or brothers and may not be accustomed to sharing adult attention with others. I will have to watch Ricky very carefully so that I can help him find ways to cope with his feelings, and I can anticipate and intervene better in situations where he might hurt another child.*

What observations can you make from this picture? (Hint: Look at the children's facial expressions and body postures.)

What Is a Running Account?

In a running account, a specific type of behavior is noted each time it occurs. A mother who worries that her child is not eating properly may keep a running account for a period of time, keeping track of when, where, and what her child eats during and between meals each day. After a few days or weeks she could begin to see if specific eating patterns emerge. Does the child pick at meals but consume high-calorie junk food during frequent snacks? Does the child eat a well-balanced lunch and afternoon snack but often refuse supper? Does the child eat whatever is offered at home but get into power struggles over food with a caregiver in the child care center?

Following is an example of a running account of a four-year-old girl's incidences of nail biting:

Observations: *Monday, 8:00 A.M.—Celia bit her nails while watching cartoons on television; she had a very tense facial expression.*

Monday, 3:30 P.M.—Celia and her best friend Joel had an argument; after he told her he wouldn't play with her anymore, she sat by herself on the steps for a long time, biting her nails; again, she appeared very tense.

Tuesday, 11:30 A.M.—Celia bit her nails while she waited for lunch; she appeared more bored than tense.

Tuesday, 4:30 P.M.—Celia bit her nails the whole time she watched a television cartoon; her whole body appeared to be tense as she sat on the edge of her chair and strained toward the TV.

Comments/Interpretations: *Tension (and possibly boredom) seems to be triggering Celia's nail biting. She was not seen biting her nails when she was coloring, playing dolls, or putting together puzzles. It may be helpful to redirect Celia to more active play and to discourage her watching television cartoons on a regular basis.*

What Is Time sampling?

The purpose of time sampling is to determine the patterns of occurrence and general frequency of specific behaviors either in an individual or in the entire group. In time sampling, a particular interval of time is selected—five minutes, thirty minutes, an hour, and so on. Then, at the designated time intervals, a checklist is marked to show whether the chosen behavior is or is not occurring at that moment. For example, an individual child could be watched at intervals to determine whether the child is spending more time actively engaged in play or passively watching others. An entire class could be watched to see how often the reading center is used as compared to the block center. This procedure can give factual evidence to back up or refute an adult's intuitive impressions about the occurrence of various patterns of behavior.

Following is a time sampling checklist used by a preschool teacher to help her study her students' patterns of being "on task" (involved in productive skill development or learning activity) rather than misbehaving, wandering aimlessly, or just watching:

Classroom Observations

Time	Misbehaving	Wandering	Watching
8:15 A.M.	James, Jill	Suzette, Amy, Tyler	Ben, Ann
8:30 A.M.	James	Amy	Suzette
8:45 A.M.	Amy, Suzette	—	—
9:00 A.M.	Tyler	—	—
9:15 A.M.	—	—	—
9:30 A.M.	—	Suzette	—
9:45 A.M.	Amy, Ben	Jill, Tyler	Suzette
10:00 A.M.	Suzette, Ann	Tyler	Jill, Amy
10:15 A.M.	Suzette	Ann, Tyler, Ben	Amy

Comments/Interpretations: *This group of children have more difficulty staying on task at the beginning and the end of the morning. Their most productive time is between 8:45 and 9:30. Suzette, Amy, and Tyler may need special attention to help them focus on productive activity. James seemed able to avoid misbehavior after he settled into productive activity.*

What observations can you make from this picture? (Hint: What can you tell about their relationships with each other? What can you tell about their mood?) (Photograph provided courtesy of CHILDREN AT RISK.)

What Is Event Sampling?

The purpose of event sampling is to determine the precise number of times a specific behavior occurs within a set period of time as well as the pattern of occurrence. Individual children can be observed for occurrences of a specific behavior, or an entire group can be watched, and a total number of occurrences of a behavior (such as aggression) can be recorded and tallied. In event sampling, a specific action (or actions) is designated for observation. When the behavior occurs, a checklist is marked so that after a given period of time, the adult can tally the exact number of times the behavior took place.

Following is an event sampling checklist used by a child care worker to determine the individual daily progress of several toddlers in their toilet training (each accident has been recorded as an x):

Toileting Accidents

Names	Monday	Tuesday	Wednesday	Thursday	Friday
Reily	xxx	xxx	xxx	x	
Joseph	xx				
Mariette	xxx	xx	x	x	
Ella	xxxx	xxxxx	xxxx	xxxx	xxxx
Prichart			x	xx	
Bethany	xx		x		

Comments/Interpretations: *Ella may not really be ready for toilet training at this time. It may be helpful to observe Mariette more closely to determine if she is having difficulty at a specific time of day or under specific circumstances. Reily had difficulty early in the week but managed to stay dry most of the day Thursday and all day Friday. He should probably be watched further to see what happens the following week.*

Which Method of Recording Observations Works Best?

Checklists and narrative accounts can be used as tools for gathering information in many different situations. The particular advantage of narrative accounts is that they create word pictures that may provide insight into a child's behavior far beyond that originally anticipated when the event was recorded.

The adult can look back over several anecdotal records and discover new, previously overlooked relationships or details each time. The biggest drawback to narratives is, of course, that they are very time consuming and so can only be relied on for recording occasional rather than routine occurrences. Narratives collect qualitative information while checklists collect quantitative information. Qualitative information is focused on the descriptive qualities or characteristics of behaviors. Quantitative information is focused on numerical and statistical calculations that tell how often or to what degree behaviors occur.

Checklists leave out all of the details surrounding behaviors and focus only on the frequencies and distributions of occurrences. They are especially useful for making comparisons—not only of one child's behaviors to that of other children, but to the child's own behaviors at other times of day, in other settings, or at an earlier age. The major advantage of checklists is the ease with which they can be used. The major drawback is that a great deal of important information about the extenuating background circumstances of a behavior are not recorded.

The checklist examples provided earlier gave a great deal more factual information about many more children than the anecdotal record and the running account; however, you probably feel that you know much more about what Ricky and Celia (described in the narrative accounts) are really like than any of the children listed on the checklists.

Practical Application/Discussion

The Mysterious Case of the Spinning Peg

Felicia, an afternoon assistant in an infant/toddler child care center, is sitting on the floor and pulling the string of a "See and Say" toy. Lisa is laughing. Felicia asks, "Where are the fish? Can you see the fish? There they are—seven of them." She laughs and tickles Lisa's tummy. Other toddlers push close to Felicia as they laugh and interact with her. They watch every move that Felicia makes.

Lisa, who is eighteen-months-old, wanders away from them toward me as I sit on the vinyl padded tunnel. Lisa accidentally drops a large plastic peg she is carrying. When it hits the wooden stair by her it spins for about five seconds. She stares at it with a look of wonder. She carefully picks it up and with great concentration drops it on the step again, but this time it does not spin. She stares at it, squats beside the stairs, then proceeds to drop it again and again on the carpet.

It does not spin. She stands up and throws it down on the carpet. It does not spin! She bites it hard, throws it two more times, but still it does not spin. She leaves the peg lying on the floor and walks away. Felicia picks it up and puts it away.

Lisa comes over to me, looks at my writing and at my face. She pats my tablet and then pulls at the pages. She looks very seriously at my eyes. She then walks away. I hear her whine as she walks over to the play sink. She stops abruptly, looks at a plastic fruit, then with great interest she watches it as she drops it to the floor. It does not spin.

She sucks her finger and starts to cry. Felicia picks her up and comforts her then walks away saying, "You're getting a little fussy. I wonder if you're hungry. Let me see if you get an afternoon bottle."

Questions for Discussion

1. What are the objective observations you could have actually seen, heard, and so on if you had been observing this interaction?

2. What are your own personal interpretations of the interaction?

3. Why do you think Lisa started to cry?

4. What can you tell about the relationship between Lisa and her caregiver, Felicia?

Points to Remember

- We see children differently because we are different.

- Everything that we perceive with our senses (eyes, ears, and so on) is filtered through layers upon layers of our own personal point of view (our bias).

- One way to increase objectivity is to make a conscious effort to separate facts from opinions.

- Observations help us evaluate how effective a chosen guidance technique has been in solving a problem.

- We need a workable plan for finding out the "what, when, where, and why" of children's problem behaviors so that we can respond effectively and appropriately.

- An anecdotal record is a narrative description of a specific episode.

- A running account describes a type of behavior each time it occurs.

- Time sampling records patterns of occurrence and frequency of specific behaviors.

- Event sampling determines the number of times a specific behavior occurs within a set period of time.

Related Readings

Developmentally Appropriate Assessment

Benjamin, A. C. (1994). Observations in early childhood classrooms: Advice from the field. *Young Children, 49*(6), 14–20.

Bentzen, W. R. (1997). Seeing young children: A guide to observing and recording behavior (3d ed.). Albany, NY: Delmar Publishers, an International Thomson Publishing company.

> Seeing Young Children *is designed to provide essential background information on many aspects of child development and recording techniques. These two bodies of information then form the basis for the individual to observe and record young children's behavior in child care centers, early childhood classrooms, homes, public schools, and various other kinds of settings.*

Billman, J., Sherman, J. A. (1997). *Observation and participation in early childhood settings: A practicum guide, birth through age five.* Needham Heights, MA: Allyn & Bacon.

Feinburg, S. G., & Mindess, M. (1994). *Designing and evaluating developmentally based programs for young children.* Needham Heights, MA: Brooks/Cole.

> *This book describes what makes a quality early childhood program, and explains the proce-dures through which quality programs can be developed, nurtured, and maintained. The authors discuss the process of designing and maintaining excellent programs that develop children's full potential throughout the curriculum and offer a guide for an ongoing process of evaluation.*

Gaustad, J. (1996). Assessment and evaluation in the multiage classroom [Special issue]. *OSSC Bulletin, 39*(3–4).

Hills, T. W. (1992). Reaching potentials through appropriate assessment. In S. Bredekamp and T. Rosegrant (Eds.), *Reaching potentials: Appropriate curriculum and assessment for young children.* Washington, DC: National Association for the Education of Young Children.

Hills, T. W. (1993). Assessment in context—Teachers and children at work. *Young Children, 48*(5), 20–28.

> *To be developmentally appropriate and to best serve children's needs, assessment should be included as an integrated part of an overall program. It is most effective when it contributes*

positively to children's self-esteem and developmental process, recognizes children's individuality, and respects their family and community backgrounds.

Katz, Lilian G. (1995). *Talks with teachers of young children: A collection.* Norwood, NJ: Ablex.

Katz, L. G., & Chard, Sylvia C. (1996). The contribution of documentation to the quality of early childhood education. *ERIC Digest.* Urbana, IL: ERIC Clearinghouse on Elementary and Early Childhood Education.

McLean, M. E., Bailey, D. B., Jr., & Wolery, M. (1997). *Assessing infants and preschoolers with special needs* (2d ed.). Upper Saddle River, NJ: Merrill Education/Prentice-Hall.

A text written for early childhood special educators and other professionals who work with infants and preschoolers, focusing on assessment for the purpose of planning effective intervention programs.

National Association for the Education of Young Children (1991). Guidelines for appropriate curriculum content and assessment in programs serving children ages 3 through 8. *Young Children, 46*(3), 21–38.

Shepard, L. A. (1994). The challenges of assessing young children appropriately. *Phi Delta Kappan, 76*(3), 206–212.

Southern Association on Children Under Six (1990). *Developmentally appropriate assessment.* Little Rock, AR: Author.

We celebrate our cultural and physical differences, and remember that underneath the skin, we are all very much the same. (Photograph provided courtesy of CHILDREN AT RISK.)

Chapter 10

Culturally Sensitive Guidance

Chapter Outline

Historical Perspectives
The Child in Society
Preparation for Participation in a Democracy
The Strain of Changing Disciplinary Traditions
Cultural Influences on Child Rearing
Preparing Children for the Realities of an Adult World
Parent Expectations Related to Social and Economic Settings
Understanding Cultural Differences
Philosophies of Guidance

> The Nature Versus Nurture Controversy
> The Behaviorist Approach
> The Maturationist Approach
> The Developmental Interactionist Approach

Practical Application/Discussion

Bringing Home a Baby Bumblebee

Questions for Discussion
Points to Remember
Related Readings

Objectives

This chapter will assist you in

- Recognizing historical events related to beliefs about children

- Outlining the child's role in society

- Identifying the role of child guidance in a democracy

- Listing changes in disciplinary strategies over time
- Outlining tenets of various folk ideologies of child guidance
- Recognizing cultural differences that affect child rearing
- Identifying behaviorist approaches to guidance
- Identifying maturationist approaches to guidance
- Identifying developmental interactionist approaches to guidance

Historical Perspectives

Child care and guidance practices have changed drastically through the years. Many child care traditions from the past would seem strange, even cruel, to modern parents. For example, swaddling, the snug wrapping of infants in strips of cloth or blankets, is an ancient custom that has persisted for centuries in many parts of the world. While snugly wrapping newborns in blankets is considered to be a very appropriate tradition in most modern cultures, the old practice of swaddling was intended to control the baby's movement and routinely continued until the child was old enough to walk. John Locke (1699) described the customary child care of his day:

> rolled and swathed, ten or a dozen times round; then blanket upon blanket, mantle upon that; its little neck pinned down to one posture; its head more than it frequently needs, triplecrowned like a young page, with covering upon covering; its legs and arms as if to prevent that kindly stretching which we rather ought to promote . . . the former bundled up, the latter pinned down; and how the poor thing lies on the nurse's lap, a miserable little pinioned captive (cited in Cunnington and Buck, p. 103).

In western Europe during the first half of the eighteenth century, infants were seen not only as somehow less human than older people, but also as somewhat expendable. A wealthy mother usually sent her newborn infant to the care of a hired wet nurse, who was expected to breastfeed and care for the child, often at the expense of the life of the wet nurse's own infant. Infant mortality rates reportedly reached as high as eighty percent in some areas as wetnurse mothers, in order to ensure their livelihood, gave birth to stimulate the production of breast milk, then sent their own infants to poorly maintained foundling homes (Weiser, 1982).

The writings of Rousseau toward the end of the eighteenth century both influenced and reflected a change in the cultural perception of childhood. He insisted that "everything is good as it comes from the hands of the Author of Nature" (Rousseau, 1893, p. 1). He argued that rather than being an evil creature who must have sin beaten out of him, the young child is born good and innocent. He believed that the harsh discipline techniques of that day, which were intended to provide the child salvation from original sin, tainted the child rather than provided healthy, normal growth. Rousseau's prescription for child care included breastfeeding by the natural mother, fresh air, loose clothing, and a minimum of interference from adults. Certain tribes of Native Americans in the 1900s particularly valued physical toughness in their children. To build up the child's resistance, newborns were plunged into cold water several times at birth, regardless of the weather. Their version of swaddling was to fasten the baby securely onto a cradleboard that could be conveniently hung inside the lodge, from a tree branch, from a saddlebow, or wherever family members were clustered. Babies were not released from the confines of cradleboards until they were able to walk (Weiser, 1982).

American mothers of European descent sent their infants and young children to the neighborhood widow or spinster for care and teaching. In these "dame schools," a baby might nap on a quilt in a corner of the kitchen while older children practiced reading from the New Testament (Weiser, 1982). Farm and slave children were valued as a source of free labor. Toddlers barely able to walk were assigned chores and held accountable for them. By the early 1900s, momentum had begun to build promoting the scientific study of the development of children and the dissemination of pertinent information to parents. Some of the writings of that day foretold future trends in thinking about young children. For example, a book produced by The Institute of Child Welfare at the University of Minnesota in 1930 warned parents that children's personal characteristics were not necessarily inborn:

> As a matter of fact, the modern study of young children is indicating that such traits are in large part due to the manner in which the child is treated by adults and other children, rather than to inheritance. The parent who has the ideal of complete and unquestioning obedience, and who is forceful and consistent enough to obtain it, is likely to have a child who, when he goes to school, distresses a good teacher and delights a poor one by always doing what he is told and furthermore by always waiting to be told what to do. His whole attitude is that of finding out what authority requires and then complying, an attitude which, if maintained, is apt to result in incompetence, inefficiency, and unhappiness in adulthood (Faegre & Anderson, 1930, pp. 45).

The early 1900s brought changes in people's beliefs about childhood, and their expectations for children.

How Has The Modern World Influenced Thinking About Child Guidance?

During the twentieth century, ideas about children have been influenced by two world wars, alternating periods of economic depression and prosperity, and by growing scientific interest in child development research. At the end of World War II, Maria Montessori wrote such books as *Peace and Education* (1971) and *Reconstruction in Education* (1968) to express her view that the hope for world peace lay in a new education for young children. Montessori (1971) wrote:

> Certainly we cannot achieve [peace] by attempting to unite all these people who are so different, but it can be achieved if we begin with the child. When the child is born he has no special language, he has no special religion, he has not any national or racial prejudice. It is men [sic] who have acquired all these things. (p. 6)

In the late 1940s and into the 1950s researchers began to unlock some of the mysteries of early learning. The common belief that experiences of the first years of life were inconsequential to later development was pushed aside by more complex theories explaining the development of intelligence and personality. These new theories placed greater emphasis on early social interaction and exploration of the physical environment (Erikson, 1963; Harlow & Zimmerman, 1959; Piaget, 1952, 1962, 1963, 1968, 1970; Skinner, 1953; Wolff, 1963). In the 1960s, research into the learning processes of children from birth to school age flourished, and an estimated 23 million books on child rearing were sold during the mid-1970s (Clarke-Stewart, 1978). Since the

Over the years, the educators, philosophers, and scientists have profoundly influenced our views on child guidance.

1970s, there has been a mushrooming growth of parental as well as scientific interest in the processes of child growth and development (Elkind, 1997; Petersen, 1996).

The Child in Society

Children occupy a very special niche in our society (Cowan & Cowan, 1992; Gutek, 1997; Hoffman & Manis, 1979). They are dressed in fancy clothing, photographed, given many colorful objects made especially for children (toys), fed special foods from tiny glass jars, and equipped with elaborate contraptions designed for sitting, swinging, strolling, eating, and crawling. Compared with previous cultures, children today are pampered and indulged. A bright-eyed baby decked out in several yards of lace, scented leakproof disposable diapers, and a huge bonnet will bring oohs and ahhs from shoppers in a supermarket and comments such as, "Oh, isn't it adorable! Look at its little shoes and its tiny earrings!"

The practice of referring to infants (and sometimes toddlers) with impersonal pronouns, such as *it,* tell us a lot about our perception of babies. The use of such descriptors as "it" and "thing" in reference to children gives a subtle indication that babies are not perceived as real persons. Several centuries ago, impersonal references to children were even more pervasive than they are today. Children were commonly referred to as "it" well into early childhood—"in this age [birth to seven years] it cannot talk well or form its words perfectly, for its teeth are not yet well arranged or firmly implanted" (Le Grand Proprietaire, cited in Aries, 1962, p. 21). At the present time, in spite of indications that infants may generally be seen as somewhat less than fully human, we place a great deal more emphasis on the value and importance of individual children's lives than was evident in the past.

A contemporary baby finds himself the center of attention. (Photograph provided courtesy of CHILDREN AT RISK.)

Parents may refer to a fetus as an "it" before the child's birth, but one almost never hears parents refer to their own baby as "it" afterward, especially after they have come to know and love him. Strangers are always more likely to refer impersonally to a baby or child. For example, a newspaper account of an alleged brutal child abuse murder quoted a district attorney explaining to shocked citizens why the murder victim, a two-year-old boy, had been given back to his natural mother after having been removed since early infancy for neglect: "Most reasonable people . . . might say the decision to put it [the child] back was probably a bad call. . . ." (Krupinski & Weikel). When asked about the use of impersonal references for babies, people often explain that "it" is used because the baby's sex may not be known. Interestingly, in discussing older children and adults, even if that person's gender is not known, it would be considered highly inappropriate to refer to that person (a salesperson, a mail carrier, or an acquaintance's teenager) as an "it." Only after an older child or adult dies is that person's body referred to as an "it."

How Is Life Different for Contemporary Children in Today's Changing World?

Children today are not only valued but are usually thought to have a fairly carefree existence, in contrast to earlier generations' use of child labor. In past years, young children have generally been allowed to spend a good portion of their days playing, fooling around, romping in the sunshine, and generally occupying themselves (sometimes in front of a television set). Child care has brought new levels of structure to many children's lives. In many early childhood programs, this structure has enriched children's lives and assisted in their development of healthy and productive habits. In other child care settings, children spend a considerable amount of time sitting, waiting, being berated, standing in line, and taking part in activities that are initiated and controlled by adults and are carried out by lockstep groups of children (Werner, 1987).

A young child is a full-fledged human being with personal rights and needs.

Since many affluent parents are having fewer children, and waiting until their professional careers are well established before having them, there is new pressure on some children to live up to the "fast lane" expectations of their parents. In the push for superbabies and superior children, many youngsters may be given gymnastics, music lessons, dance lessons, tutoring, and yoga before they ever start kindergarten. Their lives may become so full of "enrichment" activities that they run out of time to lie in the clover and experience wonder as they watch clouds go by. In an era when parents feel pressured to create a "superchild," they may inadvertently destroy some of the wonder and magic of early childhood.

The young child's role in contemporary society sometimes approaches that of a pet or a possession rather than a person deserving respect and dignity. From time to time, that role may mean that the child is indulged, pampered, forgotten, rushed, herded, and pushed (Kantrowitz & Wingert, 1997; Ladd, 1996; Silvers, 1997; Stengel, 1997). She may be expected to be perfect at all times, or be coerced to perform cute tricks on cue to entertain or impress adults. Our growing knowledge of and emphasis on early childhood has put youngsters on a pedestal. But, of course, being on a pedestal has distinct disadvantages as well as advantages—being on a pedestal means that every move one makes is watched, judged, and managed. Early childhood experts have growing concern that children are not being allowed the freedom to "just be children."

Preparation for Participation in a Democracy

Settings where young children live, work, and play (whether in a home or a child care facility) function as their small version of the world. As has been previously discussed, interaction in familial, educational, and caregiving communities helps children learn how to participate later in adult community life. Child guidance is the process by which adults help children learn appropriate ways to function as part of a group. In an **autocracy,** people would only need to learn blind obedience in order to function appropriately. People are dominated by a dictator who demands submission. In an **anarchy,** one could follow one's own desires and interests. Chaos prevails because no one governs. In a **democracy,** however, educated, responsible citizens are needed to provide effective self-governance through active participation.

The guidance practices carried out by adults can help children learn how to participate in a democracy by developing the necessary skills.

Critical Skills for Good Citizenship

- *Concept of citizenship—being cooperative, having a sense of fair play, and respecting the rights of others*
- *Initiative and self-reliance—being a self-starter, a lifelong learner, and a creative problem solver*
- *Responsible work habits—having established habits of promptness, effort, and pride*
- *Sense of loyalty—recognizing that sometimes one's own immediate interests and desires must be pushed aside for the good of the whole community*

How Do Early Influences Affect Children's Growth and Development in Terms of Their Learning Appropriate Behavior?

Modern researchers only recently, during the 1970s and 1980s, began studying how various approaches in early childhood programs affect children's development of characteristics, attitudes, and values. However, some educators have been focusing on personal development and citizenship as a part of early learning and guidance for more than a hundred years. John Dewey wrote dozens of books describing his theories of learning as a part of daily living. His world-famous school, which included preschool and kindergarten, was specifically designed to foster the characteristics that are essential for living in a democracy. His school opened in 1894 (Dewey, 1966).

It is essential for those parents, caregivers, and teachers who supervise young children to recognize that guidance is not just a process for getting children to behave appropriately today, but rather a process for helping children learn to live happy, productive lives. Guidance strategies cannot be judged only by how expedient they are at the moment but also by how effective they are in instilling functional living skills that relate to the "real" world.

Disciplinary tactics are aimed at controlling children's behaviors, often by the use of punishment. Guidance procedures are focused on the development of children's self-control and self-discipline. They rely on authentic experiences, logical consequences, and intrinsic rewards. Positive guidance is not a "bag of tricks" for coaxing or coercing children to do what we want them to do.

In a democracy, people have rights. If I break a law by driving in excess of a speed limit, I still have rights. A police officer is authorized to use only as much force as is appropriate and necessary to stop me. He or she is forbidden to hurt me, harass me, or humiliate me as a punishment or to "get me back" for what I did. In fact, many police officers patiently persist with recalcitrant "perpetrators" by politely but firmly insisting, "I know you don't like being pulled over, sir, but you were exceeding the speed limit. May I see your license?"

If officers of the law behaved the way some adults do in handling misbehaving children, we would be shocked. Imagine an officer yanking a driver out of the car, angrily shaking the driver while yelling at him or her, and snapping, "If you ever do this again, I'll use a paddle on you and you won't be able to sit down for a week!" We would probably feel very angry and misused. Children feel that same way too. It takes time and practice for children to grasp rules, but they can learn to be good citizens by the same technique that our judicial system is supposed to use— by consistent persistence and by guiding as firmly as necessary but as respectfully as possible.

The Strain of Changing Disciplinary Traditions

Changing one's methods of dealing with misbehaving children is not easy. During our own childhoods, we absorbed a great deal of unconscious information about how adults and children are expected to interact. It is as if we had mental videotapes of disciplinary interactions stored

A hundred years ago, a strong back and a willing attitude were generally considered to be all one needed to make a living—success in today's world requires a complicated set of skills and attitudes.

unconsciously but ready for instant replay at any time. Without thinking, we sometimes hear the voices of our parents and teachers as we scold the young children in our care. However, the disciplinary methods that were appropriate and functional generations ago may be inappropriate and nonfunctional in preparing today's children for life in the next century (deMelendez & Ostertag, 1997; Hildebrand, Phenice, Gray & Hines, 1996; Thorne, 1997).

The world is changing at an astonishing rate. As it changes, children need different kinds of experiences to prepare them for the future. A hundred years ago, children were not expected to prepare for a technological world where adaptability and flexibility were more valued than adherence to set routines. Minorities and females were not expected to prepare for the likelihood that they would be competing ambitiously in the business world. And females were not expected to prepare for the distinct possibility that they would, at some time or other, function as head of household and sole breadwinner.

Once we recognize the necessity for updating strategies for guiding and teaching children, it can be difficult to change our old habits. Unfortunately, we adults experience confusion and stress when the methods for dealing with children that begin to seem logical and right intellectually do not match the methods we experienced and lived in our own childhoods. Beliefs cannot be turned on and off like a light switch. Instead, they must be studied and practiced for years:

> Beliefs are altered primarily by experience, learning over a long period of time, and confidence in the authority of someone considered more knowledgeable (Costley & Todd, 1987).

Human beings, adults and children alike, are influenced by life experiences. But, as human beings we also have the ability to make choices, to take control of our lives, and even to make unexpected changes in our life journey. We are not merely leaves floating in the stream of life. Instead, we are fish, strongly influenced by currents and tides, but free to swim upstream if we have the strength and motivation. We can choose to break old habits and establish new ones, but it is not easy—it requires stamina, determination, and a great deal of persistent practice over time.

Cultural Influences on Child Rearing

The ideas that we take for granted about the nature of infancy and childhood are different from those held by others in different places in the world and at different times in history. Current views on early childhood are not universal and have not always existed. By carefully examining our own beliefs and assumptions about children, we can recognize and put into perspective biases that interfere with effective child guidance.

Child care practices have been strikingly different over time for various social classes. A long period of protected childhood has largely been a luxury of the middle and upper classes, and views of infancy have fluctuated according to cultural and class settings (Bremner, 1974; Cole, 1950; Froebel, 1887; Glubok, 1969; McGraw, 1941; Osborn, 1980; Rousseau, 1893; Ulich, 1954). Much of what is written about child rearing, infant care, and early day care curriculum is intended to present a generic model for quality care. That assumes, of course, that all parents hold a similar idea about what kind of care is good and right for babies and young children. To the contrary, there is growing evidence that strategies for guiding young children hold significant cultural importance to parents from different backgrounds, and parents have very diverse ideas about what is and is not appropriate for guiding and disciplining children.

People from different cultural and economic backgrounds often hold starkly contrasting views about what proper child care really is. Methods of caring for and educating young children routinely expected by families in one community may shock and repel families in another community—and vice versa. A mother in one cultural setting may be astonished that a mother in another setting still allows her two-year-old to nurse at the breast, while the nursing mother may be horrified that the first mother allows her two-year-old to eat candy and drink soda. In some settings, people expect infants to be taken everywhere the parents go. They think that is good for babies. In other settings, people expect infants to be left safely at home in their cribs with a "babysitter." They think that is best for babies.

Routines considered very desirable by one parent may be seen as inane by another. Guidance strategies believed by some early childhood educators to be essential to healthy growth may be considered inhumane or manipulative by others. Some people believe misbehaving children should be spanked. Some people believe children should be made to sit in a chair for a few minutes for punishment. Some people do not like either of those two ideas. Practices can vary dramatically within a single family. Parents may be very protective and controlling with a first child, but relaxed and indulgent with the fourth. Hence, we see some typical personality patterns develop in children based on their birth order. First-born children tend to be more highly motivated and success-oriented than later-born children, possibly because of the increased attention and pressure they received from parents. Later-born children tend to be more interested in pleasing peers than pleasing authority figures.

Training and experience are not the only factors that shape our views on child guidance. Our cultural values profoundly influence our perceptions about what guidance practices are most appropriate for children.

What some consider to be essential experiences for effective early learning others consider utter nonsense. Some people think infants can be made to learn at an accelerated pace by being shown flashcards of letters and numbers. Others think no child of any age should be subjected to flashcards. Social workers, early educators, and child care professionals have often felt the tension among these opposing views and have sometimes been snagged unknowingly by their own culturally biased assumptions.

Cultural perceptions of desirable and appropriate care for children reflect the perceptions and beliefs of a person at a given time and place in history. The socialization of a new generation reflects the goals, philosophies, and values of the parent generation related to their specific social and economic circumstances. In other words, culture plays a key role in defining acceptable methods for dealing with children. Cultural bias is inescapable. In order to create a supportive and **pluralistic cultural** environment, however, cultural differences must be understood, accepted, and respected. And they must also sometimes be compromised when strong evidence emerges indicating that a culturally based tradition is harmful or ineffective in reaching desired goals.

If the only tool you have is a hammer, you tend to treat everything as if it were a nail.

Abraham Maslow (1993)

Preparing Children for the Realities of an Adult World

From earliest childhood, children take in information about the roles and relationships of people and things in their environment. Consciously or unconsciously adults are teaching children indirect lessons as a part of every interaction they have with children.

For example, a frustrated father at a gas station vending machine has explained to his toddler patiently over and over that the machine is broken and he has no more money so he cannot get M&M candies for her. After the little girl falls on the floor kicking and screaming for M&Ms, the father finds an attendant and insists that the machine be opened so his daughter can have the candy she wants. The tiny girl has learned two important lessons—one, sometimes authority figures do not tell the whole truth, and, two, if you make enough fuss people sometimes find a way to get you what you want.

On one hand, we adults could rationalize any kind of harsh or careless behavior with children by explaining that we are simply preparing children for the "real" world. On the other hand, we could attempt to prepare children for what we believe would be a better world. Research into a phenomenon called self-fulfilling prophecy indicates that the expectation that something will occur actually increases the chances that it will occur (Rosenthal & Jacobson, 1968).

If children, therefore, grow up expecting to be treated with respect and fairness, they may actually behave in a way that evokes that treatment. If children grow up expecting to be treated harshly and unfairly, their behavior may trigger that response from others. The self-fulfilling prophesy may also occur because we are attracted to people and situations that match those of our childhoods. An abused child may feel familiar and comfortable with the idea that someone who says he loves you can also beat and hurt you "for your own good." That child may consequently grow up and marry an abusing spouse. People tend to be drawn toward that which is familiar and repelled from that which seems strange and unfamiliar.

How Do Young Children Learn About Their Role in the World?

From birth to school age, children develop basic assumptions about how the world works and what their role is in that world. Children glean different sets of perceptions from different settings.

> *If a child's early childhood environment is rigid and children are herded through the day with no allowance for individual choice, they learn that the world is impassive and individual needs and interests do not matter.*

For example, children are all required to sit down at a long table. They are told and shown exactly how to glue precut pieces of a Santa Claus face onto a paper plate. If a child does this differently than the adult intends, the adult makes the child do it over or the adult does it herself and puts the child's name on it.

If, on the other hand, the environment is flexible and geared to individual needs, choices, and responsibilities, children learn that the world is malleable and that, with persistence and effort, they can have impact on the world around them.

For example, winter holiday craft materials such as paper plates, glue, glitter, cotton balls, and bits of colored construction paper are made available in the art center. Children are not shown an adult model to copy, but rather are encouraged to use their own imaginations to create Christmas, Hanukkah, or other seasonal decorations. The children each responsibly clean up the materials they have used when they are finished. Unique differences in the finished products are recognized and honored, and all are displayed with pride.

 If early authority figures are aloof from the children and control them by issuing steady streams of imperative commands ("Be quiet," "Sit up straight,.""Stand in line," "Don't talk"), children develop a perception of authority figures as omnipotent powers to be obeyed without question, enemies to be rebelled against, obstacles to be avoided, or irrelevant annoyances to be ignored.

For example, the adult attempts to maintain total control by having children do everything in unison—they must all sit and wait passively while the adult has children come up to the front of the class one by one to point out letters of the alphabet or say numbers. Children must all line up to wash hands and use the toilet at the same time. Even if their food becomes stone cold, no child is allowed to eat lunch until all are given the signal to begin together. Children may even be required to stand in straight lines on the playground and do calisthenics for exercise (rather than running and playing freely). The adult imagines that no learning is taking place unless he is in charge and the children are quiet, controlled, and attentive.

 If caring adults are warm, responsive, and assertive, children develop a perception of authority figures as dependable and resourceful allies to rely upon for protection and help.

For example, the adult structures the environment and the schedule to encourage children to function independently and individually as well as part of a cohesive group. Children choose learning materials from learning centers and work at their own pace during large, uninterrupted periods of time. They generally use the restroom according to their own body needs rather than group routines. Transitions from one activity to the next are flexible rather than abrupt. If a child finishes lunch earlier than others, she can throw away her trash, sponge off her area of the table, and then curl up and look at picture books until it is time for nap.

Cultural pluralism means accepting, honoring, and valuing cultural differences. (Photograph provided courtesy of CHILDREN AT RISK.)

 If adults treat children as underlings with few rights and are careless, degrading, or threatening in their treatment of children, children learn to treat others with rudeness and aggression and fail to develop self-respect.

For example, adults often talk to each other as if the children weren't even present, sometimes laughing at or making fun of individual children. Adults order children around without saying please or thank you. Punishment is meted out according to the adults' moods and whims rather than based on fair and consistent rules. The adults act as if they are above rules.

☺ *If adults treat children with respect and concern for their comfort, dignity, and basic human rights, then children learn to expect politeness and civility in their dealings with others, and they learn to function with confidence and self-esteem.*

For example, adults behave as if children are the focal point of the environment and adults are facilitators or helpers. Adults are careful not to talk about children in a critical or humiliating way. Adults maintain a role of clear adult leadership while treating children with dignity and respect. All discipline is based on fair, consistent rules, and adults also show respect for class rules. If children are not allowed to eat, adults do not walk around in front of them drinking coffee and eating a doughnut. If an adult has to stand in a chair to change a light bulb, he explains why it was necessary for him to break a class rule about standing on furniture.

If an early childhood environment offers prepackaged curriculum kits, ditto sheets, and rote memorization as learning, children come to see learning as something irrelevant and external that is imposed by authority figures.

For example, the adult stands over children, telling them exactly what to do and what will result from each action. Adults see "free play" as recess, fun but a waste of valuable time. Adults believe that children have little capacity for or interest in learning and so must be taught directly through adult-controlled and educationally preplanned initiatives.

 If early curriculum is individualized, discovery-oriented, and based on developmentally appropriate practice, children come to see learning as something actively sought after and knowledge as something one can create. Their learning is spurred by intrinsic curiosity rather than by pressure from parents and teachers.

For example, adults point out to children the possibilities of various materials and how to use them safely and appropriately, but they allow children to explore freely and to make spontaneous discoveries on their own. Adults trust children's ability to learn on their own as well as with adult assistance and direction.

 If early role models limit their verbal communication to clipped criticism and commands, children, who are in the most formative period for language development of their lives, may be discouraged in the development of a level of vocabulary, grammar, and expression that is necessary for school success later.

For example, adults use worn out clichés, sarcastic overstatements, and meaningless threats. They say things like, "Move, or you're really going to get it!" "Shut up and sit down!" "Hush, I don't want to hear your voice!" "Everybody freeze this instant." "You'd better straighten up and get your act together." These imperative commands do not require any thinking, only blind obedience.

 If early role models are articulate, accurate, and expressive in their verbal communication with children, and if they are responsive and supportive of children's attempts to express themselves, children can blossom in their development of linguistically elaborate communication skills, which form the basis for all later academic learning.

For example, adults use meaningful statements of cause and effect, descriptions of actual events or consequences, and expressions of honest feelings. The adult's words are relevant to the actual situation. Children are expected to think, understand, predict, and evaluate actions and reactions. Children are exposed to a descriptive and elaborate vocabulary through the adult expressions. Adults say things such as, "If you stand up at the top of the slide, you may fall down." "If you hurt Genevieve, she may not want to play with you next time." "People have to wash their hands after they use the toilet to keep from spreading germs." "You must walk slowly and quietly here in the library because other people are trying to read." "I feel really sad when I see all the blooms pulled off our pretty petunia."

 If early caregivers stereotype children by gender, ethnicity, or other characteristics, children build false assumptions about their limitations in the world.

For example, adults may only select boys to act out the role of the fire marshal in a song or skit, totally ignoring girls who have their hands raised. Picture books are used that only show one ethnic, cultural, regional, or economic background. Adults take it for granted that all children celebrate Christmas and Easter. A particularly tall three-year-old is expected to behave more responsibly than a particularly tiny five-year-old. Children are singled out and treated differently according to how they look, how they dress, or what their parents do for a living.

 If early caregivers see all children as unique individuals who can be helped to reach their own special potential, the children develop high expectations for themselves and the self-esteem needed to master challenges they set for themselves.

For example, children are all seen as unique and valuable individuals. Books, puppets, and dolls are multicultural. Children are helped to appreciate various cultures through food, music, and holiday celebrations that expose them to many perspectives. Adults respect and help the children learn about religious and ethnic differences in children and their families. Girls and boys are expected to participate fully in all activities, and girls are especially encouraged to be competent and confident.

When Does Cultural Learning Begin?

Learning is important and possible for human beings at all stages, from birth to death. However, during the earliest years of life, people are in a particularly fertile period for learning (Baillargeon, 1997; Begley, 1997a; Berk, 1997; Berndt, 1997; Boyatzis, 1997; Bruner, 1978a, 1978b; French, 1996; Hildebrand, 1997; Leong & Bodrova, 1996). In the first half-dozen years of children's lives, they absorb the cultural beliefs and values of their parents and early caregivers. As they grow older, they begin to take in cultural perceptions more and more from external sources—other children, books, television, movies, records, role models, and folk heroes. Because child care by caregivers

Children not only imitate what we do, but also how we do it.

other than parents plays an important role in the development of most children today, we must look carefully at the kind of social and emotional nurturance child care settings provide children.

Parent Expectations Related to Social and Economic Settings

A basic survival mechanism for the species is the process through which adults recreate for children miniature communities that reflect and represent the adults' perceptions of the larger adult community. For example, if parents perceive that their own successful participation in the society hinges on being obedient and taking orders or taking control and giving orders, then they will expect their children to be exposed to imperative commands. If, on the other hand, parents perceive that giving and taking orders are inappropriate in their own adult dealings, then they will probably feel more comfortable with their children being allowed to negotiate and make compromises rather than being told what to do (Miller, 1986).

Parents who endure long hours of crushing boredom in repetitive jobs may see nothing wrong with their children being pressured early in life to sit still for long periods without complaining or resisting. These adults may also be very tolerant of rowdy "cutting loose" behavior when it is the children's free-play time, since work and play are totally separate and unrelated in the adults' lives. If extreme financial limitations in a community cause parents to depend for their very survival on cohesion, cooperation, and frequent help from their relatives and neighbors, then it is likely that they will expect their children at an early age to accept major responsibility for chores like tending farm animals, cooking, cleaning, or taking caring of younger children. If these parents are expected in their jobs to follow set procedures and are not encouraged to think or evaluate, then it is natural that they will expect rote memorization rather than creative thinking as the core to their children's learning. If parents perceive that the world is full of hard knocks, unfair practices, and personal insults, then they may unconsciously toughen their children for survival by exposing them early to a world that is harsh and not always fair or logical. The children learn early that they will not always get whatever they want when they want it (Cook-Gumperz, 1973).

At the opposite extreme, parents with abundant financial resources and stimulating jobs live in a very different world and thus expect a very different environment for their children. Their work may be creative and self-directed. Their hobbies may also be creative and self-directed and require as much concentration and effort as their work, so there is not a clear distinction between work and play for them. These parents probably expect a creative environment for their children in which children can initiate their own self-fulfilling activities through innovative thinking and active involvement. Children are expected to master challenges simply for the fun of it.

Since comfort and individuality are priorities in this cultural viewpoint, a young child would probably not be expected to care for younger siblings; that would be someone else's responsibility. Parents may expect their children's desires to be met quickly and fully. Parents would unconsciously condition children to be prepared for a world in which they will expect to be treated fairly and respectfully (perhaps even preferentially) and to get what they want much of the time. Our culture includes many variations of adult life other than the two extremes described here. Parents, caregivers, and teachers approach their work with children from many different cultural perspectives. One cultural perspective is not necessarily any better than any other. However, it is clear that early experiences prepare children to fit into existing cultural settings (Beaty, 1997; Cárdenas, 1995; Clark, DeWolf, & Clark, 1992; Denby, 1997; Derman-Sparks & the A.B.C. Task Force, 1989; Flynn, 1996; Gaetano, Williams, & Volk, 1998; Gonzales-Mena, 1998; Gordon & Browne, 1996b; Krogh, 1995; National Association for the Education of Young Children, 1993; Phillips, 1988).

Unfortunately, preparation for one cultural setting may make it difficult for a child to function in a totally different cultural setting (Lubeck, 1985). The child conditioned to obedience and rote memorization may be very confused and overwhelmed if she, as an adult, finds herself in a situation that requires initiative, innovation, and creative problem solving. And a child who has been conditioned to a pliable world where he always has his needs met immediately may be cruelly unprepared for adversity in a tough, unfair "real world" situation. Ideally, all children from all settings could have enough multicultural exposure to various perceptions of the world that they could learn the skills to function in whatever setting they choose or find themselves in and not be limited to functioning in only one strata in the diverse cultural rainbow available. The day is long gone when children could be reared to stay in the community of their birth, to live their entire lives and to die without ever venturing out into the larger world and dealing with people whose perceptions are quite different (Gough, 1993; Harrison et al., 1990; Howard, 1993; Majors & Billson, 1992; McLoyd, 1990; Stevenson, Chen, & Uttal, 1990). Children can be helped to appreciate differences by learning more about how all people are the *same,* regardless of color, clothes, language, size, food preferences, or disability.

Understanding Cultural Differences

Cultural differences affect the way a person perceives or thinks about things. Almost every aspect of human existence is affected by culture to some extent. Culture defines for us what is right and what is wrong, our values, our day-to-day behavior, our relationships with others, and our perception of our own worth. Religion, ethnic customs, political affiliations, gender roles, social rituals, food preparation, literature, art, and music all express cultural uniqueness and serve to pass cultural traditions from one generation to the next. **Cultural pluralism** is a term used to describe the process of accepting and honoring cultural differences. If the concept of cultural pluralism is made an integral part of the first years of children's lives, they may be better able as they grow up to avoid being pulled into struggles with racial hatred, prejudice, or the stereotyping of individuals based on gender, religion, ethnic origin, age, or handicapping conditions.

Honoring cultural differences involves recognition and **respect.** While few people openly admit to prejudice, most of us consciously or unconsciously lump people together to some extent—boys are aggressive, the French are romantic, southern whites are prejudiced against blacks, overweight people are jolly and good-hearted. Some generalizations are patently untrue, while others revolve around some kernel of truth, but all generalizations have exceptions. There are boys who are gentle and nonaggressive, French lovers who are clods, southern whites who fight for racial equality, and overweight people who are crabby and mean.

Children should see materials and books in the classroom that show people who have skin colors, hair styles, special holidays, clothing, and disabilities much like they and their own families have.

Respect means being given the opportunity to be seen as a unique individual rather than as a stereotypical caricature of some larger group. Underneath all the cultural and physical differences, we are all just people. We all put on our pants (or pantyhose) the same way—one leg at a time! We all want food, comfort, security, fulfillment, and most of all the sense of belonging that comes with being loved and respected.

It is possible to urge children to better behavior and more functional habits while clearly letting them know that we accept and respect them as they are. Sometimes adults label children by saying things like, "Vanessa, you are being so bad. Look how good Jeremy is." This sets an example for stereotyping people whose appearance or behavior is different. We can say instead, "Vanessa, hitting hurts. Use words instead of hitting, please." This way, an unacceptable behavior can be identified without lumping Vanessa into the category of "bad people."

By the age of three, children can recognize and identify different skin colors (Katz, 1982; Landreth & Johnson, 1953; Morland, 1972; Parrillo, 1985; Werner & Evans, 1971). They are very sensitive to subtle nonverbal as well as verbal indications from adults about the meaning and importance of differences in people. Adults may unconsciously show a more solicitous way of responding to people who are of similar ethnic and religious backgrounds while at the same time inadvertently snubbing those whose background is different.

Ethnicity and religion are not the only characteristics that generate prejudice. Some of us have difficulty showing warmth and respect for children whose parents behave in a way that is foreign to us, live a lifestyle we disapprove of, or are unappealing to us because of hygiene or style of dress. Some of us are obvious in our preference of girls over boys or boys over girls. We make comments such as, "The boys can go first because all the girls want to do is talk" or "You boys go on and find something to do. The girls just want to play by themselves without you causing trouble."

In order to provide a multicultural and nonsexist environment for young children, adults must consider all aspects of cultural exposure—foods, books, toys, songs, rhymes, television shows, language, and clothing. Children can be helped to know and understand traditions of their own heritage as well as to know and honor the traditions of other cultures. They can be given dolls that are male and female as well as black, white, and brown. They can be exposed to books, songs, and television shows that show girls tackling adventurous challenges and boys expressing feelings. Doll house furniture can be combined with blocks and men's dress-up clothing can be mixed with dishes and doll beds.

Young children can be exposed to terms like *police officer, mail carrier,* and *repairperson* rather than *policeman, mailman,* and *repairman.* Teachers, doctors, nurses, and secretaries can be referred to as "he or she" rather than in a stereotypical way implying that all doctors are men and all secretaries are women. Children can learn nursery rhymes and songs in Spanish or Swahili as well as in English. Foods can be offered that sensitize children to regional and national dishes, ways of preparing foods, and food-related traditions and rituals.

The Antibias Curriculum

The purpose of multicultural, nonsexist, and antidiscrimination exposure for children is not to force children into any specific mold, but rather to enhance their respect for others who are different and to empower them to be whatever they have the talent and motivation to become. By fully appreciating differences in others and by recognizing that different does not necessarily mean inferior, children may become stronger in their own beliefs and traditions and more resistant to peer pressure for conformity.

Children who have disgust for or fear of differences in others may be cruel in their treatment of handicapped or ethnically different peers. They may also be very vulnerable in adolescence to popular peers who insist that anyone is a "nerd" who does not conform to group standards—smoking, drinking, taking drugs, participating in premarital sex, or driving at illegal speeds. Sometimes it takes a great deal of courage to be different and to know that being different is okay (Teaching Tolerance Project, 1997; Trawick-Smith, 1997).

Philosophies of Guidance

Culture plays an important role in shaping parents', teachers', and caregivers' philosophies about children and child rearing. A person's philosophy affects his or her perception of children, how they learn, what their intentions are, and why they behave as they do. Ideas about child guidance

Our philosophy determines how we answer questions that have no right answer, and make decisions in situations that have no easy solution.

that immediately seem logical and appropriate or sound ridiculous have been filtered by the set of beliefs and assumptions that make up one's philosophy.

Although parents, teachers, or caregivers may think that they have no particular philosophy, it is likely that they simply have never really analyzed how their beliefs compare with those held by others. Some people may mistakenly assume that everyone in the world naturally shares their same underlying beliefs about how things should be and why they are as they are. The process of acquiring appropriate behavior is a learning process just as surely as the process of learning to read and write. It is, therefore, essential for us to explore various philosophies related to how and why learning takes place.

Is a Child's Personality Mostly the Result of Nature or Nurture?

One of the oldest debates related to children is the old nature versus nurture controversy. People who believe in "nature" believe that children become whatever they become based on heredity, inborn traits, and inner motivation. People who believe in "nurture" believe that children become whatever they become based on parental guidance, teaching effectiveness, television, and other external influences.

Whenever adults compare children, they can hardly resist venturing opinions about how children grow to be so different. Some will say, "Jennifer was born to be a little terror! She's just like her dad, never still for a minute" or "Rahul will undoubtedly be a talented musician. He has inherited musical ability from both sides of his family." These people emphasize the importance of children's internal nature in their development. They believe that children are predestined at birth to certain talents and personality traits because of genetic inheritance or inborn characteristics.

Others disagree. They say things like, "Of course Ming Li has become potty trained so early. Her child care teachers have trained hundreds of toddlers. They know how to do it" or "If that were my child, he wouldn't be whining and sucking his thumb. His parents must be overindulgent or he wouldn't behave that way." These people emphasize the importance of external nurturing in the development of children. They believe that children are all born pretty much the same and their differences evolve because of differences in their treatment and teaching.

In past decades, cultural perceptions dictated that personality and potential were inborn. Some people even worried that an adopted child could carry a "bad seed." While human nature is such that we are often tempted to take credit for accomplishments and exemplary behavior, we have routinely blamed failures and unacceptable behaviors on either the inborn traits of the child or on his or her conscious choice to be bad.

As research into human learning has mushroomed over recent years, a dawning awareness has blossomed in parents and caregivers of the role of **environment** (everything and everyone the child encounters) in child development. The pendulum has swung to the extreme opposite direction from blaming fate for child behaviors to attempting to manipulate them artificially—speeding the process of development and even attempting to create "better babies."

In the early 1980s, a culturally popular trend began that has been referred to as the "super-baby phenomenon." As many parents had only one or two children well after both parents' careers were established, they began to place more and more emphasis on the optimum development of the child or children they had. People bought or made flashcards with abstract number concepts, names of famous composers, and anatomy terms to use in stimulating their infants. Some parents began to fear that their toddler would be left behind if she had not been enrolled in baby gymnastics, French tutoring, and violin lessons by the age of two. Guilt became a national pastime for trend-setting parents. Perhaps the pendulum will settle to a middle ground where popular culture encourages adults to recognize and appreciate the uniqueness of every individual child and his or her natural rate of development but also to take seriously the critically important role of play experiences and social interactions for the child's development to his or her fullest potential.

For example, cognitive stimulation is to psychic development much like food is to physical development. If enough food is not available, development will be stunted. However, forcing as much food as possible on a child is probably equally destructive. Making appropriate quantities of developmentally appropriate foods (or learning experiences) available while respecting the child's hunger (or readiness for learning) makes a great deal of sense (Elkind, 1997).

What Do Current Experts Say About the Origin of Intelligence and Personality?

Lately, educators have been placing more emphasis on the range of philosophies that underlie various theoretical explanations of the origin of human intelligence and personality. These experts trace the ancient nature versus nurture controversy and add a new interactionist point of view that assumes a reciprocal relationship between nature and nurture.

How Do They Deal with Nature Versus Nurture?

If human thinking could be neatly separated into simple categories, we would find three contrasting views:

- The **behaviorists**—those who believe that behavior and learning result from external forces such as reinforcement and punishment

- The **maturationists**—those who believe that behavior and learning hinge on internal processes such as physiological maturation and intrinsic motivation

- The **developmental interactionists**—those who believe that behavior and learning result from complex and dynamic reciprocal interactions involving both internal processes and external forces

What Is the Behaviorist Approach?

The behaviorists incorporate the seventeenth-century tradition of John Locke, who viewed the newborn's mind as a tabula rasa, or empty slate. These theorists, the behaviorists, positivists, and empiricists, believe that human learning comes from outside the learner. They believe that environment accounts for nearly all that a person becomes.

Nature lays the groundwork for a child's potential, but nurturing makes it possible for the child to achieve that potential.

Watson (1930), Skinner (1953, 1974), and others have theorized that human beings are really products of their environments. People become scholars or cat-burglars, not because of their genetic makeup or by choice, but because their environment has conditioned them to behave as they do. Subscription to this view has powerful implications for parents and educators. It implies that human beings can be molded or shaped by the controlling of environmental experiences. This view also shifts emphasis away from focus on human will and predisposition.

Behaviorists view the development of appropriate behavior as the responsibility of the adult. The adult is responsible to identify and select specific behavior goals for the child. Then the adult observes the child and monitors any spontaneous behaviors that are slightly closer to the desired goal behavior, reinforcing each subsequent step closer to the desired goal by giving praise, treats, or **tokens** (that can be traded later for special prizes or privileges). The adult maneuvers the child's surroundings in order to **modify** (or change) specific behaviors in the child.

Behaviorists leave nothing to chance. They choose goal behaviors, select reinforcers, and even plan a reinforcement schedule of when, how often, and under exactly what circumstances reinforcers will be given. Behaviorist views are all focused on the idea that learning is an external process, that learning takes place in the child as a result of influences from the child's environment. Child guidance is seen as an adult-directed process.

What Is the Maturationist Approach?

From a point of view opposite to that of the behaviorists, the maturationists borrow from the tradition of Plato. These maturationists, innatists, and nativists believe that learning emerges from within. These educators and philosophers have theorized that human beings are born to be whatever they become; the human infant in this conception is like the rosebud, naturally unfolding into a preordained blossom as long as it is kept healthy. Well into the 1920s and the 1930s, Arnold Gesell, a researcher at Yale, maintained that children's external environment did not control developmental outcomes. He claimed that children's own genetic and biological characteristics determined their intelligence and personality (Gesell, Halvorson, Thompson, & Ilg, 1940).

The maturationists view the development of appropriate behavior as a natural process. They believe that as long as basic needs are met, the child will automatically develop the social skills, the intelligence, and the physical control necessary for the child to behave properly. They see the role of the adult as that of a facilitator. The adult studies children, carefully observing and monitoring their behaviors and abilities. When there is a problem, the adult steps in to help the child understand what has happened in a specific situation and to help the child resolve the problem as independently as possible.

Maturationists perceive that learning comes from inside the child. They believe that the processes of learning cannot be rushed. Adults view themselves as role models, guides, and consultants. They believe children are ultimately responsible for their own decision to behave properly. Personality and growth traits inherited genetically and the child's own willpower play an important role in the maturationists' views on how children learn to behave appropriately. The maturationists see the development of proper behavior as a child-directed process.

Obviously, this type of perception has broad implications for parents and educators concerned with guiding children. If early experiences are relatively inconsequential to one's later development, then adults need only be concerned with providing the basic necessities for safety and health—custodial care—in the earliest years. This view implies that growth and learning proceed

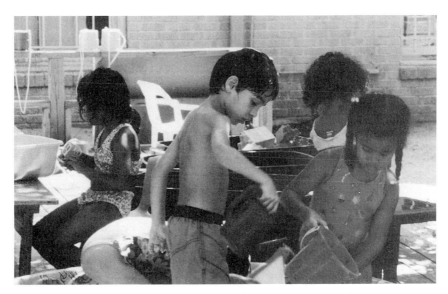

Children create their own learning; we are only their guides.

according to internal rules of physiological growth and as a result of personal decision making, in spite of specific environmental circumstances.

What Is the Developmental Interactionist Approach?

Debate over the previous two contrasting views of human learning (the nature versus nurture controversy) has been complicated recently by a growing body of research compiled toward the end of the twentieth century by the developmental interactionists who believe that human learning results from the interaction between the learner and his or her environment.

The work of Vygotsky (Berk, 1997; Gutek, 1997; Leong & Bodrova, 1996; Seefeldt & Barbour, 1998; Spafford, Pesce, & Grosser, 1998), Piaget (1952, 1962, 1963, 1970, 1983), Chomsky (1965), Kohlberg (1966), Hunt (1976), Bloom (1964), Kagan (1962, 1971; Kagan, Kearsley, & Zelazo, 1978), and White (1975, 1995; White & Watts, 1973; White, Kaban & Attanucci, 1979) has made it clear that environmental factors influence human development, but the research also supports the importance of individual readiness, personal learning styles, and reciprocal interaction as a part of the process. This new stream of thought has gained scientific credibility and is now recognized to be neither a maturational nor a behaviorist view of learning. Piaget (1952), for example, termed himself a constructionist or cognitive interactionist (developmental interactionist). He asserted that infants are born with predispositions to certain kinds of thought and behavior but that they must create their own knowledge through stages of interaction with the environment. Play is the concept we use to refer to this early exploratory interaction with the environment.

Vygotsky, on the other hand, focused on the critical role adults and peers play in the child's creation of "mental tools." He believed that adults and peers challenge the child by presenting and modeling skills just outside the child's reach.

White (1975) said that newborn children come into the world with an internal structure that sets an upper limit to their potential, but that the internal structure is not a guarantee of any level of development or learning. The child is programmed to learn, but without stimulation and reinforcement from the environment, no learning can take place (Petersen, 1996). This way of thinking about young children creates pressure on parents and child care providers to produce high-quality early experiences so that optimum experiences can be made available. Chugani (1993) has further emphasized the importance of early environments by showing that a baby's brain uses information from sensory experiences to design its own architecture. A kind of "mapping" takes place inside the brain with astounding rapidity as the number of synapses (or connections) among brain cells multiplies by the trillions in a very few months.

Lorenz (1966), Hess (1972), von Frisch (1974), and Lamb (1978, 1981) are ethologists (researchers who study behaviors in terms of natural processes and in natural settings). They have refined the idea of sensitive periods for learning in which environmental stimuli can have a maximum impact on a child's learning. Hunt (1976) described what he called the "match." He said that a match must be created between a child's level of readiness and the exact level of difficulty or discrepancy in a specific learning situation in order for optimum learning to take place.

By analyzing what we know about child development in the context of day-to-day observations of the children in our care, we strive constantly to match the right activities and materials to the emerging abilities that we identify in each child.

If interactions in the environment are too difficult, children become frustrated and discouraged. If they are too easy, children become bored. Children actively seek out materials and activities that match their own level. They enjoy and learn well from an environment that offers a fairly wide range of difficulty in which they are allowed the freedom to choose toys, games, and interactions that are matched to their own ability level as well as the freedom to reject materials or activities that seem too easy or too difficult.

In terms of child guidance, the interactionists believe that children can only learn to behave appropriately when they have inner maturity as well as suitable external influences. Adults must study children and plan carefully, but they must also focus on the child's own interests and abilities. Some areas of child guidance seem more responsive to external control and some areas to internal control. Mindless habits a child really wants to change can probably be treated quickly and effectively through behaviorist strategies. More general problems that seem to have deeply rooted emotional causes are usually best treated with maturationist support of the natural processes of development.

The interactionist approach integrates the processes for inner and outer development. Interactionists see child guidance not as an adult-directed or a child-directed process, but rather as an interaction in which either can lead or follow. It is like a waltz with give and take, leading and following. The adult respects the child's interests and abilities but is also not afraid to take control when necessary. The child feels free to express herself but also knows and respects clearly defined limits. The interactionist approach includes the best of both worlds—nature and nurture.

If There Are Different Views About How Children Develop, How Do I Know Which Philosophy Is Right?

Within any group of people who care for and teach young children, there will be many successful and effective adults who tend to lean a bit toward either a more maturationist or a more behaviorist view of early growth and development. Generally, however, a predominant view in the field of early childhood education revolves around the belief that early development results from the interaction between children's inner capacity and motivation and their external environment.

Two basic assumptions that build a foundation for the procedures throughout this book are the beliefs that:

- Babies and children develop skills and concepts by interacting (playing and living) in a stimulating and supportive environment, and

- The way children interact in their environment is triggered by their particular stage of development as well as their own interests and motives.

In other words, one might say that healthy, well-developed children come into the world preprogrammed to learn (Chomsky, 1965). They will automatically be motivated to explore the physical properties of the environment around them by using their senses, they will seek human social contact, and they will quickly absorb any language they hear. If these components of the environment are abundantly available, the interactions that ensue will foster development in a healthy and natural way. Children who come into the world without all of the five senses intact,

Wouldn't it be a wonderful world if all children grew up remembering to be safe, kind, and neat?

with developmental delays, or with impaired motor capabilities need special equipment, extra stimulation, and skilled teaching to reach their full potential for development. Children with disabilities do not usually learn as easily and naturally as their peers.

Tragically, however, even an infant who is perfectly healthy at birth may eventually suffer from the effects of a hostile or non-nurturing environment. Lack of a healthy emotional environment can cause:

- Failure-to-thrive syndrome

- **Marasmus** (a severe condition of underweight and poor health)

- Developmental delay

- Permanent mental retardation

- Death

Any of these can afflict potentially normal, healthy children if they are deprived of the essential elements of a normal environment—nurturing human contact, a sense of being wanted and accepted, the opportunity to share thoughts and feelings in verbal or nonverbal communication with others, and exposure to interesting things to explore by seeing, touching, tasting, feeling, smelling, and moving around.

The development of an intelligent, responsible human being is not an automatic internal process that takes place in spite of environmental factors, and it is not an external process of molding a pliable child into a predetermined shape chosen by parents and teachers. It is a lively process of give and take in which children explore their boundaries and limits. Sometimes they accommodate to adult expectations, and sometimes, quite naturally, they resist.

Children come equipped with individual personalities, likes, dislikes, interests, and motives. The role of the adult is to guide, assertively and respectfully, never forgetting that even the youngest child is truly a person with all the rights befitting any other human being (even the right to be negative and recalcitrant on occasion). In the developmental interactionist perspective, child guidance is intended to give children feedback about the realities of their world, to allow them choices within reasonable limits, and to help them confront the logical consequences of their own actions.

We mark our progress as a civilization by what we see as advances in hardware, and that criterion, assumed so readily by the population at large, blinds us to other possible values such as community, reverence, wisdom, the care and education of children, and the condition of the natural world.

I would wish to be a member of a community that judged itself on the happiness of its children rather than on the unhindered flow of its mechanical inventions.

Thomas Moore (1994)

Practical Application /Discussion

Bringing Home a Baby Bumblebee

In a medium-sized neighborhood child care center, a group of preschool-aged children cluster around their teacher and sing with her. They snatch invisible bumblebees out of the air and pretend to trap them in their clasped hands as they sing:

> I'm bringing home a baby bumblebee. Won't my mommy be so proud of me?
> I'm bringing home a baby bumblebee—bzzz bzzz bzzz bzzz. Ouch! [slap] He
> stung me!

In another part of town, in a child care center located in a tiny, dilapidated building that is part of a low-income housing project, a group of children sit on chairs around long, wobbly tables as they enthusiastically sing:

> I'm bringing home a baby bumblebee. Won't my mama be surprised of me?
> I'm bringing home a baby bumblebee—bzzz bzzz bzzz bzzz. Ouch! [slap] He
> stung me! I'm squashing up the baby bumblebee. Now there's bumblebee
> blood all over me. I'm wiping off the blood of the bumblebee. Now there's no
> more blood all over me.

In still another part of town, in a tastefully decorated private preschool, a third group of children sit cross-legged on the floor in a circle singing happily with their teacher:

> I'm bringing home a baby bumblebee. Won't my daddy be so proud of me?
> I'm opening up the window carefully, so my bee can fly away free—bzzz bzzz
> bzzz bzzz. Bye bye, baby bumblebee.

Questions for Discussion

1. How do the words to each of these songs reflect the differences in perspectives and expectations of childhood in these different communities?

2. Do you think that songs and games parents and child care workers use simply to entertain children pass cultural perceptions from one generation to the next?

3. What are your own cultural perceptions of children? Do you see children as innocent and pure, to be protected from anything violent, scary, or disgusting? Do you see children as regular people who enjoy raucous humor and vicarious aggression? Do you see children as "born sinners" who sometimes can have evil or cruel impulses?

4. Compare versions of songs and stories you have heard. Do the different versions reflect cultural experiences of children?

5. Why do you think the third teacher in the example replaced the word *mommy* or *mama* with the word *daddy*?

6. Do you think that children growing up in inner-city slums might like different songs and games than other more sheltered children who have not experienced the discomfort and fear associated with poverty?

7. How are songs and stories purposely used by adults to instill in children an awareness of cultural values?

8. Identify a song or story you would feel uncomfortable using with children. What
   would you do to change it? Why?

Points to Remember

- Child care and guidance practices have changed dramatically through the
  years.

- Parents who depend on help from others in rearing their children want to be
  assured that their children will receive proper guidance.

- Settings where children live, work, and play (whether homes or child care
  facilities) function as a small representation of the world for young children.

- Adults may have difficulty changing old habit patterns in dealing with children, but change is possible with motivation and practice.

- People from different cultural and economic backgrounds often hold starkly
  contrasting views about the parameters of proper child care.

- During the earliest years, children are in a particularly fertile period for
  learning.

- Honoring cultural differences involves recognition and respect for the appearances, customs, and beliefs of others.

- Contemporary educators identify three philosophical perspectives, that of the
  behaviorists, the maturationists, and the developmental (cognitive) interactionists.

- The developmental interactionist view assumes that external environment and
  internal processes of development and motivation interact to determine a
  child's development of personality and intelligence.

Related Readings

Respecting Cultural Differences

Aoki, E. M. (1981). Are you Chinese? Are you Japanese? Or are you just a mixed-up kid? Using Asian
American children's literature. *The Reading Teacher, 34,* 382–385.

Beaty, J. J. (1997). *Building bridges with multicultural picture books: For children 3–5*. Upper Saddle
River, NJ: Merrill Education/Prentice-Hall.

> *Focusing on the common bonds between children, this book shows future teachers how to
> bring multicultural values and ideas into early childhood programs using appropriate picture
> books. In addition to providing criteria for selecting appropriate books, the author describes
> how to lead children into book-related activities and, eventually, how to create a more multi-
> cultural curriculum through picture books.*

Bel Geddes, J. (1997). Childhood and children: A compendium of customs, superstitions, theories, profiles,
and facts. Phoenix, AZ: Oryx Press.

Bishop, R. S. (1987). Extending multicultural understanding through children's books. In B. Cullinan (Ed.), *Children's literature in the reading program* (pp. 60–67). Newark, DE: International Reading Association.

Bishop, R. S. (1991). African American literature for today's children: Anchor, compass, and sail. *Perspectives, 7,* ix–xii.

Cárdenas, J. A. (1995). *Multicultural education: A generation of advocacy.* Needham Heights, MA: Allyn & Bacon.

> *José Cárdenas has brought together a compilation of articles that span the last twenty-five years and seek insights into the history and development of multicultural education. The articles address the education needs of minority and disadvantaged students, with a special emphasis on Hispanic Americans.*

de Melendez, W., & Ostertag, V. (1997). *Teaching young children in multicultural classrooms: Issues, concepts, and strategies.* Albany, NY: Delmar Publishers, an International Thomson Publishing company.

> *This book addresses the historical, theoretical, and practical aspects of multicultural education as it relates to young children. It includes current and future trends, addresses the current as well as future directions of multicultural education, and provides practical classroom ideas for implementation.*

Derman-Sparks, L. (1989). *Anti-bias curriculum: Tools for empowering young children.* Washington, DC: National Association for the Education of Young Children.

Emberton, S. (1994, Fall). Do your cultural homework. *National Center for Family Literacy Newsletter* 6(3), 5–6.

Feeney, S. S., Christensen, D., & Moravcik, E. R. (1996). *Who am I in the lives of children? An introduction to teaching young children* (5th ed.). Upper Saddle River, NJ: Merrill Education/Prentice-Hall.

> *The authors cover such topics as career development initiatives, changes in professional preparation, and the movement to increase developmentally appropriate practice in primary grades. This book focuses on the value of a professional code of ethics and encourages readers to compare and contrast the field's values with their own and select ways of teaching that are consistent with their own values.*

Gutek, G. L. (1997). *Historical and philosophical foundations of education: A biographical introduction* (2d ed.). Upper Saddle River, NJ: Merrill Education/Prentice-Hall.

> *This book explores notable personalities and philosophies in education from a variety of areas and cultures by identifying leading contributors to educational thought in an international setting; developing key philosophies of education through the lives of those who developed them; and relating education to global trends that have helped shape human history.*

Harris, V. (Ed.). (1993). *Teaching multicultural literature in grades K–8.* Norwood, MA: Christopher Gordon.

Ingoldsby, B. B., & Smith, S. (Eds.). (1995). *Families in multicultural perspective.* New York: Guilford.

> *This book explores the diversity of the world's families in structure, processes, history, as well as social and environmental contexts. It covers contemporary Third World and Western families.*

King, E. W., Chipman, M. F., & Cruz-Janzen, M. (1994). *Educating young children in a diverse society.* Needham Heights, MA: Allyn & Bacon.

This text presents information, techniques, strategies, and incentives needed to generate an awareness of cultural diversity, including race, ethnicity, gender, and social class in very young children. It uses incidents in the lives of various people as examples to illustrate how early encounters with the forces of ethnic, social, and gender identification shaped their lives. The text clearly shows how cultural conditioning inherent in families or religious, linguistic, or ethnic groups may influence learning outcomes.

Konner, M. (1991). *Childhood: A multicultural view.* Boston, MA: Little, Brown.

Lynch, E. W., & Hanson, M. J. (1992). *Developing cross-cultural competence: A guide for working with young children and their families.* Baltimore: Paul Brooks.

Miller, D. F. (1989). First steps toward cultural difference: Socialization in infant/toddler day care. Washington, DC: Child Welfare League of America.

Miller-Lachmann, L. (Ed.). (1992). *Our family, our friends, our world: Annotated guide to significant multicultural books for children and teenagers.* New Providence, NJ: Bowker.

Ramirez, G., Jr., & Ramirez, J. L. (1994). *Multiethnic children's literature: A comprehensive resource guide.* Albany, NY: Delmar Publishers, an International Thomson Publishing company.

Silvers, J. (1997). Child labor in Pakistan. In E. N. Junn & C. Boyatzis (Eds.), *Annual editions: Child growth and development 97/98* (4th ed.). New York: McGraw-Hill. (Original work published in *The Atlantic Monthly,* February 1996)

The exploitation of children as laborers illustrates the influence of economic and political factors on how children are viewed and treated in a society. Jonathan Silvers describes how Pakistan's recent laws limiting child labor are generally ignored, leaving an estimated eleven million children toiling in that country's factories.

Slapin, B., & Seale, D. (1992). *Through Indian eyes: The native experience in books for children.* Philadelphia: New Society.

Strickland, D., & Strickland, M. (1994). *Families: Poems celebrating the African-American experience.* Honesdale, PA: Boyds Mills Press.

Swick, K. J., Boutte, G., & Van Scoy, I. (1997). Families and schools: Building multicultural values together. In K. M. Paciorek & J. H. Munro, *Annual editions: Early childhood education 97/98* (18th ed.). New York: McGraw-Hill. (Original work published in *Childhood Education,* Winter 1995/96)

If families and teachers looked down the road thirty years and developed a list of qualities they would like to see in their children, they could begin to plan collaboratively the types of experiences needed today. A multicultural society requires all families to advocate and work together.

United Nations. (1994). *International year of the family.* New York: Department of Public Information.

Wagoner, S. A. (1982). Mexican Americans in children's literature since 1970. *The Reading Teacher, 36,* 274–279.

Weis, L., & Fine, M. (Eds.). (1993). *Beyond silenced voices: Class, race, and gender in United States schools.* New York: State University of New York Press.

York, S. (1991). *Roots and wings: Affirming culture in early childhood programs.* St. Paul, MN: Redleaf Press.

Appendix A
Resources for Helping Contemporary Families Deal with Stress

Action Alliance for Children—A nonprofit organization dedicated to informing and empowering people who work with and on behalf of children.

Action Alliance for Children
The Hunt House
1201 Martin Luther King Jr. Way
Oakland, CA 94612-1217
Phone: 510-444-7136

Alliance for Parental Involvement in Education, Inc. (ALLPIE)—A parent network helping parents explore educational options, including public, private, and home schooling. In addition to a newsletter, ALLPIE publishes pamphlets on educational options and parents' rights.

Seth Rockmuller
Alliance for Parental Involvement in
  Education, Inc.
P.O. Box 59
East Chatham, NY 12060-0059
Phone: 518-392-6900
E-mail: allpiesr@aol.com

Center on School, Family, and Community Partnerships—A program located at Johns Hopkins University that is designed to help schools develop and maintain strong school, family, and community partnerships. They maintain a variety of resources, including videos and manuals to assist individual schools and communities.

Joyce L. Epstein, Director
Center on School, Family and Community
  Partnerships
Johns Hopkins University
3505 N. Charles Street
Baltimore, MD 21218
Phone: 410-516-8800

Children's Foundation (CF)—Provides information for caregivers, children, families, and policy makers on issues of critical concern, such as affordable, high-equality child care (especially family child care), federal food programs, health care, and enforcement of court-ordered child support at the national and local levels. CF also provides training to family day care providers and parents. Publications available in English or Spanish include a newsletter, training manuals, brochures, and fact sheets.

Kay Hollestelle
725 15th Street, NW, #505
Washington, DC 20005-2109
Phone: 202-347-3300
Fax: 202-347-3382

Families and Work Institute—A national nonprofit research, strategic planning, and consulting organization that conducts policy and worksite research on the changing workforce and changing family/personal lives.

Family and Work Institute
330 Seventh Avenue
New York, NY 10001
Phone: 212-465-2044
Fax: 212-465-8637
http://www.familiesandworkinst.org

The Family Development program (FDP)—A nonprofit organization dedicated to empowering low-income families, children, and communities.

Edith Menning, Program Manager
Family Development Program
University of New Mexico
Onate Hall, #217
Albuquerque, NM 87131

Phone: 505-277-6943
Fax: 505-277-6282

Full-Time Dads—A group providing networking and support for fathers who are the primary caregivers for their children.

Stephen Harris
Full-Time Dads
P.O. Box 577
Cumberland, ME 04021
Phone: 207-829-5260

National Organization of Single Mothers, Inc. (NOSM)—A not-for-profit network committed to helping single parents meet the challenges of daily life with wisdom, wit, dignity, confidence, and courage. NOSM seeks to unite single parents and their families primarily through its bimonthly newsletter.

National Organization of Single Mothers,
    Inc.
P.O. Box 68
Midland, NC 28107
Phone: 704-888-KIDS
Fax: 704-888-1752
E-mail: solomother@aol.com

9 to 5, National Association for Working Women—A national organization for working women, mobilizing women for improved public and workplace policies, 9 to 5 also has a toll-free hotline to discuss job issues, legal rights, and experiences with trained counselors.

9 to 5, National Association for Working
    Women
614 Superior Avenue, NW
Cleveland, OH 44113-1387
Phone: 216-566-9308 (membership)
Toll-free: 800-522-0925 (job problems
    hotline)

Parent Information Center (PIC)—Funded by the U.S. Department of Education to provide information, referral, training, and support to parents of children with disabilities. PIC services are available to all parents and family members, whether or not they have a child with a disability.

Parent Information Center
Central Office
P.O. Box 2405
Concord, NH 03302-2405
V/TDD: 603-224-7005
Phone: NH only: 800-232-0986
Phone: NH only: 800-947-7005
Fax: 603-224-4365
E-mail: picnh@aol.com

Parents Anonymous—A national organization founded to help parents who are having difficulty and would like to learn more effective ways of parenting their children.

Parents Anonymous
675 W. Foothill Blvd., Suite 220
Claremont, CA 91711-3416
Phone: 909-621-6184
Fax: 909-625-6304
E-mail: hn3831@handsnet.org

The Parents as Teachers (PAT) National Center—Serves parent educators and parents of children from birth to age five. PAT uses a research-based curriculum, providing age-appropriate information to parents on child development and ways to encourage development and learning as well as information on language, hearing, and vision screenings.

Parents as Teachers National Center
10176 Corporate Square Drive, Suite 230
St. Louis, MO 63132
http://www.patnc.org

Stepfamily Association of America, Inc. (SAA)—A nonprofit educational organization that promotes personal and family support through information, education, and advocacy for stepfamilies. SAA publishes materials on divorce and stepfamilies written for adults and children in stepfamilies and for professionals.

Stepfamily Association of America, Inc.
215 Centennial Mall S., Suite 212
Lincoln, NE 68508
Phone: 402-477-7837

Appendix B
Resources for Creating a Prosocial Environment

Association for Child Development—A federally funded nonprofit organization that publishes a monthly newsletter called "Potpourri" with articles on nutrition, child development, menu ideas, and craft projects. They offer free technical assistance in setting up a child care business.

Association for Child Development
Central Office
P.O. Box 1491
East Lansing, MI 48826-1491
Phone: 517-332-7200
Toll-free: 800-234-3287
Fax: 517-332-5543

Association for Childhood Education International (ACEI)—A not-for-profit professional association that disseminates information on education and child development; promotes a sensitive and comprehensive perspective on child development from birth through early adolescence; facilitates professional growth of educators; and focuses public attention on the needs and rights of children.

Association for Childhood Education
  International
11501 Georgia Avenue, Suite 315
Wheaton, MD 20902
Phone: 301-942-2443
Toll-free: 800-423-3563
Fax: 301-942-3012
E-mail: aceihq@aol.com

Atrium Society—Nonprofit, nonsectarian, and nonpolitical organization committed to peace education around the world; produces the *Education for Peace* books and programs for young people.

Atrium Society
P.O. Box 816
Middlebury, VT 05753
Phone: 800-848-6021

Educational Resources Information Center (ERIC)—A national information system designed to provide users with ready access to an extensive body of education-related literature. The ERIC Clearinghouse on Elementary and Early Childhood Education (ERIC/EECE) is one of sixteen clearinghouses in the ERIC system, which is part of the National Library of Education, funded by the Office of Educational Research and Improvement (OERI), U.S. Department of Education. ERIC clearinghouses are the world's most frequently used collection of information on education.

The ERIC Clearinghouse on Elementary and
  Early Child Education (ERIC/EECE)
University of Illinois at Urbana-Champaign
Children's Research Center
51 Gerty Drive
Champaign, IL 61820-7469
Phone: 800-583-4135
TTY: 217-333-1386
Fax: 217-333-3767
http://ericps.crc.uiuc.edu/eece/index.html
E-mail: ericeece@uiuc.edu

National Association for the Education of Young Children (NAEYC)—The nation's largest membership organization of early childhood professionals and others dedicated to improving the quality of services for young children and their families. Founded in 1926, NAEYC membership grew to more than 101,000 in 1997 and includes a national network of more than 425 local, state, and regional early childhood organizations affiliated with NAEYC. NAEYC Affiliate Groups share and help to implement NAEYC's primary goals of improving professional practice and working conditions in early childhood education and building public understanding and support for high-quality early childhood programs.

NAEYC
1509 16th Street, NW
Washington, DC 20036-1426
Phone: 202-232-8777
Toll-free: 800-424-2460
Fax: 202-328-1846
http://www.naeyc.org/about/about_index.
    htm

National Early Childhood Technical Assistance System (NEC*TAS)—Funded by the Office of Special Education Programs of the U.S. Department of Education. NEC*TAS provides technical assistance to eligible programs for infants, toddlers, and preschoolers with disabilities.

National Early Childhood Technical
    Assistance System
500 NationsBank Plaza
137 E. Franklin Street
Chapel Hill, NC 27514
Phone: 919-962-2001
TDD: 919-966-4041
Fax: 919-966-7463
E-mail: nectas@unc.edu
http://www.nectas.unc.edu/

National Institute on Out-of-School Time (formerly The School-Age Child Care Project)—A group working to improve the quantity and quality of school-age child care programs nationally through collaborative work with communities, individuals, and organizations. Initially concerned with raising awareness and establishing school-age child care programs, the multifaceted project today focuses on meeting policy and implementation challenges as well as on enhancing the quality of existing programs.

National Institute on Out-of-School Time
Center for Research on Women
Wellesley College
Wellesley, MA 02181
Phone: 617-283-2547
Fax: 617-283-3657
E-mail: lcoltin@wellesley.edu
http://www.wellesley.edu/WCW/CRW/SAC/
    index.html

Zero to Three—Dedicated to helping children navigate their first three years of life in order to develop a solid intellectual and emotional foundation. This site provides information on the growth and development of infants and toddlers for parents and for child care providers.

Zero to Three: National Center for Infants,
    Toddlers and Families
734 15th Street, NW
Washington, DC 20005-2101
Phone: 202-638-1144
Fax: 202-638-0851
Publications: 800-899-4301
http://www.zerotothree.org

Appendix C
Resources for Keeping Toddlers Safe

Alliance to End Childhood Lead Poisoning—A national educational, policy, and advocacy organization dedicated exclusively to ending the epidemic of childhood lead poisoning.

Alliance to End Childhood Lead Poisoning
227 Massachusetts Avenue, NE, Suite 200
Washington, DC 20002
Phone: 202-543-1147
Fax: 202-543-4466
http://www.aeclp.org

American Academy of Pediatrics (AAP)—
A "voice for children" dedicated to the health, safety, and well-being of infants, children, adolescents, and young adults. The academy supports breastfeeding and offers medical updates, information, and services for pediatricians and health professionals as well as for parents and educators.

American Academy of Pediatrics
141 NW Point Blvd.
Elk Grove Village, IL 60007-1098
Phone: 847-228-5005
http://www.aap.org

Centers for Disease Control and Prevention (CDC), National AIDS Clearinghouse, U.S. Department of Health and Human Services—An agency that makes a collection of scientific and educational HIV/AIDS materials available to people working in the HIV/AIDS field as well as those living with HIV/AIDS.

CDC National AIDS Clearinghouse
P.O. 6003
Rockville, MD 20849-6003
Phone: 800-458-5231
Fax: 301-738-6616
TTY: 800-243-7012
E-mail: aidsinfo@cdcnac.aspensys.com
http://www.cdcnac.org

Appendix D
Resources for Responding to Special Needs and Interests

Active Parenting—A publishing company producing videos and materials for professionals in parent education, parent involvement, teacher-in-service, loss, and self-esteem for children.

Barbara L. Propst
Active Parenting
810 Franklin Court, Suite B
Marietta, GA 30067
Phone: 800-825-0060
Fax: 404-429-0334
E-mail: cservice@activeparenting.com
http://www.activeparenting.com/

Adoptive, Foster, and Biological Parents of FAS/FAE Children—A support network for adoptive, foster, and biological parents of children affected by fetal alcohol syndrome or prenatal drug use.

Ronnie Jacobs
Adoptive, Foster, and Biological Parents of FAS/FAE Children
Bergen County Council on Alcoholism and Drug Abuse Inc.
P.O. Box 626
Paramus, NJ 07653
Phone: 201-261-2183 or 201-261-1450

Allergy and Asthma Network—Mothers of Asthmatics, Inc. (AAN-MA)—An international nonprofit organization dedicated to educating families dealing with asthma and allergies. Members of AAN-MA receive a monthly newsletter that includes information on medical research, current treatments and therapies, new products, and coping techniques.

Allergy and Asthma Network
Mothers of Asthmatics, Inc.

3554 Chain Bridge Road, Suite 200
Fairfax, VA 22030
Phone: 703-385-4403
Toll-free: 800-878-4403
Fax: 703-352-4354
E-mail: aanma@aol.com
http://www.podi.com/health/aanma/

American Academy of Child and Adolescent Psychiatry—Professional organization for child and adolescent psychiatrists conducting research and diagnosing and treating psychiatric disorders of children, adolescents, and their families. It publishes "Facts for Families," a series that includes over fifty informational sheets on topics such as the depressed child, suicide, discipline, and child sexual abuse.

Terri Baxter, Deputy Director of Research Development
American Academy of Child and Adolescent Psychiatry
3615 Wisconsin Avenue NW
Washington, DC 20016
Phone: 202-966-7300
Fax: 202-966-7300
E-mail: 74003.264@Compuserve.com
http://www.aacap.org/web/aacap/

The Arc of the United States—The country's largest voluntary organization committed to the welfare of all children and adults with mental retardation and their families.

The Arc of the United States
500 East Border Street, Suite 300
Arlington, TX 76010
Phone: 817-261-6003
TDD: 817-277-0553
Fax: 817-277-3491

E-mail: thearc@metronet.com
http://TheArc.org/welcome.html

ASPIRA Association, Inc.: An Investment in Latino Youth—A national nonprofit organization serving Puerto Rican and other Latino/a youth and their families through leadership and education. ASPIRA is taken from the Spanish word *aspirar,* which means to aspire to something greater). It provides bilingual publications at low cost related to Hispanic health, education, violence, and so on.

ASPIRA Association, Inc.
1444 I Street, NW
Suite 800
Washington, DC 20005
Phone: 202-835-3600
Fax: 202-835-3613
E-mail: aspiral@aol.com
http:www.incacorp.com/aspira/

Association of Birth Defect Children (ABDC)—A charitable organization that provides free telephone information to parents and professionals about birth defects. ABDC sponsors the National Birth Defect Registry, a birth defect prevention project that provides information on possible links between specific birth defects and their causes (e.g., exposures to chemicals during the Gulf War). Members of ABDC receive publications (e.g., fact sheets), special reports, and a newsletter.

The Association of Birth Defect Children, Inc.
827 Irma
Orlando, FL 32803
Phone: 407-245-7035
Toll-free: 800-313-2232

Association for the Care of Children's Health (ACCH)—A network of individuals, programs, and organizations whose vision is to humanize health care for children and families through education, dissemination of resources, research, and advocacy. ACCH publishes resources that address the pyschological, emotional, social, and spiritual needs of children and their families, and maintains an information clearinghouse for infants with disabilities and life-threatening conditions.

Association for the Care of Children's Health
7910 Woodmont Avenue, Suite 300
Bethesda, MD 20814
Telephone: 301-654-6549
Toll-free: 800-808-ACCH
Fax: 301-986-4553
http://Look.net/ACCH/

Association for Special Kids, Inc. (A.S.K.)—A financial planning organization dedicated to helping parents of children with disabilities to protect their children's future. Counselors work individually with parents, and with a network of qualified attorneys and accountants, to set parents' plans into action. There is no fee for these services. Most of the counselors are parents of children with disabilities.

A.S.K.
107 West Hill Street
Baltimore, MD 21230
Phone: 800-832-0467

Asthma and Allergy Foundation of America (AAFA)—An organization supporting families by providing a bimonthly newsletter with practical articles on asthma and allergies. AAFA also maintains a clearinghouse of current and affordable educational materials, funds medical research, and sponsors a nationwide network of affiliated AAFA chapters.

Asthma and Allergy Foundation of America
1125 Fifteenth Street, NW, Suite 502
Washington DC 20005

Phone: 202-466-7643
Toll-free: 800-7-ASTHMA
Fax: 202-466-8940

Attention Deficit Disorders Association, Southern Region (ADDA Southern Region)—An independent, nonprofit organization providing a resource network for parents, educators, and health care professionals in Texas, Louisiana, Arkansas, Oklahoma, and New Mexico. ADDA—Southern Region keeps the public informed about ADD/ADHD through a newsletter and referral service, monthly meetings, educational programs, parent support services, conferences and workshops.

Attention Deficit Disorders Association—
   Southern Region
12345 Jones Road, Suite 287
Houston, TX 77070
Phone: 713-955-3720

Center for Child Welfare (CCW)—An organization dedicated to promoting and advancing interdisciplinary knowledge and policy in child, youth, and family welfare, with a focus on Hispanic/Latino children, youth and families at-risk in Latin America and the United States. CCW conducts interdisciplinary comparative research; integrates research knowledge into existing and developing programs; disseminates papers, resource manuals, and curriculum guides; and provides training to increase knowledge and skills in child, youth, and family welfare issues to individuals from Latin America and the United States.

Ruth E. Zambrana
Center for Child Welfare
College of Nursing and Health Science
George Mason University
4400 University Drive MS 2E8
Fairfax, VA 22030-4444
Phone: 703-993-1951
Fax: 703-993-1970

Child Attention Deficit Disorder/ Attention Deficit Hyperactivity Disorder (CH.A.D.D.)—Support organization for families coping with ADD/ADHD.

CH.A.D.D.
S499 NW 70th Avenue, Suite 101
Plantation, FL 33317
Phone: 800-233-4050
http://chadd.org/

Children's Hospice International—A nonprofit organization providing medical, psychological, emotional, and spiritual support to seriously ill children and their families, as well as to families recovering from the loss of a child.

Children's Hospice International
Alexandra, VA 22301
Phone: 703-684-0330 or 800-24-CHILD
Fax: 703-684-0226

The Council for Exceptional Children (CEC) and ERIC Clearinghouse on Disabilities and Gifted Education—CEC provides information through its library and database of professional literature to those concerned with the education of children who are gifted and handicapped. CEC also convenes conferences, assists lawmakers, and effects coordination of the North American Political Action Network.

The Council for Exceptional Children
1920 Association Drive
Reston, VA 20191-1589
Phone: 800-328-0272

Education for Parents of Indian Children with Special Needs (EPICS)—A national project providing parent training and information for American Indian families with special needs children.

Indian Children with Special Needs
P.O. Box 788

Bernalillo, NM 87004
Phone: 505-867-3396
Toll-free (parents only): 800-765-7429

Educators for Social Responsibility (ESR)—Develops curricula and trains teachers with a particular focus on conflict resolution.

ESR
23 Garden Street
Cambridge, MA 02138
Phone: 617-232-1595

Families Anonymous—A national group that provides support for individuals who are concerned about drug and related behavioral problems of friends or relatives.

Families Anonymous
P.O. Box 3475
Culver City, CA 90231-3475
Phone: 800-736-9805 or 310-313-5800
Fax: 310-313-6841

Family Service America, Inc. (FSA)—An international nonprofit association that assists individuals and families through education, services, and advocacy. The FSA network helps families solve problems related to parenting skills, parent-child tensions, teenage pregnancy, child abuse and neglect, family violence, and work-related problems.

Family Service America, Inc.
11700 W. Lake Park Drive
Milwaukee, WI 53211

Family Violence and Sexual Assault Institute (FVSAI)—A nonprofit, international resource center functioning as a clearinghouse on all aspects of family violence and sexual abuse. Information and materials are reviewed and the information is disseminated in the "Family Violence and Sexual Assault Bulletin." FVSAI also works with crisis centers, agencies, and counseling clinics to develop treatment programs for spouse/partner abuse and sexual abuse. The FVSAI Book Club offers *Flip Flops: A Workbook for Children Who Have Been Sexually Abused* (ages 7–9).

Family Violence and Sexual Assault Institute
1310 Clinic Drive
Tyler, TX 75701
Phone: 903-595-6600

Federation for Children with Special Needs—A center for parents and parent organizations to work together on behalf of children with special needs and their families.

Federation for Children with Special Needs
95 Berkeley Street, Suite 104
Boston, MA 02116
Phone: 617-482-2915 or 800-331-0688 (in MA)
E-mail: fcsninfo@fcsn.org

Federation of Families for Children's Mental Health—A national organization, run by parents, that focuses on the needs of children and youth with emotional, behavioral, or mental disorders, and their families.

Federation of Families for Children's Mental Health
1021 Prince Street
Alexandria, VA 22314-2971
Phone: 703-684-7710
Fax: 703-836-1040
E-mail: ffcmh@crosslink.net
http://www.crosslink.net/pub/users/f/ffcmh/enghome.htm

National Association for Visually Handicapped—A private, nonprofit organization serving visually impaired—not totally blind—children, their parents, and professionals who work with them, as well as adults with vision loss. The organization provides large-print visual aids, a newsletter, and brochures with information about commercially manufactured optical aides.

National Association for Visually Handi-
capped
22 West 21st Street
New York, NY 10010
Phone: 212-889-3141
Fax: 212-727-2931

**National Black Child Development Insti-
tute (NBCDI)**—An organization providing
community and direct services to African
American children, families, and advocates

National Black Child Development Institute
1023 15th Street, NW, Suite 600
Washington, DC 20005
Phone: 202-387-1281
Fax: 202-234-1738
E-mail: moreinfo@nbcdi.org
http://www.nbcdi.org

**National Burn Victim Foundation
(NBVF)**—A program providing advocacy
and services to burn victims and their families, at no charge. NBVF provides burn-relat-
ed information and referrals and community
burn-prevention resources. It also conducts
seminars on how to determine if child burns
are a result of child abuse.

National Burn Victim Foundation
246A Madisonville Road
P.O. Box 409
Basking Ridge, NJ 07920
Phone: 908-953-9091
Fax: 908-953-9099
E-mail: NBVF@intac.com
http://www.nbvf.org

**National Clearinghouse for Alcohol and
Drug Information (MCADI)**—Serves as
the world's largest resource for current information and materials concerning substance
abuse prevention. NCADI has an information
services staff equipped to respond to the public's alcohol, tobacco, and illicit drug
inquiries. The program is a service of the

Center for Substance Abuse Prevention,
Substance Abuse and Mental Health Services
Administration, U.S. Public Health Service,
U.S. Department of Health and Human
Services.

National Clearinghouse for Alcohol and
Drug Information
P.O. Box 2345
Rockville, MD 20847-2345
Phone: 800-NCADI-64 (622-3464)
Fax: 301-468-6433
http://www.health.org/index.htm
http://www.health.org/kidsarea/index.htm
("Just for kids")

**National Clearinghouse on Child Abuse
and Neglect**—A clearinghouse providing
resources for professionals related to the prevention of child abuse and neglect. It is a
service of the National Center on Child
Abuse and Neglect (NCCAN), Administration on Children, Youth and Families, Administration for Children and Families, U.S.
Department of Health and Human Services.

National Clearinghouse on Child Abuse and
Neglect
P.O. Box 1182
Washington, DC 20013-1182
Phone: 703-385-7565 or 800-FYI-3366
(394-3366)
Fax: 703-385-3206
E-mail: nccanch@calib.com
http://www.calib.com/nccanch/

**National Latino Children's Institute
(NLCI)**—Promotes and implements the
National Latino Children's Agenda, which is
a statement of principles essential for the
health and complete development of Latino
children. NLCI identifies and recognizes
"best practice" in the areas of children's
health, environment, economic, and educational conditions that are respectful of Latino
cultural values and language.

National Latino Children's Institute
1611 West Sixth Street
Austin, TX 78703
Phone: 512-472-9971
Fax: 512-472-5845
E-mail: nlca@inetport.com

National Organization of Parents of Blind Children (NOPBC)—Facilitates the sharing of experience and concerns among parents of blind children and visually impaired children, to provide information and support, and to develop resources for them. NOPBC conducts seminars and workshops and publishes free or low-cost brochures.

Barbara Cheadle, President
National Organization of Parents of Blind
   Children
1800 Johnson Street
Baltimore, MD 21230
Phone: 410-659-9314
Fax: 410-685-5653

The Stuttering Foundation of America (SFA)—Maintains a toll-free Hotline on Stuttering. Call for free information brochures and a nationwide referral list of speech-language pathologists who specialize in stuttering. SFA has also produced

Stuttering and Your Child: A Videotape for Parents, which is offered free of charge to public libraries. Provide your local library with the toll-free telephone number below, and ask that they obtain a copy of the video for their collection. The video is geared toward parents, teachers, day care professionals, and others interested in helping a child who stutters.

Stuttering Foundation of America
3100 Walnut Grove, Suite 603
P.O. Box 11749
Memphis, TN 38111-0749
Phone: 901-452-7343
Toll-free: 800-992-9392
http:///www.stuttersfa.org/index.html

The Women's Educational Equity Act (WEEA) Resource Center—A federal program dedicated to reducing educational disparity for women and girls.

Womens Educational Equity Act (WEEA)
Education Development Center
55 Chapel Street
Newton, MA 02158-1060
E-mail: weeapub@edc.org
http://www.edc.org/CEEC/WEEA

Appendix E
Resources for Understanding and Dealing with Child Abuse

CHILDREN'S LEGAL RIGHTS AND ADVOCACY

American Bar Association (ABA), Center on Children and the Law, 740 15th Street, NW, Washington, DC 20005, phone: 202-662-1720, fax: 202-662-1755, e-mail: ctchildlaw@abanet.org, website: http://www.abanet.org/child. This is a program of the American Bar Association, Young Lawyers Division, that provides consultation, technical assistance, and training for professionals in using the legal system to protect children. The center also publishes materials on child abduction.

American Civil Liberties Union (ACLU), Children's Rights Project, 132 W. 43rd Street, New York, NY 10036, phone: 212-229-0540, fax: 212-229-0749. The Children's Rights Project is a national program of litigation, advocacy, and education to ensure that when government child welfare systems must intervene in the lives of troubled families and children, they do so according to constitutional and statutory standards of fairness and due process.

The National Children's Advocacy Center, Local Intervention Program, 106 Lincoln Street, Huntsville, AL 35801, phone: 205-533-KIDS. This center provides child protective services, law enforcement, prosecution, mental health, medicine, education, and other resources in a model community response to child sexual abuse. The center sponsors training conferences, disseminates research findings, and provides technical assistance.

CULTURE-SPECIFIC ORGANIZATIONS

American Indian Institute (AII), College of Continuing Education and Public Service, The University of Oklahoma, 555 Constitution Street, Suite 237, Norman, OK 73072-7820, phone: 405-325-4127, fax: 405-325-7757. The institute serves North American Indian tribes and bands through workshops, seminars, and consultation and technical assistance on a state, regional, national, and international basis. It also cosponsors annually the National American Indian Conference on Child Abuse and Neglect. E-mail: aii@cce.occe.ou.edu

COSSMHO, 1501 16th Street, NW, Washington, DC 20036, phone: 202-387-5000, fax: 202-797-4353. COSSMHO is a national nonprofit coalition of Hispanic organizations serving the Mexican American, Puerto Rican, Cuban, and Latino communities in the area of health and human services, substance abuse prevention, and family strengthening. Coalition affiliates include 220 local agencies in 32 states, the District of Columbia, and Puerto Rico.

National Black Child Development Institute, Inc. (NBCDI), 1023 15th Street, NW, Suite 600, Washington, DC 20005, phone: 202-387-1281, fax: 202-234-1738. NBCDI, together with its forty-two affiliates composed of volunteers, works to improve the quality of life for African American children and youth through public education and services in the areas of child care, education, child welfare, and health. Publications on issues in these areas are also available.

People of Color Leadership Institute (POCLI), 714 G Street, SE, Washington, DC 20003, phone: 202-544-3144, fax: 202-547-3601. POCLI's mission is to increase knowledge, skills, and competency in ethnic and cultural issues among child and family welfare professionals and agencies, and to promote leadership among professionals of color in the fields of child and family welfare juvenile justice, mental health, and preventive services. POCLI has developed an agency self-assessment tool that allows agencies to assess their level of cultural competence and a staff training curriculum guide. Both are available for cost. POCLI staff also provides training in the areas of child abuse and neglect, attitude competency, domestic violence, substance abuse, and family support preservation.

DIRECTORIES

The National Directory of Children, Youth and Families Services lists over 30,000 agencies, both public and private. State by state and county by county professional contacts are listed for Human/Social Services, Health, Mental Health/Substance Abuse, Juvenile Justice, Treatment Centers, and Specialized Hospitals. Sections include: National Organizations, Runaway Shelters, Clearinghouses, Federal Resources, Hotlines, Information/Referral. For information, call 303-776-7539 or fax: 303-776-5831. National Directory of Children, Youth and Families Services, P.O. Box 1837, Longmont, CO 80502-1837.

The North American Directory of Programs for Runaways, Homeless Youth and Missing Children can be obtained from the American Youth Work Center, 1200 17th Street W., 4th Floor, Washington, DC 20036, phone: 202-785-0764, fax: 202-728-0657. Runaway centers are crucial defenses that protect street children form potentially abusive and exploitative situations. This directory lists 500 programs; price and ordering information is available upon request.

The Public Welfare Directory lists state and local human service agencies, including information on children, immigration, family support, adoptions, Medicaid, and correctional institutions. For price information, contact

Public Welfare Directory, American Public Welfare Association (APWA), 810 First Street, NE, Suite 500, Washington, DC 20002-4267, phone: 202-682-0100, fax: 202-289-6555.

FAMILY RESOURCES

AARP Grandparent Information Center, 601 E Street, NW, Room B5436, Washington, DC 20049, phone: 202-434-2296, fax: 202-434-6474. AARP Grandparent Information Center is a national organization that targets grandparents raising grandchildren, professionals, support groups, researchers, and policy makers. Referrals to local support groups, technical assistance, newsletter, national calendar of events, conference, fact sheets, brochures, and pamphlets.

Family Development Resources, Inc., 3160 Pinebrook Road, Park City, UT 84060, phone: 801-649-5822. Offers programs for professionals and paraprofessionals working in mental health, social work, education, medicine, and legal aid. They work with parents, infants, children, and adolescents to reduce dysfunction and build healthy positive interactions. Methods include role play, discussion, audiovisual, parent handbooks, activities manuals, and games. These programs cover multicultural families and substance abuse issues. For a catalog of programs and resources, call or write.

Family Resource Coalition (FRC), 200 S. Michigan Avenue, 16th Floor, Chicago, IL 60604, phone: 312-341-0900, fax: 312-341-9361. FRC is a membership organization of social service agencies concerned with strengthening families through preventive services. FRC maintains a clearinghouse for information on family resource programs throughout the United States, publishes a quarterly newsletter, sponsors conferences, and provides technical assistance.

Fatherhood Project (FP), Families and Work Institute, 330 7th Avenue, 14th Floor, New York, NY 10001, phone: 212-465-2044, fax: 212-465-8637, website: http://www. fatherhoodproject.org. The Fatherhood Project encourages the participation of males in child rearing through research, demonstration, and dissemination of materials.

National Exchange Club Foundation, 3050 W. Central Avenue, Toledo, OH 43606-1700, phone: 419-535-3232 or 800-760-3413. The foundation coordinates a network of over seventy-two parent aide programs in thirty-one states and Puerto Rico. Professionally trained and supervised parent aides work with abusive families and families considered at risk, to help parents develop positive parenting skills.

The foundation also coordinates the National Parent Aide Network, an organization designed to develop and support parent aide programs nationwide, promote activities that strengthen families, offer support to parents, and prevent child abuse and neglect. E-mail: nechq@nol.com, website: QL: RTPnet.Org/~nec/

The Office of Family Policy (OFP), Military Family Resource Center, Ballston Tower, Suite 3, 4015 Wilson Blvd., Suite 903, Arlington, VA 22203, phone: 703-696-6806. OFP is an international center supporting family advocacy in the military services. It collects and disseminates information on programs that support the needs of military families, publishes a newspaper, and provides assistance to professionals serving military families.

Parents Without Partners, Inc. (PWP), 401 N. Michigan Avenue, Chicago, IL 60611-4267, phone: 312-644-6610, for local chapters: 800-637-7974. PWP provides single parents and their children with an opportunity for enhancing personal growth, self-confidence, and sensitivity toward others by offering an environment for support, friendship, and the exchange of parenting techniques. Visit their website at http://www.parentsplace.com/readroom/pwp/

Stepfamily Association of America (SAA), 215 Centennial Mall S., Suite 212, Lincoln, NE 68502, phone: 402-477-7837 or 800-735-0329, fax: 402-477-8317. SAA provides information, education, and support for stepfamilies. Catalog of resources available. Members receive a quarterly publication, discount on resources, and a free copy of the book Stepfamilies Stepping Ahead. Quarterly newsletter also available by subscription. Local chapters sponsor monthly meetings. For further information or to locate an SAA chapter near you, call or write.

Stepfamily Foundation, Inc., 333 West End Avenue, Apt. 11C, New York, NY 10023, phone: 212-877-3244. Founded in 1975, its goals include creating awareness of the predictable patterns and problems of stepfamily members, acting as a clearinghouse for information, conducting research, providing a speaker's bureau, publishing a newsletter, and conducting workshops and professional counseling training sessions. Visit their website at http://www.stepfamily.org

EXCEPTIONAL CHILDREN

The Association for Persons with Severe Handicaps (TASH), 29 W. Susquehanna, Suite 210, Baltimore, MD 21204, phone: 410-828-8274, fax: 410-828-6706, TDD: 410-828-1306. TASH is an international organization concerned with human dignity, education, and independence for individuals who have traditionally been labeled "severely intellectually disabled." TASH provides information that keeps the public aware of legal issues affecting the handicapped.

Boys Town National Research Hospital, 555 N. 30th Street, Omaha, NE 68131-9909, phone: 402-498-1657, fax: 402-498-1654.

Center for Abused Children with Disabilities (CACD)/Psych. Services provides assessment and intervention of abused children with disabilities and their families and conducts research on child maltreatment and disability issues.

PACER Center, 4826 Chicago Avenue S., Minneapolis, MN 55417, phone: 612-827-2966. The Let's Prevent Abuse project features three puppet shows for children (grades K–4) on abuse, and training for professionals who work with children (birth–12) with and without disabilities. The project also offers workshops and written materials to groups and parent organizations about child maltreatment and the increased vulnerability for children with disabilities.

The Shield Abuse and Trauma Project, 3909 214th Place, Bayside, NY 11361, phone: 718-229-5757 ext. 216, fax: 718-225-3159. The Shield Abuse and Trauma Project provides a unique program of services to individuals with developmental disabilities who have experienced abuse or other traumatic experiences resulting in emotional, behavioral, or interpersonal difficulties. The project provides individual and group treatment services in addition to organizational training and consulting services. Organizational training and consulting are geared to helping agencies understand the impact of abuse and/or trauma on these individuals and to assist in creating more effective intervention in all settings.

HOTLINES

Childhelp USA/IOF Foresters National Child Abuse Hotline, toll-free: 800-422-4453 or 800-4-A-Child. The National Child Abuse Hotline provides crisis counseling, child abuse reporting information, and information and referrals for every county in the United States. Referrals include national, state, and local agencies. The hotline is staffed

twenty-four hours a day, seven days a week, by mental health professionals.

Father Flanagan's Boys Home (Boys Town) can be contacted at 14100 Crawford Street, Boys Town, NE 68010, phone: 402-498-1301. Boys Town operates a variety of in- and out-of-home services for children and families, including a residential treatment center, residential services, emergency shelter, family preservation, treatment foster care, and parenting classes in thirteen states. The Boys Town National Training Center offers training to child care professionals, school districts, mental health facilities, and other organizations. Boys Town also operates a national toll-free hotline for youth problems: 800-448-3000.

National Directory of Hotlines and Crisis Intervention Centers can be contacted at Covenant House Nineline, 346 W. 17th Street, New York, NY 10011, phone: 800-999-9999, TDD: 800-999-9915. It provides a twenty-four-hour nationwide hotline for runaways and troubled youth and their families and offers referrals to services in a caller's local area as well as conference calls and message relays to runaways who wish to speak with their parents.

LEGAL RESOURCES

National Association of Counsel for Children (NACC), 1205 Oneida Street, Denver, CO 80220, phone: 303-322-2260, fax: 303-329-3523, e-mail: NACCNATL@ aol.com, website: http://electricstores.com/ kempe/nacc.htm. The NACC is a professional organization for lawyers and other practitioners who represent children in court. NACC publishes "The Guardian," a monthly newsletter for members, and a variety of books dealing with children's legal rights. NACC also holds annual conferences on children's legal issues.

National Center for Prosecution of Child Abuse, American Prosecutors Research Institute (APRI), 99 Canal Center Plaza, Suite 510, Alexandria, VA 22314, phone: 703-739-0321. APRI provides training and technical assistance to prosecutors and others handling child abuse cases. Resources include state statutes, case law, expert witness, court reform, topical files, and the authoritative manual "Investigation and Prosecution of Child Abuse."

National Center for Youth Law (NCYL), 114 Sansome Street, Suite 900, San Francisco, CA 94104, phone: 415-543-3307. NCYL provides information, training, and consultation on youth law matters to legal services attorneys and other professionals serving poor children and youth. Areas of expertise include abuse and neglect, termination of parental rights, public benefits for children, children's health, and the rights of children living in institutions.

The National Conference of State Legislatures (NCSL), Children Families Program, 1560 Broadway, Suite 700, Denver, CO 80202, phone: 303-830-2200, fax: 303-863-8003. NCSL is a nonpartisan organization serving the nation's 7,500 state legislators and their staffs. NCSL's child research services include publications, and technical assistance available to legislators for assessing problems and identifying solutions to improve state programs. Visit their website at http://www.ncsl.org/public/cfh.htm

National Council of Juvenile and Family Court Judges (NCJFCJ), P.O. Box 8970, Reno, NV 89507, phone: 702-784-6012. NCJFCJ represents America's 9,000 plus judges who exercise jurisdiction over delinquency, abuse and neglect, divorce, custody, support, domestic violence, and similar types of cases throughout the country. The National Council conducts training programs at its headquarters' training facility, the National College of Juvenile and Family Law.

National Court Appointed Special Advocates Association (National CASA), 100 W. Harrison Street, North Tower, Suite 500, Seattle, WA 98119-4123, phone: 800-628-3233 or 206-270-0072, fax: 206-270-0078, e-mail:staff@nationalcasa.org, website: http://www.nationalcasa.org. National CASA is a nonprofit, membership organization that supports and develops local CASA programs. **Local programs** train community volunteers who are appointed by a judge to speak up for abused and neglected children in court. Contact National CASA for start-up or local program information.

State Laws related to child abuse are available either by contacting individual states or in a single volume compilation that includes all fifty states, the District of Columbia, American Samoa, Guam, Puerto Rico, and the Virgin Islands. To purchase *State Statutes Related to Child Abuse and Neglect: 1988,* contact the Clearinghouse on Child Abuse and Neglect Information, P.O. Box 1182, Washington, DC 20013, phone: 703-385-7565.

LITERATURE SEARCH

For an annotated bibliography of documents about specific aspects of child abuse or neglect (e.g., the relationship between alcohol abuse and child maltreatment), contact the **Clearinghouse on Child Abuse and Neglect Information,** P.O. Box 1182, Washington, DC 20013, phone: 800-FYI-3366 or 703-385-7565, fax: 703-385-3206, http://www.calib.com/nccanch

MATERIALS ON CHILD ABUSE AND PARENTING

The National Committee to Prevent Child Abuse (NCPCA) publishes a variety of materials on child abuse, child abuse prevention, and parenting. For a free catalog describing publications, contact NCPCA, Publications Department, P.O. Box 2866, Chicago, IL 60690, phone: 800-55-NCPCA, or call 800-CHILDREN to see how you can stop child abuse before it starts.

MEDICAL RESOURCES

American Academy of Pediatrics (AAP), Department C—Sexual Abuse, P.O. Box 927, Elk Grove Village, IL 60009-0927, phone: 847-228-5005, fax: 847-228-5097. The AAP provides numerous materials for professionals working in the child abuse field, including policy statements, a visual diagnosis of child physical abuse program, and resources for prevention, recognition and treatment available on CD-ROM. The AAP also publishes a public education brochure on child sexual abuse. To obtain a free copy of the brochure, send a stamped, self-addressed, business-size envelope to the above address. Visit their website at http://www.aap.org

American Medical Association, Department of Mental Health, 515 N. State Street, Chicago, IL 60610, phone: 312-464-5066. Provides information to health professionals about family violence, including child abuse/ neglect, child sexual abuse, and media violence, among other topics. AMA members may receive materials free by calling the number above. Others may order materials from 312-464-5563. A website with information and resources is available at http://www. psy.bsd.uchicago.edu/~larry/uchome.htm

MISSING CHILDREN

National Center for Missing and Exploited Children, 2101 Wilson Blvd., Suite 550, Arlington, VA 22201, toll-free: 800-843-5678. The center was established by congressional mandate in 1984 to locate and recover missing children and reduce crimes against children. To report information about a missing child or to request free brochures on child protection, call the toll-free number.

ORGANIZATIONS

American Humane Association, Children's Division, 63 Inverness Drive E., Englewood, CO 80112-5117, phone: 303-792-9900, fax: 303-792-5333, e-mail: children@amerhumane.org, website: http:www.amerhumane.org. The American Humane Association is a national center promoting responsive child protection services in every community through program planning, training, education, and consultation. It operates the National Resource Center on Child Abuse and Neglect. Please contact for free general information.

American Professional Society on the Abuse of Children (APSAC), 407 S. Dearborn, Suite 1300, Chicago, IL 60605, phone: 312-554-0166. APSAC is a multidisciplinary professional membership society founded to promote support among professionals who work with victims of child abuse.

American Public Welfare Association (APWA), 810 First Street, NE, Suite 500, Washington, DC 20002-4267, phone: 202-682-0100, fax: 202-289-6555. APWA is an organization concerned about effective administration of publicly funded human services. Its affiliate, the National Association of Public Child Welfare Administrators (NAPCWA), is a membership organization designed to promote and enhance the delivery of public child welfare services.

C. Henry Kempe National Center for the Prevention and Treatment of Child Abuse and Neglect, 1205 Oneida Street, Denver, CO 80220, phone: 303-321-3963. The center emphasizes the development of treatment programs for abused children, conducts training and consultation programs, and offers technical assistance. A catalog of materials and services is available upon request. Visit their website at http://electricstores.com/kempe/default.htm

Child Welfare League of America (CWLA), 440 First Street, NW, Suite 310, Washington, DC 20001-2085, phone: 202-638-2952, fax: 202-638-4004. CWLA is a membership association of almost 1,000 public and private nonprofit agencies, which together serve over two million children and their families across the United States annually. CWLA's member agencies provide a wide range of services to protect abused, neglected, and otherwise vulnerable children and youth.

Extension Service, U.S. Department of Agriculture (USDA), 14th and Independence Avenue, SW, Washington, DC 20250, phone: 202-720-0987. Cooperative Extension, working through land-grant universities, provides research-based information on critical issues such as child abuse and neglect. Professionals and paraprofessionals work with nearly three million volunteers to provide prevention programs throughout the United States and its territories.

International Society for Prevention of Child Abuse and Neglect (ISPCAN), 401 N. Michigan Avenue, Suite 2200, Chicago, IL 60611, phone: 312-644-6610 ext. 3273 and ext. 4713. ISPCAN is a membership organization that pro vides a forum for the exchange of information on child abuse and neglect globally. Benefits include the monthly "Child Abuse and Neglect: The International Journal," a newsletter, and the biennial international congress on child abuse and neglect.

National Association of Social Workers (NASW), 750 1st Street NE, Washington, DC 20002-4241, phone: 800-638-8799. NASW supports protection of social service consumers, advances the quality of social work practice, and proposes and promotes sound public policies and programs. NASW also participates in annual public service campaigns and publishes social work books and journals. NASW provides referrals to social services.

National Center on Child Abuse and Neglect (NCCAN), U.S. Department of Health and Human Services, P.O. Box 1182, Washington, DC 20013, phone: 800-FYI-3366. NCCAN conducts research, collects and analyzes information, and provides assistance for activities on the prevention of child abuse. Visit their website at http://www.calib.com/nccanch

National Child Abuse and Neglect Clinical Resource Center, 1205 Oneida Street, Denver, CO 80220, phone: 303-321-3963. Part of the U.S. National Center on Child Abuse and Neglect resource system, the center provides clinical consultation, referrals, training, and literature to aid in the multidisciplinary diagnosis and treatment of child abuse.

National Coalition to Abolish Corporal Punishment in Schools (NCACPS), Center for Effective Discipline, 155 W. Main Street, Suite 100-B, Columbus, OH 43215, phone: 614-221-8829, fax: 614-228-5058. NCACPS is an organization of parents, child advocates, and professional associations that seeks to have corporal punishment banned as a means of discipline in schools. NCACPS provides fact sheets, resource materials, and consultation on state and local actions to ban corporal punishment. NCACPS is how heading

E.P.O.C.H.-USA a multinational federation to End Physical Punishment on Children in the United States.

National Crime Prevention Council (NCPC), 1700 K Street, NW, Second Floor, Washington, DC 20006-3817, phone: 202-466-NCPC, fax: 202-296-1356. NCPC publishes books, kits of camera-ready program materials, posters, and informational and policy reports on a variety of crime prevention and community-building subjects. NCPC offers training, technical assistance, and national focus for crime prevention. Visit their website at http://www.weprevent.org

PARENTING EDUCATION

American Guidance Service (AGS), 4201 Woodland Road, Circle Pines, MN 55014, phone: 800-328-2560 or 612-786-4343, fax: 612-786-9077. AGS produces classroom materials for the program Systematic Training for Effective Parenting (STEP). The STEP materials include books for parents and volunteer leaders as well as a newsletter. AGS also produces additional publications and videos for parents of teens and preschoolers. Call to receive a catalog on parenting.

Family Communications, Inc., 4802 5th Avenue, Pittsburgh, PA 15213, phone: 412-687-2990. Written by Fred Rogers, creator of Mister Rogers' Neighborhood, its "Let's Talk About It" booklet series facilitates communication between parents and children on subjects such as moving, going to school, discipline, divorce, and death. For one free booklet, indicate the subject and self a self-addressed, stamped, business-sized envelope.

Gordon Training International, 531 Stevens Avenue, W., Solana Beach, CA 92075, phone: 800-628-1197, or 619-481-8121, fax: 619-481-8125. Provides an eight-session course taught by instructors throughout the United States and in thirty countries. It teaches how to

raise self-disciplined, responsible, cooperative children, how to resolve family conflicts amicably, and how to set rules children follow willingly. It also is available in a home-study program.

PARENT RESOURCES

Big Brothers/Big Sisters of America, 230 N. 13th Street, Philadelphia, PA 19107, phone: 215-567-7000. Families under stress and single parents can find support in parenting responsibilities through the Big Brothers/Big Sisters program. Volunteers support families by working with children in need of additional attention and friendship.

Center for the Improvement of Child Caring, 11331 Ventura Blvd., Suite 103, Studio City, CA 91604, phone: 818-980-0903, fax: 818-753-1054 or 800-325-2422. The center provides training for parents and training of parenting instructors nationwide. It offers workshops nationwide, including two ethnic programs, effective Black Parenting, and Los Ninos Bien Educados.

Effective Parenting Information for Children (EPIC), Program, Inc., Buffalo State College, 1300 Elmwood Avenue, 340 Cassety Hall, Buffalo, NY 14222, phone: 716-886-6396, fax: 716-886-0221. EPIC provides parenting education to help young people develop strength of character, self-esteem, and skills necessary for facing difficult decisions throughout their lives. The program also includes teachers' training and classroom activities infused into mandated curricula, workshops for parents, and networking activities with community agencies.

National Coalition Against Domestic Violence (For members): P.O. Box 34103, Washington, DC 20043-4103, phone: 202-638-6388, TTY: 202-737-3033. To order publications: P.O. Box 18749, Denver, CO 80218-0749, phone: 303-839-1852. The coalition is a national organization that works to end violence in the lives of battered women and their children. The coalition provides information, technical assistance, publications, newsletters, and resource materials. Call or write for membership information.

National Institute of Mental Health, Public Inquiry Section, 5600 Fishers Lane, Room 15C-05, Rockville, MD 20857. For more information on mental health topics such as stress, anxiety, and depression, and for general parenting materials, write to the above address. **Parents Anonymous (PA)** is a self-help program for parents under stress and for abused children. There are no fees, and no one is required to reveal his or her name. Group members support each other in searching out positive alternatives to the abuse behavior in their lives. To locate a group in your area, look in the white pages of your telephone directory under Parents Anonymous or contact National Parents Anonymous, 675 W. Foothill Blvd, Suite 220. Claremont, CA 91711, phone: 909-621-6184.

Salvation Army. Call your local office listed in the telephone book, or contact one of the following territorial offices: Eastern Territory, 440 W. Nyack Road, P.O. Box C-635, West Nyack, NY 10994-0635, phone: 914-620-7200; Southern Territory, 1424 NE Expressway, Atlanta, GA 30329, phone: 404-728-1300; Central Territory, 10 W. Algonquin, Des Plaines, IL 60016, phone: 708-294-2000; Western Territory, 30840 Hawthorne Blvd., Rancho Palos Verdes, CA 90274, phone: 213-541-4721. The Salvation Army offers such services as emergency shelter, temporary foster-home care for children, temporary housing and transitional residential programs, family, prenatal, and postnatal counseling, care and guidance for unwed and expectant mothers, and counseling for unmarried fathers.

PROGRAM SUPPORT FOR NEW PARENTS

Birth to Three, 3875 Kincaid Street, #15, Eugene, OR 97405, phone: 541-484-4401, fax: 541-484-1449 or 800-680-7888. This organization is dedicated to strengthening families and preventing child abuse and neglect in families from all socioeconomic backgrounds. Programs are for parents of infants, toddlers, and teenage parents. The organization also offers support and education groups, operates a warmline, publishes a newsletter, and writes a parenting column for a local newspaper.

The Family Institute (TFI), 1833 Kalahau Avenue, Suite 1001, Honolulu, HI 96815, phone: 808-944-9000. The Family Institute was established in 1996 by the Hawaii Family Stress Center at Kapiolani Medical Center and the Consuelo Zobel Alger Foundation. TFI's mission is to enhance the ability of home-based family support, early childhood, and other family service providers to provide quality services that produce positive outcomes for children and their families in the United States and abroad.

First Steps, Georgia Council on Child Abuse, 1475 Peachtree Street, NE, Suite 200, Atlanta, GA 30309, phone: 404-870-6565. Volunteers offer emotional support, parent education, referrals, and follow-up contacts to expectant and new parents in hospital and clinic settings. Program also includes a twenty-four-hour helpline, extended support to families of neonatal intensive care unit infants, and home visitors for high-risk families.

Healthy Families America (HFA), 332 S. Michigan Avenue, Chicago, IL 60604, phone: 312-663-3520. NCPCA in partnership with Ronald McDonald Children's Charities has implemented HFA, an innovative initiative designed to support and educate new parents through the establishment of intensive home visitor services nationwide.

MELD, 123 N. Third Street, Suite 507, Minneapolis, MN 55401, phone: 612-332-7563 or 612-344-1959. MELD offers parent information and support groups in locations around the country. Groups are led by carefully selected and trained volunteer peer facilitators. Programs include MELD's New Parents, MELD's Young Moms, MELD for Hearing Impaired Parents, MELD Special for parents of children with special needs, and Nueva Familia for Hispanic families.

Teen Parent Connection (a program of Child Abuse Prevention Services), 3308 Broadway, Suite 100, San Antonio, TX 78209, phone: 210-829-KIDS, fax: 210-829-5882. The Teen Parent Connection is a multi-service program of self-help, peer support groups for first-time teen parents and their infants.

Zero to Three: National Center for Infants, Toddlers and Families, 734 15th Street, NW, 10th Floor, Washington, DC 20005, phone: 202-638-1144, fax: 202-638-0851, publications: 800-899-4301. Zero to Three's urgent mission is to advance the healthy development of America's babies and young children. They strengthen and support professionals, policy makers, and parents by increasing public awareness, fostering professional excellence through training, promoting the discovery and application of new knowledge concerning early child development, and educating parents. Visit their website at http://www.zerotothree.org

PUBLIC INFORMATION

The National Committee to Prevent Child Abuse (NCPCA) and the **Advertising Council, Inc.,** produce and make available public service announcements (PSAs) for radio, television, and print media. The goal of these advertisements is to make the public more aware of child abuse and to teach alternatives to abusive behavior. PSAs are often provided free when individuals and organizations from the immediate area contact their local stations and newspapers and request their usage. For more information on how you can help prevent child abuse by involving the media in your area, contact NCPCA, Public Awareness Department, P.O. Box 2866, Chicago, IL 60690, phone: 312-663-3520.

SELF-HELP GROUPS

Self-help groups may be beneficial to parents with children who have special needs. Such families can find extra support and learn new ways of handling difficult situations by communicating with others in similar situations. For listings of self-help groups, send a stamped, self-addressed business-sized envelope to **The National Self-Help Clearinghouse.** Graduate School, City University of New York, 25 W. 43rd Street, Room 620, New York, NY 10036, phone: 212-642-2944.

SUBSTANCE ABUSE

Alcoholics Anonymous (AA), General Service Office, P.O. Box 459, Grand Central Station, New York, NY 10163, phone: 212-870-3400. AA is a worldwide fellowship of men and women who help each other maintain sobriety through AA's Twelve-Step Program of recovery. The only requirement for membership is a desire to stop drinking. AA is a nonprofessional, self-supporting, nondenominational, apolitical organization with 90,000 groups in 133 countries.

Children of Alcoholics Foundation, 555 Madison Avenue, 20th Floor, New York, NY 10163, phone: 212-754-0656 or 800-359-2623. The foundation promotes public and professional awareness of children of alcoholics' problems and develops programs and materials to break the cycle of family alcoholism. Free information packet provided on request.

National Clearinghouse for Alcohol and Drug Information (NCADI), 11426 Rockville Pike, Suite 200, Rockville, MD 20852, phone: 800-729-6686 or 301-468-2600. NCADI is a communications service of the Center for Substance Abuse Prevention. NCADI provides information to thousands of requestors on the latest research results, popular press and scholarly journal articles, prevention and education resources, and prevention programs. Call to receive a catalog.

Appendix F
Parent Training and Information Projects

Following is a list of federally funded parent training and information projects in the United States. These groups serve the entire state in which they are located unless otherwise noted. They are useful resources for parents and professionals caring for young children with behavioral difficulties due to psychological or physical disabilities.

Alabama

Special Education Action Committee, Inc.
Carol Blades, Director
600 Bel Air Blvd., #210
Mobile, AL 36606-3501
Phone: 334-478-1208
TDD: 334-473-7877
Fax: 800-222-7322 (in-state only)
E-mail: seacmob1@juno.com
www.hsv.tis.net/~cja/

Alaska

P.A.R.E.N.T.S. Resource Center
Faye Nieto
4743 E. Northern Lights Blvd.
Anchorage, AK 99508
Phone: 907-337-7678
TDD: 907-337-7671
Fax: 800-478-7678 (in-state only)
E-mail: parents@alaska.net
www.alaska.net/~parents/

American Somoa

American Samoa PAVE
Fa' Anati Penitusi
P.O. Box 3432
Pago Pago, AS 96799
Phone: 011-684-633-2407
Fax: 011-684-633-2408

Arizona

Pilot Parent Partnerships
Mary Slaughter/Judy Walker
4750 N. Black Canyon Hwy., Suite 101
Phoenix, AZ 85017-3621
Phone: 602-242-4366 (TDD available)
Fax: 602-242-4306 or 800-237-3007
    (in-state only)

Arkansas

Arkansas Disability Coalition
Wanda Stovall
2801 Lee Avenue, Suite B
Little Rock, AR 72205
Phone: 501-614-7020 (TDD available)
Fax: 501-614-9082 or 800-223-1330
    (in-state only)
E-mail: adc@cei.net

FOCUS, Inc.
Elizabeth Stafford
305 W. Jefferson Avenue
Jonesboro, AR 72401
Phone: 870-935-2750
Fax: 870-931-3755
E-mail: focusinc@ipa.net

California

Central California
Exceptional Parents Unlimited
Marian Karian, Executive Director
4120 N. First Street
Fresno, CA 93726
Phone: 209-229-2000
Fax: 209-229-2956
E-mail: epul@cybergate.com

Nine Counties in the San Francisco Bay Area

Parents Helping Parents of San Francisco
Lois Jones
594 Monterey Blvd.
San Francisco, CA 94127-2416
Phone: 415-841-8820
Fax: 415-841-8824

Northern California

DREDF
Diane Lipton
2212 Sixth Street
Berkeley, CA 94710
Phone: 510-644-2555 (TDD available)
Fax: 510-841-8645 or 800-466-4232
  (in-state only)
E-mail: dredf@dredf.org
www.dredf.org

Matrix
Deidre Hayden
555 Northgate Drive, Suite A
San Rafael, CA 94903
Phone: 415-499-3877
TDD: 415-499-3854
Toll-free: 800-578-2592 (in-state only)
Fax: 415-507-9457
E-mail: matrix@matrixparents.org
www.matrixparents.org

Parents Helping Parents of Santa Clara
Mary Ellen Peterson
3041 Olcott Street
Santa Clara, CA 95054-3222
Phone: 408-727-5775
TDD: 408-727-7655
Fax: 408-727-0182
E-mail: info@php.com
www.php.com

San Diego and Imperial Counties

TASK, San Diego
Richard Miller, Codirector
3750 Convoy Street, Suite 303
San Diego, CA 92111-3741

Phone: 619-874-2386
Fax: 619-874-2375

San Francisco

Support for Families of Children with Disabilities
Juno Duenas
2601 Mission #170
San Francisco, CA 94110-3111
Phone: 415-282-7494
Fax: 415-282-1226
E-mail: sfcdmiss@aol.com

Southern California

TASK
Joan Tellefsen
100 W. Cerritos Avenue
Anaheim, CA 92805
Phone: 714-533-8275
Fax: 714-533-2533
E-mail: taskca@aol.com

Colorado

PEAK Parent Center, Inc.
Barbara Buswell/Judy Martz
6055 Lehman Drive, Suite 101
Colorado Springs, CO 80918
Phone: 719-531-9400 (Voice)
  719-531-9403 (TDD)
Toll-free: 800-284-0251 (in-state only)
Fax: 719-531-9452
E-mail: PKPARENT@aol.com

Connecticut

CPAC
Nancy Prescott
338 Main Street
Niantic, CT 06357
Phone: 860-739-3089 (Voice and TDD)
Toll-free: 800-445-2722 (in-state only)
Fax:860-739-7460 (Call first to dedicate line)
E-mail: cpacinc@aol.com
members.aol.com/cpacinc/cpac.htm

Delaware

Parent Information Center (PIC)
Marie-Anne Aghazadian
700 Barksdale Road, Suite 3
Newark, DE 19711
Phone: 302-366-0152 (Voice)
    302-366-0178 (TDD)
Fax: 302-366-0276
E-mail: PEP700@aol.com

Florida

Family Network on Disabilities
Jan LaBelle
2735 Whitney Road
Clearwater, FL 33760-1610
Phone: 813-523-1130
Toll-free: 800-825-5736 (in-state only)
Fax: 813-523-8687
E-mail: fnd@gate.net
www.gate.net/~fnd

Georgia

**Parents Educating Parents and
    Professionals for All Children (PEPPAC)**
Linda Shepard
8318 Durelee Lane, Suite 101
Douglasville, GA 30134
Phone: 770-577-7771
Fax: 770-577-7774
E-mail: peppac@bellsouth.net

Hawaii

AWARE
Jennifer Schember-Lang, Executive Director
200 N. Vineyard Blvd., Suite 310
Honolulu, HI 96817
Phone: 808-536-9684 (Voice)
    808-536-2280 (Voice and TTY)
Fax: 808-537-6780
E-mail: Idah@gte.net

Idaho

Idaho Parents Unlimited, Inc.
Ruth Griggs

4696 Overland Road, Suite 478
Boise, ID 83705
Phone: 208-342-5884 (Voice and TDD)
Toll-free: 800-242-4785 (in-state only)
Fax: 208-342-1408
E-mail: ipul@rmci.net
home.rmci.net/IPUL

Illinois

Designs for Change
Donald Moore/Jim McGovern
6 N. Michigan Avenue, Suite 1600
Chicago, IL 60602
Phone: 312-857-9292 (Voice)
    312-857-1013 (TDD)
Toll-free: 800-851-8728 (in-state only)
Fax: 312-857-9299
E-mail: dfcl@aol.com

Family Resource Center on Disabilities
Charlotte Des Jardins
20 E. Jackson Blvd., Room 900
Chicago, IL 60604
Phone: 312-939-3513 (Voice)
    312-939-3519 (TTY and TDY)
Toll-free: 800-952-4199 (in-state only)
Fax: 312-939-7297

**National Center for Latinos with
    Disabilities**
Maria Elena Rodriguez-Sullivan
1921 South Blue Island Avenue
Chicago, IL 60608
Phone: 312-666-3393 (Voice)
    312-666-1788 (TTY)
Toll-free: 800-532-3393 (in-state only)
Fax: 312-666-1787
E-mail: ncld@interaccess.com

Central and Southern Illinois
Family T.I.E.S. Network
Deb Kunz
830 S. Spring
Springfield, IL 62704
Phone: 217-544-5809

Toll-free: 800-865-7842 (in-state only)
Fax: 217-544-6018
E-mail: ftiesn@aol.com

Indiana

IN*SOURCE
Richard Burden
8009 N. Michigan Street
South Bend, IN 46601-1036
Phone: 219-234-7101
Fax: 219-234-7279 or 800-332-4433
E-mail: insour@speced.doe.state.in.us
home1.gte.net/insource

Iowa

SEEK Parent Center
Kate Payne
406 SW School Street, Suite 207
Ankeny, IA 50021
Phone: 515-965-0155
Toll-free: 888-431-4332 (in-state only)
Fax: 515-276-8470 (call first)

Kansas

Families Together, Inc.
Connie Zienkewicz
3340 W. Douglas, Suite 102
Wichita, KS 67203
Phone: 316-945-7747
Toll-free: 888-815-6364 (in-state only)
Fax: 316-945-7795
E-mail: fmin@feist.com
www.kansas.net/~family

Kentucky

Family Training and Information Center
Paulette Logsdon
2210 Goldsmith Lane, Suite 118
Louisville, KY 40218
Phone: 502-456-0923
Toll-free: 800-525-7746 (in-state only)
Fax: 502-456-0893
E-mail: FamilyTrng@aol.com

Louisiana

Project PROMPT
Leah Knight
4323 Division Street, Suite 110
Metairie, LA 70002-3179
Phone: 504-888-9111
Toll-free: 800-766-7736 (in-state only)
Fax: 504-888-0246
E-mail: lafhforg@iamerica.net

Maine

Special Needs Parents Info Network
Janice LaChance
P.O. Box 2067
Augusta, ME 04338-2067
Phone: 207-582-2504
Toll-free: 800-870-SPIN (in-state only)
Fax: 207-582-3638
E-mail: info@mpf.org
www.mpf.org

Maryland

Parents Place of Maryland, Inc.
Josie Thomas
7257 Parkway Drive, Suite 210
Hanover, MD 21076-1306
Phone: 410-712-0900 (Voice and TDD)
Fax: 410-712-0902
E-mail: parplace@aol.com
www.somerset.net/ParentsPlace

Massachusetts

Federation for Children with Special Needs
Richard Robison
95 Berkeley Street, Suite 104
Boston, MA 02116
Phone: 617-482-2915 (Voice and TTY)
Toll-free: 800-331-0688 (in-state only)
Fax: 617-695-2939
E-mail: fcsninfo@fcsn.org
www.fcsn.org/

Michigan

CAUSE
Sue Pratt/Patrick Strong
3303 W. Saginaw, Suite F-1
Lansing, MI 48917-2303
Phone: 517-886-9167 (Voice, TDD, and TDY)
Toll-free: 800-221-9105 (in-state only)
Fax: 517-886-9775
E-mail: info-cause@voyager.net
www.taalliance.org/ptis/mi/

Wayne County
Parents Are Experts
Jessie Mullins
23077 Greenfield Road, Suite 205
Southfield, MI 48075-3744
Phone: 248-557-5070 (Voice and TDD)
Fax: 248-557-4456
E-mail: ucpdetroit@aol.com

Minnesota

PACER Center, Inc.
Paula Goldberg/Marge Goldberg/Virginia
   Richardson
4826 Chicago Avenue S.
Minneapolis, MN 55417-1098
Phone: 612-827-2966 (Voice)
   612-827-7770 (TTY)
Toll-free: 800-537-2237 (in-state only)
Fax: 612-827-3065
E-mail: pacer@pacer.org
www.pacer.org

Mississippi

Parent Partners
Aretha Lee, Director
3111 N. State Street
Jackson, MI 39216
Phone: 601-366-5707
Toll-free: 800-366-5707 (in-state only)
Fax: 601-362-7361
E-mail: ptiofms@misnet.com
www.taalliance.org/ptis/ms/

Project Empower
Agnes Johnson
1427 S. Main, Suite 8
Greenville, MS 38701
Phone: 601-332-4852
Toll-free: 800-337-4852 (in-state only)
Fax: 601-332-1622

Missouri

Missouri Parents Act
Kent Kolaga, Executive Director
208 E. High Street, Room I
Jefferson City, MO 65101
Phone: 573-635-1189
Fax: 573-635-7802

Greater Kansas City
Parent Education and Advocacy Resource
MPACT
Carolyn Stewart
1 W. Armour, Suite 301
Kansas City, MO 64111
Phone: 816-531-7070
Fax: 816-531-4777
E-mail: mpactcs@coop.crn.org

Montana

Parents Let's Unite for Kids
Katharin Kelker
1500 N. 30th Street, Room 183
Special Education Building
Billings, MT 59101-0298
Phone: 406-657-2055 (Voice and TDD)
Toll-free: 800-222-7585 (in-state only)
Fax: 406-657-2061
E-mail: PLUKMT@aol.com

Nebraska

Nebraska Parents Center
Glenda Davis
1941 S. 42nd Street, #122
Omaha, NE 68105-2942
Phone: 402-346-5253 (Voice and TDD)

Fax: 402-346-5253
Toll-free: 800-284-8520 (in-state only)
E-mail: npc@uswest.ne.net
techlab.esu3.k12.ne.us/npc/ParentsCenter.
  html

Nevada

Nevada Parents Encouraging Parents (PEP)
Karen Taycher
601 S. Rancho Drive, Suite C25
Las Vegas, NV 89106
Phone: 702-388-8899
Toll-free: 800-216-5188 (in-state only)
Fax: 702-388-2966
E-mail: nvpep@vegas.infi.net

New Hampshire

Parent Information Center
Judith Raskin
P.O. Box 2405
Concord, NH 03302-2405
Phone: 603-224-7005 (Voice and TDD)
Toll-free: 800-232-0986 (in-state only)
Fax: 603-224-4365
E-mail: picnh@aol.com
www.taalliance.org/ptis/nhpic.text.htm

New Jersey

Statewide Parent Advocacy Network (SPAN)
Diana MTK Autin
35 Halsey Street, 4th Floor
Newark, NJ 07102
Phone: 973-642-8100
Toll-free: 800-654-SPAN (in-state only)
Fax: 973-642-8080
E-mail: autind@aol.com

New Mexico

Parents Reaching Out, Project ADOBE
Sally VanCuren

1000-A Main Street, NW
Los Lunas, NM 87031
Phone: 505-865-3700 (Voice and TDD)
Toll-free: 800-524-5176 (in-state only)
Fax: 505-865-3737

*Parents of Indian Children with Special
  Needs Nationwide*
EPICS Project
Martha J. Gorospe
P.O. Box 788
Bernalillo, NM 87004
Phone: 505-867-3396
Toll-free: 800-765-7320 V/TDD (in-state
  only)
Fax: 505-867-3398
E-mail: epics@highfiver.com

New York

Five Boroughs of New York City
Advocates for Children of New York
Ana Espada/Galen Kirkland
105 Court Street, Suite 402
Brooklyn, NY 11201
Phone: 718-624-8450
Fax: 718-624-1260
E-mail: advocat1@idt.com

New York City
Resources for Children with Special Needs
Karen Schlesinger, Director
200 Park Avenue, S., Suite 816
New York, NY 10003
Phone: 212-677-4650
Fax: 212-254-4070
E-mail: resourcesnyc@prodigy.net
www.epsty.com/resourcesnyc

Sinergia/Metropolitan Parent Center
Richard Lash, Executive Director
15 W. 65th Street, 6th Floor
New York, NY 10023
Phone: 212-496-1300

Fax: 212-496-5608
E-mail: Sinergia@panix.com
www.panix.com/~sinergia

Statewide Except in New York City
Parent Network Center
Joan Watkins
250 Delaware Avenue, Suite 3
Buffalo, NY 14202
Phone: 716-853-1570 (Voice)
    716-853-1573 (TTD)
Toll-free: 800-724-7408 (in-state only)
Fax: 716-853-1574

North Carolina

ECAC, Inc.
Connie Hawkins
P.O. Box 16
Davidson, NC 28036
Phone: 704-892-1321
Toll-free: 800-962-6817 (in-state only)
Fax: 704-892-5028 (Call first to dedicate line)
E-mail: ECAC1@aol.com

North Dakota

Native American Family Network System
Arrowhead Shopping Center
1600 2nd Avenue, SW
Minot, ND 58701
Phone: 701-852-9426 (Voice)
    701-852-9436 (TTY)
Toll-free: 800-245-5840 (in-state only)
Fax: 701-838-9324
E-mail: ndpath01@minot.ndak.net
www.ndcd.org/pathfinder

Pathfinder Family Center
Kathryn Erickson
Arrowhead Shopping Center
1600 2nd Avenue, SW
Minot, ND 58701
Phone: 701-852-9426 (Voice)
    701-852-9436 (TTY)
Fax: 701-838-9324

E-mail: ndpath01@minot.ndak.net
www.ndcd.org/pathfinder

Ohio

OCECD
Margaret Burley
Bank One Building
165 West Center Street, Suite 302
Marion, OH 43302-3741
Phone: 740-382-5452 (Voice and TDD)
Toll-free: 800-374-2806 (in-state only)
Fax: 740-383-6421
E-mail: ocecd@edu.gte.net
www.taalliance.org/PTIs/regohio/text.htm

Southwestern Ohio, Northern Kentucky,
*   Dearborn County, Indiana*
Child Advocacy Center
Cathy Heizman
1821 Summit Road, Suite 303
Cincinnati, OH 45237
Phone: 513-821-2400
Fax: 513-821-2442
E-mail: CADCenter@aol.com

Oklahoma

Parents Reaching Out in Oklahoma
Sharon Bishop
1917 S. Harvard Avenue
Oklahoma City, OK 73128
Phone: 405-681-9710
Fax: 405-685-4006
E-mail: prook1@aol.com
www.ucp.org/probase.htm

Oregon

Oregon COPE Project
Jill Crawford
999 Locust Street, NE
Salem, OR 97303
Phone: 503-581-8156 (Voice and TDD)
Toll-free: 888-505-COPE (in-state only)
Fax: 503-391-0429
E-mail: orcope@open.org

Pennsylvania

Parent Education Network
Louise Thieme
333 E. Seventh Avenue
York, PA 17404
Phone: 717-845-9722 (Voice and TTY)
Toll-free: 800-522-5827 (in-state only) or
    800-441-5028 (Spanish, in-state only)
Fax: 717-848-3654
E-mail: pen@parentednet.org
www.homepagecreations.com/pen/

Philadelphia; Occasional Service to
    Surrounding Counties
Parents Union for Public Schools
Janet Lonsdale
311 S. Juniper Street, Suite 200
Philadelphia, PA 19107
Phone: 215-546-1166
Fax: 215-731-1688
E-mail: ParentsU@aol.com

Puerto Rico

Island of Puerto Rico
Parents Training Parents by APNI
Carmen Sells deVil
P.O. Box 21301
San Juan, PR 00928-1301
Phone: 787-250-4552
Toll-free: 800-981-8492 (in-state only) or
    800-949-4232 (in-state only)
Fax: 787-767-8492
E-mail: APNIPR@PRTC.net

Rhode Island

RI Parent Information Network
Elizabeth Priestley/Cheryl Collins
500 Prospect Street
Pawtucket, RI 02860
Phone: 401-727-4144 (Voice)
    401-727-4151 (TDD)
Toll-free: 800-464-3399 (in-state only)
Fax: 401-727-4040

South Carolina

PRO-PARENTS
Mary Eaddy
2712 Middleburg Drive, Suite 203
Columbia, SC 29204
Phone: 803-779-3859 (Voice and TDD)
Toll-free: 800-759-4776 (in-state only)
Fax: 803-252-4513
E-mail: pro-parents@aol.com

South Dakota

South Dakota Parent Connection
Bev Schreck
3701 West 49th Street, Suite 200B
Sioux Falls, SD 57106
Phone: 605-361-3171 (Voice and TDD)
Toll-free: 800-640-4553 (in-state only)
E-mail: jdiehl@sdparentconnection.com
Fax: 605-361-2928
dakota.net/sdpc

Tennessee

STEP
Nancy Diehl
424 E. Bernard Avenue, Suite 3
Greeneville, TN 37745
Phone: 423-639-0125 (Voice)
    636-8217 (TDD)
Toll-free: 800-280-STEP (in-state only)
Fax: 423-636-8217
E-mail: tnstep@aol.com
www.tnstep.org

Texas

Partners Resource Network Inc.
Janice Meyer
1090 Longfellow Drive, Suite B
Beaumont, TX 77706-4819
Phone: 409-898-4684 (Voice & TDD)
Toll-free: 800-866-4726 (in-state only)
Fax: 409-898-4869
E-mail: Kakitkat@aol.com
www.salsa.net/~path

*Comprised of Various Community
    Groups Nationwide*

Grassroots Consortium
Agnes A. Johnson
6202 Belmark
P.O. Box 61628
Houston, TX 77208-1628
Phone: 713-643-9576
Fax: 713-643-6291
E-mail: SpecKids@aol.com

*San Antonia, Hondo, and Catroville;
    Cameron, Hidalgo, Willacy, and Starr
    Counties*

Project PODER
Yvette Hinojosa
1017 N. Main Avenue, Suite 207
San Antonio, TX 78212
Phone: 210-222-2638
Toll-free: 800-682-9747 (in-state only)
Fax: 210-222-2638
E-mail: poder@world-net.com

Utah

Utah Parent Center
Helen Post
2290 E. 4500 South, Suite 110
Salt Lake City, UT 84117
Phone: 801-272-8907
Toll-free: 800-468-1160 (in-state only)
Fax: 801-272-8907
E-mail: upc@inconnect.com

Vermont

Vermont Parent Information Center
Connie Curtin
1 Mill Street, Suite A7
Burlington, VT 05401
Phone: 802-658-5315 (Voice and TDD)
Toll-free: 800-639-7170 (in-state only)
Fax: 802-658-5395
E-mail: vpic@together.net
www.together.net/~vpic

Virgin Islands

V.I. FIND
Catherine Rehema Glenn
#2 Nye Gade
St. Thomas, US VI 00802
Phone: 340-775-3962 or 340-774-1662
Fax: 340-775-3962
E-mail: vifind@islands.vi

Virginia

**Parent Educational Advocacy Training
    Center**
Cheri Takemoto
10340 Democracy Lane, Suite 206
Fairfax, VA 22030-2518
Phone: 703-691-7826
Toll-free: 800-869-6782 (in-state only)
Fax: 703-691-8148
E-mail: peatcinc@aol.com
members.aol.com/peatcinc/index.htm

Washington

Washington PAVE
Joanne Butts
6316 S. 12th
Tacoma, WA 98465-1900
Phone: 253-565-2266 (Voice and TDD)
Toll-free: 800-572-7368 (in-state only)
Fax: 253-566-8052
E-mail: wapave9@idt.net
idt.net/~wapav9

Serves U.S. Military Installations

PAVE/STOMP
Heather Hebdon
6316 S. 12th Street
Tacoma, WA 98465
Phone: 253-565-2266 (VOICE AND TTY)
Toll-free: 800-572-7368 (in-state only)
Fax: 253-566-8052
E-mail: wapave9-2@idt.net
idt.net/~wapave9

West Virginia

West Virginia PTI
Pat Haberbosch
371 Broaddus Avenue
Clarksburg, WV 26301
Phone: 304-624-1436 (Voice and TTY)
Toll-free: 800-281-1436 (in-state only)
Fax: 304-624-1438
E-mail: wvpti@aol.com

Wisconsin

Parent Education Project of Wisconsin
S. Patrice Colletti, SDS
2192 S. 60th Street
West Allis, WI 53219-1568

Phone: 414-328-5520 (Voice)
  414-328-5525 (TDD)
Toll-free: 800-231-8382 (in-state only)
Fax: 414-328-5530
E-mail: PMColletti@aol.com
members.aol.com/pepofwi/

Wyoming

Parent Information Center
Terri Dawson
5 N. Lobban
Buffalo, WY 82834
Phone: 307-684-2277 (Voice and TDD)
Toll-free: 800-660-9742 (in-state only)
Fax: 307-684-5314
E-mail: tdawsonpic@vcn.com

Appendix G

National Disability Organizations and Agencies

American Association on Mental Retardation
444 N. Capitol Street, NW, #846
Washington, DC 20001-1570
Phone: 202-387-1968 or 800-424-3688
Fax: 202-387-2193
info@aamr.org

American Speech-Language-Hearing Assocation
10801 Rockville Pike
Rockville, MD 20852
Phone: 301-897-5700
Consumer Affairs: 800-498-2071
TTY: 301-897-0157
Fax: 301-571-0457
actioncenter@asha.org

Assocation of Birth Defect Children, Inc. (ABDC)
827 Irma Avenue
Orlando, FL 32803
Phone: 407-245-7035 or 800-313-2232
Fax: 407-245-7087
abdc@birthdefects.org

Autism Society of America, Inc.
7910 Woodmont Avenue, #650
Bethesda, MD 20814
Phone: 301-657-0881 or 800-3-AUTISM (328-8476)
Fax: 301-657-0869

Better Hearing Institute, Hearing Helpline
P.O. Box 1840
Washington, DC 20013
Phone: 800-327-9355
Fax: 703-750-9302
mail@betterhearing.org

Brain Injury Association
1776 Massachusetts Avenue, NW
Alexandria, VA 22314
Phone: 703-236-6000
PublicRelations@biausa.org

Challenge (Attention Deficit Disorder Assocation)
The River Road
West Newbury, MA 01985
Phone: 508-462-0495

Child and Adolescent Service System Program (CASSP)
National Insititute of Mental Health (NIMH)
Parklawn Building
5600 Fishers Lane, Room 11C-09
Rockville, MD 20857
Phone: 301-443-1333

Children and Adults with Attention Deficit Disorders (CH.A.D.D.)
499 NW 70th Avenue, Suite 101
Plantation, FL 33317
Phone: 800-233-4050
Fax: 954-587-4599

Council for Exceptional Children (CEC)
1920 Association Drive
Reston, VA 22091-1589
Phone: 703-620-3660/703-264-9446 (TTY)/888-CEC-SPED (232-7733)
Fax: 703-264-9494
service@cec.sped.org

Epilepsy Foundation of America (and National Epilepsy Library and Resource Center)
4351 Garden City Drive
Landover, MD 20785

Phone: 301-459-3700/800-332-1000
Toll-free: 800-332-2070 (TTY)
Fax: 301-577-2684

ERIC Clearinghouse on Disability and Gifted Education
1920 Association Drive
Reston, VA 22091
Phone: 800-328-0272 (V/TTY)
Fax: 703-264-9494
ericec@cec.sped.org

Federation of Families for Children's Mental Health
1021 Prince Street
Alexandria, VA 22314-2971
Phone: 703-684-7710
Fax: 703-836-1040
ffcmh@crosslink.net

Learning Disabilities Association of America
4156 Library Road
Pittsburgh, PA 15234
Phone: 412-341-1515 or 412-341-8077
Fax: 412-344-0224
ldanatl@usaor.net

Learning Disabilities On-line
ldonline@weta.com

National Autism Hotline
P.O. Box 507
Huntington, WV 25710-0507
Phone: 304-525-8014
Fax: 304-525-8026

National Brain Injury Research Foundation
14408 Newton Patent Court
Centreville, VA 22020
Phone: 703-818-0078 or 800-447-8445

National Down Syndrome Congress
1605 Chantilly Drive, NE, #250
Atlanta, GA 30324-3269

Phone: 404-633-1555 or 800-232-NDSC
Fax: 404-633-2817

National Down Syndrome Society
666 Broadway, #810
New York, NY 10012-2317
Phone: 212-460-9330 or 800-221-4602
Fax: 212-979-2873
info@ndss.org

National Information Center for Children and Youth with Disabilities (NICHCY)
P.O. Box 1492
Washington, DC 20013
Phone: 202-884-8200 (V/TTY) or 800-695-0285 (V/TTY)
Fax: 202-884-8441
nichcy@aed.org

National Information Center on Deafness
Gallaudet University
800 Florida Avenue, NE
Washington, DC 20002-3625
Phone: 202-651-5051 or 202-651-5052 (TTY)
Fax: 202-651-5054
nicd@gallux.gallaudet.edu

National Tourette Syndrome Assocation
4240 Bell Blvd., Suite 205
Bayside, NY 11361
Phone: 718-224-2999 or 800-237-0717
Fax: 718-279-9596

Orton Society (Dyslexia)
8600 LaSalle Road
Chester Building, #382
Baltimore, MD 21286-2044
Phone: 301-296-0232

Research and Training Center on Family Support and Children's Mental Health
Portland State University
P.O. Box 751
Portland, OR 97207-0751
Phone: 503-725-4040
Fax: 503-725-4180

United Cerebral Palsy Association
1660 L Street, NW, Suite 700
Washington, DC 20036
Phone: 800-872-5827
Fax: 800-776-0414
ucpnatl@ucpa.or

Appendix H
Bilingual Children's Books Affirming Cultural Differences

All the Colors of the Earth
Author: Sheila Hamanaka

From the "whispering golds of late summer grasses" to "the roaring browns of bears and soaring eagles," children come in all colors. The author likens different skin colors and hair textures to things found in nature and, in the process, affirms the beauty of every child.

Morrow Junior Books
1350 Avenue of the Americas
New York, NY 10019
Phone: 800-237-0657
http://www.williammorrow.com

All the Colors We Are/Todos los Colores de Nuestra Piel
Author: Katie Kissinger

This book uses simple language to explain how we get skin color. Photographs by Wernher Krutein present a diverse array of skin hues.

Redleaf Press
450 N. Syndicate, Suite 5
St. Paul,. MN 55104-4125
Phone: 800-423-8309
Fax: 800-788-3123

Black Is Brown Is Tan; Black, White, Just Right!; and Real Sisters
Author: Arnold Adoff

These stories wee written especially to address the needs of children of multiracial families, but they are appropriate for helping all children respect and understand ethnic differences.

Great Owl Books
33 Watchung Plaza
Montclair, NJ 07042-4111
Phone: 800-299-3181
Fax: 201-783-5899

Bread, Bread, Bread; Shoes, Shoes, Shoes; Houses and Homes; and Loving
Author: Ann Morris

This series of books is focused on the way different people all around the world meet the universal human needs of food, clothing, housing, and love. Photographs from around the globe foster a respect for individual differences.

My Song Is Beautiful: Poems and Pictures in Many Voices
Editor: Mary Ann Hoberman

This collection of poems from different cultures celebrates childhood. The illustrations reflect the cultural diversity of the various poems.

Little, Brown & Company
200 West Street
Waltham, MA 02154
Phone: 800-759-0190

Multicultural Connections—Provides a selection of children's books written with Spanish and English appearing side by side. These books introduce bilingual skills, increase language and learning abilities, and positively heighten awareness of many cultures. This publisher also makes available musical and language-learning tapes and games that depict multicultural images in an affirmative manner.

Libros Bilingües para Niños
P.O. Box 653
Ardsley, NY 10502
Phone/Fax: 800-385-1020
E-mail: bilingbk@mhv.net
http://www.make-a-store.com/cgi-bin/mall/BilingualBooks/Make-a-Store.cgi

Bastante grande/Big Enough
Author: Ofelia Dumas Lachtman

Everyone in this story discovers that although Lupita is too little for some tasks, for others she is just the right size.

32pp
Ages: 3–7

Diez Deditos/Ten Little Fingers and Other Play Rhymes and Action Songs from Latin America
Selected, arranged, and translated by: Jose-Luis Orozco

Children can sing, chant, clap, wiggle, wave, and dance to more than thirty finger rhymes and action songs adapted from the traditional to the new. The bilingual lyrics, background notes, and simple pictographs show the children how to move. Guitar and piano music included.

55pp
Ages: 2+
(Audiotape and compact disc also available)

Esos desagradables detestables sucios completamente asquerosos pero . . . invisibles germanes/Those Mean Nasty Dirty Downright Disgusting but . . . Invisible Germs
Author: Judith Anne Rice

Through playful and colorful illustrations, this book tells about the germs that cause illness and the importance of hand washing to good health.

32pp
Ages: 4–8

Esos sucios pegajosos olorosos causantes de caries pero . . . invisibles germenes/Those Icky Sticky Smelly, Cavity-Causing but . . . Invisible Germs
Author: Judith Anne Rice

This companion to the above selection is intended to help children develop good teeth brushing habits. Lively, colorful illustrations tell about the germs that cause activities and

demonstrate how important brushing is to good dental health.

32pp
Ages: 4–8

Fiesta!
Author: Sesame Street

Sesame Street presents a fiesta, complete with floats, costumes, and Elmo's favorite new dance—The Conga-Wiffle. All the songs are in English and Spanish. It presents familiar characters, Maria, Gabi, Rosita, and their Sesame Street friends, as well as special performances by Linda Ronstadt and Celia Cruz.

Ages: 2–6
VHS tape—30 minutes
(Audiotape and compact disc also available)

Hola Amigos
Trio of VHS recordings with Paco and his friends presented in a series of bilingual adventures designed to introduce the Spanish language. In his first adventure, Paco and his sister Lupe learn about numbers with Pepe the Clown. In Volume 2, Paco starts in the kitchen and travels throughout his house learning about letters. In Volume 3, Paco and his friends go to a farm, to the city, and to Monkey Island.

All ages
Videotape—55 minutes

La lagartija y el sol/The Lizard and the Sun
Author: Dr. Alma Flor Aida

Traditional folktale of ancient Mexico. Youngsters will enjoy the story of the brave little lizard who, after the sun disappeared, would not rest until she brought back the light and warmth to everyone. (Dr. Flor Aida is an authority on bilingual and multicultural education.)

36pp
Ages: 4+

Pepita y el color rosado/Pepita Thinks Pink
Author: Ofelia Dumas Lachtman

Pepita likes every color but pink, so she just cannot bring herself to make friends with her new neighbor, Sonya—a little girl in a pink dress with pink balloons. Pepita soon learns, however, that the things that make people different from one another are the very things that make a friendship special.

32pp
Ages: 5–7

Thinking Stories
Author: Jackie Scott

Series of three books, each containing four stories presented in bilingual format. The stories promote inductive and deductive reasoning, flexibility of thought, predictive strategies, and increase confidence in problem solving. Teacher's guides, lesson plans, discussion questions, and follow-up activities follow each selection to promote categorization and associative thinking objectives.

64pp each
Ages: 4–8

Un regalo de Papa Diego/A Gift from Papa Diego
Author: Benjamin Alire Saenz

Little Diego loves his grandfather, but does not see him often because Papa Diego lives in Mexico. Diego asks for a Superman outfit for his birthday because he wants to fly across the border to Mexico to be with his grandfather. Includes author notes, a glossary, and claymation illustrations.

24pp
Ages: 5–9

Appendix I
Internet Starting Points for Parents and Caregivers

CYE-L@cunyvms1.gc.cuny.edu
Children, Youth, and Environment
ssi@cunyvms1.gc.cuny.edu

CYFERNET
http://www.cyfernet.mes.umn.edu/
Children, youth, and family information:
  includes ADOPTINFO, FATHERNET,
  and PAVNET (Partnerships Against
  Violence)

ECENET-L@postoffice.cso.uiuc.edu
Young children, birth to age 8
ericeece@uiuc.edu

ECEOL-L@postoffice.cso.uiuc.edu
Early childhood educators online
  bonnieb@maine.bitnet

ECPOLICY-L@postoffice.cso.uiuc.edu
Early childhood policy issues
ericeece@uiuc.edu

FAMILY WORLD
http://family.disney.com/
Electronic magazine from Parent
  Publications of America, Inc.

MCHNet
Information on health and young children
http://www.ichp.edu/distance/

MULTIAGE@Services.dese.state.mo.us
Mixed-age grouping
catchley@mail.coin.missouri.edu

NCCIC
National Child Care Information Center
  publications and directories
http://nccic.org/

NPIN
Information for parents and educators
http://npin.org/

PARENTING-L@postoffice.cso.uiuc.edu
Parenting of children from infancy through
  adolescence
ericeece@uiuc.edu

REGGIO-L@postoffice.cso.uiuc.edu
The Reggio Emilia (Italy) approach to early
  education
ericeece@uiuc.edu

SAC-L@postoffice.cso.uiuc.edu
School-age care
ericeece@uiuc.edu

U.S. Department of Education
gopher://gopher.ed.gov
U.S. Department of Education publications
  and announcements
http://www.ed.gov

U.S. Department of Health and Human
  Services
U.S. Department of Health and Human
  Services publications, program descrip-
  tions, and services
http://www.acf.dhhs.gov

ERIC/EECE. (1995). *A to Z: The Early
  Childhood Educator's Guide to the
  Internet.* ERIC Clearinghouse on
  Elementary and Early Childhood
  Education. University of Illinois at
  Urbana-Champaign, Children's Research
  Center, 51 Gerty Drive, Champaign, IL
  61820-7469.

Glossary

Active listening   A form of attentive listening in which one concentrates on what is being said, then reflects the ideas back to the speaker to show an understanding of what the speaker is feeling and saying.

Anarchy   Absence of any form of control; chaos and disorder.

Antisocial   Behavior that detracts from the welfare of others or has a generally negative effect on persons with whom one comes in contact. Antisocial personality behaviors are typically marked by lack of ethical restraint, lack of moral control, impulsiveness, and an inability to experience feelings of guilt.

Apnea   The occurrence of a breathing abnormality marked by momentary delays in breathing.

Appropriate   Suitable for the occasion and the person affected, nonexploitative, and having no concealed intention.

Auditory physiology   The physical makeup of the ear that enables hearing. Sounds are channeled through the external auditory canal to the tympanic membrane (ear drum) and the middle ear (ossicles), and then through the auditory nerve to the brain for interpretation of what has been heard. Auditory perception encompasses the ability to understand what has been heard.

Autocracy   Control by a single person having unlimited power.

Behaviorists   Those holding the view that the environment is the primary determinant of human behavior and that objectively observable behavior constitutes the essential psychological makeup of a human being.

Biases   One's own set of beliefs, values, perceptions, and assumptions that develop from one's upbringing, past experience, and personal philosophy of life.

Bonding   The process of becoming emotionally attached to another.

Cephalocaudal   The process of developing in a pattern from the head downward toward the feet (head to toe).

Child-directed   Learning activity instigated by the child's natural curiosity and desire to learn rather than by the adult's manipulation or coercion.

Classical conditioning   Training in which a neutral stimulus produces an expected response, a learned association between a stimulus and a response. This term derives from an experiment originally performed by Ivan Pavlov in which a bell was rung just as food was offered to a hungry dog. Soon the dog would salivate at the sound of the bell whether or not food was offered, demonstrating how this association becomes learned.

Concept   An idea, understanding, or belief formed by organizing images or mental pictures from specific occurrences and experiences.

Concrete operational   The third stage of cognitive development in Jean Piaget's theory that begins with the ability to analyze thoughts concerning a concrete idea (as opposed to an abstract idea).

Cues   Words, facial expressions, or gestures that trigger certain behaviors. A technique used to help children remember what is expected by giving them a specific signal.

Cultural pluralism   The peaceful coexistence of numerous distinct ethnic, religious, or cultural groups within one community or society.

Delay gratification   The process of putting off something desired until a later time. This skill can be learned gradually during early childhood by children who develop a strong sense of trust that their essential needs will be met.

Democracy   The principles of social equality and respect for the individual within a cohesive community.

Developmental interactionists   Those holding the Piagetian view that, rather than only passively absorbing information or emerging into a predestined form, a human being's essential psychological makeup derives from a dynamic interactive process, based on both innate cognitive structures and external experiences.

Dysfunctional   Inappropriate or self-destructive behavior not serving any positive or productive function in a child's life.

Egocentric   Seeing oneself as the center of the universe; self-centered; selfish. This point of view is a perfectly normal development characteristic of babies and very young children.

Egocentrism   The inability to view reality from the standpoint of another person that is an intellectual limitation of children in the preoperational stage of cognitive growth in Piaget's theory.

Emotional growth   Learning to understand the feelings that affect how we behave.

Empathy   The ability to understand or have concern for someone other than oneself, marked by identification with and understanding of another's situation, feelings, and motives.

Environment   The physical surroundings or conditions around a child that influence his or her growth, development, and learning. The young child's environment can be described as everything the child sees, hears, touches, and experiences.

Ethologists   Scientists who study the behavior of animals living under normal conditions. Ethology is the scientific study of animal behavior. (Ethnology is the science of depicting the character or disposition peculiar to a particular culture.)

Expressive language   The ability to communicate with others by oral or written language.

External environment   A term that refers to one's physical surroundings experienced through the senses, including daily routines and patterns of interactions.

Functional   Appropriate actions or behaviors that serve some productive or positive function in a child's life.

Habituated   The process of becoming accustomed to something by frequent repetition or pattern of behavior.

Hyperactivity   Also called *hyperkinesia* or *attention deficit disorder;* a behavior disorder marked by excessive physical activity at inappropriate times. Typically the child cannot sit still, fidgets compulsively, and shows a persistent lack of attention or focus on the task at hand.

Industry   One's motivation to work constructively, to be diligent and productive.

Inferiority   The process of feeling incapable, having a pervasive sense of inadequacy, and experiencing a tendency toward self-diminishment.

Inferring meaning   The act of drawing conclusions from evidence perceived by one's senses or through communication.

Intermittent reinforcers The presence of a reinforcer after some, but not all, occurrences of a particular behavior. This process tends to result in an increase in the specific behavior that is reinforced, even if the reinforcement is only sporadic.

Internal sensations The feelings sensed by one's own body, such as hunger or fear.

Internalize The process of taking in experiences and absorbing learning, then making them part of one's own behavior or belief.

Learned behavior The process of learning to repeat an action that has produced a favorable response in the past. A behavior that is taught by the reinforcing response of another person.

Manipulative Using trickery to coerce another person into doing something that he or she really does not want to do.

Marasmus A disease associated with inadequate or inadequately assimilated nutrition that affects infants and causes a wasting away of the child's body. Also referred to as *failure to thrive syndrome,* this condition can result from prolonged absence of emotional nurturance as well as from malnutrition, and affected infants typically evidence delays in motor and intellectual development.

Maturationists Those holding the view that internal predisposition, physiological characteristics, or inherited traits account for the essential psychological makeup of a human being.

Metacognition The ability to reflect or evaluate one's own behavior or actions.

Mirror Reflecting back the feelings expressed by someone else—repeating what you understood *See also* Active listening.

Modeling The process of following a guided example, imitating a role model. In positive child guidance, the adult demonstrates appropriate behavior, teaching by providing an example of appropriate or desired behaviors.

Modify The process of bringing about a change. In behavior modification, modifying is the process of changing a specific behavior through external reinforcement of some kind.

Moral affect The ability to feel guilt or shame; feelings associated with a guilty or clear conscience.

Moral reasoning The thinking processes that guide people in deciding what is or is not moral behavior.

Negotiate The process of settling disputes through interactive verbal exchanges rather than by physical force.

Nonverbal communication Communicating ideas without the use of speech through such cues as gesture, tone of voice, facial expression, or body posture.

Object permanence The knowledge that something hidden from view is not gone forever, but rather is in another location at that time and likely to reappear.

Osmosis A gradual, often unconscious mental process of assimilating ideas or absorbing information that resembles the tendency of fluids to gradually flow through an absorbent material.

Perceive To become aware of something by directly using one's senses; to notice or to understand in one's own mind.

Pluralistic culture *See* Cultural pluralism.

Preoperational The second stage of cognitive development in Jean Piaget's theory that begins with the achievement of object permanence. This stage is typified by imaginative play, egocentricity, the inability to take another person's point of view, and the belief that the number or amount is changed when objects are rearranged.

Prosocial Behavior that improves the welfare of others or has a generally positive effect on persons with whom one comes in contact.

Proximodistal The process of developing in a direction from closest to the body's trunk to the farthest, such as controlling the muscles of the trunk, and then learning how to control the muscles down the arms and finally, in the hands (close to far).

Receptive language The ability to understand written or spoken communication expressed by others.

Redirection The process of offering a substitute focus to distract the child from a current undesirable one. For example, a child may be offered a developmentally appropriate water play activity to refocus his or her inappropriate interest in pouring milk from a cup onto the floor.

Replaces Substitutes one action for another when both cannot be done at the same time, so that an undesired behavior must be given up or suspended for the new action to take place.

Rescued A situation in which one has been removed from experiencing the logical consequence of an inappropriate behavior.

Typically a child has acted improperly without any negative results because an adult has intervened to extricate the child from a precarious situation he or she has created.

Respect The process of showing regard for the rights and needs of another; to display polite expressions of consideration for another.

Self-concept One's own perception of oneself in terms of personal worth, life and school successes, and perceived social status.

Self-esteem Seeing oneself as a worthwhile individual.

Social growth Learning to understand and function appropriately in one's social environment; learning how to effectively interact with others.

Stimuli Things taken in through the senses that might incite activity or thought; things seen, smelled, heard, felt, or tasted; incentives for action.

Tokens Objects (e.g., stars, points, stickers) given to children for performing specified behaviors that are then exchanged at prearranged times for their choice of activities or items from a "menu" of rewards (e.g., toys, special food treats, field trips).

Unconscious reactions Actions that are unplanned, devoid of forethought.

References

A

Adlam, D. (1977). *Code in context.* London: Routledge & Kegan Paul.

Adler, A. (1964, originally published 1931). Compulsion neurosis. In H. L. Ansbacher & R. R. Ansbacher (Eds.), *Superiority and social interest.* Evanston, IL: Northwestern University Press.

Aidman, A. (1997). Television violence: Content, context, and consequences. Champaign, IL: ERIC Clearinghouse on Elementary and Early Childhood Education.

Ainsworth, M. D. S. (1973). The development of the infant-mother attachment. In B. M. Caldwell & H. N. Ricciuti (Eds.), *Review of child development research, 3,* 1–94. Chicago: University of Chicago Press.

Alley, T. (1981). Head shape and the perception of cuteness. *Developmental Psychology, 17,* 650–654.

Altenor, A., Kay, E., & Richter, M. (1977). The generality of learned helplessness in the rat. *Learning & Motivation, 8,* 54–61.

Amato, P. R. (1997). Life-span adjustment of children to their parents' divorce. In E. N. Junn & C. Boyatzis (Eds.), *Annual editions: Child growth and development 97/98* (4th ed.). New York: McGraw-Hill. (Original work published in *The Future of Children,* Spring 1994)

American Academy of Pediatrics. (1995). *Caring for your school-age child: Ages 5–12.* New York: Bantam Books.

Anyon, J. (1983). Intersections of gender and class: Accommodation and resistance by contradictory sex-role ideologies. In S. Walker and L. Barton (Eds.), *Gender, class and education* (pp. 21–37). London: Falmer.

Aries, P. (1962). *Centuries of childhood.* New York: Random House.

B

Bagley, C., Verma, G. K., Mallick, K., & Young, L. (1979). *Personality, self-esteem and prejudice.* Westmead, Farnborough, Hants, England: Saxon House.

Baillargeon, R. (1997). How do infants learn about the physical world? In E. N. Junn & C. Boyatzis (Eds.), *Annual editions: Child growth and development 97/98* (4th ed.). New York: McGraw-Hill. (Original work published in *Current Directions in Psychological Science,* October 1994)

Bandura, A. (1977). *Social learning theory.* Englewood Cliffs, NJ: Prentice-Hall.

Barko, N. (1997). Labeled for life? In K. M. Paciorek & J. H. Munro, *Annual editions: Early childhood education 97/98* (18th ed.). New York: McGraw-Hill. (Original work published in *Parents,* September 1996)

Beaty, J. J. (1997). *Building bridges with multicultural picture books: For children 3–5.* Upper Saddle River, NJ: Merrill Education/Prentice-Hall.

Beck, R. (1973). White House conferences on children: An historical perspective. *Harvard Educational Review, 43,* 4.

Begley, S. (1997a). Your child's brain. In K. M. Paciorek & J. H. Munro, *Annual editions: Early childhood education 97/98* (18th ed.). New York: McGraw-Hill. (Original work published in *Newsweek,* February 19, 1996)

Begley, S. (1997b). The IQ puzzle. In E. N. Junn & C. Boyatzis (Eds.), *Annual editions: Child growth and development 97/98* (4th ed.). New York: McGraw-Hill. (Original work published in *Newsweek,* May 6, 1996)

Begley, S., & Springen, K. (1997). Life in a parallel world. In E. N. Junn & C. Boyatzis (Eds.), *Annual editions: Child growth and development 97/98* (4th ed.). New York: McGraw-Hill.

(Original work published in *Newsweek,* May 13, 1996)

Bentzen, W. R. (1997). Seeing young children: A guide to observing and recording behavior (3d ed.). Albany, NY: Delmar Publishers, an International Thomson Publishing company.

Berk, L. E. (1997). Vygotsky's theory: The importance of make-believe play. In E. N. Junn & C. Boyatzis (Eds.), *Annual editions: Child growth and development 97/98* (4th ed.). New York: McGraw-Hill. (Original work published in *Young Children,* November 1994)

Berk, L. E. (1997). *Child development* (4th ed.). Needham Heights, MA: Allyn & Bacon.

Berndt, T. J. (1997). *Child development* (2d ed.). New York: McGraw-Hill.

Bianchi, S. M. (1990, June). America's children: Missed prospects. *Population Bulletin, 45*(1), 7–10.

Billman, J., & Sherman, J. A. (1997). *Observation and participation in early childhood settings: A practicum guide, birth through age five.* Needham Heights, MA: Allyn & Bacon.

Blankenhorn, D. (1997). Life without father. In K. M. Paciorek & J. H. Munro, *Annual editions: Early childhood education 97/98* (18th ed.). New York: McGraw-Hill. (Original work published in *USA Weekend,* February 24–26, 1995)

Bloom, B. S. (1964). *Stability and change in human characteristics.* New York: Wiley.

Bodrova, E., & Leong, D. J. (1996). *Tools of the mind: The Vygotskian approach to early childhood education.* Englewood Cliffs, NJ: Prentice-Hall.

Bond, J. T., Galinsky, E., & Swanberg, J. E. (1998). *The 1997 National Study of the Changing Workforce.* New York: Families & Work Institute.

Bornstein, M. H., & Lamb, M. (1992). *Development in infancy: An introduction* (3d ed.). New York: McGraw-Hill.

Bowlby, J. (1958). The nature of the child's tie to his mother. *International Journal of Psychoanalysis, 39,* 350–373.

Bradburn, E. (1989). *Margaret McMillan: Portrait of a pioneer.* New York: Routledge.

Brazelton, T. B. (1985). *Working and caring.* Reading, MA: Addison-Wesley.

Brazelton, T. B., Koslowski, B., & Main, M. (1974). The origins of reciprocity. In M. Lewis & L. Rosenblum (Eds.), *The effect of the infant on its caregiver.* New York: Wiley-Interscience.

Bredekamp, S., & Copple, C. (Eds.). (1997). *Developmentally appropriate practice in early childhood programs* (Rev. ed). Washington, DC: National Association for the Education of Young Children.

Bredekamp, S., & Shepard, L. (1989). How to best protect children from inappropriate school expectations, practices, and policies. *Young Children, 44* (3), 14–24.

Bremner, R. H. (Ed.). (1974). *Children and youth in America: A documentary history* (Vols. 1–3). Cambridge, MA: Harvard University Press.

Brewer, A. (1998). *Introduction to early childhood education: Preschool through primary grades* (3d ed.). Needham Heights, MA: Allyn & Bacon.

Brookings Institution. (1999, April 21). Creating a better start for children: A new look at child care and early childhood education. Read by Senator Chris Dodd (D-CT) from Brookings Naitonal Issues Forum. Washington, DC: The Brookings Institution (http:www.brook.edu/es/cr/events.htm).

Brown, J. L., & Pollitt, E. (1997). Malnutrition, poverty, and intellectual development. In E. N. Junn & C. Boyatzis (Eds.), *Annual editions: Child growth and development 97/98* (4th ed.). New York: McGraw-Hill. (Original work published in *Scientific American,* February 1996)

Bruner, J. (1978a, September). Learning the mother tongue. *Human Nature,* 11–19.

Bruner, J. (1978b). Learning how to do things with words. In J. S. Bruner & A. Garton (Eds.), *Human growth and development: Wolfson College lectures.* Oxford: Clarendon Press.

Bullock, J. R. (1997). Children without friends. In E. N. Junn & C. Boyatzis (Eds.), *Annual editions: Child growth and development 97/98*

(4th ed.). New York: McGraw-Hill. (Original work published in *Childhood Education,* Winter 1992)

C

Cairns, R. B. (1979). *Social development: The origins and plasticity of interchanges.* San Francisco: Freeman.

Campos, J. J., Bertenthal, B. I., & Kermoian, R. (1997). Early experience and emotional development: The emergence of wariness of heights. In E. N. Junn & C. Boyatzis (Eds.), *Annual editions: Child growth and development 97/98* (4th ed.). New York: McGraw-Hill. (Original work published in *Psychological Science,* January 1992)

Cárdenas, J. A. (1995). *Multicultural education: A generation of advocacy.* Needham Heights, MA: Allyn & Bacon.

Carnegie Corporation of New York. (1994, April). Starting points: Meeting the needs of your youngest children. In *The report of the Carnegie task force on meeting the needs of young children.*

Charlesworth, R. (1996). *Understanding child development* (4th ed.). Albany, NY: Delmar Publishers, an International Thomson Publishing company.

Chomsky, N. (1965). *Aspects of the theory of syntax.* Cambridge, MA: MIT Press.

Chugani, H. (1996, June). Positron emission tomography scanning in newborns. *Clinics in Perinatology, 20* (2), 398.

Clark, L., DeWolf, S., & Clark, C. (1992). Teaching teachers to avoid having culturally assaultive classrooms. *Young Children, 47*(5), 4–9.

Clarke, J. I. (1978). *Self-esteem: A family affair.* New York: Winston Press.

Clarke-Stewart, A. (1978). Popular primer for parents. *American Psychologist, 33,* 359.

Cole, L. (1950). *A history of education.* New York: Rinehart.

Collins, W. A., & Gunnar, M. (1990). Social and personality development. In M. R. Rosenaweig

& L. W. Partner (Eds.), *Annual Review of Psychology, 44,* 387–416.

Condon, W. S., & Sander, L. (1974). Neonate movement is synchronized with adult speech: Interactional participation and language acquisition. *Science, 183,* 99–101.

Cook-Gumperz, J. (1973). *Social control and socialization.* London: Routledge & Kegan Paul.

Coontz, S. (1997). Where are the good old days? In K. M. Paciorek & J. H. Munro, *Annual editions: Early childhood education 97/98* (18th ed.). New York: McGraw-Hill. (Original work published in *Modern Maturity,* May/June 1996)

Coopersmith, S. (1967). *The antecedents of self-esteem.* San Francisco: W. H. Freeman.

Copeland, M. L., & McCreedy, B. S. (1997, January–February). Creating family-friendly policies: Are child care center policies in line with current family realities? *Child Care Information Exchange, 113,* 7–10, 12.

Corsaro, W. A. (1981). Friendship in the nursery school: Social organization in a peer environment. In S. R. Asher and J. M. Gottman (Eds.), *The development of children's friendships.* New York: Cambridge University Press.

Costley, D., & Todd, R. (1987). *Human relations in organization* (3d ed.). New York: West.

Cotton, N. (1984). The development of self-esteem and self-esteem regulation. In J. E. Mack and S. L. Ablon (Eds.), *The development and sustaining of self-esteem in childhood.* New York: International Universities Press.

Cowan, C. P., & Cowan, P. (1992). *When partners become parents.* United States: Basic Books.

Crockenberg, S. (1997). How children learn to resolve conflicts in families. In E. N. Junn & C. Boyatzis (Eds.), *Annual editions: Child growth and development 97/98* (4th ed.). New York: McGraw-Hill. (Original work published in *Zero to Three,* April 1992)

Cunnington, P., & Buck, A. (1965). *Children's costume in England.* New York: Barnes & Noble.

Curran, D. (1985). *Stress and the healthy family.* Minneapolis, MN: Winston Press.

D

Dean, A. L., Malik, M. M., Richards, W., & Stringer, S. A. (1986). Effects of parental maltreatment on children's conceptions of interpersonal relationships. *Developmental Psychology, 22,* 617–626.

DeCasper, A. J., & Fifer, W. P. (1980). Of human bonding: Newborns prefer their mothers' voices. *Science, 208,* 1174–1176.

deMelendez, R., & Ostertag, V. (1997). *Teaching young children in multicultural classrooms: Issues, concepts and strategies.* Albany, NY: Delmar Publishers, an International Thomson Publishing company.

Denby, D. (1997). Buried alive. In E. N. Junn & C. Boyatzis (Eds.), *Annual editions: Child growth and development 97/98* (4th ed.). New York: McGraw-Hill. (Original work published in *The New Yorker,* July 15, 1996)

Dennis, W. (1960). Causes of retardation among institutional children: Iran. *The Journal of Genetic Psychology, 96,* 47–59.

Dennis, W. (1973). *Children of the creche.* New York: Appleton-Century-Crofts.

Derman-Sparks, L., & the A.B.C. Task Force. (1989). *Anti-bias curriculum: Tools for empowering young children.* Washington, DC: National Association for the Education of Young Children.

deSales, F., & Ryan, J. (1972). *Introduction to the devout life by St. Francis de Sales* (Reissue Ed.). New York: Image Books.

Dewey, J. (1966). *Experience and education.* New York: Collier.

Dinkmeyer, D., & McKay, G. D. (1982). *Systematic training for effective parenting: Parent's handbook.* Circle Pines, MN: American Guidance Service.

Dreikurs, R., & Cassel, P. (1972). *Discipline without tears* (2d ed.). New York: Hawthorn Books.

Duis, S. S., et al. (1997, Spring). Parent versus child stress in diverse family types: An ecological approach. *Topics in Early Childhood Special Education, 17*(1), 53–73.

E

Eddowes, E. A., & Ralph, K. S. (1998). *Interactions for development and learning: Birth through eight years.* Upper Saddle River, NJ: Merrill Education/Prentice-Hall.

Edwards, C. H. (1997). *Classroom discipline and management* (2d ed.). Upper Saddle River, NJ: Merrill Education/Prentice-Hall.

Ehrensaft, D. (1997). *Spoiling childhood: How well-meaning parents are giving children too much—but not what they need.* New York: Guilford.

Eisenberg, R. B. (1976). *Auditory competence in early life.* Baltimore, MD: University Park Press.

Eisenberg-Berg, N. (1979). Development of children's prosocial moral judgment. *Developmental Psychology, 15,* 128–138.

Elkind, D. (1997). School and family in the postmodern world. In E. N. Junn & C. Boyatzis (Eds.), *Annual editions: Child growth and development 97/98* (4th ed.). New York: McGraw-Hill.

Erikson, E. (1963). *Childhood and society* (2d ed.). New York: W. W. Norton.

Erikson, E. (1982). *The life cycle completed: A review.* New York: W. W. Norton. (Original work published in Erikson, E., 1959. Identity and the life cycle. *Psychological Issues, 1*(1), Monograph 1)

F

Faegre, M., & Anderson, J. (1930). *Child care and training* (3d ed.). Minneapolis Institute of Child Welfare. Minneapolis, MN: University of Minnesota Press.

Feeney, S. S., Christensen, D., & Moravcik, E. R. (1996). *Who am I in the lives of children? An introduction to teaching young children* (5th ed.). Upper Saddle River, NJ: Merrill Education/Prentice-Hall.

Ferguson, T. J., & Rule, B. G. (1982). Influence of inferential set, outcome intent, and outcome severity on children's moral judgments. *Developmental Psychology, 18,* 843–851.

Field, T. M. (1982). Affective and physiological changes during manipulated interactions of high-risk infants. In T. Field & A. Fogel (Eds.), *Emotion and early interaction.* Hillsdale, NJ: Erlbaum.

Fields, M. V., & Boesser, C. (1998). *Constructive guidance and discipline: Preschool and primary education* (2d ed.). Upper Saddle River, NJ: Merrill Education/Prentice-Hall.

Finkelhor, D., & Dziuba-Leatherman, J. (1997). Victimization of children. In E. N. Junn & C. Boyatzis (Eds.), *Annual editions: Child growth and development 97/98* (4th ed.). New York: McGraw-Hill. (Original work published in *American Psychologist,* March 1994)

Finkelstein, N. W., & Ramey, C. T. (1977). Learning to control the environment in infancy. *Child Development, 48,* 806–819.

Flynn, C. (1996). Regional differences in spanking experiences and attitudes: A comparison of northeastern and southern college students. *Journal of Family Violence, 11*(1), 59–80.

Francke, L. B. (1983). *Growing up divorced.* New York: Fawcett Crest.

French, L. (1996). "I told you all about it, so don't tell me you don't know." *Young Children, 5* (2), 17–20.

Froebel, F. (1887). *The education of man: The art of education, instruction and training.* New York: Appleton.

G

Gaetano, Y. D., Williams, L. R., & Volk, D. (1998). *Kaleidoscope: A multicultural approach for the primary school classroom.* Upper Saddle River, NJ: Merrill Education/-Prentice-Hall.

Gallo, N. (1997). Why spanking takes the spunk out of kids. In E. N. Junn & C. Boyatzis (Eds.), *Annual editions: Child growth and develop-*

ment 97/98 (4th ed.). New York: McGraw-Hill. (Original work published in *Child,* March/April 1989)

Galston, W. (1993, Winter). Causes of declining well-being among U.S. children. *Aspen Institute Quarterly.*

Gartrell, D. (1997). Misbehavior or mistaken behavior? In K. M. Paciorek & J. H. Munro, *Annual editions: Early childhood education 97/98* (18th ed.). New York: McGraw-Hill. (Original work published in *Young Children,* July 1995)

Gartell, D. (1998). *Guidance approach for the encouraging classroom* (2d ed.). Albany, NY: Delmar Publishers, an International Thomson Publishing company.

Gazda, G. M., Asbury, F. S., Balzar, F. J., Childers, W. C., & Walters, R. P. (1990). *Human relations development* (4th ed.). Boston: Allyn & Bacon.

Gerbner, G., & Gross, L. (1980). The violent face of television and its lessons. In E. L. Palmer and A. Dorr (Eds.), *Children and the faces of television: Teaching, violence, selling.* New York: Academic Press.

Gesell, A., Halverson, H. M., Thompson, H., & Ilg, F. (1940). *The first five years of life: A guide to the study of the preschool child.* New York: Harper & Row.

Gestwicki, C. (1999). *Developmentally appropriate practice.* Albany, NY: Delmar Publishers, an International Thomson Publishing company.

Gibbs, N. (1997). The EQ factor. In E. N. Junn & C. Boyatzis (Eds.), *Annual editions: Child growth and development 97/98* (4th ed.). New York: McGraw-Hill. (Original work published in *Time,* October 2, 1995)

Glubok, S. (Ed.). (1969). *Home and child life in colonial days.* New York: Macmillan.

Gonzalez-Mena, J. (1998a). *The child in the family and in the community* (2d ed.). Upper Saddle River, NJ: Merrill Education/Prentice-Hall.

Gonzalez-Mena, J. (1998b). *Foundations: Early childhood education in a diverse society.* Mountain View, CA: Mayfield.

Gordon, A., & Browne, K. W. (1996a). *Guiding young children in a diverse society.* Needham Heights, MA: Allyn & Bacon.

Gordon, A., & Browne, K. W. (1996b). *Beginnings and beyond* (4th ed.). Albany, NY: Delmar Publishers, an International Thomson Publishing company.

Gordon, T. (1970). *Parent effectiveness training.* New York: Peter Wyden.

Gough, P. B. (1993). Dealing with diversity. *Phi Delta Kappan, 75*(1), 3.

Green, V., & Stafford, S. H. (1997). Preschool integration: Strategies for teachers. In K. M. Paciorek and J. H. Munro, *Annual editions: Early childhood education 97/98* (18th ed.). New York: McGraw-Hill. (Original work published in *Childhood Education,* Summer 1996)

Gronlund, G. (1997). Families and schools: Bringing the DAP message to kindergarten and primary teachers. In K. M. Paciorek & J. H. Munro, *Annual editions: Early childhood education 97/98* (18th ed.). New York: McGraw-Hill. (Original work published in *Young Children,* July 1995)

Grusec, J. E., Kuczynski, L., Rushton, J. P., & Simutis, Z. (1979). Learning resistance to temptation through observation. *Developmental Psychology, 15,* 233–240.

Gutek, G. L. (1997). *Historical and philosophical foundations of education: A biographical introduction* (2d ed.). Upper Saddle River, NJ: Merrill Education/Prentice-Hall.

H

Hamburg, D. A. (1992). *Today's children.* New York: Times Books.

Harding, C. G., & Golinkoff, R. M. (1979). The origins of intentional vocalizations in prelinguistic infants. *Child Development, 50,* 33–40.

Harlow, H., & Zimmerman, R. (1959). Affectional responses in the infant monkey. *Science, 130,* 421–432.

Harms,T., & Clifford, R. (1998). *Early childhood environment rating scale* (Rev. ed.). New York: Teachers College Press.

Harrison, A. O., et al. (1990, April). Family ecologies of ethnic minority children. *Child Development, 61,* 347–362.

Hartshorne, H., & May, M. A. (1928). *Studies in the nature of character* (Vol. 1). New York: Macmillan.

Heineman, R. V. (1998). *The abused child psychodynamic: Understanding and treatment.* New York: Guilford.

Hernandez, D. J. (1997). Changing demographics: Past and future demands for early childhood programs. In K. M. Paciorek & J. H. Munro, *Annual editions: Early childhood education 97/98* (18th ed.). New York: McGraw-Hill. (Original work published in *The Future of Children,* Winter 1995)

Hess, E. (1972). Imprinting in a natural laboratory. *Scientific American, 227,* 24–31.

Hess, R., & Shipman, V. (1967). Parents as teachers: How lower and middle class mothers teach. In C. S. Lavatelli & F. Stendler (Eds.), *Readings in child behavior and development* (3d ed., pp. 436–446). New York: Harcourt Brace Jovanovich.

Hildebrand, V. (1997). *Introduction to early childhood education* (6th ed.). Upper Saddle River, NJ: Merrill Education/Prentice-Hall.

Hildebrand, V., Phenice, L. A., Gray, M. M., & Hines, R. P. (1996). *Knowing and serving diverse families.* Upper Saddle River, NJ: Merrill Education/Prentice-Hall.

Hills, T. W. (1993). Assessment in context—Teachers and children at work. *Young Children, 48* (5), 20–28.

Hoffman, L., & Manis, J. D. (1979). The value of children in the United States: A new approach to the study of fertility. *Journal of Marriage and the Family, 41,* 583–596.

Hoffman, M. L. (1979). Development of moral thought, feeling, and behavior. *American Psychologist, 34,* 958–967.

Hoffman-Plotkin, D., & Twentyman, C. T. (1984). A multimodal assessment of behavioral and cognitive deficits in abused and neglected preschoolers. *Child Development, 55,* 794–802.

Honig, A. S. (1986). Stress and coping in children: Part 2. Interpersonal family relationships. *Young Children, 41*(5), 47–60.

Honig, A., & Wittmer, D. (1992). *Prosocial development in children: Caring, sharing, and cooperation: A bibliographic resource guide.* New York: Garland.

Honig, A. S., & Wittmer, D. S. (1997). Helping children become more prosocial: Ideas for classrooms. In K. M. Paciorek & J. H. Munro, *Annual editions: Early childhood education 97/98* (18th ed.). New York: McGraw-Hill. (Original work published in *Young Children,* January 1996)

Howard, G. R. (1993). Whites in multicultural education: Rethinking our role. *Phi Delta Kappan, 75*(1), 36–41.

Hunt, J. (1976). The psychological development of orphanage-reared infants: Interventions with outcomes (Teheran). *Genetic Psychology Monographs, 94,* 177–226.

I

Ingrassia, M., & McCormick, J. (1997). Why leave children with bad parents? In E. N. Junn & C. Boyatzis (Eds.), *Annual editions: Child growth and development 97/98* (4th ed.). New York: McGraw-Hill. (Original work published in *Newsweek,* April 25, 1994)

Isenbeerg, J., & Jalongo, M. R. (1997). *Creative expression and play in the early childhood curriculum* (2d ed.). New York: Macmillan.

J

Jackson, B. R. (1997, November). Creating a climate for healing in a violent society. *Young Children, 52*(7), 68–70.

Junn, E. N., & Boyatzis, C. (1997). *Annual editions: Child growth and development 97/98.* New York: McGraw-Hill.

K

Kagan, J. (1971). *Change and continuity in infancy.* New York: Wiley.

Kagan, J., Kearsley, R. B., & Zelazo, P. R. (1978). *Infancy: Its place in human development.* Cambridge, MA: Harvard University Press.

Kagan, J., & Moss, H. (1962). *Birth to maturity.* New York: Wiley.

Kagan, S. L. (1997, May). Support systems for children, youths, families, and schools in inner-city situations. *Education and Urban Society, 29*(3), 277–295.

Kantrowitz, B., & Wingert, P. (1997). How kids learn. In E. N. Junn & C. Boyatzis (Eds.), *Annual editions: Child growth and development 97/98* (4th ed.). New York: McGraw-Hill. (Original work published in *Newsweek,* April 17, 1989)

Katz, L., & McClellan, D. (1997). *Fostering children's social competence: The teacher's role.* Washington, DC: National Associaiton for the Education of Young Children.

Katz, P. A. (1982). Development of children's racial awareness and intergroup attitudes. In L. Katz (Ed.), *Current topics in early childhood education* (Vol. 4). Norwood, NJ: Ablex.

Kaye, K. (1982). *The mental and social life of babies.* Chicago: University of Chicago Press.

Kempe, R. S., & Kempe, C. H. (1966). A cognitive-developmental analysis of children's sex-role concepts and attitudes. In E. E. Maccoby (Ed.), *The development of sex differences.* Palo Alto, CA: Stanford University Press.

Kempe, R. S., & Kempe, C. H. (1978). *Child abuse.* Cambridge, MA: Harvard University Press.

Knowlson, J. (1996). *Damned to fame: The life of Samuel Beckett.* New York: Simon & Schuster.

Kohlberg, L. (1966). A cognitive-developmental analysis of children's sex-role concepts and attitudes. In E. E. Maccoby (Ed.), *The development of sex differences.* Stanford, CA: Stanford University Press.

Kohlberg, L. (1969). Stage and sequence: The cognitive-developmental approach to socialization. In D. Goslin (Ed.), *Handbook of socialization theory and research.* Skokie, IL: Rand-McNally.

Kohlberg, L. (1976). Moral stages and moralization: The cognitive-developmental approach. In T. Lickona (Ed.), *Moral development and behavior.* New York: Holt, Rinehart & Winston.

Kokenes, B. (1974). Grade level differences in factors of self-esteem. *Developmental Psychology, 10,* 954–958.

Kolb, B. (1989). Brain development, plasticity, and behavior. *American Psychologist, 44*(9), 1203–1212.

Krogh, S. (1995). *The integrated early childhood curriculum* (2d ed.). New York: McGraw-Hill.

Krupinski, E., & Weikel, D. (1986). *Death from child abuse and no one heard.* Winter Park, FL: Currier-Davis.

Kuhl, P. K. (1981). Auditory category formation and developmental speech perception. In R. Stark (Ed.), *Language behavior in infancy and early childhood.* New York: Elsevier.

L

Ladd, R. E. (Ed.). (1996). *Children's rights revisioned: Philosophical readings.* Belmont, CA: Wadsworth.

Lamb, M. E. (1978). Infant social cognition and "second-order" effects. *Infant Behavior and Development, 1,* 1–10.

Lamb, M. E. (1981). *The role of the father in childhood development* (2d ed.). New York: Wiley.

Lamb, M. E., Gaensbauer, T. J., Malkin, C. M., & Schultz, L. A. (1985). The effects of child maltreatment on security of infant-adult attachment. *Infant Behavior and Development, 8,* 35–45.

Landreth, C., & Johnson, B. (1953). Young children's responses to a picture inset test designed to reveal reactions to persons of different skin color. *Child Development, 24,* 63–80.

Leach, P. (1996, July 9). *Spanking: A shortcut to nowhere* [WWW document]. http://cnet.unb.ca/orgs/prevention_cruelty/spank.htm

Lefkowitz, M. M., & Tesiny, E. P. (1980). Dejection and depression: Prospective and contemporaneous analyses. *Developmental Psychology, 20,* 776–786.

Leland, J. (1997). Violence, reel to real. In E. N. Junn & C. Boyatzis (Eds.), *Annual editions: Child growth and development 97/98* (4th ed.). New York: McGraw-Hill. (Original work published in *Newsweek,* December 11, 1995)

Leong, D., & Bodrova, E. (1996). *Tools of the mind: A Vygotskian approach to early childhood education.* Upper Saddle River, NJ: Merrill Education/Prentice-Hall.

Lindjord, D. (1997, November–December). Child care: The continuing crisis for working families and child care teachers. *Journal of Early Education and Family Review, 5(2),* 6–7.

Lorenz, K. (1966). *On aggression.* New York: Harcourt, Brace & World.

Lubeck, S. (1985). *Sandbox society: Early education in black and white America.* London: Falmer.

M

Majors, R., & Billson, J. M. (1992). *Cool pose: The dilemmas of Black manhood in America.* New York: Touchstone.

Marshall, R. (1991). *The state of Families: 3. Losing direction, families, human resource development, and economic performance.* Milwaukee, WI: Family Service America.

Maslow, A. H. (1943, July). A theory of human motivation. *Psychological Review, 50,* 370–396.

Maslow, A. (1993). *The farther reaches of human nature* (Esalen Book Reprint ed.). Manhattan Beach, CA: Arkana.

McAlister, B. G. (1997, Spring). Growing up in a violent world: The impact of family and community violence on young children and their families. *Topics in Early Childhood Special Education, 17*(1), 74–102.

McCloskey, C. M. (1997). Taking positive steps toward classroom management in preschool: Loosening up without letting it all fall apart. In K. M. Paciorek & J. H. Munro, *Annual editions: Early childhood education 97/98* (18th ed.). New York: McGraw-Hill. (Original work published in *Young Children,* March 1996)

McGraw, M. (1941). *The child in painting.* New York: Greystone Press.

McLean, M. E., Bailey, D. B., Jr., & Wolery, M. (1997). *Assessing infants and preschoolers with special needs* (2d ed.). Upper Saddle River, NJ: Merrill Education/Prentice-Hall.

McLoyd, V. C. (1990). The impact of economic hardship on Black families and children; Psychological distress, parenting, and socioemotional development. *Child Development, 61,* 311–346.

Meece, J. (1997). *Child and adolescent development for educators.* New York: McGraw-Hill.

Miller, D. (1986). *Infant/toddler day care in high, middle, and low socio-economic settings: An ethnography of dialectical enculturation and linguistic code.* Unpublished doctoral dissertation, University of Houston, Houston, TX.

Mindes, G., Ireton, H., & Mardell-Czudnowski, C. (1996). *Assessing young children.* Albany, NY: Delmar Publishers, an International Thomson Publishing company.

Montessori, M. (1968). *Reconstruction in education.* India: Theosophical Publishing House.

Montessori, M. (1971). *Peace and education.* India: Theosophical Publishing House.

Montessori, M., & Hunt, J. M. (1989). *The Montessori method.* New York: Schocken Books.

Moore, T. (1994). *Care of the soul: A guide for cultivating depth and sacredness in everyday life* (Reprint ed.). New York: Harper.

Morland, J. (1972). Racial acceptance and preference in nursery school children in a southern city. In A. R. Brown (Ed.), *Prejudice in children.* Springfield, IL: Charles C. Thomas.

Mussen, P. H., & Eisenberg-Berg, N. (1977). *Roots of caring, sharing and helping.* San Francisco: Freeman.

N

National Association for the Education of Young Children (NAEYC). (1993). Enriching classroom diversity with books for children, indepth discussion of them, and story-extension activities. *Young Children, 48*(3), 10–12.

National Commission on Children. (1991). Speaking of kids: A national survey of children and parents. Washington, DC: Author.

National Committee to Prevent Child Abuse. (1998). *Child abuse and neglect statistics.* Chicago, IL: Author.

O

Osborn, D. (1980). *Early childhood education in historical perspective.* Athens: Education Association.

Owen, R. (1958). *Life of Robert Owen written by himself.* New York: Augustus M. Kelley.

P

Papousek, H. (1967). Conditioning during postnatal development. In Y. Brackbill & G. G. Thompson (Eds.), *Behavior in infancy and early childhood* (pp. 259–284). New York: Free Press.

Parrillo, V. (1985). *Strangers to these shores: Race and ethnic relations in the United States/Vincent N. Parrillo* (2d ed.). Boston: Houghton Mifflin.

Parke, R. D., & Slaby, R. G. (1983). The development of aggression. In E.M. Hetherington (Ed.), *Handbook of child psychology: Socialization, personality and social development* (4th ed., Vol. 4, pp. 537–643). New York: Wiley.

Petersen, E. A. (1996). *A practical guide to early childhood planning, methods and materials: The what, why and how of lesson plans.* Needham Heights, MA: Allyn & Bacon.

Peterson, L. (1983). Influence of age, task competence, and responsibility focus on children's altruism. *Developmental Psychology, 19,* 141–148.

Phillips, C. B. (1988). Nurturing diversity for today's children and tomorrow's leaders. *Young Children, 43*(2), 42–47.

Piaget, J. (1952). *The origins of intelligence in children.* New York: International University Press.

Piaget, J. (1962). *Play, dreams, and imitation in childhood.* New York: W. W. Norton.

Piaget, J. (1963). *The origins of intelligence in children.* New York: W. W. Norton.

Piaget, J. (1965, originally published 1932). *The moral judgment of the child* (M. Gabain, Trans.). New York: Free Press.

Piaget, J. (1968). *On the development of memory and identity.* Barre, MA: Clark University Press.

Piaget, J. (1970). *Science of education and the psychology of the child.* New York: Orion Press.

Piaget, J. (1983). Piaget's theory. In P. H. Mussen (Ed.), *Handbook of child psychology: Vol. 1. History, theory, and methods* (2d ed., W. Kessen [Vol. Ed.]). New York: Wiley.

Pouissant, A. F., & Linn, S. (1997, Spring/Summer). Fragile: Handle with care. *Newsweek* [Your Child: From Birth to Three, Special Issue], *33.*

Pransky, J. (1991). *Prevention: The critical need.* Springfield, MO: Burrell Foundation and Paradigm Press. (Available from NEHRI Publications, Cabot, VT, phone: 802 563 2730)

Prothrow-Stith, D., & Quaday, S. (1995). *Hidden casualties: The relationship between violence and learning.* Washington, DC: National Health & Education Consortium and National Consortium for African American Children, Inc. (ED 390 552).

R

Raikes, H. (1996). A secure base for babies: Applying attachment concepts to the infant care setting. *Young Children, 51,*(5), 59–67.

Randy, L., Hoover, R. L., & Kindsvatter, R. (1997). *Democratic discipline: Foundation & practice.* Upper Saddle River, NJ: Merrill Education/Prentice-Hall.

Roberts, P. (1997). Fathers' time. In E. N. Junn & C. Boyatzis (Eds.), *Annual editions: Child growth and development 97/98* (4th ed.). New York: McGraw-Hill. (Original work published in *Psychology Today,* May/June 1996)

Rosenblith, J. F., Sims-Knight, J. (1985). *In the beginning: Development in the first two years.* Monterey, CA: Brooks/Cole.

Rosenthal, R., & Jacobson, L. (1968). *Pygmalion in the classroom: Teacher expectations and pupils' intellectual development.* New York: Holt, Rinehart & Winston.

Rousseau, J. (1893). *Emile: Or treatise on education.* New York: Appleton.

Rutter, M. (1976). Family, area, and school influences in the genesis of conduct disorders. In L. Hersov, M. Berber, & D. Shaffer (Eds.), *Aggression and antisocial behavior development.* Oxford: Pergamom Press.

S

Salk, L. (1992). *Familyhood.* New York: Simon & Schuster.

Sameroff, J. J., & Cavanagh, P. J. (1979). Learning in infancy: A developmental perspective. In J. D. Osofsky (Ed.), *Handbook of infant development* (pp. 344–392). New York: Wiley.

Santrock, J. W. (1997). *Children.* New York: McGraw-Hill.

Sears, R. R., Maccoby, E. E., & Lewin, H. (1957). *Patterns of child rearing.* Evanston, IL: Row & Peterson.

Seefeldt, C., & Barbour, N. (1998). *Early childhood education: An introduction* (4th ed.). Upper Saddle River, NJ: Merrill Education/Prentice-Hall.

Shore, R. (1997). *Rethinking the brain: New insights into early development.* [Executive Summary]. New York: Families & Work Institute.

Silvers, J. (1997). Child labor in Pakistan. In E. N. Junn & C. Boyatzis (Eds.), *Annual editions: Child growth and development 97/98* (4th ed.). New York: McGraw-Hill. (Original work published in *The Atlantic Monthly,* February 1996)

Skinner, B. (1953). *Science and human behavior.* New York: Macmillan.

Skinner, B. (1974). *About behaviorism.* New York: Knopf.

Skolnick, A. (1991). Embattled paradise: The American family in an age of uncertainty. United States: Basic Books.

Spafford, C. S., Pesce, A. I., & Grosser, G. (1998). *The cyclopedic education dictionary.* Albany, NY: Delmar Publishers, an International Thomson Publishing company.

Sroufe, L. A. (1979). Socioemotional development. In J. Osofsky (Ed.), *Handbook of infant development.* New York: Wiley.

Sroufe, L. A. (1996). *Child development: Its nature and course.* New York: McGraw-Hill.

Sroufe, L. A., Cooper, R., & Dehart, G. (1996). *Child development: Its nature and course* (3d ed.). New York: McGraw-Hill.

Steinberg, L. (1995). *Childhood.* New York: McGraw-Hill.

Stengel, R. (1997). Fly till I die. In K. M. Paciorek & J. H. Munro, *Annual editions: Early childhood education 97/98* (18th ed.). New York: McGraw-Hill. (Original work published in *Time,* April 22, 1996)

Stern, D. N. (1974). Mother and infant at play: The dyadic interaction involving facial, vocal and gaze behaviors. In M. Lewis & L. Rosenblum (Eds.), *The effect of the infant on its caregiver.* New York: Wiley-Interscience.

Stevenson, H. W., Chen, C., & Uttal, D.H. (1990). Beliefs and achievement: A study of Black, White and Hispanic children. *Child Development, 61,* 508–523.

Stevenson, H. W., & Lee, S. (1990). Contexts of achievement. *Monograph of the Society for Research in Child Development, 55*(1–2).

Stott, L. H., & Ball, R. S. (1957). Consistency and change in ascendance-submission in the social interaction of children. *Child Development, 28,* 259–272.

Stringer-Seibold, T., et al. (1996, Fall). Strengths and needs of divided families. Research Highlights. *Dimensions of Early Childhood, 24*(4), 22–29.

T

Teaching Tolerance Project. (1997). *Starting small: Teaching tolerance in preschool and the early grades.* Montgomery, AL: Southern Poverty Law Center.

Thomas, A., & Chess, S. (1977). *Temperament and development.* New York: Brunner/Mazel.

Thomas, A., Chess, S., & Birch, H. G. (1970). The origin of personality. *Scientific American, 233,* 102–109.

Thorne, B. (1997). Girls and boys together but mostly apart. In E. N. Junn & C. Boyatzis (Eds.), *Annual editions: Child growth and development 97/98* (4th ed.). New York: McGraw-Hill. (Original work published in *GenderPlay: Girls and Boys in School,* Rutgers University Press, 1993)

Toner, I. J., Parke, R. D., & Yussen, S. R. (1978). The effect of observation of model behavior on the establishment and stability of resistance to deviation in children. *Journal of Genetic Psychology, 132,* 283–290.

Toner, I. J., & Potts, R. (1981). Effect of modeled rationales on moral behavior, moral choice, and level of moral judgment in children. *Journal of Psychology, 107,* 153–162.

Trawick-Smith, J. (1997). *Early childhood development in multicultural perspective.* Upper Saddle River, NJ: Merrill Education/Prentice-Hall.

Trehub, S. (1973). Infants' sensitivity to vowel and tonal contrasts. *Developmental Psychology, 9,* 81–96.

U

Ulich, R. (1954). *Three thousand years of educational wisdom.* Cambridge, MA: Harvard University Press.

V

von Frisch, K. (1974). Decoding the language of the bee. *Science, 185,* 663–668.

von Goethe, W. (1995). Conversations of German refugees: Wilhelm Meister's journeyman years, or the renunciants (J. Van Heurck, Trans.). In J. K. Brown (Ed.), *Goethe's collected works* (Reprint Ed., Vol. 10). Princeton, NJ: Princeton University Press.

W

Wallach, L. B. (1997). Breaking the cycle of violence. In K. M. Paciorek & J. H. Munro, *Annual editions: Early childhood education 97/98* (18th ed.). New York: McGraw-Hill. (Original work published in *Children Today, 23*[3], 1994–1995).

Wang, C. T. and Daro, D. (1998). *Current trends in child abuse reporting and fatalities: The results of the 1997 Annual Fifty State Survey.* Chicago, IL: National Committee to Prevent Child Abuse.

Watson, J. (1930). *Behaviorism* (2d ed.). Chicago: University of Chicago Press.

Watson, J. (1973). Smiling, cooing and "the game." *Merrill-Palmer Quarterly, 18,* 323–339.

Weiser, M. (1982). *Group care and education of infants and toddlers.* St. Louis, MO: Mosby.

Weiss, C. D., & Lillywhite, H. S. (1976). *Communicative disorders: A handbook for prevention and early intervention.* St. Louis, MO: Mosby.

Werner, E. E. (1987). Vulnerability and resiliency in children at risk for delinquency: A longitudinal study from birth to adulthood. In J. D. Burchard & S. N. Burchard (Eds.), *Primary prevention of psychopathology: Vol. 10. Prevention of delinquent behavior* (pp. 16–43). Newbury Park, CA: Sage.

Werner, N. E., & Evans, I. M. (1971). Perception of prejudice in Mexican-American preschool children. In N. N. Wagner & M. J. Haug (Eds.), *Chicano: Social and psychological perspectives.* St. Louis, MO: Mosby.

White, B. L. (1975). *The first three years of life.* New York: Avon.

White, B. L. (1995). *The new first three years of life* (Rev. ed.) New York: Simon & Shuster.

White, B., Kaban, B., & Attanucci, J. (1979). *The origins of human competence: The final report of the Harvard Preschool Project.* Boston: Lexington Books.

White, B., & Watts, J. (1973). *Experience and environment: Major influences on the development of the young child* (Vol. 2). Englewood Cliffs, NJ: Prentice-Hall.

Whitehead, B. D. (1993, May/June). The new family values. *Utne Reader.*

Wittmer, D. S., & Honig, A. S. (1997). Encouraging positive social development in young children. In K. M. Paciorek & J. H. Munro, *Annual editions: Early childhood education 97/98* (18th ed.). New York: McGraw-Hill. (Original work published in *Young Children,* July 1994)

Wolff, P. (1963). Observations on the early development of smiling. In B. M. Foss (Ed.), *Determinants of infant behavior* (Vol. 2). London: Methuen.

Y

Yarrow, A. (1991). *Latecomers: Children of parents over 35.* New York: Free Press.

Index